T0358295

Revised Edition

PUBLIC FINANCE

AN INTERNATIONAL PERSPECTIVE

Revised Edition

PUBLIC FINANCE

AN INTERNATIONAL PERSPECTIVE

Joshua E. Greene, Ph.D.

Visiting Professor, Singapore Management University

NEW JERSEY • LONDON • SINGAPORE • BEIJING • SHANGHAI • HONG KONG • TAIPEI • CHENNAI

Published by

World Scientific Publishing Co. Pte. Ltd.

5 Toh Tuck Link, Singapore 596224

USA office: 27 Warren Street, Suite 401-402, Hackensack, NJ 07601

UK office: 57 Shelton Street, Covent Garden, London WC2H 9HE

British Library Cataloguing-in-Publication Data
A catalogue record for this book is available from the British Library.

PUBLIC FINANCE
An International Perspective
Revised Edition

ISBN 978-981-120-993-2 (hardcover)
ISBN 978-981-120-994-9 (ebook for institutions)
ISBN 978-981-120-995-6 (ebook for individuals)

For any available supplementary material, please visit
https://www.worldscientific.com/worldscibooks/10.1142/11543#t=suppl

Desk Editor: Sandhya Venkatesh

Typeset by Stallion Press
Email: enquiries@stallionpress.com

Printed in Singapore

Preface

The first two decades of the 21st century have increased the appreciation for public finance. Always an issue in developing and emerging market countries, the Financial Crisis and subsequent global downturn in 2009 made fiscal policy a prime concern among countries at all income levels. With monetary policy of limited help in addressing a recession triggered by falling asset prices and rising debt burdens, countries turned to tax cuts and expenditure increases to support demand and cushion the decline in employment. The resulting budget deficits caused public debt levels to soar, particularly in advanced economies. Adding to the fiscal pressures resulting from aging populations, many of these countries faced strong pressures to curb future debt increases. By mid-2011, several countries had introduced controversial programs to restrain public debt over the medium term. Others were debating the proper mix of spending cuts, revenue increases, and restraints on pension and health programs to address future debt problems while maintaining an appropriate level of public services and protection for vulnerable groups. Since that time, many advanced economies have trimmed deficits, and countries in the Eurozone have reduced public debt–GDP ratios. However, deficits and debt have risen in emerging market and economies middle- and low-income economies, and debt ratios have increased in the United States. The COVID-19 pandemic of 2020 led to further increases in deficits and debt.

This book aims to promote a better understanding of public finance. Based on courses delivered at Singapore Management University, the text incorporates examples from a variety of countries in different regions and at different income levels. Although some mathematics is inevitable in explaining such topics as fiscal (public debt) sustainability, the goal has been to minimize the technical demands on readers and focus on policy issues. Thus, this book should be suitable for students at the master's and upper undergraduate levels, as well as civil servants interested in enhancing their understanding of public finance. Besides limiting the use of jargon, the book contains an extensive glossary that defines most of the technical terms used. This revision was largely written before the start of the COVID-19 pandemic. Thus, the data presented do not reflect the impact of the pandemic on government budgets and debt.

Writing a book is an extended undertaking, and thanks are due to many people who contributed to its realization. I would like to thank professors Wallace Oates, Harvey Brazer, and Mancur Olson, for demonstrating the excitement and relevance of public finance; former colleagues at the International Monetary Fund, and especially the IMF Institute for Capacity Development and the IMF's training department, for providing an opportunity to develop and refine training programs on public finance; Singapore Management University and former Dean Roberto Mariano, for offering the chance to develop master's level courses reflecting my views on how the subject should be taught; Eugene Steuerle, William Gale, Mukul Asher, Parthasarathi Shome, Phua Kai Hong, Eduardo Ley, Angel Antonaya, and Ling Hui Tan, for sharing insights on public finance issues; Max Phua of World Scientific Publishing, for his willingness to undertake publication of the initial and revised versions of this book; and several professional colleagues who reviewed a preliminary version of the text. I also want to acknowledge the World Bank and International Monetary Fund for granting permission to reproduce several charts and tables from World Bank and IMF publications. Finally, I would like to thank my children, Ashira and Alex, and particularly my dear wife, Dara, for their support, encouragement, and patience during the many hours needed to update and revise the text. This revised version is dedicated to all of them.

Contents

Chapter One: The Role of Government in a Modern Market Economy

Public finance is the study of the goods and services provided through the public sector and their financing. Countries around the world face similar challenges in determining what activities their governments should pursue and how these activities should be financed. Economists have thought long and hard about this issue. Thus, it is useful to begin the study of public finance by reviewing how economists view the appropriate role of government in a modern market economy.

1.1. The Economic Justification for Government Activity

Non-economists with conservative political leanings sometimes argue that government has only two legitimate functions: providing public safety and order (military and police service, with related court activities) and foreign relations. Classic socialists, in contrast, traditionally believe that government should undertake most, if not all, economic activities in a country and own the bulk of all resources. For most economists, the justification for government rests on *market failure*: the belief that various imperfections will make private markets unable to supply all goods and services people want in an optimal fashion and that government can improve the outcome by addressing these imperfections.

1.1.1. *Conditions for private markets to yield an optimal allocation of goods and services*

Economic theory states that, if certain critical assumptions are satisfied, private markets should provide an optimal allocation of goods and services. The key assumptions are as follows:

1. A market exists for every good and service.
2. Every market is characterized by perfect competition, meaning that no individual or small group of agents has the power to influence prices.
3. Everyone in each market has ready access to the same information ("everyone knows what anyone in the market knows").
4. Contract negotiation and enforcement have negligible costs.
5. Production functions exhibit decreasing returns to scale in production, meaning that, beyond some point, the cost per unit of production of every good or service begins to rise. (This makes it efficient to have more than one producer of each item.)
6. There are no externalities, meaning that the production and/or consumption of an item by one party will not affect the well-being of those not producing or consuming it.
7. Producers can prevent those who do not pay for goods from having access to them. In other words, there are no goods for which, if one person has access to them, everyone does.

Besides these seven assumptions, some would add an eighth: that people have similar preferences (and similar welfare functions).

1.1.2. *Consequences of market imperfections*

What happens if the above assumptions are violated?

1. *Not all goods have ready markets.* For example, private insurers may be unwilling to provide health insurance for all individuals without restrictions, because the required premiums will drive away healthy

customers, and only the sick (who will impose high costs) will pay. Economists call this situation "adverse selection."

2. *Many markets are characterized by imperfect competition*, in which there are few enough buyers or sellers that some have the power to influence the price of what is bought and sold. In this case, the market price will typically exceed marginal cost, distorting the allocation of resources, as some people buy (or sell) less than they would like if the market were competitive and price equaled marginal cost. A monopolist, for example, raises the market price of an item above marginal cost, causing less to be purchased than in a perfectly competitive market.

3. *Imperfect information characterizes many markets*, particularly in the financial sector. In these markets the more knowledgeable party can extract abnormal profits from others, raising costs, reducing sales, and again distorting the allocation of resources. Shrewd doctors, for example, can order unnecessary tests and services if not subject to review, while clever financiers can hide information from the public if not supervised. In extreme cases, the information imbalance makes it hard for a market to function. For example, purchasers of used cars may worry that the only cars offered are "lemons," thereby driving down market valuations and discouraging owners of "good" cars from offering them for sale.[1]

4. *Contract negotiation and enforcement are usually costly.* While private arbitration can resolve some claims, courts of law may be needed to resolve conflicts peaceably.

5. *A few services*, such as electricity generation, landline telephone service, and railroads, *exhibit steadily decreasing average costs*, because the marginal cost of supplying another customer is very low and overhead costs are virtually fixed, up to the capacity of the system. For such items, markets will tend toward monopoly, and monopoly

---

[1] This is the classic "market for lemons" problem first discussed by George Akerlof. See Akerlof, G. A. (1970), "The Market for 'Lemons': Quality Uncertainty and the Market Mechanism," *Quarterly Journal of Economics*, vol. 84(3), pp. 488–500.

prices will prevail unless government supplies the item itself or regulates the behavior of a private monopoly supplier.

6. *Many goods have externalities, either negative or positive.* On the negative side, for example, the production of many items generates waste and pollution, while every car on a crowded highway contributes to congestion. Many other items have positive externalities. For example, basic research provides unknown benefits that others can tap through commercialization, while public vaccination programs protect everyone by reducing the incidence of communicable diseases. If left solely to the market, people may find themselves with too much pollution and congestion, because those generating the negative externalities will not bear the costs they impose on others. Likewise, there may be too little basic research, and too few people will find it worthwhile bearing the cost of being vaccinated.

7. A few goods have the characteristic that, *if anyone has access to them, everyone does,* even those who have not paid for them. For example, everyone in a community benefits from an effective police force and court system that contribute to a low-crime environment, whether or not they pay taxes. Likewise, a strong and properly functioning military protects all of a country's citizens. Because it is hard to exclude those who have not paid for such goods, private firms will have difficulty producing them.

8. *Sellers may have incentives to engage in market manipulation,* providing misleading information that distorts consumer choices — what Akerlof and Shiller call "phishing".[2]

Besides the above considerations, *markets may not yield a politically acceptable distribution of income and wealth.* Differences in skills, combined with consumer preferences, can allow for widespread poverty and substantial inequality of income and wealth. In addition, private insurance may be unavailable to help individuals cope with severe income loss during economic downturns. Massive inequality may inhibit the free and voluntary exchange required for markets to work

---

[2]Akerlof, G. A., and R. J. Shiller (2015), *Phishing for Phools* (Princeton, NJ: Princeton University Press), p. xi.

well. It may also have undesirable political consequences, giving far greater political access to the wealthy than to others and possibly undermining the support for democracy as a consequence.

Finally, *markets can experience large swings* — pronounced business cycles and large booms and busts in asset markets — *if left unattended*. The high resulting costs can justify government stabilization efforts.

Because the key assumptions do not characterize reality, most economists would argue that *there is an economic case for government, even in a market economy*. Governments should do what markets cannot. From an economic perspective, governments should devote effort to the following (see Figure 1.1):

---

1. Address externalities
2. Address monopolies, natural and otherwise
3. Provide public goods
4. Address information failures
5. Provide macroeconomic stabilization
6. Provide social safety nets, to address concerns about the distribution of income
7. Provide a supportive legal framework and other services needed for markets to operate effectively

---

Figure 1.1. Key tasks for government in a market economy.

1. **Address externalities.** Governments should use their powers to tax and subsidize, or regulate (prohibit or compel), activities, to limit negative externalities such as pollution and congestion and stimulate the production of more goods with positive externalities, such as public health and basic research, than private markets will create on their own. Taxing negative externalities and subsidizing positive externalities are the best ways to do this, because they internalize to the producer and consumer the external costs and benefits of their actions. This approach allows the populace to determine how much of these goods and services is produced, through the interaction of supply and demand in markets, because the taxes and subsidies are factored into costs and prices.

When taxes and subsidies are infeasible, regulation may be necessary. However, regulation, which appeals instinctively to non-economists, is often less desirable, because it imposes fixed limits on the offending (or desirable) items, rather than letting the interaction of people's preferences in markets determine how much of the items is produced or consumed.[3]

2. **Address monopolies.** Because monopolies impose heavy social costs, governments should either (a) acquire and operate them, to secure the optimal outcome (setting price at marginal cost, possibly with some charge for overhead) or (b) regulate them, letting a private owner produce the good or service but setting the price at a socially desirable level (cost-covering, plus a modest profit margin).

3. **Provide public goods.** Government needs to ensure an adequate supply of basic infrastructure (roads, highways, clean water and sewage services), military and police protection, judicial services, public health services, and the like, because difficulties in pricing and excluding those who do not pay (what economists call "free riders") will make it hard for the private sector to provide these goods in adequate quantities. Whether education is a public good raises separate issues (Box 1.1).

4. **Address information failures.** It usually takes a government to intervene and correct information failures, since those benefiting will not want to correct them. Self-regulation is notoriously ineffective and often makes a bad situation worse (for example, guilds frequently create cartels, and doctors are typically loath to punish one of their own). At the same time, those who are hurt may benefit too little as individuals to finance the necessary oversight services, or they may lack the power to contend effectively with those disseminating misleading information. These reasons explain why many economists who oppose other government activities favor appropriate government regulation and supervision of the financial sector (which also provides a public good). It also gives

---

[3]For a classic analysis of this issue, comparing the costs and benefits of using taxes and subsidies, rather than regulation, see Schultze, C. (1977), *The Private Use of Public Interest* (Washington: Brookings Institution).

a justification for a government to compel people to save for their retirement, since an inherent focus on the short term will cause many young people to save too little voluntarily.

Besides the above four concerns, the shortcomings of markets justify three other government activities: stabilization, creating appropriate social safety nets, and providing a supportive legal and regulatory framework for private markets.

5. **Stabilize the economy.** Experience shows that markets are subject to wide swings that individuals have no incentive to address through counter-cyclical behavior. When times are good, people usually benefit by borrowing and investing in the expectation of ever-higher profits, or assuming that prices of stocks and other assets will continue to rise. Absent perfect foresight, there is little gain for individuals to act contrarily and limit the excesses of over-optimism. Likewise, in a recession, when the economy looks bleak, individuals have little to gain by taking a risk and investing, since there is no assurance that the economy will turn around. In these situations, government intervention (through monetary and fiscal policies) can cool an overheated economy or provide new demand to a weak one (by lowering interest rates, cutting taxes, and increasing government spending). This is an argument against requiring a balanced budget every fiscal year, at least at the central government level. However, as noted in Chapter 14, a less restrictive fiscal rule, such as a ceiling on the government's debt-to-GDP ratio or a requirement that the government balance its budget over the business cycle, may have benefits, particularly if some flexibility is allowed during severe recessions.

6. **Create a social safety net.** Market economies will not automatically create what most people consider a just distribution of income and assets. People whose skills are highly valued and in short supply will earn high incomes, while those with few marketable skills will earn little, if anything. Moreover, the distribution of income also reflects the initial distribution of wealth and power, which can be highly unequal. For this reason, there is usually support for measures to narrow the gaps left by the market. At a minimum, most societies provide at least a modicum of support for the poor and disabled.

Wealthier societies often do more, providing such social services as highly subsidized access to basic health care, child care, and services for the elderly. Most but not all also provide benefits for the unemployed, to reduce the costs of involuntary joblessness. In addition, many societies try to reduce inequities of wealth by taxing estates and inheritances and use progressive income taxes to lessen the inequality of income. Different countries have different views on these issues, with the extent of the safety net varying from one nation to another.

7. **Provide a supportive legal framework and other services for markets.** It is hard for markets to work properly without a supportive legal framework, including the enforcement of property rights. Individuals will be reluctant to produce and invest if others can steal their property or wrest control of the companies they have built or purchased. Hence, government can play a key role by providing effective legal enforcement of property rights, including protections for intellectual property (patents and trademarks). Government protection of creditors' rights, through the courts and bankruptcy procedures, is important to support banking, while government support for the rights of minority shareholders may be critical to promote stock markets and the widespread ownership of company shares.

To be sure, government activity comes at a price, so the costs of government activity must be considered alongside the benefits.

1. **Virtually any government action interferes with the outcome of private markets.** Taxation changes prices. Subsidies affect people's incentives about purchases and spending. Regulation either compels or prohibits activity, limiting freedom of action. All of these distort markets.
2. **Government action imposes financial costs and administrative burdens.** Workers are needed to carry out government programs, and budgets are required to pay for them and the cost of any materials and supplies needed for workers to do their jobs. In addition, private individuals and firms bear the cost of paying

taxes and complying with any rules associated with government programs. Heavy regulation or taxation can prohibit useful private activity, while corruption can raise costs, reduce investment, and curb growth.

Thus, it is important that the benefits from government activity outweigh these costs.

1.2. Specific Activities for Governments

1.2.1. *Addressing natural monopolies*

Natural monopolies arise when the identified fixed costs and a low marginal cost of accommodating another customer lead to declining marginal and average costs of service. In this situation, provision by a single entity is the most efficient way to supply the service. Electricity generation and distribution and landline telephone service are common examples of natural monopolies.

As shown in Figure 1.2, a monopolist can be expected to choose a market price at the level of output where marginal cost equals marginal revenue. When the demand curve slopes downward, the market price will exceed marginal revenue, and the monopolist earns a profit indicated by the area between the demand curve and the average cost curve for each unit sold. Because market price exceeds marginal revenue, consumers opt for less of the item than they would in the more optimal case where price equals marginal cost. In such a situation the government can intervene and improve consumer welfare, either by operating the company and setting price at marginal cost or by imposing a similar regulation on the existing private supplier. Because average cost exceeds marginal cost, the government must offset the loss with a budgetary transfer (at the expense of taxpayers) or set price at average cost (which yields a second-best result). In the case of private utilities, many governments set the market price such that the company can earn a modest but appropriate rate of return on its capital.

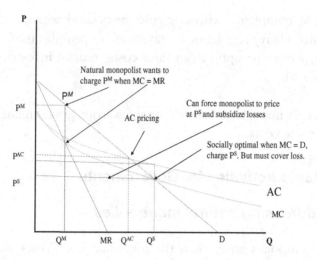

Figure 1.2.   Natural monopoly pricing issues.

1.2.2. *Public goods*

As explained earlier, public goods have two main characteristics. First, they are what economists call "non-rival in consumption," meaning that many people can use them at the same time, and no one's consumption is reduced when another user is added. Second, the goods exhibit "non-excludability," meaning that it is hard to keep people from using them once they are available, even if they do not pay for them. This gives rise to what economists call the "free rider" problem, where people can get something without having to pay for it (Box 1.2).[4] Because public goods are available to anyone, it is hard for private suppliers (who need to exclude those who don't pay from having access) to provide them. In addition, the social benefits from public goods will typically far exceed the private benefits to any single user, making it unattractive for any one user to bear the cost of providing them. Lighthouses, public parks, clean air, and an unspoiled environment are classic public goods, usually requiring either

---

[4]For a discussion of the free rider problem, see Hardin, R. (2008), "The Free Rider Problem", *Stanford Encyclopedia of Philosophy* (Fall Edition), at http://plato.stanford.edu/archives/fall2008/entries/free-rider/.

a government or a club of identified users (who force each person in the club to contribute) to finance them. A classic example is the so-called "tragedy of the commons," in which a common resource that no one owns will deteriorate from overuse unless government or a club of individuals agrees to enforce rules that maintain the resource.[5] Similarly, a commonly used resource, such as a public park or fishing area, may deteriorate from overuse unless a government intervenes to provide maintenance and regulate usage. Proper valuation requires that the benefits and costs to every affected individual be summed, to see whether the collective benefit justifies the cost.[6] Failure to do so can lead to undervaluing public goods and, hence, spending too little for them. Infrastructure spending in the United States may provide an example (Box 1.3).

1.2.3. Creating an economic framework that allows private markets to work well

Some public goods are important enough to be worth mentioning separately. One is creating an economic framework that allows private markets to work well. This involves three critical elements.

(1) **Property rights.** The first element is the *enforcement of property rights.* A key breakthrough in economic history was the acknowl-edgment by sovereigns that private firms could retain the bulk of the earnings from businesses.[7] Without such assurances, firms are unlikely to invest. Indeed, experiences in Eastern Europe and the former Soviet Union during the 1990s have shown the chilling effects on foreign investment when investors find that companies

---

[5]The classic analysis is in Hardin, G. (1968), "The Tragedy of the Commons," *Science*, vol. 162, no. 3859, pp. 1243–1248; also at http://www.garretthardinsociety.org/articles/art_tragedy_of_the_commons.html.

[6]See Samuelson, P. (1954), "The Pure Theory of Public Expenditure," *Review of Economics and Statistics*, vol. 36, no. 4, pp. 387–389.

[7]See, for example, Heilbroner, R., and L. Thurow (1998), *Economics Explained* (New York: Simon and Schuster), Chapter 1.

or investments they have created or renovated can be taken over at will by local mafias.

(2) **Effective judicial system.** A second element is the creation of an *honest and efficient judicial system.* The World Bank lists the prompt and efficient resolution of commercial disputes as one of the important criteria for assessing a country's business climate.[8] In many developing countries, the long time periods needed for commercial disputes to come to trial or perceptions that courts are biased have been serious impediments to foreign investment. Similarly, problems in the domestic court system led many foreign investors in Romania during the early 1990s to develop elaborate (and costly) provisions in contracts as a way of resolving commercial disputes. An efficient legal system is also critical for developing respect for the rule of law, including the recognition of contracts. Thus, an effective court system is a key aspect of economic development.

(3) **Competitive markets.** A third element involves *measures to promote competitive markets.* As noted earlier in this chapter, competitive markets are essential for consumers to achieve the benefits possible from a market economy. Monopoly, whether by sellers or buyers, restricts the opportunities available in markets and drives up prices. This in turn affects the allocation of resources, as consumers (or sellers, in the case of a monopoly buyer) change their buying or selling patterns in response to relative prices. By enacting anti-monopoly laws and taking other measures to promote competition (for example, opening markets to foreign suppliers), governments can help markets work better. Since government-owned firms may have "unfair advantages" relative to private producers, governments can also promote healthy competition by leaving most markets to private firms.[9]

---

[8]See World Bank, "Doing Business: Measuring Business Regulation," http://www. doingbusiness.org.

[9]For further discussion of state-owned enterprises, see Chapter 8.

1.2.4. *Managing public goods and services*

Providing public goods and services raises certain management issues for the government, including financing, how much to supply, and the operation and maintenance of facilities.

Financing is perhaps the most fundamental management decision facing government provision of public services. *Cost recovery* is an option where the government can identify those actually using the goods. In this case, the government can finance the goods through user fees or special levies. Many bridges, roads, and public parks have tolls or entrance fees, for example. Similarly, in some countries the costs of public schooling or sanitation service are fully or largely covered by special taxes levied on those in the area receiving the service.

Optimal pricing theory would suggest basing prices on *marginal costs*. However, in the case of an item with flat or declining marginal costs, marginal cost pricing will fail to recover the fixed costs of providing the good. Unless the government subsidizes these costs through the budget, pricing at *average cost* (for cost recovery) offers a second-best alternative. If public facilities experience congestion, the government may want to use *peak-period pricing*, recovering the average cost of provision (including construction or capital costs) through a series of charges that are higher than average cost during busy periods and somewhat below average cost during periods of less use. Another option, which many private clubs follow, is to levy a two-part tariff that combines both a "cost of use" and a capital (or overhead) charge.

If users cannot be clearly identified, or if an item (such as primary education) has substantial positive externalities and user charges would be prohibitively expensive for many potential users, *budget financing through taxation* may be preferable. In this case, the taxpaying public bears the cost of provision, with individual burdens depending on the level and composition of taxes used to fund the government. Where users of the service can be identified, the government may choose to impose a *combination of user charges and budget subsidies*. In many countries, for example, tuition at government-run universities is set at modest levels, so that low-income students can attend.[10] In this case, a substantial budget subsidy covers the remaining costs. Similarly, many government printing offices set the price of official publications at close to marginal cost and use general budget financing to cover the overhead expenses of the printing agency.

Closely related to the financing issue is *how much to supply*. In democracies, various methods are available to address this issue. *Planning officials*, for example, can propose the level of service based on certain criteria. Governments can also *survey the public* for information. In some cases, the public decides by voting. In the United States, for example, voters in many jurisdictions are asked at the time of state or national elections to vote on proposed bond issues whose proceeds are to be used to fund public facilities such as parks or schools. *Elections* themselves sometimes resolve the issue, as one party or set of candidates may favor one level (or allocation) of services, while another favors a different level or combination of services. Where budget financing is involved, the quantity of services also depends on the *amount of revenue available*. Governments with little revenue, or where existing budget responsibilities absorb virtually all the available funds, will be less able to finance expenditures than those with room to expand spending ("fiscal space"). Indeed, the level of service provision is often linked to decisions about taxation, with some voters favoring lower taxes and service levels and others willing to accept higher taxes in order to fund more services.

When considering public services, it is important to remember that creating a facility is often just the beginning of many future

---

[10]However, as university students often come disproportionately from higher income families, subsidized tuition at public universities frequently benefits the wealthy much more than the poor. This has led some economists to claim that subsidies to higher education are regressive. However, a more complete analysis that takes into account the taxes that higher income households pay to finance these subsidies suggests that the net impact of these subsidies on the income distribution is neutral or slightly progressive. See Johnson, W. (2005), "Are Public Subsidies to Higher Education Regressive?" *Education Finance and Policy*, vol. 1, pp. 288–315.

financial obligations. For example, *public services involve expenses for operations and maintenance* that can be substantial. Indeed, for many government programs (for example, schools or public medical facilities) operating costs — salaries for employees, expenses for supplies, and costs of upkeep and management — far exceed those of construction, certainly if aggregated over the life of a project. Proper management also requires appropriate incentives for employees to provide good service (e.g., competitive salaries, perhaps with bonuses) and for users to make effective use of facilities — for example, through charges for water usage and fines for not returning library books. In some cases, efficiency may involve having government *contract out* all or part of the service to the private sector. In many countries, for example, *public–private partnerships* are used to construct facilities such power plants or toll roads, letting private parties receive tolls or charges in return for constructing and operating the facility. In some localities, private firms are used in place of government employees to collect rubbish. Indeed, private firms are sometimes used in place of government agencies as a way of avoiding "entrenched bureaucracies," since in principle it may be easier to change private contractors than to fire public employees.

Because government has its own monopoly power, it is important that public goods not become "public bads." Widespread corruption, for example, can make a public agency worse than having none at all. A corrupt court system or a highly complicated tax system can make doing business more difficult. Similarly, an inefficient public utility can impose heavy costs, or subject users to poor service. In addition, allowing a government regulatory authority to be controlled by those it is supposed to regulate can reduce competition and the provision of services to the public. Thus, it is critical that the delivery of public services meet certain standards of quality and efficiency. In practice, the quality of services varies widely, both across and within countries.[11]

---

[11] For details on the World Bank's assessment of government effectiveness and governance, see its "Worldwide Governance Indicators", website https://info.worldbank.org/governance/wgi/.

1.2.5. *Externalities*

Externalities — benefits or costs that accrue to third parties from the economic activities of a producer or consumer that are not reflected in the market price — represent still another area that private markets cannot handle efficiently. Consumers and producers normally have no incentive to take externalities into account when they decide what to buy or produce, because they rarely experience the effects of their activities on others. Unless third parties intervene, through regulation or by imposing penalties or providing subsidies, producers and consumers of the good or service will make their production or purchasing decisions solely on the benefits and costs to themselves. Thus, goods with negative externalities (e.g., pollutants) will be over-produced, and those with positive externalities (e.g., those generating benefits to others that the producer or consumer cannot realize) will be under-produced, relative to where the externalities are recognized and valued appropriately. As noted earlier, classic negative externalities include air and water pollution from production, traffic congestion (such as from the construction of free highways that attract too many cars during peak travel periods), and "sprawl" (outward, low-density growth of urban areas that destroys scenic rural areas and farmland) from unregulated building projects. Positive externalities are less well known but equally important. Examples include the social benefits from having an educated population (positive externalities from primary and secondary education) and the better environment that results from such public health programs as vaccination drives and mosquito eradication measures.

As with public goods, government is an appropriate agent to address most externalities, because it can represent the interests of third parties and use its taxing and regulatory powers to address them. Because externalities affect the costs and benefits of an activity, the most efficient way to address them is to for government to *impose taxes or provide subsidies* that change the price of the activity. This approach "internalizes the externalities," by embedding them in the price the consumer faces. For example, if government determines that the pollution generated by a manufacturing firm imposes costs equivalent to 100 Euros per metric ton, it can impose a "pollution tax" of that amount on the producer, who in turn can be expected to reflect the tax in the price of the firm's products. Likewise, government can convey the cost of congestion to others by charging peak-period tolls for highway usage (see Box 1.4 on Singapore's approach to this issue, for an example). On the positive side, the social value of literacy can be made tangible through subsidies or free tuition for primary education. Similarly, government can fund "beautification" (e.g., tree planting) programs or provide tax benefits to underwrite the cost of certain research projects.

Although in principle taxes and subsidies are the most efficient way to address externalities, in practice it may not always be possible to do so. For example, it may be hard to measure the amount of pollutants. In addition, the cost of pollution may vary from one area to another and depend on air currents and the time of the year. In the case of global warming, the risk from heat-generating activities is difficult to assess, although carbon usage can be measured. Similarly, it may be difficult to require producers to install pollution-measuring devices. In other cases, people may doubt that charges will be able to deter noxious activities.

For all of these reasons, many governments prefer to address externalities by *regulation*, for example, prohibiting activities with negative externalities and mandating those with positive side benefits. The problem with this approach is that it does not allow for the possibility that the public would prefer to have some goods, even with the negative externalities, than none at all. A regulatory approach, such as zoning, may restrict the number of houses per hectare as a way of limiting the need for school construction. This can make house prices very expensive. An alternate approach, levying "public service fees" on developers that will be passed onto consumers in the price of housing, allows the market to determine how much housing the public wants by having the price reflect the cost of public services that will be required, such as access to sewage and water supply lines.

When addressing externalities, it is important that policy not constrain access to other worthwhile goods and services. For example, free public education should not prevent investment in private education. More generally, state-owned enterprises should not have an unfair advantage in competing with private producers.

1.2.6. *Merit goods*

An interesting concept closely related to the idea of externalities is the notion of *merit goods*. These are goods that are thought to confer strong benefits to society as a whole and thus "deserve" to be provided. Hence, a case can be made for subsidizing their creation and distribution. Typical merit goods include fine art, serious theater, opera and symphonic music, and national historical institutions, because they are seen as contributing to a society's culture. Some analysts in democratic countries would also consider "liberal education" as a merit good, because it encourages careful reading and critical thinking, which are important for the analysis of ideas in a free society. A few might add not-for-profit, independent news and cultural media networks, such as Corporation for Public Broadcasting in the United States or the BBC in the United Kingdom, since they offer non-partisan but intellectually serious information free of charge to the public.

A key question for those promoting the concept of merit goods is whether these are just a special class of goods with positive externalities. Like basic research and public health programs, merit goods are considered to benefit not just those who consume them but also others. What is arguably different is that these goods are often said to have intrinsic cultural value. In practice, merit goods often appeal mainly to an elite segment of society. Thus, one can argue whether merit goods are simply things that have positive value for a small but influential part of the population.

Because of the controversy surrounding merit goods, the case for public support requires strong factual justification. One should ask, for example, whether the activity truly benefits the public. This can raise a variety of issues involving public tastes. The government should think carefully about the process for determining which activities merit support. It may be important to establish certain criteria for making decisions, to ensure that minority and controversial but high-quality projects can be considered, in addition to those that a wide segment of the population considers worthwhile. One can also ask whether the public sector needs itself to supply these goods (for example, through a state-owned museum, opera company, or television network). It may be equally or more effective for the state to subsidize private providers, as is common in Singapore (through the National Council for the Arts) and the United States (through the National Endowment for the Arts). Another option is to provide vouchers to students or low-income households, so that they find it easier to attend designated cultural activities.

1.2.7. *Addressing distributional issues*

Because markets reward those who supply highly desired goods and services, they need not produce a "just" distribution of income. Those with few marketable skills, or for whose skills there is little demand, or who happen to be competing with many others for a limited number of positions, will inevitably earn less than those whose skills are in much demand and short supply. The distribution of assets is often even more unequal, as it usually requires a fair amount of financial capital to have access to high-earning investment opportunities.

Because the so-called basic needs typically require a minimum amount of income, a case can be made for government intervention to create a social safety net for the most vulnerable, if not to adjust the distribution of income more extensively. Income can be redistributed through both tax and expenditure measures, although most experience suggests that it is easier to provide support to those with low incomes through government spending.

On the revenue side, most governments have a progressive income tax, with higher marginal rates as income increases, so that higher income taxpayers pay a higher share of their incomes in tax than do those with lower incomes. A few countries (e.g., Romania and Russia) have so-called *flat* income taxes, with only a single rate applied to taxable income. However, even these taxes can be progressive, if they exempt the bottom slab of income from tax, because the percentage of income subject to tax rises with income. Besides income taxes, countries can address the distribution of income and wealth through estate, inheritance, and gift taxes, which can impose a high tax rate on large estates or inheritances, and on large gifts to individuals, unless the deceased (or living donors) give a large share of their property to approved charitable activities. Finally, the United States provides a significant amount of support to low-income households with earnings through its Earned Income (Tax) Credit. Under this program, households with earned income (wages and salaries) can actually receive money from the government by filing a tax return if their incomes are sufficiently low and they meet certain criteria regarding citizenship and family composition.

Governments have a wide variety of expenditure programs to address distributional concerns. These include food distribution and subsidy programs for low-income households, income support and temporary employment projects for the unemployed, and income support for the disabled. Most high-income countries and many countries transitioning from central planning have government-sponsored pension programs for the elderly, and many of these provide more-than-proportionate benefits to low-income, compared to higher income, households and individuals. In many countries, government support for health and education particularly benefits lower income households, as they are more likely to use state health clinics and public schools. In addition, government subsidies for transit (bus, rail, and jitney fares) help low-income families disproportionately, since they rely more on public transportation. For the same reason, general fuel subsidies more often assist upper income households, who are more likely to own and use automobiles. More generally, to address distributional concerns, government subsidies must be *targeted* toward low-income households. In many low- and middle-income countries, identifying low-income households can be challenging, although various strategies are available to help identify and reach the poor. Targeting, however, may render benefit programs politically unpopular, particularly when powerful groups (such as government employees or rich farmers) find their interests threatened. Even in advanced economies, governments sometimes have to enact benefit programs that assist middle- and even upper income families, to secure the political support needed to aid the poor.

Programs to redistribute income, like tax measures, impose costs that must be considered. These include the cost of administering the program, such as creating offices and hiring staff, and the costs of compliance. Meeting the many requirements needed to qualify for assistance can be difficult and time consuming. In addition, many individuals feel stigmatized if they receive benefits. Accordingly, some who are eligible choose not to apply. At the same time, expenditure programs invite fraud and abuse, and governments may have to accept a certain amount of wrongdoing in order to make it simpler for those who do qualify to receive benefits. Governments must also take into account the effect that programs have on the incentives to work and save. Jobless workers may be hesitant to accept job offers if unemployment benefits are too generous (too high a percentage of the person's last wage), for example. Similarly, overly generous state pension benefits may reduce the incentives to develop private savings for retirement, although economists are divided over whether the evidence supports this claim. Finally, measures to require employers to pay a minimum wage may reduce the demand for low-skilled workers, although in some countries research suggests that current minima may be too low to have much effect on employment levels.

Assessing the impact of government programs on the distribution of income requires considering both tax and spending measures. For example, a less-than-progressive tax system, in which income and profits are taxed more lightly than consumption, may be accompanied by a large number of spending programs that assist the poor, such as food and employment subsidies, free public schools, government health clinics, and support for the elderly. Thus, the combined impact of tax and spending programs on households at different income levels must be assessed. Doing so is hard, because tax systems and spending programs are complex, and determining who bears the burden of different taxes and who benefits from various programs may be difficult. Two tax systems with similar tax rates but different sets of exclusions — for example, one that taxes interest and capital gains, and one that does not — may have affect households very differently, because households at different income levels derive different shares of their incomes from wages and salaries, interest and dividends, and capital gains. Similarly, the distributional effect of social expenditures depends on the quality of benefits provided to households at different income levels. Thus, public education programs may appear to favor the poor. In fact, however, as noted earlier in footnote 10, middle- and upper income families benefit disproportionately if their schools receive much higher outlays per pupil, or if better services are provided to higher than to lower income households.

In practice, it may be harder for government to address distributional concerns by fostering opportunity and wealth holding than by providing minimum levels of consumption through subsidies and income transfer programs. Nevertheless, certain programs can provide greater opportunities for higher earnings. These include free and high-quality primary and secondary education, effective job training and retraining programs, public health programs and health clinics that provide effective and inexpensive health services, subsidies for pensions and homeownership, and civil rights laws that help overcome discrimination in the marketplace.

1.2.8. *Stabilization*

Macroeconomic stabilization represents still another area where government has a role to play in a market economy. It is widely acknowledged that markets are subject to a variety of shocks and can therefore experience significant fluctuations. *External shocks*, such as changes in weather, world interest rates, or market perceptions of a country's economy, can have a dramatic impact on a nation's economic growth and inflation rate. Indeed, during late 2008 and much of 2009 many developing and emerging market countries found that turbulence originating in the United States and other advanced economies adversely affected their exports, growth rates, and in some cases exchange rates. *Domestic business cycles*, which can reflect shifts in investment behavior or changing consumer sentiment, also affect an economy's macroeconomic performance.

Economic fluctuations can have serious repercussions for a country's citizens. Recessions typically bring not only slower or negative economic growth but also losses in household income, higher unemployment, and more business failures. Poverty rates often increase when economic growth declines. Indeed, losses are often spread unevenly, with the poor and those in specific industries affected more than others. A sharp rise in GDP that causes an economy to overheat can trigger higher inflation and, in some cases, asset bubbles that can trigger subsequent collapse when equity or real estate prices can no longer be maintained. Higher inflation has particularly adverse effects on the poor, since whatever assets they have are more likely to be in cash, and thus especially subject to the inflation tax.

Free markets have few "natural" ways to respond to economic shocks. Many developing country economies, for example, are often poorly diversified. Even small advanced economies with high ratios of trade to GDP, such as Singapore, are highly exposed to changes in the global economy. In addition, private parties have little incentive to "lean against" the prevailing market pressures. Private parties typically benefit from asset booms and overheating and are unlikely to gain from delaying investments and other projects. Similarly, private parties may have trouble judging when a depressed economy will begin to revive. Thus, there is little incentive to invest or spend aggressively while the economy looks weak.

For all of these reasons, counter-cyclical policy by government can help stabilize a nation's economy. Loosening monetary policy, by providing liquidity and lowering interest rates, can make investment projects more attractive and promote borrowing. Similarly, counter-cyclical fiscal policy, involving tax cuts and spending increases, can boost demand directly and give firms and households more after-tax income to support private investment and consumption. When inflation accelerates or an economy threatens to overheat, monetary tightening can help cool demand by raising interest rates and discouraging borrowing. Similarly, tightening fiscal policy, by raising taxes and non-tax revenues and reducing government expenditure, can decrease demand through reductions in private and government spending. Although politicians are especially fond of relaxing policies during recessions, it is important for policy also to be tightened during economic booms, so that the government has sufficient credibility for policy relaxation to boost growth and not trigger a loss in confidence that can provoke a capital outflow and sharp depreciation in the national currency. Research has shown that many developing countries lack the ability to implement expansionary fiscal policy during recessions because they have been unsuccessful at limiting expenditure during good times.[12] In other words, pro-cyclical policy during booms limits the ability to implement counter-cyclical policy during slowdowns.

Although many options are available for stimulating output during recessions, the 2007–2009 economic crisis demonstrated that some policies are more effective than others at boosting demand. A 2008 study by staff at the International Monetary Fund (IMF), for example, contended that increased spending, including higher transfer payments, and tax cuts targeted on lower income households, are likely to have larger positive effects on jobs and incomes than more general tax cuts or increases in subsidies.[13] A subsequent IMF staff paper argued that infrastructure projects may have the largest payoffs in

---

[12]See, for example, Ilzetzki, E., and C. A. Végh (2008), "Procyclical Fiscal Policy in Developing Countries: Truth or Fiction?" NBER Working Paper No. 14191 (Cambridge, MA: National Bureau of Economic Research).

[13]See Spilimbergo, A. *et al.* (2008), "Fiscal Policy for the Crisis," IMF Staff Position Note SPN/08/01 (Washington, DC: International Monetary Fund, December), http://www.imf.org/external/pubs/ft/spn/2008/spn0801.pdf.

terms of income and jobs created for each unit of spending.[14] One reason may be that such projects create a stream of expenditures for inputs that in turn lead to considerable hiring, not just for the project itself but also for firms that supply goods and services for the projects. The second highest multiplier is for transfers targeted on low-income (borrowing-constrained) households. Cuts in labor taxes and untargeted transfers have noticeably smaller multipliers. Research also shows that expansionary fiscal policy is more powerful when supported by accommodating monetary policy. The inflationary consequences are also greater, although inflation remained subdued in many countries during 2009 and 2010.

1.2.9. *Addressing information failures: Regulation and social insurance*

Limited or asymmetric information in private markets offers still another justification for government involvement in the economy. For example, the inability of lenders to assess borrowers limits lending to lower income households, while richer households and established firms can obtain loans, some of which will prove uncollectable (non-performing assets). Similarly, without regulation, unequal access to information can lead to a wide variety of ills in financial markets, including fraud and insider dealing. Myopia (short-sightedness) and adverse selection (the tendency of those needing coverage to be the ones to apply for it) can make it harder for private markets to make available health insurance and annuities (pensions for life). Finally, inadequate and unequal information can enable medical providers to "create demand" for their services or get patients to request medically unnecessary tests and procedures because patients lack the information to determine whether they are receiving appropriate care or whether a particular medical procedure has value or is "worth the cost." Following are examples of this general principle.

---

[14]See Freedman, C. *et al.* (2009), "The Case for Global Fiscal Stimulus," IMF Staff Position Note SPN/09/03 (Washington, DC: International Monetary Fund, March), http://www.imf.org/external/pubs/ft/spn/2009/spn0903.pdf.

1.2.9.1. *Deposit insurance*

Most economists acknowledge that asymmetric information makes it hard for the private sector to provide deposit insurance, i.e., insurance that depositors will not lose their funds if a bank fails. The reason is that bank managers know their own risk profile far better than do outsiders, who have only limited information about a bank's asset portfolio. Potential insurers typically know only the information that a bank releases, usually through periodic reports. Likewise, few depositors typically know the "true" condition of their bank, unless they have inside information. For these reasons, it is hard to assess the risk that a bank might fail and, thus, price that risk before it happens. However, at least one economist has argued that it may be possible to infer such risk by requiring banks to issue subordinated debt and then looking at its "price" (i.e., the spread between interest rates on that debt and on relatively secure assets, such as short-term government securities).[15]

To maintain confidence, particularly after bank runs have led to bank closures, the government must intervene appropriately. Because bank failures can have serious repercussions for the rest of a nation's economy, government should regulate and supervise the activities of individual institutions. This includes a variety of measures, including standards for opening banks, rules mandating minimum capital levels and the disclosure of information to regulators, and limitations on how much of a bank's capital may be lent to any one borrower (or, perhaps, industry). In addition, because regulation and supervision cannot prevent all bank failures, a case can be made for government-provided deposit insurance. Because unlimited deposit insurance can create incentives for risky behavior by financial institutions,[16] deposit insurance should ideally be limited in scope. Most countries provide full coverage only for small depositors, as they cannot be expected to be aware of the condition of different financial institutions. Large

---

[15] See, for example, Calomiris, C. W. (1989). "Deposit Insurance: Lessons from the Record," *Economic Perspectives* (May), Federal Reserve Bank of Chicago, pp. 10–30.
[16] *Ibid.*

depositors should receive only partial coverage for their deposits. This will give them an incentive to police the behavior of individual banks and remove their funds if they consider a particular institution unsafe.

1.2.9.2. Pensions

Individuals are often shortsighted when it comes to providing for their old age. Young adults can have difficulty envisioning that they will eventually reach an age when it is difficult to continue working and earning an income. Yet, experience shows that aging is inevitable, and that declining health makes it hard for people to anticipate remaining in the workforce. Thus, government can play a role by requiring individuals to set aside funds for retirement, whether through mandatory savings programs or through state pension programs that impose taxes to finance retirement benefits. Each approach has advantages and disadvantages (see Chapter 12 for discussion), and current recommendations from the World Bank suggest that countries develop multiple ways of providing support for the elderly.[17] A potential advantage of a government pension program is that benefits can be skewed toward lower income households, who may find it especially hard to accumulate savings.

To be sure, any pension program poses potential costs. For example, a government-provided pension regime may discourage private retirement savings, although the empirical research on this issue is inconclusive. In addition, a pay-as-you-go pension program, in which current workers are taxed to support benefits for the elderly, can impose a heavy burden on future generations in a country with an aging population. The reason is that, over time, the number of workers per retiree will decline, requiring either higher taxes, lower benefits, or an increase in the retirement age to keep the system solvent. Many

---

[17]See Holtzmann, R., and R. Hinz (2005), *Old Age Income Support in the 21st Century* (Washington: World Bank), http://siteresources.worldbank.org/INTPENSIONS/Resources/Old_Age_Inc_Supp_Full_En.pdf.

advanced economies face serious budget problems because they have pay-as-you-go pension systems, and the problems are particularly acute in Germany, Italy, and Japan.[18]

1.2.9.3. Health care

Still another area where asymmetric information helps justify government involvement is health care. Because consumers rarely know what treatments they need and have difficulty assessing the accuracy of what physicians recommend, they can be persuaded to accept more care than they need, or unnecessarily costly care — what is sometimes termed "supplier-induced care." It is especially hard for consumers to shop for treatment or assess a physician's recommendation when care is needed immediately. Even if decisions can be deferred, requesting a "second opinion" may leave the consumer uncertain as to which recommendation is correct.

In theory, consumers may find it easier to choose providers when they are well than when ill. Even then, however, making an informed choice can be difficult. Individuals may have heard of certain physicians or practices by word of mouth or reputation, and the comments may not be what doctors would offer if asked in confidence. Sometimes, popular magazines publish articles listing physicians that other doctors would recommend. However, verifying the comments is difficult. Moreover, in large markets, it can be very hard identifying the most skilled physicians and specialists.

The private market for health insurance, similarly, may work less than optimally. Insurers may find that those seeking health insurance are more likely to need coverage than those who do not — an example of what economists call *adverse selection*. As a result, health insurance may be relatively expensive, discouraging younger and healthier people from applying. Insurers can try to reduce adverse

---

[18]See Chand, S. K., and A. Jaeger (2000), *Aging Populations and Public Pension Schemes*, Occasional Paper No. 147 (Washington: International Monetary Fund).

selection by restricting benefits — for example, denying coverage for the so-called "preexisting conditions." In this case, however, those needing insurance cannot get it and must instead pay out of pocket for care. Limiting the ability of insurers to deny such coverage was a key objective in the Patient Protection and Affordable Care Act (Pub. Law 111–152) approved in United States in 2010.

Government programs can address many of the shortcomings of private health care markets. For example, governmental organizations can review the care given by different medical providers and publish information about relative costs and rates of success with different treatments or types of care. Similarly, governments can encourage cost-saving innovations that private markets have not undertaken — for example, computerizing medical records — via subsidies and, if necessary, regulation. Governments can also create "insurance exchanges," to facilitate the comparison of insurance policies and promote competition among insurers.[19] In addition, governments can also offer health insurance themselves, addressing the adverse selection problem by offering coverage to the community at large or creating large pools of individuals, so that the costs of those needing care can be spread across the population. Such coverage can be offered at cost to those unable to buy private health insurance, or at highly subsidized prices in the case of low-income households.

Government involvement in health care can create costs as well as benefits. Regulation — for example, overseeing physician behavior or mandating that certain procedures be followed — imposes burdens that can raise costs. In addition, subsidized health care or health insurance adds to the government's budget, requiring higher taxes, lower spending elsewhere, or higher public debt. In addition, providing health insurance can increase demand unless coverage is well structured, because patients will no longer face the full cost of care.

---

[19]Blumberg, L. (2009), "Improving Health Insurance Markets and Promoting Competition under Health Care Reform," Committee on Ways and Means, U.S. House of Representatives (April 22), http://www.urban.org/uploadedpdf/901246_improving{\%}20healthinsurance.pdf.

This can make patients less sensitive to cost comparisons and encourage physicians to recommend unnecessary or unduly expensive care. It can also create moral hazard, to the extent that patients, knowing that they have insurance, are less careful — for example, not practicing oral hygiene or not being as careful about activities that increase the risk of heart disease. Moreover, health insurance can inflate the demand for health care generally, encouraging consumers to spend more for medical services than they might otherwise. The reason is that it can be very difficult disputing the value of medical treatments that offer some benefit, even if they are very costly. Thus, governments sometimes find it necessary to impose restrictions — for example, limiting insurance to well-established remedies and screening, rather than experimental treatments whose success remains to be validated.[20]

For these and other reasons, such as the goal of ensuring access to health care for all citizens, governments in most economies have intervened in the health care market, providing insurance, financing, and health care facilities. The specific combinations vary from country to country. The United Kingdom, for example, has created its own National Health Service, which provides a wide range of care at public hospitals and medical facilities. Canada's health care system provides full coverage for a broad array of services provided by private physicians. In France, public insurance covers 70–80% of all medical costs; most persons buy supplementary insurance, which covers nearly all the remaining charges. The Ministry of Health establishes set budgets and regulates many aspects of care, including prices for procedures and pharmaceuticals.[21] In Singapore, the government provides funding for public hospitals and health clinics and requires that a portion of each person's Central Provident Fund contributions be used for their

---

[20]For further discussion of these issues, see Hsiao, W., and P. Heller (2007), "What Macroeconomists Should Know about Health Care Policy," Working Paper No. 07/13 (Washington, DC: International Monetary Fund, January), http://www.imf.org/external/pubs/ft/wp/2007/wp0713.pdf.

[21]Carroll, A. E., and A. Frakt (2017), "The Best Health Care System in the World: Which One Would You Pick?" *New York Times*, September 18, https://www.nytimes.com/interactive/2017/09/18/upshot/best-health-care-system-country-bracket.html.

own Medisave account, which can be used to pay for approved health insurance premiums, hospital care, and certain types of outpatient and long-term care. In the United States, the federal government provides care directly to veterans at government-operated veterans' hospitals, offers hospitalization insurance and voluntary medical and drug insurance (at a cost) to the elderly, funds (with state participation) medical insurance for the poor through Medicaid, and supports medical research. It also supports an extensive system of privately supplied insurance coverage through tax subsidies and the organization of medical exchanges (some provided by the states) to facilitate the sale of private health insurance for those not offered insurance by their employers.

1.3. Summary

Even in a well-functioning market economy, government has a clear role to play in providing goods and services that markets cannot be expected to make available in sufficient quantities. Government also supports the "social contract" by establishing the framework in which markets can operate. This framework includes creating and protecting property rights, establishing rights for minority as well as majority shareholders in private firms, promoting competition in markets, and creating institutions that allow the peaceful resolution of commercial disputes. Government also plays a role in establishing vital "non-economic" rights, such as protection from discrimination and access to key sources of opportunity, such as primary and secondary education and reasonable health care services. In addition, government is needed to provide public goods, address externalities, and handle cases of natural monopoly, all examples of classic "market failure." Government is also essential to address the distributional inequities that result from the working of private markets; to create and apply policies that can help stabilize output and prices; and to provide financial sector regulation. Together, these activities help make the outcomes of the market politically acceptable, thereby facilitating the acceptance of private markets as the main means for allocating goods and services.

Government action comes at a cost, however. Regulations designed to address market failures impose burdens on market participants. Similarly, the taxes needed to fund public goods, regulation, stabilization policies, and redistribution reduce the returns to work, saving, and investment, potentially diminishing private sector activity unless the government services provided offset these negative effects. To minimize these costs, policymakers should think dynamically, recognizing that today's solutions can create new problems for an economy. For example, the ability to use fiscal policy to stabilize output in a recession may also make government a source of inflation. Thus, policy responses should be adaptable, and government programs should be capable of modification or elimination if changing circumstances require new approaches. Many policy variants, including options ranging from near-market to government provision, can be developed to meet the need for public goods or the supply of services characterized by natural monopoly. Thus, governments should consider the many options available when deciding how to perform their role in doing what markets cannot be expected to do well.

Box 1.1: Is Education a Public Good?

Periodically, the question arises whether education is a public good. Primary and secondary education provide substantial benefits, not only to students and their families but also to the society in general. The general populace benefits from having a citizenry able to read and write and knowledgeable about basic rules for human interaction, skills imparted during primary school. Likewise, the economy benefits generally from having a population with the basic skills needed for employment and knowledgeable about the national history and culture, skills that secondary school provides. Because it is easy to exclude individuals from school and because resources provided to some students preclude their provision to others, it is difficult to see education as satisfying the tests of non-excludability and non-rivalrous consumption that normally apply

---

Box 1.1: (*Continued*)

to public goods. However, the strong positive externalities from primary and secondary schooling and the value of having children at all income levels acquire these skills explain why most governments provide primary and secondary education to all citizens, usually at little or no cost.

Box 1.2: The Free Rider Problem

An issue that inevitably arises with the provision of public goods is the "free rider" problem. Because public goods are available to everyone when available to anyone, there is a strong incentive for individuals to avoid contributing to their cost. Accordingly, people are encouraged to become "free riders" — those gaining benefits without paying for them. If free riding becomes too prevalent, it will be hard to finance a good or service.

Free riding occurs in many settings. Classic examples include the following:

1. *The tragedy of the commons*: Government or a kind benefactor provides a good or service that needs maintenance. Unless maintenance can be enforced, or people are required to pay for it, the good or service will deteriorate. A good example is the recent provision of very inexpensive bicycles in several European cities, where many people have stolen or damaged the bicycles with impunity, thereby challenging the viability of the service.
2. *People "holding up an agreement" for pay*: When unanimous consent is needed for an agreement, the last few individuals can force the remainder to pay a very high price for their agreement, much more than their share of any benefits from its implementation.
3. *Negotiating passage of a bill in a parliament*: Members of parliament who are not that interested in a bill's main issues can use it as a way to get approval of a side issue that interests them.

Box 1.3: Infrastructure Spending in the United States

In 2017, the IMF estimated that the United States spent less than 2.5% of GDP annually on infrastructure from 1990 through 2015, and only 1.6% in 2015.[22] The OECD reported a noticeably smaller figure of about 0.6% for 2015, less than the estimated outlays in Japan and the United Kingdom (0.9%) and France (0.8%).[23] The World Economic Forum's *Global Competitiveness Report* for 2018 ranked the United States ninth in infrastructure, behind Singapore, Hong Kong SAR, Switzerland, Netherlands, Japan, Republic of Korea, Germany, and France.[24] In 2017, the American Society of Civil Engineers (ASCE) gave United States infrastructure an overall grade of D+, with grades ranging from B for rail to D− for transit. The ASCE estimated that US$2.0 trillion would be needed over a 10-year period to fill the shortfall in infrastructure, corresponding to raising expenditure to between 2.5% and 3.5% of GDP annually.[25]

Box 1.4: Singapore's Approach to Addressing Traffic Congestion

Singapore offers an interesting example of how to address traffic congestion: its "electronic road pricing" or ERP system. This small island country has erected overhead gantries at the entrance to many potentially congested areas. All vehicles are required to have installed on the dashboard a small device that holds an electronic cash card, and a vehicle that passes under a gantry incurs a toll that is deducted from the balance on the card. The amount of

---

[22] International Monetary Fund (2017), *United States: 2017 Article IV Consultation — Press Release; Staff Report*, Washington, July, p. 27.
[23] OECD Data, "Infrastructure Investment," https://data.oecd.org/transport/ infrastructure-investment.htm.
[24] World Economic Forum (2018), *Global Competitiveness Report 2018*.
[25] American Society of Civil Engineers (2017), "2017 Infrastructure Report Card," https://www.infrastructurereportcard.org/.

Box 1.4: (*Continued*)

the toll depends on the location, time of day, and type of vehicle. For example, a car pays a modest toll when entering a downtown area during a relatively uncongested part of the workday; a much higher toll during rush hour; and no toll on Sundays, when traffic is normally very low. Tolls are typically higher for larger vehicles (e.g., trucks and private busses) than smaller ones (e.g., cars and motorcycles). Taxis also pay the tolls, which are then passed on to passengers. From time to time, Singapore adjusts the level of tolls, to reflect changes in driving patters. Although the ERP system does not eliminate congestion, at least one study claims that it has reduced it.[26]

In 2003, London, the British capital, adopted a similar system, the London Congestion Charge, in which vehicles pay a flat toll of 8 pounds when entering the central business district. Despite much grumbling, studies suggest that it, too, has reduced congestion in the central business district.[27]

---

[26]See Chin, Kiang Kong (2002), "Road Pricing — Singapore's Experience," Singapore Land Transport Authority, http://www.imprint-eu.org/public/Papers/IMPRINT3_chin.pdf.
[27]See Transport for London (2003), "Congestion Charging Six Months On," http://web. archive.org/web/20060515194436/ http://www.tfl.gov.uk/tfl/downloads/pdf/congestion-charging/cc-6monthson.pdf.

Chapter Two: How Fiscal Policy Affects the National Economy

Government economic activity affects a nation's economy, and vice-versa. This chapter analyzes the impact of government economic policy, in particular fiscal policy, on the national economy. A variety of models and experiences will be used to suggest how fiscal policy affects the rate of economic growth and inflation, the balance of payments, and the working of monetary policy. In addition, the chapter reviews how fiscal policy can be used for macroeconomic management, including ways by which fiscal policy can promote the economic growth.

2.1. Fiscal Policy: An Introduction

Fiscal policy represents the government's efforts to shape economic activity through the government budget. Traditionally, fiscal policy has focused on the government's *budget balance* — whether the budget is in surplus or deficit and by how much. However, fiscal policy encompasses much more than this. Fiscal policy also involves the size and composition of the government's *revenues;* the level and composition of government *expenditures;* and the nature of budget *financing,* including the amount and composition of *public debt.* Each of these elements can affect an economy's stability, including its rate of inflation and economic growth. In addition, assessing the stance of fiscal policy requires knowing the position not just of the central government but also of state or provincial and local governments, since they all collect revenues, make expenditures, and, in some cases, incur debt. It can also be useful to understand the financial position of state-owned (public) enterprises, since their profits help finance government expenditure and their outlays can burden government budgets and add to public debt. Together, the financial activities of the different units of government and the public enterprises comprise the financial position of a country's public sector.

Fiscal policy affects the non-government sector in a variety of ways.

Government revenues and revenue policy, in addition to providing the main source of funding for government activity, have an effect on incentives and alter the behavior of private firms and individuals. *The level and composition of taxes* affect household decisions about work, saving, investment, and consumption. They also influence firms' decisions about production, investment, hiring, and financing. All other things equal, higher taxes will likely mean less consumption, less investment, and reduced work effort. The *type of taxation* also matters. Income taxation will have a greater impact on work effort, savings, and investment, while sales and value-added taxes will affect consumption but have less impact on work and saving. Differential taxation — for example, higher taxes on some kinds of goods than others — may steer people toward the more lightly taxed items, possibly distorting behavior and encouraging firms and individuals to engage in fundamentally less productive activities.

Government expenditures also affect behavior, particularly when subsidies (policies that reduce the price of something) and transfers (payments to individuals or institutions) are involved. For example, subsidies for gasoline and expenditures for highways (as opposed to public transit) encourage more driving and greater consumption of petroleum, thereby increasing petroleum imports (or reducing petroleum exports) and worsening a country's balance of payments. Certain transfer payments, for example, unemployment benefits for those out of work, can reduce the incentives to look for and accept employment if they are set too close to an individual's last wage or salary level. Expenditures can also have positive effects. Expenditures for productive infrastructure, such as mass transit facilities or electrical power lines, can improve the business climate and encourage investment. Effective spending for primary education boosts literacy, while spending for financial regulation can lead to a stronger banking system and less risk of panics or bank failures.

The government's fiscal balance has an important bearing on aggregate demand in an economy. As we will see in Section 2.2, a budget deficit, other things being equal, will tend to stimulate demand, because the government is injecting more resources into the economy than it is removing. A budget surplus, by contrast, tends to contract demand.[1] The government budget balance also bears a relationship to the current account of a country's balance of payments. The reason is that the classic cash or overall budget balance is equal to the difference between government savings and investment (see Box 2.1). When combined with the savings minus investment balance for the non-government sector, the two add up to the current account balance of the balance of payments. We will discuss this point in Section 2.4 of this chapter. Finally, the fiscal balance and its financing affect a country's monetary sector. A larger fiscal deficit, unless financed by non-bank sources, increases the demand for budget financing from the banking system. This in turn can drive up interest rates and reduce the availability of lending for private investment, unless the monetary authority (central bank) accommodates the financing need by providing more money.

2.2. Fiscal Policy and Aggregate Demand

To understand how fiscal policy affects aggregate demand in an economy, it is useful to draw on a simple macroeconomic model that allows the use of diagrams. We begin with the classic *IS–LM* model developed by John Hicks to illustrate Keynes's *General Theory*. This model draws on the notion of the circular flow of income, in which the income received by workers, firms, and investors flows through the economy as it is spent (consumed or invested).

In this model, government spending adds to income, while taxation reduces it (by draining resources from the private sector). Hence, the key fiscal parameter that affects aggregate demand is net government

---

[1]The impact of the budget on demand can be assessed further using the *cyclically adjusted budget balance*, i.e., the balance adjusted by the economy's position in relation to the business cycle. This concept will be explored later, in Chapter 4.

spending (total expenditure less revenue). Because it is a model of comparative statics, it lacks dynamics and expectations, and its results are often complemented with other analysis. Nevertheless, this model remains the mainstay used in many textbooks.[2]

2.2.1. *Fiscal policy in a closed economy*

A closed economy model, with no external sector, can be modeled using the following expressions:

(1) $w/p = F_N(K, N)$: the real wage increases as the capital stock expands but decreases as labor supply increases;

(2) $\Upsilon = F(K, N)$: output (income) is a positive function of both the capital stock and labor supply;

(3) $C = C(\Upsilon - T, r)$, where private consumption increases with after-tax income ($\Upsilon - T$) but decreases as the interest rate increases;

(4) $I = I(r)$, where private investment declines as the interest rate increases;

(5) $M/p = L(r, \Upsilon)$: demand for real money is a negative function of the interest rate but a positive function of income (higher interest rates shift demand from money to interest-bearing assets);

(6) $C + C_g + I + I_g = \Upsilon$: national income (GDP) equals private plus public consumption plus private and public investment.

In the above model, expressions (1) and (2) define the production relationships; expressions (3) and (4) define private demand; expression (5) is the money demand function; and expression (6) provides the expenditure definition of GDP. Note that, in a closed economy, GDP excludes net exports ($X - M$).

In this very simple, closed economy model, the so-called investment–saving (IS) curve summarizes equilibrium in the goods market. Higher interest rates (higher r) reduce private consumption (C) and investment (I). Higher income corresponds to higher private

---

[2] See, for example, Mankiw, N. G. (2006), *Macroeconomics* (New York: Worth Publishers).

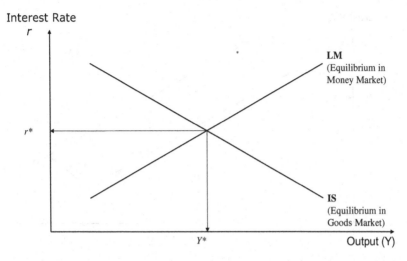

Figure 2.1. *IS–LM* model closed economy: Determination of equilibrium.

consumption (C) and possibly higher private investment (I). Thus, the *IS* curve slopes downward in a graph with r on the vertical axis and Y on the horizontal axis (Figure 2.1). The *LM* (liquidity preference) curve summarizes equilibrium in the money market. In the money market, higher interest rates reduce the demand for real money balances, while higher income levels increase money demand. However, as income increases, the demand for money balances (to finance transactions) increases, triggering the sale of other financial assets, which lowers their price and, implicitly, increases the rate of interest. Thus, the *LM* curve slopes upward (see Figure 2.1). Equilibrium exists at the point where both the goods and money markets are in equilibrium. In Figure 2.1, this occurs at the intersection of the *IS* and *LM* curves, where r has the value r^* and Y has the value Y^*.

Suppose now that the government enacts some type of fiscal stimulus — for example, cutting taxes. The stimulus increases the demand for private consumption and/or investment. In Figure 2.2, this appears as an upward shift in the *IS* curve to *IS'*. Higher demand will, in turn, generate more spending and a higher demand for money.

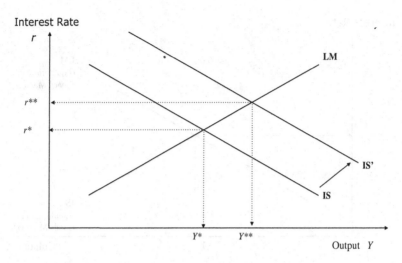

Figure 2.2.　*IS–LM* closed economy: Fiscal expansion.

A new economy-wide equilibrium occurs at the intersection of *IS'* with the *LM* curve, where income (Y^{**}) and the interest rate (r^{**}) are both higher than those before. Income is higher because higher demand leads to additional sales, production, and income. The interest rate is higher, because the fiscal stimulus worsens the budget deficit, creating excess demand in the money market. As we move along the *LM* curve, private demand for funds (for investment and consumption) is crowded out to some extent, until a new equilibrium is reached (where money demand and supply are again equal). The degree of crowding out depends on the slope of the *LM* curve. If the *LM* curve were to be completely vertical (full crowding out), fiscal stimulus would simply increase interest rates, without creating additional real income (real GDP).

2.2.2. *Fiscal policy in an open economy*

Because the closed economy model characterizes very few economies, it is worthwhile to consider an open economy variant. In this case, we introduce a new equation to represent the balance of payments, the *BP* schedule:

(7) $BP = BP(r, \Upsilon)$, since the balance of payments improves with r (because higher interest rates lead to an increase in net capital inflows) and weakens with Υ (because higher Υ generates higher imports)

In addition, we adjust expression (6), so that GDP includes net exports:

(6) $C + C_g + I + I_g + X - M = \Upsilon$: national income (GDP) equals private plus public consumption plus private and public investment plus net exports (exports minus imports of goods and services)

The BP schedule, like the LM schedule, slopes upward, because higher national income requires a higher rate of interest to induce the higher net capital inflows needed to finance the additional imports that the increased income generates.

The open economy model, shown in Figure 2.3, allows us to consider not just internal but also external equilibrium. Full equilibrium, of course, requires simultaneous internal and external balance. This corresponds to the intersection of the IS, LM, and BP curves. It also allows consideration of a variety of exchange rates and payment regimes, i.e., different degrees of capital market openness.

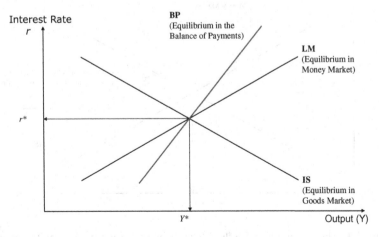

Figure 2.3. Open economy: Internal and external equilibrium.

2.2.2.1. *Open economy with limited capital mobility and flexible exchange rate*

Consider first the case of an economy with a flexible exchange rate and limited capital mobility. In this economy, the exchange rate is allowed to adjust to equilibrate the balance of payments, but capital account restrictions give the monetary authorities control over domestic interest rates. Suppose in this economy the government provides fiscal stimulus — a tax cut, or an increase in government spending not financed by higher taxes, which shifts the *IS* curve to *IS'*. In this situation, shown in Figure 2.4, the economy can move initially to internal balance (where *IS'* and *LM* intersect). However, the economy will not be at full equilibrium, because the interest rate at the intersection of *IS'* and *LM* is too low to equilibrate the balance of payments: not enough additional capital flows are generated to cover the increase in imports corresponding to higher real GDP. The interest rate would have to be higher still — at that corresponding to the intersection of *IS'* with the *BP* schedule. However, at this interest rate, the money market would be out of equilibrium: there would be too little money to finance domestic transactions.

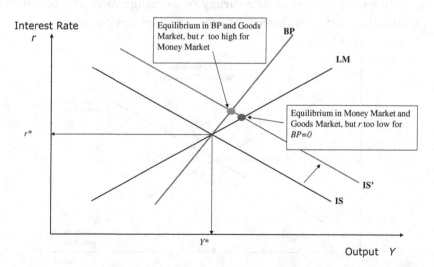

Figure 2.4.   Fiscal stimulus with flexible exchange rates and limited capital mobility.

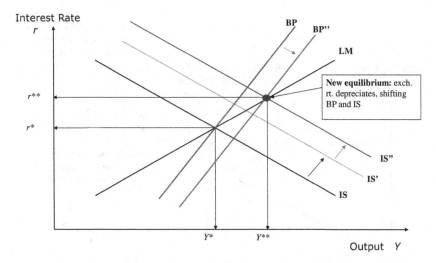

Figure 2.5.   New equilibrium achieved via exchange rate depreciation.

How can both internal and external equilibrium be achieved? Figure 2.5 describes the situation. Where the exchange rate can adjust, the increase in demand exerts downward pressure on the exchange rate, so that imports decrease and exports increase sufficiently for the *BP* schedule to shift to the right, meaning that equilibrium can be achieved at a lower interest rate. The increase in net exports also shifts the *IS* curve upward to *IS″*, which in turn prompts a further adjustment in the *BP* curve to *BP″*. After these adjustments, the economy is at a new equilibrium, where *IS″*, *BP″*, and *LM* all intersect. At this point, real GDP, at Y^{**}, is higher than that seen initially, while the new interest rate, r^{**}, is higher than what would have initially cleared the goods and money markets but possibly lower than the market clearing interest rate before the depreciation of the exchange rate. Note that equilibrium is achieved with a flexible exchange rate.

2.2.2.2. *Open economy with limited capital mobility and a fixed exchange rate*

Suppose instead that the economy has limited capital mobility and a fixed exchange rate. In this case, a fiscal stimulus again increases the *IS*

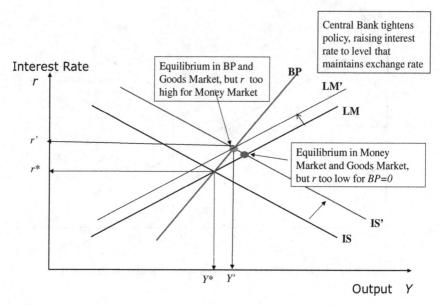

Figure 2.6. Equilibrium with fixed exchange rate achieved by tightening monetary policy.

schedule to *IS'*. As before, the equilibrium interest rate in the goods market will be too low for equilibrium in the balance of payments, while the interest rate that attains equilibrium in the balance of payments will be too high to equilibrate the goods market. To attain both internal and external balance without changing the exchange rate, the monetary authority must tighten monetary policy, shifting the *LM* schedule to *LM'*, thus increasing the interest rate to the level required for external equilibrium (Figure 2.6).

2.2.2.3. *Open economy with perfect capital mobility*

Consider now the situation of an economy with perfect capital mobility. In this case, represented by Figure 2.7, the interest rate is determined as a fixed markup (reflecting market perceptions of the country's riskiness for investment) over a benchmark, relatively riskless international rate such as the London Interbank Offer Rate (LIBOR) or the rate paid on short-term U.S. Treasury securities. With the interest rate set by

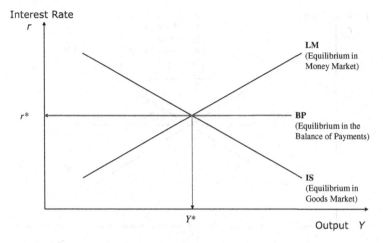

Figure 2.7. *IS–LM* model with perfect capital mobility.

the market, the *BP* curve is now flat, rather than upward sloping. As before, fiscal stimulus will make the interest rate that generates simultaneous equilibrium in the goods and money markets too high to achieve equilibrium in the balance of payments.

Where perfect capital mobility characterizes the economy, the impact of a fiscal stimulus will depend on the economy's exchange rate regime. Consider first the case of a fixed exchange rate regime — one in which the authorities use monetary policy to set the exchange rate. In this situation, described by Figure 2.8(a), the fiscal stimulus puts upward pressure on the interest rate, which in turn encourages an increase in capital inflows. Higher inflows in turn encourage an appreciation of the exchange rate. To keep the exchange rate from appreciating, the monetary authorities must expand the money supply so that the interest rate remains at its initial level (Figure 2.8(b)). This corresponds to an outward shift in the *LM* curve to *LM′*. At the new equilibrium, where the *IS′*, *LM′*, and *BP* schedules all intersect, real income is higher (Y^{**}) but the interest rate remains at its initial level (r^*). Thus, monetary expansion is needed to support the fiscal stimulus. One could even argue that it is the monetary expansion in this case that makes the fiscal stimulus effective at increasing real GDP.

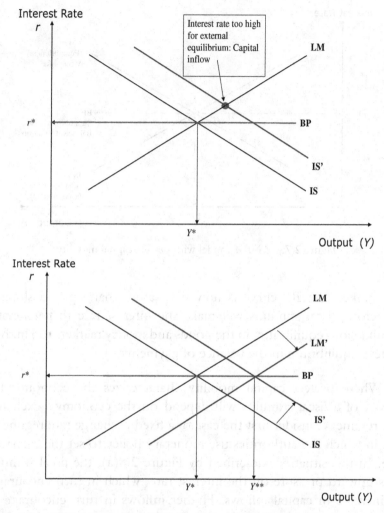

Figure 2.8. (a) Fiscal expansion: Perfect capital mobility, fixed exchange rate — part 1. (b) Perfect capital mobility, fixed exchange rate: After money expansion.

Suppose, however, that the economy follows a floating exchange rate regime — for example, an economy practicing inflation targeting. In this situation, shown in Figure 2.9, fiscal stimulus may prove ineffective. The reason is that, if the interest rate cannot adjust, and the monetary authorities do not adjust the money supply to accommodate the fiscal stimulus, the only way to achieve simultaneous internal and

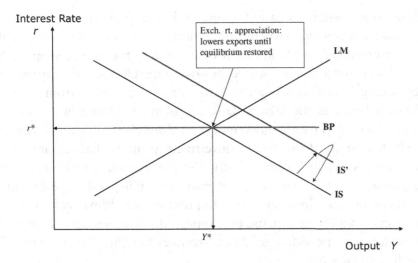

Figure 2.9.   Perfect capital mobility, flexible exchange rate: Full crowding out.

external balance is for the aggregate demand to remain unchanged. As before, the fiscal stimulus exerts upward pressure on the interest rate, which in turn promotes an appreciation of the exchange rate. If the monetary authorities do not intervene, the appreciation causes net exports to contract, lowering aggregate demand. The appreciation will continue until net exports decline enough to offset the effect of fiscal stimulus on aggregate demand, indicating that real income returns to its initial level. In Figure 2.9, this corresponds to the arrow showing that the *IS'* curve eventually returns to its initial level, *IS*, as fiscal stimulus "crowds out" an equivalent amount of net exports. Thus, fiscal stimulus is ineffective in increasing GDP if the capital is perfectly mobile and the exchange rate is fully flexible.

2.2.2.4. *Impact of budget financing*

The above two situations represent two polar cases regarding the impact of fiscal policy. They prompt the assumption that a fiscal stimulus is *bond financed*, meaning that any increase in the deficit triggers some crowding out of private sector activity, as the requirement for additional budget financing increases interest rates. In practice, this is but one possible scenario for budget financing. A second possibility is *money financing* (where the central bank buys the additional government debt and pays for it by expanding the money supply). A third is *foreign financing*, where the government finances the expansion by selling bonds to foreign investors or by borrowing from official lenders (such as the World Bank or Asian Development Bank). A fourth option is for the government to *draw down its official reserves* (which it might do to finance investment projects that require a lot of imports). A fifth option is for the government to "finance" an expansion with *arrears*, i.e., not paying its bills, and imposing the costs on others. However, this last option would ultimately have little impact on aggregate demand over time, if the arrears were to domestic suppliers who provided goods and services but then had to contend with not being paid.

Each type of budget financing has its own consequences. As noted earlier, *bond financing* typically increases interest rates and crowds out private sector activity, unless the economic outlook is poor and the demand for private goods and services is low.[3] This situation in particular characterizes *non-bank financing*, when the government sells bonds mainly to the public or to institutions, such as savings banks and insurance companies, lacking access to the rediscount facility of the monetary authorities. If the bonds are sold primarily to commercial banks (*bank financing*), the macroeconomic impact depends on whether the commercial banks continue to hold them (or exchange them to domestic parties with no recourse to the monetary authority's rediscount facility) or whether they use them to secure central bank refinancing. In the latter case, the rediscounting causes the monetary authority to expand the money supply. This would have the same impact as if the monetary authority had bought the

---

[3]There may also be no crowding out if, because of a collapse in asset prices or the exchange rate, many firms find their liabilities far exceeding their assets, meaning that they must recapitalize to avoid bankruptcy. Some economists have argued that, in this type of situation, what could be called a "balance sheet" recession, fiscal policy can be very powerful at restoring demand, while monetary policy may have little effectiveness. See Koo, R. C. (2009), *The Holy Grail of Macroeconomics: Lessons from Japan's Great Recession* (New York: Wiley).

bonds initially (*central bank financing*). Central bank financing avoids crowding out. However, it is potentially far more inflationary than non-bank financing, since it involves monetary expansion.

External financing avoids both crowding out and monetary expansion, but it has its own consequences. *Foreign borrowing*, from investors or official lenders, exposes most governments to exchange rate risk, since few developing or emerging market economies can sell bonds denominated in their own currency to non-domestic buyers. Many countries have suffered heavily from this type of financing, with the Russian Federation being a prime example. During the first half of 1998, the Russian government refinanced most of its ruble-denominated government debt, which carried relatively high interest rates, for dollar-denominated debt with much lower interest rates. While this reduced the government's interest costs, it opened the possibility of a sharp jump in the domestic value of this debt if the exchange rate depreciated. In August 1998, after the government was unable to approve tax increases and the International Monetary Fund did not agree to further financing, investor fears led to a sharp depreciation in the value of the ruble, which fell from about 6 rubles per U.S. dollar to 21 rubles. Following the depreciation, the government defaulted on its dollar-denominated debt, triggering a variety of adverse consequences, both for the economy and for the foreign investors who had bought the bonds.[4]

Financing additional government spending by *drawing down official foreign exchange reserves* represents a fourth option. This can occur, for example, if the government draws on reserves to finance imports for development projects. It can also occur if the authorities transfer foreign exchange resources to domestic banks as part of recapitalization. The Chinese authorities did this in 2003–04, for example, when recapitalizing several state-owned banks that needed

---

[4]For more details on the Russian collapse, see Kharas, H. *et al.* (2001), "An Analysis of Russia's 1998 Meltdown: Fundamentals and Market Signals," *Brookings Papers on Economic Activity*, #1.

to write-off uncollectable debts from state-owned enterprises.[5] This approach works for countries such as China, with huge foreign exchange reserves. The typical developing country lacks such resources, however. For the typical developing country, drawing down reserves may jeopardize the country's balance of payments and possibly trigger a currency collapse.

2.2.2.5. *Other factors affecting the impact of fiscal policy*

Besides the degree of openness and the exchange rate regime, research has identified several other factors that determine the effectiveness of fiscal policy. In general, fiscal policy will be more effective (a) when the economy is operating below potential output; (b) when the ratio of public debt to GDP is considered moderate, so investors have little fear that government will default on its debt; (c) when consumers are credit constrained; and (d) when policy changes are considered permanent, rather than temporary.[6]

The last two conditions decrease the extent to which taxpayers will reduce spending in the present, in anticipation of future tax increases to repay the public debt resulting from fiscal stimulus.

2.2.3. *Fiscal policy in countries with limited credibility*

The above analysis and the ability to provide fiscal stimulus to address a recession apply to countries with "credibility," meaning that financial markets view them as basically sound, with no risk that debt might not be repaid. What happens if the country lacks "credibility?" In this case, expansionary fiscal policy, rather than increasing aggregate demand,

---

[5]See Setser, B. and A. Pandey (2009), "China's $1.7 Billion Bet" (New York: Council of Foreign Relations Working Paper 6), http://www.cfr.org/content/publications/attachments/CGS_WorkingPaper_6_China.pdf.
[6]See, for example, Hemming, R. *et al.* (2002), "The Effectiveness of Fiscal Policy in Stimulating Economic Activity: A Review of the Literature," IMF Working Paper 02/28, http://www.imf.org/external/pubs/ft/wp/2002/wp02208.pdf.

could provoke a crisis. The fiscal stimulus triggers a loss of confidence, leading to a capital outflow or currency substitution, as investors fear a sharp increase in inflation or an unsustainable balance of payments position. The resulting movements may trigger a large depreciation in the exchange rate and force the currency to be devalued if the country has a fixed exchange rate regime. As a result, real output may actually decrease, rather than increase. Many low-income countries have had such experiences. Indeed, during the financial crisis of 2008–2009, countries such as Pakistan, which faced a sharp worsening of their balance of payments, had to tighten fiscal policy in response to a loss of exports, rather than implement the fiscal expansion that many other developing countries, including India, were able to introduce. Such situations suggest that fiscal contraction can sometimes be expansionary. In advanced economies, this has occurred only in a few countries, mainly Ireland and Denmark during the 1980s, where spending cuts to allow lower taxes and reduce high debt levels, accompanied by exchange rate depreciation, improved economic performance.

2.2.4. *Fiscal multipliers*

The impact of fiscal policy under different exchange rates and capital mobility regimes leads naturally to a discussion of fiscal multipliers. The *fiscal multiplier* represents the change in national income (GDP) in response to a change in fiscal activity, typically a change in revenue or expenditure. Because revenue and expenditure are measured in current prices, the fiscal multiplier represents the change in nominal GDP for a given change in revenues or outlays, with revenue cuts or expenditure increases adding to GDP and the inverse reducing GDP.

A variety of factors influence the size of the multiplier. These include the following:

- the type of fiscal measure,
- whether the measure is considered temporary or permanent,
- the openness of the economy (the ratio of total trade to GDP),
- the type of exchange rate regime,

- how close the economy is to potential GDP (full employment),
- the stance of monetary policy,
- the type of budget financing (via debt or money expansion),
- the degree of confidence in the authorities, as measured by the government's debt-to-GDP ratio and financing constraints, and
- whether the measure is coordinated with other countries.

Depending on the type of measure and other factors, the multiplier may range in absolute value from less than 1 to perhaps 3 or even 4 over time, when the full impact of the measure is felt.

(1) *The type of fiscal measure* — Measures involving government expenditure typically have larger multipliers than revenue measures. The reason is that government spending adds directly to aggregate demand, while some taxpayers often save part of any tax cut or use some of the cut to repay existing debt. Thus, infrastructure spending typically has a high multiplier. In addition, the main group affected by a measure can influence the multiplier. Higher benefits for the poor or unemployed, who will likely spend most of a tax cut, will typically have a larger multiplier than a tax cut for the wealthy, much of which may be saved.

(2) *Whether the measure is considered temporary or permanent* — Temporary tax cuts usually have smaller multipliers than permanent changes, because taxpayers may anticipate a return to the previous situation and thus not change their spending as much.

(3) *The openness of the economy* — An economy in which trade and particularly imports are a large proportion of GDP will likely have a smaller multiplier than one in which trade is a smaller share of GDP. The reason is that a larger proportion of any tax cut or increase in benefits will likely be spent on imports, thereby having less impact on domestic demand and GDP.

(4) *The type of exchange rate regime* — As suggested in the prior analysis, the multiplier will likely be smaller with a flexible exchange rate regime, because a larger fiscal deficit will likely increase interest rates and help appreciate the exchange rate, raising imports and decreasing exports.

(5) *How close the economy is to potential output (full employment)* — A fiscal stimulus is likely to have more impact when the economy is below potential output (full employment), because idle resources are available to satisfy the increase in aggregate demand. At potential output, the same stimulus may have little or no impact on output, because most resources are being used for production. Here, a stimulus is more likely to generate inflation than increase output.

(6) *The stance of monetary policy* — A tax cut implemented when monetary policy is accommodating will have a larger multiplier than if the policy is restrictive, i.e., focused on limiting inflation.

(7) *The type of budget financing* — A tax cut or spending increase financed by borrowing from the central bank (which is equivalent to financing by expanding the money supply) is more likely to increase demand than one financed by borrowing from commercial banks or the non-bank public. The reason is that borrowing from commercial banks or the non-bank public will generally increase interest rates, crowding out at least some private borrowing. By comparison, central bank financing expands the money supply, avoiding an increase in interest rates and thus creating less risk of crowding out.

(8) *The degree of confidence in the authorities* — Countries where market participants lack confidence in the authorities, often where the ratio of government or public debt to GDP is high (above 50 percent), typically have smaller fiscal multipliers, because many will be concerned about a possible plunge in the exchange rate or other disruption, thereby curbing new spending and the increase in demand.

(9) *Whether the measure is coordinated with similar activity in other economies* — A fiscal stimulus is likely to have a larger multiplier if other countries are also implementing stimulus measures, in which case the demand for a country's exports will likely be higher.

Research conducted before the 2007–2009 Global Financial Crisis often suggested that multipliers for tax cuts and spending increases were typically positive but small, well below 1.[7] More recent research by IMF staff has suggested that multipliers can be much larger if the economy is well below potential output, the stimulus involves productive spending that uses otherwise idle resources, monetary policy is supportive (keeping interest rates low), and the stimulus is coordinated with stimulus measures in other countries.[8] Experience during 2009–2010 in advanced economies, where fiscal policy proved potent even with flexible exchange rates and full capital mobility, supports this view. In addition, empirical research by Ilzetzki, Mendoza, and Végh (2011) supports the idea that fiscal multipliers are larger for more advanced and less open economies and for economies with fixed exchange rates.[9]

2.3. Fiscal Policy and the Supply Side

Fiscal policy can affect aggregate supply in an economy through tax policy, government expenditure, and the choice of budget financing.

Tax policy inevitably affects decisions about work, saving, and investment. High marginal tax rates can be expected to reduce work and investment, although the degree of impact will depend on the price elasticity of the good or service in question, tax rates in competing jurisdictions, and the extent to which untaxed or more lightly taxed alternatives are available. Thus, foreign investment and the work effort of secondary earners in a household are more likely to be affected. Similarly, differential taxation of similar goods and services can distort investment decisions and inhibit growth if the tax-favored activities are inherently less efficient.[10] At the same time, the composition of taxation can affect the level of economic activity. Shifting the tax burden from levies on profits and income toward consumption may

---

[7] *Ibid.*

[8] See, for example, Dell'Erba, S. *et al.* (2014), "Medium-Term Fiscal Multipliers during Protracted Recessions," IMF Working Paper 14/213 (December).

[9] Ilzetzki, E. *et al.* (2011), "How Big (Small?) Are Fiscal Multipliers?" IMF Working Paper 11/52 (March).

[10] This was a frequent criticism of the tax cuts enacted in the U.S. in 1981, in which the accelerated depreciation provided was seen as favoring industries where investment focused more on equipment than structures.

promote investment. The same applies to investment tax credits or tax rebates linked to additional investment. While selective tax benefits, such as credits for the production of energy-efficient vehicles, can influence investment decisions, tax reforms that simplify tax administration can encourage foreign direct investment. The World Bank's Doing Business website highlights countries in which tax reforms and simplification have improved the investment climate in recent years.[11]

Expenditure policy can also affect aggregate supply in an economy. Sound investments in infrastructure, in particular electricity, water, and sanitation projects, transportation networks, and communications, can dramatically facilitate doing business. The same applies to investments in primary and secondary education, public health, and legal systems. In some areas, such as the military, government spending provides the major source of demand and can encourage the development of new industries or lines of research (many commercial innovations in the United States, for example, have drawn on developments from military projects). The same can apply to government funding for non-military investment, for example, in theoretical science or engineering. Government subsidies affect production decisions and the allocation of resources: subsidies for certain crops, for example, will typically steer production toward those goods and away from others. Financial regulation can have a similar effect, promoting activity in more lightly regulated institutions, although effective regulation can also promote finance by increasing consumer confidence. Transfer payments to individuals can also affect aggregate supply. For example, very high unemployment benefits may cause jobless workers to be more selective in considering job offers, thereby increasing the unemployment rate. In the same way, generous public pension benefits may encourage early retirement, particularly if the benefits are available at an early age (e.g., 45) for workers in so-called hardship industries such as coal mining.

---

[11] https://www.doingbusiness.org/en/reports/thematic-reports/paying-taxes-2020. During 2018, 32 countries enacted major tax reforms.

Finally, government financing can also affect aggregate supply. The government's demand for financing affects interest rates and, thus, interest-sensitive investment and consumption. Large deficits that require heavy financing can drive up interest rates and crowd out private investment, possibly reducing the rate of economic growth if the government spending that is financed is less productive than the private activities that lower interest rates would induce. In a few countries, such as India, heavy demand for government finance has traditionally limited the availability of bank financing for private investment. Indeed, some researchers have argued that it is only the large pool of relatively captive savings, together with a deep capital market, that has made India's high ratio of public debt to GDP sustainable.[12]

2.4. Fiscal Policy and Globalization

Globalization has complicated fiscal policy making, as the competition for investment among economies has increased. With capital more mobile, it has become harder to impose high taxes on incomes and corporate profits. In response, some countries such as Singapore have cut corporate profit taxes and increased consumption taxes to maintain revenue levels. Downward pressure on tax rates has also made it harder to support generous social safety nets. To respond, countries need to coordinate tax policies — for example, policies toward tax holidays. Recent efforts to curb the use of tax havens may in part be a response to these developments.

2.5. Fiscal Policy and the Balance of Payments

Fiscal policy can affect the balance of payments through its impact on the economy's resource absorption, or savings–investment balance. In essence, a worse fiscal balance — in particular, a larger budget deficit — contributes to a weaker current account in the balance of payments, although the economy can still have a surplus if the savings–investment

---

[12] See Hausmann, R., and Catriona, P. (2004), "The Challenge of Fiscal Adjustment in a Democracy: The Case of India," IMF Working Paper WP/04/168 (Washington, DC: International Monetary Fund), http://www.imf.org/external/pubs/ft/wp/2004/wp04168.pdf.

balance for the non-government sector is sufficiently large and positive (in which case the non-government sector is financing the government's deficit). One can see this through a series of mathematical identities.

Begin with the expenditure-side definition of GDP (gross domestic product), including net exports

$$GDP = C + I + X - M, \qquad (2.1)$$

where C is consumption, I is investment, X represents exports of goods and services, and M denotes imports of goods and services. C and I each include components for the government and the non-government sectors:

$$C = C_g + C_p; \quad I = I_g + I_p.$$

Add net factor income (net interest and profit payments *vis-à-vis* the rest of the world) to both sides of the equation. This yields GNI (gross national income), also called gross national product (GNP):

$$GNI = C + I + X - M + Y^f. \qquad (2.2)$$

Next, add net transfers from abroad: grants received less grants given to other countries, plus net private transfers (gifts by individuals and non-governmental institutions, less similar gifts received). This yields $GNDI$ (gross national disposable income):

$$GNDI = C + I + X - M + Y^f + TR. \qquad (2.3)$$

Now note the following key relationships:

$$CAB \text{ (current account balance)} = X - M + Y^f + TR, \qquad (2.4)$$

$$GNDI = CAB + (C + I) = CAB + A \text{ (where } A$$
$$= \text{absorption} = C + I), \qquad (2.5)$$

$$CAB = GNDI - (C + I) = GNDI - A. \qquad (2.6)$$

Moreover, $GNDI$ equals domestically available resources, while $C + I$ (A) is domestic demand. Hence,

$$CAB = \text{Domestically available resources LESS domestic demand.}$$
$$(2.7)$$

Thus, the sign of the current account balance equals the difference between domestically available resources and domestic demand. Countries where *GNDI* exceeds domestic demand have a current account *surplus*. Those in which domestic demand exceeds *GNDI* have a current account *deficit*.

By recognizing that the difference between income and consumption equals savings, one can also see the relationship between the current account balance and the economy's savings — investment gap:

$$S = GNDI - C. \tag{2.8}$$

Substituting S for $GNDI - C$ into equation (2.6) yields

$$CAB = S - I. \tag{2.9}$$

Thus, the current account balance corresponds to the economy's savings — investment gap. The current account is in surplus when savings exceed investment and is in deficit when investment exceeds savings.

To see the role of the government sector in the current account balance, decompose the economy's *GNDI* into components for the non-government (Y_p) and government (Y_g) sectors. Apply equation (2.9) for the CAB and note that the difference between each sector's *GNDI* and consumption is its savings, S:

$$GNDI = Y_p + Y_g$$

$$CAB = [Y_p - C_p - I_p] + [Y_g - C_g - I_g]$$

$$CAB = \underset{\text{Private Sector Gap}}{[S_p - I_p]} + \underset{\substack{\text{Public Sector Gap=} \\ \text{(Revenue-Expenditure)}}}{[S_g - I_g]}. \tag{2.9a}$$

Thus, the economy's current account balance equals the sum of the private sector's and the public sector's (or the non-government sector's and the government sector's) savings–investment gaps.

Equation (2.9a) is what economists call an *ex post* identity, meaning that it is always true after the fact. Thus, reducing the government's budget deficit does not necessarily ensure that the current account balance improves. For example, if the budget deficit is reduced by cutting transfers to households, and households simply reduce their own savings in response, total purchases of goods and services, and therefore total imports, may not change. In this case, the deficit reduction may not improve the current account balance. By comparison, if tax increases result in lower private consumption or investment, or if the government reduces its own consumption or investment of imported goods, imports should decline. In this case, the current account balance will improve.

Similarly, a fiscal expansion can worsen the current account balance, if it leads to an increase in imports, or to borrowing and interest rate increases that reduce the economy's exports. However, if the expansion crowds out private investment, indicating that government spending merely replaces private investment, or if a higher deficit causes taxpayers to reduce their spending, in anticipation of future tax increases, then the larger deficit will be offset by a reduction in the non-government sector's savings–investment balance. In this case, the expansion would not worsen the current account balance.

Nevertheless, reducing the fiscal deficit can improve the economy's current account balance, if it leads to some decline in consumption or investment for the entire economy. Thus, fiscal adjustment can be a useful part of an economy-wide adjustment program. Private sector behavior must be modeled to determine whether fiscal tightening can, in fact, help in this situation.

2.6. The Interaction between Fiscal and Monetary Policies

Fiscal policy can affect the conduct of monetary policy. For example, the monetary authorities need to know the government's refinancing activities when determining the conduct of open market operations. If the government needs to sell X billion units of bonds to cover retiring short-term debt, and half of this amount will be coming from commercial banks, the monetary authorities should estimate the value of these bonds the banks will likely want to replace with new government debt when deciding on the volume of government securities to buy or sell (or repurchase operations to carry out) to achieve their target for the policy interest rate. Perhaps more importantly, the monetary authorities need to be aware of the government's demand for credit and how that will affect the financial markets. Large government deficits in an environment of relatively limited private savings may force the monetary authorities to accommodate the government's demand for financing, so as not to increase interest rates to unacceptable levels. Such a situation, where the authorities have to accommodate the government's demand for financing, is called *fiscal dominance.*

Fiscal dominance makes it difficult for the monetary authorities to use monetary policy to constrain inflation. Thus, an important first step for economies trying to control inflation is to end fiscal dominance, by limiting budget deficits. Poland, Bulgaria, and Romania are just three of the many emerging market countries in which overcoming fiscal dominance was the key to achieving low inflation. Of the three countries, Poland moved fastest and brought inflation down to the 20 percent range by the mid to late 1990s. Bulgaria succeeded in curbing fiscal dominance by establishing a currency board. In Romania, large deficits were finally brought under control in the first decade of the 21st century. This enabled Romania to adopt inflation targeting as its monetary regime in 2006.

To have a better understanding of how fiscal policy affects the monetary side of an economy, it is useful to consider a country's monetary accounts. These are summarized in a document called the *monetary survey*, which provides a snapshot of the assets and liabilities of a country's banking system — the monetary authorities plus the commercial banks. Table 2.1 provides a stylized sample of a country's monetary survey, using abstract entries for key variables rather than specific values.

Table 2.1. Analytical balance sheet of the banking system: Monetary survey.

Assets	Liabilities
Net foreign assets	Broad money (M2)
Net domestic assets	• Narrow money (M1)
• Net domestic credit	o Currency in circulation
o Net claims on government	o Demand deposits
o Claims on the private sector	• Quasi-money (QM)
• Other items (net)	o Time and savings deposits
	o Foreign currency deposits

In the monetary survey, note that total assets — the sum of net foreign assets (NFA) and net domestic assets (NDA) — equal total liabilities, which are essentially broad money (cash plus demand deposits or checking accounts, plus time and savings deposits, foreign currency deposits, and certificates of deposit):

$$NFA + NDA = M2 \text{ (or } M3) \tag{2.10}$$

Net domestic assets (NDA) equal the sum of domestic credit (DC) plus other items net (OIN) — a collection of items that include bank capital and an account that tracks the effect of exchange rate changes on net foreign assets, any foreign exchange deposits, and any loans made in foreign currency. Thus,

$$NDA = DC + OIN. \tag{2.11}$$

Domestic credit comprises net credit to government (NCG) plus credit to the rest of the economy (the private sector plus state enterprises), CRE:

$$DC = NCG + CRE. \tag{2.12}$$

Fiscal policy determines the government's need for financing. In most economies, the non-bank sector (savings institutions, insurance companies, other non-bank financial institutions, and private firms and households) will supply some of the financing. The banking system must provide the rest.

The monetary survey shows that the government's demand for bank financing can have one or more of the following effects:

(1) If the authorities accommodate the need for financing, broad money expands by the amount of the financing. In this case, there is no crowding out of private sector credit. However, unless the economy is operating well below potential, inflation may increase.

(2) If the authorities do not accommodate the need for financing by providing an equivalent increase in broad money, interest rates will likely increase, probably crowding out some credit to the private sector. If the private investment crowded out were to be more productive than the additional government expenditure that was financed, then the economy's growth rate may decline.

(3) If the authorities do not accommodate the need for financing by providing an equivalent increase in broad money, yet another possibility is that net domestic assets (NDA) will increase, reducing net foreign assets (NFA) to some extent. The reduction would appear as a worsening of the overall balance of payments, meaning somewhat lower official reserves. This outcome would be most likely if the budget deficit weakens the current account of the balance of payments, and the country cannot obtain foreign financing to cover the deterioration. It is one reason why the International Monetary Fund often advises countries with balance of payments difficulties to reduce their budget deficits to help address the problem.

Besides the above possibilities, *fiscal and monetary policy can also conflict*. For example, if fiscal policy is expansionary but the monetary authorities fear an increase in inflation, they may tighten policy by increasing interest rates. In this case, fiscal policy will crowd out private borrowing, possibly reducing growth. An event similar to this occurred in the United States during the early 1980s, when the Federal Reserve Board was restricting monetary policy to combat the inflation that emerged at the end of the 1970s while the U.S. Congress passed a large tax cut without significantly reducing total government spending.

Macroeconomic policy is more effective if fiscal and monetary policies have a similar orientation. In the United States during 1993, President Clinton argued that less expansionary fiscal policy might enable the Federal Reserve Board to relax monetary policy, thereby promoting economic growth. On this basis, he proposed, and the U.S. Congress approved, a tax increase that reduced the budget deficit. Sometime afterward, the Federal Reserve Board in fact reduced interest rates.

2.7. Using Fiscal Policy for Macroeconomic Management

Fiscal policy can be used to support a variety of macroeconomic objectives. A fiscal contraction, involving a combination of spending cuts and revenue (tax and non-tax) increases, can help contain inflation and reduce a current account deficit in the balance of payments. A fiscal expansion, through tax cuts, increased spending, or a combination of the two, can help a country combat recession by boosting aggregate demand, moving the economy back toward potential output. Fiscal policy can be particularly helpful when a plunge in asset prices is responsible for a recession, because a decline in capitalization may make firms reluctant to borrow and banks hesitant to lend. During 2009, many advanced and emerging market countries, having largely exhausted the possibilities of monetary policy, used expansionary fiscal policy to combat the loss in output and decline in export demand attributable to the financial crisis that began in advanced economies in 2007.[13]

---

[13]See Spilimbergo, A. *et al.* (2008), "Fiscal Policy for the Crisis," IMF Staff Position Note SPN/08/01 (Washington, DC: International Monetary Fund), http://www.imf.org/external/pubs/ft/spn/2008/spn0801.pdf; and Freedman, Charles, and others (2009), "The Case for Global Fiscal Stimulus," IMF Staff Position Note SPN/09/03 (Washington, DC: International Monetary Fund), http://www.imf.org/external/pubs/ft/spn/2009/spn0903.pdf.

Irrespective of whether fiscal policy is being tightened or relaxed, the specific policies chosen matter. Increasing consumption taxes, for example, is likely to have fewer negative effects on a country's rate of economic growth than a rise in corporate or personal income taxes. However, the increase would typically trigger a one-time rise in consumer prices that would in turn increase the inflation rate, at least temporarily. It may also worsen income inequality. On the spending side, cuts in less productive expenditure — for example, trimming low-yielding capital projects or instituting new procurement rules that cut the cost of supplies and equipment — will likely have less negative effects on the economy than cutbacks in primary education or health expenditure. Recent research by the IMF suggests that spending for infrastructure projects will likely generate the greatest increase in real GDP. Higher spending for transfers targeted on low-income households that face borrowing constraints will also have a relatively high multiplier effect. By comparison, less targeted transfer payments and general tax cuts will likely have smaller effects on real GDP, as will tax cuts perceived as temporary.[14]

2.7.1. *Relative effectiveness of tax and spending policies for adjustment*

Research has shown that certain fiscal policies are more likely to be durable as adjustment measures. Alesina and Perotti (1997), for example, have found that, in advanced economies, cuts in transfers and the government's wage bill have proved more lasting than cuts in public investment and tax increases.[15] The reason is that cuts in public investment can only be deferred so long, while most advanced economies already have relatively high revenue levels. In developing countries, Gupta and others have found that, besides cuts in transfers,

---

[14]See references identified in Note 10, plus Spilimbergo, A., S. Symansky, and M. Schindler (2009), "Fiscal Multipliers," IMF Staff Position Note SPN/09/11 (Washington, DC: International Monetary Fund, May), http://www.imf.org/external/pubs/ft/spn/2009/spn0911.pdf.

[15]Alesina, A., and R. Perotti (1997), "Fiscal Adjustments in OECD Countries: Composition and Macroeconomic Effects," *International Monetary Fund Staff Papers*, 1997, vol. 44 (2, June), pp. 210–248.

subsidies, and the government's wage bill, revenue increases from improving tax administration, curbing exemptions, and reducing tax evasion can provide lasting adjustment.[16]

Under certain circumstances, large fiscal contractions can even be growth inducing. As noted earlier, in a few advanced economies with high tax levels and high ratios of government debt to GDP, budget cuts have actually contributed to economic growth, particularly when accompanied by wage restraint and exchange rate depreciation. In both Denmark (1983–1986) and Ireland (1987–1989), fiscal tightening achieved through structural reforms helped usher in higher economic growth.[17] Australia (in 1987) and Belgium (in 1984–1985) also had periods of expansionary fiscal contraction. However, such events appear to be unusual.

2.7.2. Using fiscal policy to promote economic growth

Certain fiscal policies are considered more growth oriented than others. On the revenue side of the budget, consumption taxes are thought to be more supportive of growth than income taxes, because they avoid the "double taxation of savings." Economists have noted that, with an income tax, households are taxed initially on their income, and then again on the returns from saving — in effect, a double tax on income. With a consumption tax, such as a value-added or retail sales tax, the taxpayer pays tax only on that portion of income used for consumption. Income that is saved is not subject to tax, and the earnings from savings will only be taxed if they are consumed. Hence, savings are taxed at most once if there is a consumption tax, but twice if there is an income tax. Simulation models have shown that the double taxation of savings from an income tax can lead to lower levels of real GDP, compared to a consumption tax raising the same revenue, after several

---

[16]Gupta, S. *et al.* (2004), "The Persistence of Fiscal Adjustments in Developing Countries," *Applied Economics Letters*, vol. 11, pp. 209–212.

[17]See, for example, Alesina, Alberto, and Silvia Ardanga (1998), "Tales of Fiscal Adjustments," *Economic Policy*, no. 27 (October).

years of operation.[18] Governments should also watch the interaction of income taxes with payroll or social insurance taxes, because the combined marginal rates of the taxes can become very high. In Ukraine during the early 1990s, the combined marginal rates for the personal income tax and the social insurance tax reached 51 percent. Hence, some companies seeking to hire the limited number of well-trained, bilingual Ukrainian university graduates had to pay nearly twice the net, after-tax income of such employees, to enable them to receive their desired level of after-tax income. Finally, governments should remember that sizable tax exemptions narrow the tax base, requiring higher rates to obtain the same amount of revenue. Higher tax rates, in turn, have more negative effects on work effort and activity. They also create greater incentives for tax evasion and avoidance.

On the outlay side of the budget, research has shown that certain types of expenditures are particularly supportive of economic growth. These include efficient investments in infrastructure, spending for primary education and primary (basic) health services, and outlays for courts, public order, and effective financial regulation. Good infrastructure and legal services contribute significantly to a favorable investment climate, while the returns to having a literate and healthy population are high. In countries that have attained universal primary education, efficient spending for secondary education also contributes importantly to growth, because effective secondary education is a key ingredient for developing a well-trained and employable labor force. Research has also shown that good governance has a positive impact on private investment and growth.[19] Hence, government spending that promotes effective governance also contributes to growth.

---

[18] See, for example, Ballard, C. L. *et al.* (1985), "Replacing the Personal Income Tax with a Progressive Consumption Tax," in Ballard, C. L. *et al.*, *A General Equilibrium Model for Tax Policy Evaluation* (Cambridge, MA: National Bureau of Economic Research), Ch. 9, pp. 171–187.

[19] See, for example, Mauro, P. (1996), "The Effects of Corruption on Growth, Investment, and Government Expenditure," IMF Working Paper 96/98 (Washington: International Monetary Fund).

2.8. Limitations on Fiscal Policy

Although fiscal policy can sometimes be more effective than monetary policy, institutional features can make fiscal policy harder to adjust. In most countries, fiscal policy requires agreement by the government and approval by parliament. Even in a parliamentary system, where the government has a substantial majority, the many details involved in formulating fiscal policy mean that it takes some time to develop and implement. If the government leads a weak coalition, developing fiscal policy may require extensive and time-consuming negotiations with coalition partners. In a government setup like that of the Philippines or the United States, with a separately elected president and legislature, fiscal policy making can be even more lengthy and difficult, because different branches of government must agree on policy changes. The legislature is free to reject proposals from the president, while the president can block bills approved by the legislature, unless the legislature can override a presidential veto. Occasionally, as in the United States in 1978, tax bills approved by the legislature may bear little resemblance to the proposals initially forwarded by the president. For these reasons, most countries today rely mainly on monetary policy for day-to-day and short-term macroeconomic management.

Nevertheless, fiscal policy remains important, both for its own sake and for its interaction with monetary and exchange rate policy. Moreover, when circumstances militate, fiscal policy can sometimes be adjusted quickly. For example, the United States succeeded in approving a major stimulus bill in less than two months early in 2009.

The division of fiscal responsibilities among multiple levels of government can also complicate the management of fiscal policy. Where sub-national units of government are allowed to borrow, budget deficits at the state, regional, or local level can compromise efforts by the central government to tighten the fiscal policy. The refusal by several state governments in Argentina to meet their fiscal obligations to the central government is said to have helped trigger that country's 2002 financial crisis. In Brazil, fiscal imbalances at the state level led the central government to enact fiscal responsibility legislation. In India, until quite recently the states often turned to the central government for loans, and the center found it difficult to limit state borrowing. Since 2006, many states have adopted fiscal responsibility laws as a condition for receiving further financial assistance from the central government, and analysts hope that these laws will restrain future borrowing by the states. In China, the use of off-budget special purpose vehicles to finance local government activities has led to sharp increases in general (total) government debt despite relatively low central government deficits.

While sub-national fiscal imbalances remain an important concern, fiscal restraints can sometimes operate in the other direction. In the United States, balanced budget laws prohibit 49 of the 50 states from approving budgets in which revenues do not cover current expenditures. In many of these states, fiscal rules also require the states to adjust the approved budgets if it appears that the budget, excluding capital expenditure, will be in deficit. While these rules limit the states from borrowing for purposes other than capital expenditure (i.e., investment), they also keep the states from implementing expansionary policies during recessions. As a result, activist fiscal policy becomes the responsibility of the federal (central) government. In addition, during an economic downturn, the decline in revenues will force state governments to reduce expenditures, unless the federal government provides assistance in the form of grants or transfers to the states.

2.9. Summary

Fiscal policy can have a powerful impact on macroeconomic activity, affecting aggregate demand, the balance of payments, and monetary policy. Sound fiscal policies can make a country an attractive place for doing business, by keeping taxes and debt burdens moderate while concentrating government expenditure on goods and services that support private sector activities. Fiscal policy can also promote macroeconomic stability, by adjusting the budget deficit so as to restrain aggregate demand when inflation increases or the economy faces an unsustainable balance of payments position, and to expand demand during recessions. By selecting the right combinations of revenue and expenditure measures, governments can also promote economic growth. Increasing the role of consumption taxes relative to taxes on income and profits will encourage saving and investment, at the risk of worsening income inequality, provided the overall tax burden is competitive. On the spending side, focusing outlays on productive investments in infrastructure, efficient primary health and education services, effective legal and regulatory systems, and well-designed and targeted social safety nets will enable the government to provide services that support the private sector.

Although sound fiscal policy can support macroeconomic stability, its effectiveness depends on the institutional setting, the exchange rate regime, and the stance of monetary policy. Because of the need to determine specific changes to tax laws and expenditure programs, fiscal policy invariably takes longer to implement than monetary policy. In countries with separate executive and legislative branches, fiscal policy can take a long time to implement, because of the need for the executive and legislature to reach agreement. Similarly, fiscal policy can be harder to implement when sub-national governments have their own borrowing authority. However, economic theory suggests that fiscal policy can be more effective when exchange rates are fixed, or when monetary policy is more accommodating. In addition, as noted earlier, fiscal policy is more effective when the economy is operating below its potential, when public debt is moderate, and when households are credit constrained.

Box 2.1: The Equivalence between the Government's Savings–Investment Balance and the Cash Deficit

One can show that the government's savings–investment gap equals the difference between government revenue and expenditure as follows. Begin by recognizing that the government's disposable

---

(Continued)

Box 2.1: (*Continued*)

income (Y_g) is defined as revenues less transfers, which in the case of the government sector includes all payments for subsidies, transfers, and interest, including net lending:

(1) $Y_g = R - \text{Subs} - Tr - \text{Int} - NL.$

Government sector savings equal government disposable income less consumption:

(2) $S_g = Y_g - C_g.$

Subtracting government investment (capital) spending from government spending yields

(3) $S_g - I_g = R - \text{Subs} - Tr - \text{Int} - NL - C_g - I_g.$

The above expression, however, equals government revenue less all categories of expenditure. Hence, the government's savings–investment balance equals its cash balance, i.e., revenues less expenditure.

Chapter Three: How the National Economy Affects the Fiscal Sector

Just as fiscal policy can affect the national economy, the national economy and its interactions with the rest of the world can affect a country's government and public sector. The national economy and external forces affect the level and composition of government revenue, the magnitude and composition of government expenditure, and the type of budget financing available. Many aspects of the economy play a role, including the level of economic development, country-specific institutions, the stage of the business cycle, and internal and external economic shocks. Of these, the impact of the business cycle is arguably both the most general and the most important.

3.1. Business Cycles and the Government Budget

Business cycles affect the government budget in a variety of ways, especially on the revenue side. Revenues typically expand when the growth rate is high and the economy is operating close to its potential. This is especially true of economies where taxes on incomes and profits provide the major source of revenues, because income and particularly profits often rise more than proportionately with the rate of economic growth. However, even economies in which a broad-based consumption tax, such as a value-added tax (VAT) with few exemptions, is the main revenue source will typically see revenues rise at least proportionately with the level of economic activity. For similar reasons, revenues fall, often disproportionately, when the economy moves into recession, because profits decline sharply and layoffs cut personal income. On the expenditure side of the budget, certain programs also respond to the level of activity. Where government provides unemployment benefits, expenditures will rise automatically as layoffs increase and then decline as a strengthening economy reduces joblessness. Outlays for antipoverty programs, such as temporary work projects and short-term food assistance, will also rise as the economy worsens and diminish as private sector activity recovers. In addition, economic downturns encourage older workers who can do so to take retirement and may lead others who are eligible for it to file for disability payments. Together, the inherent responsiveness of government revenues and expenditures cause these programs often to be called the government's *automatic stabilizers.*

Table 3.1, which presents some data on fiscal performance in Thailand and the United States, provides an example of the response of the government budget to cyclical developments. As Table 3.1 indicates, revenues during Thailand's 1995 (April–March) fiscal year reached 19.5% of GDP, when GDP during the calendar year grew by 9.3%. Revenues declined to 18.6% of GDP during FY 1996, reflecting a slowdown in economic growth during calendar year 1996 to 5.9% and an even larger decline in company profits. The coming of the Asian Crisis in 1997, which saw real GDP decline, caused FY 1997 revenues to plummet to 16.2% of GDP. Revenues remained at that level in FY

Table 3.1.   Examples of fiscal response to business cycles: Thailand and the United States.

Fiscal Performance in Thailand, 1995–1999					
	1995	1996	1997	1998	1999
Pct. Chg. Real GDP	9.3	5.9	−1.4	−10.8	4.2
Fiscal Year Rev./GDP	19.5	18.6	16.2	16.2	16.4
Fiscal Year Exp./GDP	17.1	20.6	23.8	26.7	19.7
Fiscal Performance in the United States, 2007–2011					
	2007	2008	2009	2010	2011
Pct. Chg. in Real GDP	1.8	−0.3	−2.8	2.5	1.8
General Govt. Rev./GDP	33.9	32.5	30.8	31.2	31.4
General Govt. Exp./GDP	36.7	39.2	44.2	42.4	41.4

Source for data: International Monetary Fund, World Economic Outlook Database.

1998, despite a further decline in real GDP. The return to positive real growth in 1999 saw FY 1999 revenues increase slightly, to 16.4% of GDP. Fiscal year expenditures during the same period rose steadily, from 17.1% of GDP in FY 1995 to a peak of FY 26.7% in FY 1998, partly because of spending increases designed to combat the severe recession. Expenditures then declined to 19.7% of GDP in FY 1999, as many of the temporary anti-recession programs were allowed to expire.

In the United States, revenues fell and expenditures rose as the Financial Crisis triggered a recession in 2008 and again in 2009 as the recession deepened. General government revenue fell from 33.9% of GDP in 2007 to 30.8% in 2009 as the economy weakened, supplemented by a tax cut in 2009. Rising unemployment helped boost expenditure from 36.7% of GDP in 2007 to 39.2% in 2008, thanks to automatic increases in unemployment benefits and other social outlays, while further deterioration and legislated spending increases boosted outlays to 44.2% of GDP in 2009. As the economy recovered, revenues rose to 31.2% of GDP in 2010 and 31.4% in 2011, while expenditure slowed to 42.4% of GDP in 2010 and 41.4% in 2011.

Although a counter-cyclical response of government budgets to business cycles will generally promote economic stabilization, in some countries fiscal rules or debt problems may lead to pro-cyclical responses. For example, where fiscal rules, such as constitutional provisions barring deficit financing, constrain fiscal activity, an economic slowdown may trigger cuts in government spending, in response to the automatic decline in revenues. As noted in Chapter 2, most state governments in the United States are barred from running deficits on their current budgets (the difference between revenues and current expenditure). Thus, when a recession reduces fiscal revenue, government expenditure must be trimmed to avoid incurring a current deficit.

A similar problem can emerge in countries with high ratios of government or public sector debt to GDP, because financial markets

Table 3.2. Argentina: Effect of slowdown in growth and other factors on ratio of public debt to GDP (in percent of GDP).

	1998	1999	2000	2001
Public debt/GDP	40.9	47.6	50.9	62.2
Impact of growth slowdown	1.9	5.6	3.9	7.8
Growth of real primary expenditure	5.3	4.2	−3.8	−1.6
Percent change in real GDP	3.9	−3.4	−0.8	−4.4

Source: Daseking et al. (2005), Lessons from the Crisis in Argentina, Occasional Paper 236 (Washington: IMF).

may fear that additional borrowing to address recession will appreciably increase the risk of government default. Argentina provides a powerful example of this situation. Following several years of steady economic growth, toward the end of 1998 the Argentine economy slipped into a recession that continued through 2001. A fixed exchange rate regime linked to a currency board (which precluded activist monetary policy), combined with high public debt that reached 62% of GDP in 2001, made it virtually impossible for the government to implement an expansionary fiscal policy to combat the recession. As shown in line 2 of Table 3.2, the slowing of economic growth is estimated to have raised the public debt-to-GDP ratio by nearly 2 percentage points in 1998, more than 5 points in 1999, nearly 4 points in 2000, and almost 8 points in 2001. While real primary expenditure did manage to grow in 1998 and 1999, growth turned negative in 2000 and 2001. Beginning in 2008, several other developing countries found that high debt levels and a weak balance of payments forced them to cut deficits, rather than expanding them, in response to slowing growth. For example, during this period Pakistan cut expenditure and worked to raise revenues, despite declining GDP growth, as part of its 2008–2011 economic adjustment program supported by the IMF.[1]

---

[1] See IMF (2010), "Pakistan: Fourth Review under the Stand-By Arrangement," http://www.imf.org/external/pubs/ft/sca/2010/cr10158.pdf.

3.2. How the Stage of Economic Development and Other Factors Affect Fiscal Policy

A country's *stage of economic development* typically has a significant bearing on its fiscal system. Lower income countries and those at an earlier stage of development typically rely more on simpler taxes, such as excises, domestic sales taxes, and import duties, supplemented by a profits tax that mainly larger companies pay. As a result, revenue to GDP ratios are often relatively low — sometimes 15% of GDP or less. This, in turn, limits the expenditures that government can finance, sometimes compelling the country to draw on foreign assistance from countries and development banks to finance capital projects. Bangladesh, in which revenues have averaged 10–12% of GDP in recent years, provides a good example of the public sector in a low-income developing country. Higher income countries can usually raise more in revenues and thus finance not only a broader array but also a higher level of many government services. This includes more extensive health programs, schools with better facilities and smaller class sizes, and a more extensive social safety net that includes benefits for the elderly. The Republic of Korea, which is among the few Asian countries to have unemployment benefits and a public pension program for its population, offers an example of fiscal programs in a higher income country.

A country's stage of development also affects its tax administration and the ability to run efficient social welfare programs. Although countries at all income levels have succeeded in establishing VATs, higher income countries have usually found it easier to implement personal income taxes with broad scope and wage taxes or contribution programs that can fund pension savings schemes. Thus, these countries have been able to rely less on international trade taxes. Similarly, higher income countries have generally had more success in operating benefit programs that screen applicants on the basis of income and financial assets. Finally, higher income countries more often have the financial sophistication that makes possible a secondary market in government securities. Thus, higher income countries find it easier to sell government securities to non-bank financial institutions, as well as banks.

The tendency for the size of government to expand with income level is sometimes referred to as "Wagner's Law," after the German economist Adolph Wagner, who hypothesized that the relative size of a country's government (measured by the ratio of government expenditure to GDP) will rise as the country becomes industrialized. Several studies have documented that in countries such as Japan, the United Kingdom, and the United States, government expenditure as a percentage of GDP has tended to rise over the long term.[2] IMF staff economists have also found a tendency for a rising share of government expenditure in GDP in developing countries, with a considerable cyclical variation. The elasticity of government expenditure to per capita income averaged 1.26 for the countries observed, with higher elasticities for non-interest and non-interest current expenditure.[3]

External shocks also affect fiscal policy. Countries have long recognized that natural disasters, such as flooding and health epidemics, create the need for additional government expenditure. However, external macroeconomic events also affect government budgets. For example, a *drop in world growth rates*, such as that experienced during late 2008 and much of 2009, will reduce national exports and contribute to lower profits and adverse consequences for employment, personal income, and consumption. The resulting downturn will reduce revenues from corporate profits and household income taxes, as well as consumption taxes. Lower incomes will also reduce imports, thereby cutting revenue from import duties. On the expenditure side of the budget, the drop in external demand may also raise government spending for unemployment benefits in high-income countries and for food subsidies and discretionary social programs in other nations.

---

[2] See, for example, Chang, T. (2002), "Econometric Test of Wagner's Law," *Applied Economics*, vol. 34, pp. 1157–1169.

[3] See Akitoby, B. *et al.* (2004), "Cyclical and Long-Term Behavior of Government Expenditures in Developing Countries," IMF Working Paper No. 04/202 (Washington: International Monetary Fund, October), http://www.imf.org/external/pubs/ft/wp/2004/wp04202.pdf.

Higher world petroleum prices, while increasing petroleum-related tax revenues and raising growth in oil-producing countries, may slow growth in importing countries, thereby limiting revenues. Moreover, countries such as India and Indonesia that subsidize petroleum prices for consumers will find the cost of these programs rising, unless they reduce the level of subsidies, as Indonesia did in 2005. *Higher world interest rates* raise interest costs on public debt. Borrowing costs will also rise if an external crisis triggers a *sharp depreciation in the country's exchange rate*.

During the late 1990s, external shocks adversely affected the fiscal positions of many developing and emerging market countries. In 1998, for example, a sharp depreciation in the Thai baht and a decline in real GDP of more than 6% led to a plunge in revenue and heavy pressures for social expenditure. As a result, the government budget, which had been in surplus for much of the 1990s, recorded a significant deficit that continued during 1999. In Argentina, an economic slowdown, triggered partly by the August 1998 Russian crisis and also reflecting other factors, contributed to a jump in interest rates and much higher government interest payments that year.

However, external shocks can sometimes benefit countries. For example, Russia, which in 1998 suffered heavily from a plunge in the ruble exchange rate, subsequently benefited from the sharp increase in petroleum prices, to the extent that government budgets moved into surplus and the government could clear outstanding arrears in salary and other payments. However, the failure to broaden the revenue base significantly has made Russia's budget highly dependent on oil revenues, creating fiscal problems during 2009 and the period from late 2014 through 2020, when world oil prices fell sharply from earlier highs in 2008 and 2011 to the first half of 2014.

Besides short-term shocks, *long-term demographic and other trends* also affect government budgets. Aging populations pose major fiscal burdens for countries around the world, as the size and percentage of the non-working population rise and health expenditures increase.

Rising costs for public pension schemes stand particularly to burden advanced economies such as Italy, Japan, and Spain, while the cost of public health care programs poses especially great challenges for the United States. *Global warming* will also affect country budgets, as more frequent natural disasters and deteriorating agricultural yields reduce income and revenue while creating new demands for expenditure.

Finally, *globalization*, which has increased competition among countries, has strongly affected fiscal policy. With capital becoming more mobile, countries have competed to reduce corporate tax rates, and many have also lowered personal income tax rates. A few countries, such as Singapore, have followed a policy of increasing consumption taxes — in Singapore's case, the Goods and Services Tax (GST) — to offset reductions in the corporate tax rate, although Singapore has moved to mitigate the impact of a higher GST on lower- and middle-income families by providing offsetting credits and other benefits.[4] However, globalization also affects consumption taxes, as the increased sale of goods on the Internet has eroded the tax base of sales taxes and VATs, in the absence of inter-state and international agreements on how such sales should be taxed. Where not offset by higher consumption taxes, the reduction in corporate and personal income taxes has put downward pressure on government expenditure, making it harder to maintain a generous social safety net.[5] Tax competition also increases the value of having countries coordinate their tax policies. Broad tax agreements, for example, may be needed to curb the proliferation of tax holidays, particularly in small island economies that depend on foreign investors to build hotels and other tourist ventures and the use of tax havens to shield multinational corporate income from tax.

---

[4] See Government of Singapore, "GST Offset Package," http://www.gstoffset.gov.sg/Overview. htm.

[5] See, for example, Tanzi, V. (1996), "Globalization, Tax Competition, and the Future of Tax Systems," Working Paper No. 96/141 (Washington: International Monetary Fund).

3.3. Is Fiscal Policy Pro- or Counter-Cyclical?

Economic analysis generally recommends that fiscal policy be *counter-cyclical*, with revenue rising and expenditure falling during periods of high growth so that revenues can decline and outlays increase when growth slows or the economy enters a recession. In reality, many government budgets are *pro-cyclical*. In many economies, narrow tax bases and weak tax administration make it hard to raise revenue. In others, pressures to reduce the size of government have led to long-term declines in the ratio of revenue to GDP. Thus, when rapid growth leads to higher revenues, governments find it hard to resist pressures for additional spending. By comparison, the drop in revenue that accompanies slower growth forces countries to reduce outlays, because limited confidence in government and high ratios of public debt to GDP make it hard to expand government borrowing. This can also happen in countries or jurisdictions where fiscal rules limit the ability of government to run deficits, thereby forcing expenditures to fall when revenue declines.

3.3.1. *Advanced economies*

Research suggests that some, but not all, advanced economies have counter-cyclical fiscal policies. It is widely agreed that government revenue declines during recession and rises during periods of high growth. However, evidence regarding government expenditure is mixed. Some studies find that government expenditure tends, on average, to be counter-cyclical.[6] There is also evidence suggesting that the adoption of fiscal rules, such as the deficit and public debt limits in the Maastricht Treaty, has made fiscal policy more counter-cyclical.[7]

---

[6]See, for example, Galí, J. (1994), "Government Size and Macroeconomic Stability", *European Economic Review*, vol. 38, no. 1, pp. 117–132; and Galí, Jordi (2005), "Modern perspective of fiscal stabilization policies," *CESifo Economic Studies*, vol. 51, no. 4, 587–599.

[7]Galí, J., and P. Roberto (2003), "Fiscal policy and monetary integration in Europe," *Fiscal Policy*, vol. 18, pp. 533–572.

Other studies find little pattern.[8] At least one study has found that the ability of OECD countries to implement counter-cyclical fiscal policy rises with per capita income, because higher income countries are better able to control expenditure.[9] Finally, one recent study suggests that that fiscal policy tends, across more than 100 countries at different income levels, to exhibit persistence more than responsiveness to the business cycle.[10]

The variation in findings may arise because different types of government expenditure respond differently to the business cycle. Arreaza and colleagues (1998) have noted that transfers rise during recessions.[11] Lane (2003) has observed that current expenditure is somewhat counter-cyclical, while capital expenditure, which is often more discretionary, is usually more pro-cyclical. There is also evidence that government spending often exhibits a "ratcheting" effect, rising during recessions and falling less during recessions.[12]

3.3.2. Developing and emerging market countries

In developing and emerging market countries, many studies suggest that fiscal policy is often pro-cyclical. One study by IMF staff found that non-interest spending typically rises during economic booms and declines during recessions and growth slowdowns.[13] In half of the

---

[8]See, for example, Fiorito, R. (1997). "Stylized Facts of Government Finance in the G-7," IMF Working Paper 97/142; and Perotti, R. (1998), "Fiscal policy in good times and bad" (New York: Columbia University), http://didattica.unibocconi.it/mypage/upload/49621_20090119_052630_BADTIMES.PDF.

[9]Lane, P. R. (2003), "Cyclical Behavior of Fiscal Policy: Evidence from the OECD," *Journal of Public Economics*, vol. 87, pp. 2661–2675.

[10]See Afonso, A. *et al.* (2008), "Fiscal Policy Responsiveness, Persistence, and Discretion," Working Paper No. 954, European Central Bank (October), http://www.ecb.europa.eu/pub/pdf/scpwps/ecbwp954.pdf.

[11]Arreaza, A. *et al.* (1998), "Consumption Smoothing Through Fiscal Policy in OECD and EU Countries," NBER Working Paper No. 6372 (Cambridge, MA: National Bureau of Economic Research).

[12]See Lane (2003), *op. cit.*, Note 9; and Hercowitz, Z., and M. Strawczynski (2004), "Cyclical Ratcheting and Government Spending: Evidence from the OECD," *Review of Economics and Statistics*, vol. 86, no. 1, pp. 353–361.

[13]Akitoby, B. *et al.* (2004), *op. cit.*, Note 3.

countries studied, the elasticity of non-interest spending to real GDP growth was quite high, at 1.8. The elasticity for capital spending was particularly high: more than 3 for half the countries surveyed. A study of developing, emerging market, and OECD countries by Kaminsky, Reinhart, and Végh (2004) found that central and general government expenditures during the period 1960–1993 were on average positively correlated with real GDP growth in non-OECD countries and negatively correlated in OECD economies, although not every country in each group followed this trend.[14] Thus, government expenditure tended to grow much faster during good times than bad times in developing countries. More recently, Ilzetzki and Végh (2008) also found evidence that fiscal policy is typically pro-cyclical in developing countries.[15] However, there is evidence suggesting that more developing countries have adopted counter-cyclical policies since 2000, reflecting better institutions, stronger financial systems, and, in some cases, lower debt ratios.[16]

Several explanations have been offered for the pro-cyclicality of fiscal policy in developing countries. Talvi and Végh have argued that political distortions make it difficult for countries to limit spending during good times.[17] Alesina and Tabellini contend that corruption is a major factor.[18] In addition, research suggests that discretionary government spending is negatively correlated with the quality of

---

[14]Kaminsky, G. et al. (2004), "When It Rains, It Pours: Procyclical Capital Flows and Macroeconomic Policies," NBER Working Paper No. 10780 (Cambridge, MA: National Bureau of Economic Research).

[15]Ilzetzki, E., and C. A. Végh (2008), "Procyclical Fiscal Policy in Developing Countries: Truth or Fiction?" NBER Working Paper No. 14191 (Cambridge, MA: National Bureau of Economic Research).

[16]Frenkel, J. et al. (2011), "Fiscal Policy in Developing Countries: Escape from Procyclicality," VoxEU (June).

[17]Talvi, E., and C. A. Végh (2005), "Tax Base Variability and Procyclical Fiscal Policy," Journal of Economic Development, vol. 78, no. 1, pp. 156–190.

[18]Alesina, A., and G. Tabellini (2005), "Why is fiscal policy often procyclical?" Harvard Institute for Economic Research Discussion Paper No. 2090 (August), http://www.cesifo-group.de/portal/page/portal/DocBase_Content/WP/WP-CESifo_Working_Papers/wp-cesifo-2005/wp-cesifo-2005-10/cesifo1_wp1556.pdf.

political institutions in a country.[19] Thus, in developing countries, where political institutions are typically weaker, a greater quantity of government expenditure tends to be discretionary. This, in turn, contributes to greater macroeconomic volatility. As noted earlier, in many developing countries the inability of governments to resist spending during good times increases public debt and reduces their credibility. As a result, they find it much harder to borrow and expand spending during difficult times. The greater volatility of GDP in developing countries adds to the difficulty of pursuing counter-cyclical policy. Finally, there is some evidence that the greater concentration of political power in many developing countries leads to greater pro-cyclicality.[20]

3.4. Making Policy More Counter-Cyclical

A variety of measures can help make fiscal policy respond more appropriately to economic cycles. The first is to *establish credibility by strengthening fiscal balances during good times*. Reducing deficits or achieving surpluses when growth is high demonstrates that the government recognizes the need to support macroeconomic stability by curbing debt and limiting its claims on financial resources when there is strong demand for funds from the private sector. By reducing deficits or achieving surpluses during good times, governments will be in a stronger position to stimulate the economy, through tax cuts and spending increases, during difficult periods. The substantial improvement in fiscal performance beginning in the late 1990s enabled many developing and emerging market countries, including China and India, to increase budget deficits in response to the financial crisis of 2008–2009. *Greater transparency of fiscal data can also contribute to credibility.*

Fiscal rules may also prove helpful. Rigid prohibitions against budget deficits make it hard for governments to maintain expenditures

---

[19]Fatás, A., and I. Mihov (2003). "The Case for Restricting Fiscal Policy Discretion," *Quarterly Journal of Economics*, vol. 118, pp. 1419–1447.
[20]Akitoby, B. *et al.* (2004), *op. cit.*, Note 3.

when growth falters. However, less restrictive rules may be useful for establishing the credibility that enables government to support demand during recessions. Singapore, for example, prohibits the government from drawing on reserves accumulated during previous administrations without approval from the President. Since its independence, only once, in 2009, was the President asked to draw on past reserves, and the requested amount — S$4.9 billion — was quite small. However, an additional S$150 billion of past reserves was used to provide a blanket guarantee for bank deposits.[21] In the European Union, countries that are signatories to the Maastricht Treaty and the Stability and Growth Pact are ordinarily barred from incurring budget deficits above 3% of GDP or allowing public debt to exceed 60% of GDP. In principle, these rules help limit deficits during good times, thereby enabling governments to incur deficits up to the limit during recessions. In practice, many countries have employed accounting conventions to circumvent the limits, and during 2009–2010 most countries were allowed to incur large deficits to respond to the financial crisis that began in 2007–2008. More generally, a policy of balancing the budget over the business cycle should help governments limit debt accumulation while preserving the ability to incur deficits when times are difficult. The challenge with this, and any fiscal rule, lies in enforcement. There is a risk that governments will try to waive the restrictions, thereby rendering them meaningless.

Governments can also promote counter-cyclical activity through *better coordination with the monetary authorities.* Countries where the fiscal and monetary authorities meet regularly and agree on broad policy objectives can more easily adjust fiscal policy to support macroeconomic stability. The adoption of inflation targeting, which requires that countries avoid fiscal dominance (budget positions that compel the monetary authorities to finance the deficit, regardless of its effect on inflation), has promoted the coordination of fiscal and monetary policies in many countries. In the United States, which only

---

[21]Chew, V. (2009), "First Drawdown of National Reserves," Singapore Infopedia, National Library of Singapore (March 19), http://infopedia.nl.sg/articles/SIP_1489_2009-03-20.html.

adopted an inflation target in 2012,[22] the Clinton Administration used policy coordination as a key argument for proposing a more restrictive fiscal policy in 1993 and achieved better fiscal performance, including several years of budget surpluses, during the years through 2000. More recently, the monetary and fiscal authorities have worked closely to combat recession through expansionary policies, during 2001 and again during 2009, 2010, and 2020.

Finally, governments should work to *heed the lessons of budget ratcheting and Wagner's Law*. Efforts should be made to review and terminate fiscal programs that have lost their justification and preserve short-term budget reductions where these prove productive. So doing will create the flexibility for government to address new challenges as they emerge without jeopardizing the government's financial position — what economists call *fiscal space*.[23]

3.5. Summary

Just as fiscal policy can affect a nation's economy, the national economy and the international context also affect the government budget. Budget elements, in particular revenues, vary significantly with the business cycle. In advanced economies with unemployment insurance and other safety net measures, expenditures may also vary. Changes in the inflation rate, interest rates, and exchange rates, as well as external shocks, can also affect budget revenues, expenditures, and financing. Long-term demographic developments, such as population aging, can also affect revenues and expenditure.

Fiscal policy and government budgets also vary with a country's level of development. More advanced economies typically find it easier

---

[22]Following its January 2012 meeting, the Federal Open Market Committee issued a statement that a 2% annual rise in the price index for personal consumption expenditures was "most consistent over the longer run" with the Federal Reserve system's statutory mandate. See Board of Governors of the Federal Reserve System (2019), "What are the Federal Reserve's objectives in conducting monetary policy?" https://www.federalreserve.gov/faqs/money_12848.htm.

[23]See Heller, P. (2005), "Understanding Fiscal Space," Policy Discussion Paper No. 05/4 (Washington: International Monetary Fund, March), http://www.imf.org/external/pubs/ft/pdp/2005/pdp04.pdf.

to raise more revenue and therefore tend to have revenues and expenditures higher in proportion to GDP. Finally, experience shows that more advanced economies have had greater success in implementing countercyclical fiscal policy, perhaps because they have already achieved a level of revenues sufficient to finance most basic public services. In recent years, however, fiscal policy has also become counter-cyclical in a growing number of emerging market and developing countries.

Chapter Four: Fiscal Accounts, Analysis, and Forecasting

Understanding fiscal policy requires an appreciation of fiscal accounts, key fiscal indicators, and how the government budget can be forecast. This chapter addresses these issues.

4.1. Coverage of the Fiscal Sector

Before discussing the fiscal accounts, it is useful to understand what the fiscal sector of a typical economy includes. Figure 4.1 provides a useful summary that excludes public sector financial enterprises.

The *consolidated public sector* of an economy includes not only the operations of government but also the activities of *state-owned (public) enterprises*, with a focus on non-financial enterprises, i.e., enterprises excluding the central bank and any state-owned banks. It also includes what are called *quasi-fiscal activities* — activities of the central bank and state-owned enterprises that look like budgetary activities (e.g., subsidies) but take place outside the budget. While government operations typically represent the bulk of all public sector activities, non-government activities nonetheless represent an important part of the public sector. Indeed, in a few of the formerly centrally planned countries in Eastern and Central Europe, and in countries such as China, Lao PDR, and Vietnam, state-owned enterprises account for an important part of the national economy, employ a significant share of the labor force, and are responsible for much of the public sector's financing needs from the rest of the economy. Quasi-fiscal activities are typically a small share of the economy. In Zimbabwe, however, quasi-fiscal activities of the central bank have been responsible for much of the

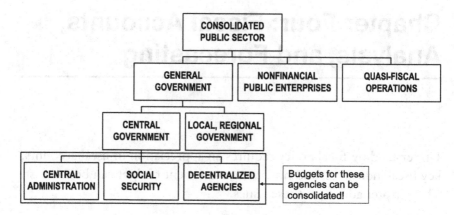

Figure 4.1.   Coverage of fiscal accounts, excluding financial public enterprises.

country's public debt and represented a main source of that country's hyperinflation during the start of the 21st century.[1]

A country's fiscal accounts should ideally cover the entire government sector, called *general government*, and the accounts of the central, regional or provincial, and local governments. Sub-national units of government are often responsible for a large share of the total government sector activities. Indeed, in countries such as China and Indonesia, sub-national governments undertake the major share of government sector expenditures, even if much of their revenue comes from the central government. Most OECD countries have data for the entire government sector, and OECD and IMF records typically provide such data, which are identified as data for the general government. Data for sub-national levels of government are often harder to find in emerging market and developing countries. Nevertheless, countries need such information to have a comprehensive view of the government's financial activities.

As with sub-national governments, one cannot have a comprehensive view of the central government's activities without knowing the full

[1]See International Monetary Fund (2009), *Zimbabwe: 2009 Article IV Consultation — Staff Report; Public Information Notice on the Executive Board Discussion; and Statement by the Executive Director for Zimbabwe*, http://www.imf.org/external/pubs/ft/scr/2009/cr09139.pdf.

range of financial operations that the central government undertakes. In many countries, the so-called state budget or central administration covers only part of the central government's activities. In Romania, for example, the central government operated many special funds with dedicated revenue sources, to undertake specific activities. The United States also has funds of this sort, such as the Federal Highway Trust Fund, which receives funding from the US federal gasoline tax and uses the money for highway construction and transit projects. Understanding the full scope of the central government's operations requires knowing and consolidating the activities of these special funds with the revenues and expenses of the main central government budget. Where the central government maintains a social insurance or social security fund, as in many of the formerly centrally planned economies, the operations of this fund (or these funds) should also be included with the other financial activities of the central government. This also applies to OECD countries with large social insurance programs, since in many of these nations these programs and the social insurance taxes funding them represent a large share of the total government budgetary activities.

4.2. Fiscal Accounts

International authorities have developed several systems for recording fiscal accounts. Most countries follow the approach outlined in the IMF's 1986 *Government Finance Statistics* (GFS) Manual. This manual presumes that countries maintain fiscal accounts on a cash basis and use a notion of budget balance linked to the government's need for budget financing. While the 1986 GFS manual has the advantage of familiarity, accounts on a cash basis are hard to reconcile with those for other sectors, in particular, the national accounts (GDP, national income, and expenditure) and the balance of payments, which are based on accrual accounting. In addition, the 1986 GFS accounts ignore arrears and fail to measure the government's net worth, since they do not take into account the accumulation and depreciation of government sector assets. To rectify these problems, international representatives have developed a newer approach to fiscal accounts embodied in the IMF's

2001 and 2014 *Government Finance Statistics Manuals.* The approach in these manuals treats fiscal accounts on an accrual basis, which has the advantage of recording arrears (unpaid government obligations) as outlays, thereby giving a fuller picture of government undertakings. Because of their different treatment of the government's acquisition of assets, many of the so-called fiscal balances in the 2001 and 2014 GFS differ from those in the more traditional 1986 approach. This book relies mainly on the 1986 GFS. However, those elements of the 2001 and 2014 GFS that may be useful for those undertaking fiscal analysis are identified.

4.2.1. *Main elements of the fiscal accounts*

For most countries using the 1986 GFS approach to fiscal accounting, the main elements of the fiscal accounts are *revenues and grants, expenditures,* and *budget financing.* These are illustrated in Table 4.1, which shows a conventional summary budget table for the government of Indonesia, based on data available as of early 2008.

Revenues and grants comprise *revenues* — all non-repayable receipts (receipts that do not create an obligation of repayment), except grants — and *grants,* which are unrequited receipts from other governments or international institutions. Revenues, in turn, include two main elements. One is *tax revenue,* which comprises compulsory and unrequited receipts collected by the government for public purposes. The other is *non-tax revenue,* which includes the operating surpluses of public enterprises, central bank profits, property income of the government, administrative fees, charges, and fines. In most countries, taxes represent the largest component of revenues. In some oil- and mineral-producing countries, non-tax revenue is larger than tax revenue, because of the substantial sums collected in royalties and leasing fees from firms that produce petroleum products or minerals.

Table 4.1.   Indonesia: Summary of government operations, 2002–2005 (in billions of rupiah).

	2002	2003	2004	2005
Government Revenues and Grants	**298,605**	**341,396**	**403,366**	**495,154**
Revenues	298,528	340,929	403,104	493,858
Tax Revenues	210,088	242,048	280,559	346,997
Domestic Taxes	199,512	230,934	267,817	331,759
Income tax	101,874	115,016	119,515	175,543
Non-oil/gas	84,404	95,293	99,020	140,403
Oil/gas	17,469	19,723	20,494	35,140
Value added tax	65,153	77,082	102,573	101,295
Land and building tax	6,228	8,677	11,684	16,184
Land and building transfer duties	1,600	2,229	3,001	3,429
Excise duties	23,189	26,277	29,173	33,256
Other domestic taxes	1,469	1,654	1,872	2,050
International trade taxes	10,575	11,114	12,742	15,239
Export duties	231	230	298	318
Import duties	10,344	10,885	12,444	14,921
Non-tax Revenues	88,440	98,880	122,546	146,860
Natural resource revenues	64,755	67,739	96,717	110,441
Profit transfers from state enterprises	9,760	12,833	10,644	12,777
Other non-tax revenues	13,925	18,308	15,185	22,643
Grants	78	468	262	1,296
Government Expenditures	**322,180**	**376,505**	**427,176**	**509,622**
Central Government Expenditures	223,976	256,191	297,454	359,158
Current Expenditures	186,651	186,944	236,003	301,557
Personnel	39,480	47,662	52,743	54,339
Other Goods and Services	12,777	14,992	15,518	29,240
Interest	87,667	65,351	62,486	65,151
Domestic debt	25,406	46,356	39,286	43,496
Foreign debt	62,261	18,995	23,200	21,655
Subsidies	43,628	43,899	91,529	120,784
o/w: Fuel	31,162	30,038	69,025	95,737
Other Current Expenditures	3,099	1,504	13,727	32,043
Development and Capital	37,325	69,247	61,450	57,601
Regional Expenditures	98,204	120,314	129,723	150,464
Primary Balance, Excluding Discrepancy	64,093	30,241	38,676	50,683

(*Continued*)

Table 4.1. (*Continued*)

	2002	2003	2004	2005
Overall balance, after rounding	−23,574	−35,110	−23,810	−14,468
Discrepancy[a]				69
Financing	**23,574**	**35,110**	**23,810**	**14,399**
Foreign financing, net	6,550	548	−28,057	−10,260
Drawings	18,809	20,360	18,434	26,870
Amortization	−12,259	−19,812	−46,491	−37,130
Domestic financing, net	17,024	34,562	51,867	24,659
Banking system, net	−8,140	10,705	25,727	700
Non-banks, net	25,164	23,857	26,141	23,959
o/w: Asset recovery (from NPLs)	19,439	19,661	15,751	6,558

Note: [a] Difference between identified revenue, expenditure, and budget financing.
Source: Bank Indonesia (2008), 2007 Economic Report on Indonesia, Appendix, Tables 30 and 31.

Expenditures and net lending comprise all the outlays of government. These can be classified according to economic or functional categories.

The *economic classification* of expenditure categorizes all outlays as current (sometimes called "recurrent"), capital or development, or net lending. *Current* expenditure, in principle, represents all payments for goods or services deemed to last not more than a year (although most military outlays are categorized as current expenditure). The main elements of current expenditure are payments for *wages and salaries*; *purchases of other goods and services*, which typically go for operations and maintenance of government programs; *subsidies and transfers*, to persons, firms, or institutions outside government; and *interest payments*. Of these elements, payments for wages and salaries and other goods and services are considered the main elements of *government consumption* and are included when determining the national GDP. *Capital* expenditure, in many countries also called development expenditure, comprises the *acquisition of fixed assets* (government investment) and *capital transfers* (transfers for the purpose of acquiring a capital asset, often to other levels of government). *Net Lending* (loans minus repayments) comprises government lending to achieve public policy purposes (e.g., subsidized loans to students or farmers). Net lending appears in expenditure only in the 1986 GFS system. The 2001 and 2014 GFS manuals consider net lending as a part of *budget financing*. Note that *expenditures exclude repayments of debt principal* (amortization), which are part of net financing. Table 4.2, taken from the staff report for the IMF's 2018 Article IV Consultation with the Philippines, offers an example of the 2001 GFS manual's approach to government finance statistics.

The *functional classification* of government expenditure categorizes government outlays by the type of program undertaken. Typical functional categories of expenditure include outlays for education, health, social insurance, transportation, military services, internal security, infrastructure, interest payments, and government administration, to mention just a few. Spending for a particular function includes all outlays for that activity, whether current, capital, or net lending. Government budget documents typically present government expenditure by function, although a growing number of governments also provide data on expenditure by economic classification.

Budget financing represents the net issuance of debt needed to cover any shortfall of revenue from expenditure. Thus, financing represents the difference between the amount of new debt issued and the amount of debt (principal or amortization) repaid during any particular time period. The main categories of financing are *foreign financing*, meaning net borrowing from sources outside the country, and *domestic financing*, which is net borrowing from residents. Domestic financing, in turn, comprises net borrowing from the *banking system* (commercial banks and the central bank or monetary authority) and net borrowing from *non-bank* sources, which can include non-bank financial institutions, non-financial companies, and households. Many analysts distinguish between bank and non-bank financing for two

Table 4.2.　Philippines: General government operations, 2013–1920.

	2013	2014	2015	2016	2017	2018 Proj.	2019 Proj.
Revenue and grants	14.8	15.1	15.4	15.2	15.6	16.0	16.2
Tax revenue	13.3	13.6	13.6	13.7	14.2	14.9	15.2
Net income and profits	6.2	6.2	6.4	6.4	6.5	5.6	5.6
Excises	1.3	1.3	1.4	1.4	1.7	2.7	2.9
VAT	4.2	4.4	4.2	4.2	4.4	4.8	4.7
Tariffs	0.3	0.4	0.4	0.4	0.4	0.4	0.4
Other 1/	1.3	1.2	1.2	1.2	1.2	1.5	1.5
Nontax revenue	1.5	1.5	1.7	1.5	1.4	1.1	1.0
Expenditure and net lending	16.3	15.7	16.8	17.6	17.9	18.8	19.4
Current expenditures	13.2	12.8	13.4	13.2	13.4	13.7	13.9
Personnel services	5.0	4.8	5.0	5.0	5.1	5.2	5.2
Maintenance and operations	2.5	2.4	3.0	2.9	2.9	2.9	3.0
Allotments to LGUs	2.1	2.2	2.3	2.4	2.5	2.5	2.5
Subsidies	0.6	0.6	0.6	0.7	0.8	0.8	0.8
Tax expenditure	0.2	0.2	0.1	0.1	0.1	0.1	0.1
Interest	2.8	2.6	2.3	2.1	2.0	2.2	2.3
Capital and equity expenditure	3.0	2.8	3.3	4.3	4.5	5.1	5.5
Capital expenditure	2.9	2.8	3.3	4.2	4.5	5.1	5.5
Equity	0.1	0.0	0.0	0.1	0.0	0.0	0.0
Net lending	0.1	0.1	0.1	0.1	0.0	0.0	0.0
Balance	-1.5	-0.6	-1.4	-2.4	-2.2	-2.8	-3.2
On the authorities' presentation 2/	-1.4	-0.6	-0.9	-2.4	-2.2	-2.8	-3.2
Financing	1.5	0.6	1.4	2.4	2.2	2.8	3.2
External financing (net)	-0.7	0.1	0.5	-0.2	0.2	-0.1	-0.1
Domestic financing (net)	3.5	1.3	0.2	1.7	4.0	3.0	3.4
Change in cash (negative=accumulation)	-1.3	-0.8	0.2	0.9	-2.0	-0.1	-0.1
Privatization	0.0	0.0	0.5	0.0	0.0	0.0	0.0
Memorandum items:							
Cyclically-adjusted primary balance 3/	1.3	1.7	1.0	-0.4	-0.3	-0.6	-0.9
Structural primary balance 3/	0.0	2.1	1.3	-0.1	-0.1	-0.5	-0.9
Gross financing requirement 4/	5.9	4.7	5.2	5.9	5.2	5.9	6.1
National government gross debt 5/	49.2	45.4	44.7	42.1	42.1	41.6	41.1
Domestic	32.4	30.2	29.2	27.2	28.1	28.3	28.9
External	16.9	15.2	15.5	14.9	14.0	13.3	12.1
GDP (in billions of pesos)	11,538	12,634	13,322	14,480	15,806	17,574	19,480

Sources: Philippine authorities; and IMF staff projections.

1/ Includes other percentage taxes, documentary stamp tax, and non-cash collections.
2/ Includes privatization receipts as revenue and excludes the operations of the Central Bank-Board of Liquidators.
3/ In percent of potential GDP. Compared to the cyclically-adjusted balance, the structural balance also controls for the effect of cyclical fluctuations
4/ Defined as the sum of deficit, amortization of medium- and long-term debt, and the stock of outstanding short-term debt.
5/ Includes national government debt held by the bond sinking fund and excludes contingent/guaranteed debt.

Source: Reproduced with permission from *Philippines: 2018 Article IV Consultation: Press Release; Staff Report; and Statement by the Executive Director for Philippines* (Washington: IMF, September), Country Report 18/287, Table 3.

reasons. First, ordinarily only financing from banks can lead to money creation: either directly (when the central bank acquires government debt) or indirectly (when commercial banks buy government securities and then use them as collateral for loans from the central bank). Second, in most countries, commercial banks are more important than non-bank financial institutions in lending to firms, so that commercial bank financing of government is more likely to crowd out private investment and drive up lending rates. This distinction is becoming less important as countries adopt inflation targeting and the growth in monetary aggregates is no longer considered an important indicator of inflationary risk.

4.3. Fiscal Analysis: Key Indicators

As with other sectors of the economy, certain variables represent key indicators of fiscal activity. This section identifies several of these variables. Among the most important are *various concepts of budget balance*; measures of *fiscal sustainability*; and indicators of *revenue and expenditure performance*.

4.3.1. *Traditional measures of budget balance*[2]

Economists have developed a variety of ways to measure the budget balance. Each reflects different concerns. Thus, certain measures may be useful for some purposes and others for different issues.

4.3.1.1. *Conventional (cash or overall) balance*

The best-known and most frequently used concept of budget balance is the *conventional* (cash) balance, sometimes called the *overall balance*. The conventional balance is defined as the difference between cash revenues and cash expenditures. Thus, it measures the government's *short-run need for financing*. If there are no budget arrears (i.e., no unpaid government obligations), the conventional balance also measures the effect of the budget on net government debt. This point highlights a key drawback to the conventional balance: since it looks only at the government's cash revenues and expenditures, the conventional balance understates the government's ultimate financing

---

[2]For an extensive discussion of alternative measures of budget balance, see Blejer, M., and A. Cheasty (1993), *How to Measure the Fiscal Deficit* (Washington: IMF).

needs in the event of arrears. This is one reason why the 2001 GFS manual moved from a cash to an accrual system of accounts. The other is that an accrual system synchronizes the government's accounts with those of other key macroeconomic sectors, in particular the national accounts (GDP) and the balance of payments.

4.3.1.2. *Primary balance*

The *primary balance* is calculated as the conventional balance with interest payments removed from expenditures. The primary balance is thus always less negative, or more positive, than the conventional balance. The primary balance serves two main purposes. First, it provides a measure of the effects of current period fiscal activity, since interest payments (which represent the carrying cost of past deficits) are excluded from expenditures. The primary balance can thus indicate whether fiscal obligations in the current period are tending either to increase or decrease public debt. Second, the primary balance is the fiscal measure most closely linked to fiscal sustainability — whether the ratio of government debt to GDP tends to rise without limit, in the absence of a change in policy. As will be shown in Chapter Five on fiscal sustainability, the primary balance bears a direct relationship with changes in the ratio of government debt to GDP. Where the average real interest rate on government debt exceeds the real growth rate for GDP, a primary deficit will make the ratio of government debt to GDP rise. In that case, to keep the debt/GDP ratio from rising, the government must incur a primary surplus, with the size of the surplus depending on the initial debt/GDP ratio and the extent to which the average real interest rate on government debt exceeds the real GDP growth rate.

4.3.1.3. *Operational balance*

The government's operational balance is defined as the conventional budget balance, with the portion of *interest payments arising from the inflationary component of nominal interest rates* excluded from expenditures. This balance thus includes the estimated "real" element of interest payments in expenditures. The operational balance is used mainly in high-inflation countries, when the authorities want to record only the "real" component of interest payments in expenditures. For most countries, the general decline in inflation has made this balance less important in recent years.

4.3.1.4. Government savings (the current balance)

Government savings represent the difference between government revenues and current government expenditure. The resulting balance shows how much revenue is left to finance capital spending and how much borrowing is needed to cover the shortfall. The government savings concept is sometimes used in development analysis to indicate the government's need for financing to cover unfunded development spending. The analysis implicitly assumes that borrowing needs arise from capital outlays. However, borrowing can also result from heavy current expenditure. Indeed, some countries have negative government savings, meaning that current expenditure exceeds revenue.

4.3.1.5. Public sector borrowing requirement

The public sector borrowing requirement represents the total borrowing needs of the public sector. Besides the government's conventional budget balance, it includes the combined balances of the public enterprises. In some countries, the combined deficits of these enterprises far exceed those of the government sector. This was typical in Romania, for example, during the early 1990s, when few state enterprises had been privatized and most incurred heavy losses. If state enterprises have large deficits, this measure can help identify the total burden imposed by the public sector on the financial system.

4.3.1.6. *Cyclically adjusted budget balance*[3]

The cyclically adjusted budget balance is an attempt to correct for the impact of the business cycle in assessing the stance of fiscal policy. The cyclically adjusted balance is calculated by estimating budget revenues and expenditures at potential output (or full employment), rather than at the current level of GDP. For an economy in recession, estimating revenues and expenditures at potential output could well lead to a smaller fiscal deficit, since revenues would likely be higher and any recession-linked expenditures (such as unemployment benefits) would be smaller. By comparison, the cyclically adjusted balance could show a smaller surplus or larger deficit for an economy with a positive output gap, since revenues would be above those at potential output while cyclically sensitive expenditures might be lower. Determining the cyclically adjusted balance requires an estimate of the economy's output gap — the difference between actual GDP and potential GDP. This in turn requires having an estimate of potential output, i.e., the maximum output consistent with relative price stability. The cyclically adjusted budget balance also requires knowing the elasticity of revenues and expenditures to changes in the output gap: the percent by which revenues and expenditures change for each 1 percent rise or fall in the output gap.

The following example shows how the cyclically adjusted budget deficit can be calculated. Assume that revenues are 200 billion units of national currency and expenditures are 220 billion units of currency, with GDP at 1,000 billion units of currency, which implies a deficit of 2 percent of GDP. Suppose that potential GDP has been estimated at 1,100 billion currency units, implying that the economy is about 9.1 percent short of potential. Suppose also that the elasticity of revenue to GDP at constant prices is 1, but that the expenditure elasticity is zero, as might be true in many developing and emerging market countries that lack unemployment insurance. If the economy were at potential

---

[3]Text in this section is reproduced from Greene, J. (2018), *Macroeconomic Accounts and Policy*, Chapter 4.

GDP, GDP would be 10 percent higher (1,100, rather than 1,000). With a revenue elasticity of 1, revenues would also be 10 percent higher at potential output, i.e., 220 billion currency units rather than 200 billion. In this case, at potential output the budget would be in balance: revenues and expenditures would both be 220 billion currency units. Thus, the cyclically adjusted budget balance would be zero.

The cyclically adjusted budget balance can be useful for judging the budget's *fiscal stance*, i.e., whether the budget is tending to expand or contract the economy when assessed at potential output, with the *fiscal impulse* being the *change* in the fiscal stance. As suggested earlier, a small budget deficit in an economy with a negative output gap could be considered contractionary at potential output. Similarly, a budget with a small surplus when the economy is overheating, i.e., has a positive output gap, could be considered expansionary at potential output. The cyclically adjusted budget balance also provides a way to assess long-term trends in fiscal policy, by smoothing out the effects of business cycles on projected levels of the budget balance. For this reason, many fiscal reports, including recent issues of the IMF's *Fiscal Monitor*, often report projections of the cyclically adjusted fiscal or primary balance.[4] Table 4.3, reproduced from a recent IMF Article IV consultation staff report for Thailand, provides an example of several fiscal balances, along with data for both general government and the public sector.

4.3.1.7. *Structural balance*

A *structural balance* is a fiscal balance obtained after removing the volatile elements from the government budget. Structural balances include fiscal balances after eliminating grants and fiscal balances after controlling for commodity or asset prices or after removing revenue from commodity exports. Structural balances are sometimes calculated

---

[4]See, for example, IMF (2020), *Fiscal Monitor, April 2020*, Tables A3, A4, A11, and A12 (Washington).

Table 4.3. Thailand: Medium-term fiscal scenario, fiscal years 2013–2023.

(In percent of fiscal year GDP, unless otherwise stated)

	FY 2013	FY 2014	FY 2015	FY 2016	FY 2017	FY 2018	FY 2019	FY 2020	FY 2021	FY 2022	FY 2023
						Projections					
General Government											
Revenue	22.2	21.4	22.3	22.0	21.1	21.4	21.5	21.5	21.5	21.5	21.5
Tax revenue	18.4	17.2	17.7	17.2	16.4	16.6	16.8	16.8	16.8	16.8	16.8
Taxes on income	7.3	6.7	6.6	6.2	5.9	6.0	6.0	6.0	6.0	6.0	6.0
Taxes on goods and services	9.8	9.3	10.0	9.9	9.6	9.6	9.6	9.6	9.6	9.6	9.6
Taxes on international trade	0.9	0.8	0.7	0.7	0.6	0.6	0.6	0.6	0.6	0.6	0.6
Other	0.4	0.4	0.4	0.4	0.4	0.5	0.7	0.7	0.7	0.7	0.7
Social contributions	0.8	1.1	1.2	1.1	1.0	1.0	1.0	1.0	1.0	1.0	1.0
Other revenue	2.9	3.1	3.4	3.7	3.7	3.7	3.7	3.7	3.7	3.7	3.7
Total expenditure	21.6	22.2	22.2	21.4	21.7	22.3	22.4	22.4	22.6	22.7	22.8
Expense	18.9	19.3	18.6	19.1	19.2	19.5	19.5	19.5	19.7	19.8	20.0
Compensation of employees	6.6	6.5	6.6	6.6	6.3	6.3	6.3	6.3	6.3	6.3	6.3
Purchase/use of goods and services	5.9	6.2	6.1	6.2	6.2	6.2	6.2	6.2	6.2	6.2	6.2
Interest	1.1	1.1	1.0	0.9	0.9	0.9	0.9	1.0	1.0	1.0	1.1
Social benefits	2.1	2.2	2.2	2.5	2.6	2.9	2.9	2.9	3.1	3.2	3.3
Other	3.2	3.3	2.7	2.9	3.1	3.1	3.1	3.1	3.1	3.1	3.1
Net acquisition of nonfinancial assets	2.8	2.9	3.6	2.3	2.6	2.8	2.9	2.9	2.9	2.9	2.8
o.w. fixed assets	3.1	2.9	3.6	3.9	2.6	2.8	2.9	2.9	2.9	2.9	2.8
o.w. nonproduced assets	-0.3	0.0	0.0	-1.6	0.0	0.0	0.0	0.0	0.0	0.0	0.0
Overall fiscal balance	0.5	-0.8	0.1	0.6	-0.6	-0.9	-0.9	-0.9	-1.1	-1.2	-1.3
SOEs											
Overall fiscal balance 2/	-1.8	-0.5	0.7	0.8	0.7	0.2	0.0	0.0	0.0	0.0	0.1
Public Sector											
Overall fiscal balance 3/	-1.3	-1.3	0.9	1.4	0.1	-0.8	-0.9	-1.0	-1.1	-1.2	-1.2
Primary balance	0.3	0.3	2.3	2.6	1.4	0.5	0.2	0.2	0.1	0.0	0.2
Cyclically adjusted primary balance	-0.1	0.4	2.7	2.9	1.6	0.6	0.3	0.3	0.2	0.0	0.2
Structural primary balance	-0.4	0.4	2.7	1.3	1.6	0.6	0.3	0.3	0.2	0.0	0.2
Debt	42.2	43.3	42.5	41.8	41.9	41.6	41.6	41.6	41.7	41.9	41.9
Memorandum items:											
Public sector investment 4/	5.8	5.3	5.9	6.4	5.2	6.0	6.4	6.4	6.3	6.3	6.0
General government	3.9	3.6	4.4	4.7	3.4	3.7	3.8	3.8	3.8	3.8	3.7
Public enterprises	1.9	1.7	1.6	1.7	1.8	2.3	2.6	2.6	2.5	2.5	2.3

Sources: Thai authorities; and IMF staff estimates and projections.
1/ Fiscal year runs from October 1 to September 30.
2/ Estimated from the evolution of SOEs debt.
3/ Includes General Government and SOEs.
4/ Official GFS data are not available for the Public Sector. Historical data are estimated based on GFS General Government official data, and information from SEPO and national accounts.

Sources: Reproduced with permission from International Monetary Fund (2018), *Thailand: 2018 Article IV Consultation — Press Release; Staff Report; and Statement by the Executive Director for Thailand,* Country Report 18/143, Table 5.

using the cyclically adjusted fiscal balance, to remove the impact of business cycles. Examples of structural fiscal balances would include the "non-oil" fiscal balance in an oil-producing country, i.e., the fiscal balance excluding revenue attributable to petroleum exports, and a cyclically adjusted fiscal balance with petroleum prices fixed at a certain level. This would show the impact of higher (or lower) oil prices on the fiscal balance estimated at potential output.

4.3.2. *Fiscal balances under the 2001 and 2014 GFS*

Under the IMF's 2001 and 2014 *Government Finance Statistics Manuals*, fiscal accounts are measured on an accrual basis, and different fiscal balances are used. Among the most important are the following:

- **Net operating balance:** This is the difference between revenues and expense, with expense defined as outlays excluding net lending and the purchase of non-financial assets.
- **Net lending/borrowing:** The net operating balance *minus* the net acquisition of non-financial assets, which is close to capital expenditure (purchases minus sales and consumption of non-financial assets, where the consumption of such assets includes depreciation and any reduction in the government's inventory of non-financial assets). In Australia, net lending/borrowing is also called the *fiscal balance*.
- **Net primary balance:** Net lending or borrowing, *excluding* net interest payments. This is an accrual version of the primary balance in the 1986 GFS approach, although it excludes policy loans granted by government (which are included as net lending in the 1986 GFS approach).
- **Cash surplus or deficit:** This is equivalent to the conventional fiscal balance in the 1986 GFS approach to fiscal accounts.

4.3.3. *A quick introduction to fiscal sustainability*

Although Chapter Five covers this issue in detail, fiscal sustainability deserves mention as an important concept in fiscal analysis. *Fiscal sustainability* — which is also called *public debt sustainability* — means that the government's budget policy can continue without risk of a dramatic reversal. If fiscal policy cannot be continued without such risk, it is unsustainable.

In practice, fiscal sustainability turns on the state of public sector debt — in particular, *the ratio of government debt to GDP*. It is widely accepted that the ratio of government debt to GDP cannot rise without limit. Such a situation would raise serious questions about the government's solvency. Hence, a government whose debt-to-GDP ratio is seen as rising steadily, to high levels, is considered as having an unsustainable fiscal policy. What constitutes a high debt-to-GDP ratio? IMF economists have noted that more than half of all government defaults have occurred in countries where the debt-to-GDP ratio exceeded 40%.[5] Moreover, until recent years, countries whose debt to GDP ratio exceeded 50% had great difficulty in reducing the ratio below that level. Hence, countries with debt-to-GDP ratios above 40–50% are considered vulnerable, and policies that would raise the debt-to-GDP ratio above that level are unsustainable over the long term. This helps explain the concern about fiscal stimulus packages implemented in many advanced economies during 2009 and the call by many economists, including the Chairman of the US Federal Reserve Board, that the US and other countries take steps to reduce their debt-to-GDP ratios to more reasonable levels (e.g., not more than 60%, for the US Federal Government) over the medium term.[6]

As Chapter Five will show, the change in government's debt-to-GDP ratio depends on the primary fiscal balance, the debt-to-GDP ratio at the start of the period, the average real interest rate on government debt, and the real growth rate of the economy's GDP

$$d_t - d_{t-1} = -pb_t + \frac{r - g}{1 + g} d_{t-1},$$

where d = debt/GDP, pb = primary balance/GDP, r = real interest rate, and g = real GDP growth rate.

---

[5]International Monetary Fund (2003). "Public Debt in Emerging Markets: Is It Too High?" in World Economic Outlook, September 2003 (Washington: IMF), Chapter III, pp. 113–152, http://www.imf.org/external/pubs/ft/weo/2003/02/pdf/chapter3.pdf.

[6]See Irwin, N. (2009), "Bernanke Presses for Fiscal Restraint," Washington Post, June 4; and IMF Fiscal Affairs Department, 2009, "State of Public Finances Cross Country Fiscal Monitor: November 2009," IMF Staff Position Note 09/25 (Washington), http://www.imf.org/external/pubs/ft/spn/2009/spn0925.pdf.

To keep the debt-to-GDP ratio unchanged, the primary balance (as a percent of GDP) must satisfy the following relationship:

$$pb_t \geq (r_t - g_t)/(1 + g_t)^* d_{t-1}.$$

For example, if $r_t = 0.04$, $g_t = 0.02$, $d_{t-1} = 0.6$, setting pb_t 1.18 (a primary surplus of 1.18% of GDP) will stabilize the debt/GDP ratio. A larger primary surplus will reduce the ratio.

4.3.4. Budget financing

How a government finances its budget deficit matters greatly for the economy and, in some cases, for fiscal sustainability. Any type of financing has economic consequences. However, some types are particularly worrisome.

4.3.4.1. Foreign financing

In many developing and emerging market countries, foreign financing is an important source for financing development expenditure. Often, financing represents a loan from an international organization such as the World Bank or Asian Development Bank, or a bilateral loan from an advanced economy, linked to a specific development project. For many low-income countries, such loans provide valuable support for infrastructure spending and other critical elements of economic development. However, many such countries have trouble selling bonds to foreign lenders in their own currencies. Instead, the countries must incur or issue debt in a widely accepted foreign currency, such as euros, US dollars, or Japanese yen. Thus, foreign financing exposes the budget to *currency risk* — the possibility that the volume of debt measured in local currency will rise because the local currency depreciates. Economists call the inability of many non-advanced economies to sell foreign debt in their own currency *original sin*. This situation arises because financial markets consider many non-advanced economies too unstable financially for debt in their domestic currencies to be viewed as marketable.[7]

In some emerging markets and many advanced economies, foreign financing is a choice the government makes about raising funds to finance a budget deficit. Besides domestic markets, governments can choose to obtain financing from foreign sources. In some countries, such as the United States, foreign financing represents a major share of the outstanding government debt.

For many countries, particularly those with high inflation rates, foreign financing can be tempting, because the interest rates on foreign debt are often lower than those on domestically held securities. Again, however, foreign financing exposes the budget to currency risk. As noted in Chapter Three, the risk can be substantial if the currency faces the possibility of a sharp depreciation.

4.3.4.2. Domestic financing

Domestic financing involves financing both from the banking system and from non-bank institutions. The two have different effects, because (under normal circumstances) only financing from the banking system can lead to money creation.

(a) **Central bank financing:** The monetary authority (central bank) finances the government budget when it buys new government securities. Because the monetary authority must create the resources to buy these bonds, this type of bank financing is pure *monetization*, i.e., money creation. Thus, it represents the most inflationary form of government finance. For this reason, many countries limit the amount of central bank financing for

---

[7]See Eichengreen, B. *et al.* (2005), "The Mystery of Original Sin," in B. Eichengreen and R. Hausmann, eds., *Other People's Money: Debt Denomination and Financial Instability in Emerging-Market Economies* (Chicago: University of Chicago Press).

the budget. A few countries prohibit central bank financing altogether.

(b) **Commercial (deposit money) bank financing:** The banking system also finances the government budget when commercial (deposit money) banks buy newly issued government debt. The monetary implications of commercial bank financing depend on what commercial banks do with the debt. When commercial banks buy and hold government debt, the effect is to *crowd out* some private sector borrowing. The reason is that commercial banks have a fixed amount of assets at any one time, and assets used to purchase government debt represent funds that cannot be used for other purposes, in particular, for providing loans to private firms and individuals. However, commercial bank holdings of government debt can lead to monetization if commercial banks draw on the monetary authority's rediscounting facility to obtain additional financing. In this case, the banks typically pledge government securities as backing for a loan from the monetary authority. In return, the monetary authority credits commercial banks with freely usable reserves. The same situation occurs when the monetary authority decides to use open market operations to expand the money supply by buying government securities. In either case, the sale or pledging of securities to the monetary authority leads to an expansion of the money supply. Thus, the consequences of commercial bank financing depend on whether the banks retain the debt (crowding out) or transfer it to the monetary authority (monetization).

(c) **Domestic non-bank financing:** When non-bank institutions, whether financial or non-financial, or individuals purchase new government securities, the result is pure crowding out. The reason is that non-bank purchasers ordinarily have no access to the monetary authority, and thus no way of generating money creation from their purchase of government debt. The purchase of government debt by a non-bank institution means that the institution is allocating part of its resources to holding government debt, rather than some other financial asset. Thus, fewer financial resources are available for other potential claimants, such as private firms or individuals. One consequence is that, except in periods of weak economic activity, interest rates for loans to the private sector will typically be somewhat higher than they would be if the government's demand for domestic financing were less.

4.3.4.3. *Drawing on foreign exchange reserves*

In some cases, countries with substantial foreign exchange reserves can use those to finance government expenditure. For example, a country with large reserves can use a portion to finance the cost of imports for development projects. Another possibility is to use foreign reserves to recapitalize a bank with heavy loan losses, as China did with several state-owned banks that had large non-performing loans from state enterprises.[8] Using foreign exchange reserves in this way may pose few problems for a country such as China, which had about US$3.1 trillion in foreign exchange reserves at the end of 2019. For most countries, however, with official reserves totaling only several months' worth of imports, drawing on foreign exchange reserves could raise questions about the sustainability of the country's balance of payments. Such questions could trigger capital flight or a sharp depreciation in the currency. Thus, few countries use foreign exchange reserves as a significant source of budget financing.

4.3.4.4. *Arrears*

Arrears represent the government's failure to pay for spending obligations it has incurred. Although governments should not, in principle, incur arrears, in practice many governments fail to pay bills promptly. In some countries, arrears have led to long delays in payments to

---

[8] In 2003, China allocated about US$45 billion of its foreign exchange reserves to recapitalize two large state-owned banks. See Knowledge Wharton, 2005, "Reform of China's Banks, Burdened by Bad Loans, is Priority for Government" (June 1), http://knowledge.wharton.upenn.edu/article.cfm?articleid=1202.

contractors. In the Russian Federation during part of the 1990s, the government incurred substantial arrears in wage and salary payments. In practice, that meant the government was often several months late in paying salaries to civil servants.

Late payments make suppliers less willing to deal with the government. Where arrears are frequent, suppliers may raise their prices, effectively charging the government the equivalent of interest payments in anticipation of receiving late payments. More importantly, arrears undermine the government's reputation and may foster an environment in which fewer people respect the law. For all these reasons, arrears are highly destructive and should be avoided wherever possible.

4.3.5. *Fiscal space*[9]

Fiscal space has been defined as "room in a government's budget that allows it to provide resources for a desired purpose without jeopardizing the sustainability of its financial position or the stability of the economy."[10] Governments with fiscal space typically have budget surpluses or deficits small enough to allow a small deterioration in the fiscal balance without undermining fiscal sustainability or macroeconomic stability.

A government can create fiscal space by raising taxes, securing outside grants, cutting lower priority expenditure, or borrowing, provided the borrowing does not raise debt to an unacceptable level or threaten a steady rise in the government's debt-to-GDP ratio. In creating fiscal space, the government must ensure it has the capacity in both the short term and the longer term to finance its expenditure programs while also servicing its debt. Following are

---

[9]Material in this section is reproduced from Greene, J. (2018), *op. cit.*, Chapter 4.
[10]Heller, P. (2005), "Understanding Fiscal Space," IMF Policy Discussion Paper No. 05/4 (Washington: International Monetary Fund, March)." Available at: http://www.imf.org/external/pubs/ft/pdp/2005/pdp04.pdf. Accessed July 16, 2017.

several examples of how governments can create fiscal space for desired programs.

1. *Expenditure substitution*: a government could reduce spending for a lower-priority program to make available funds for a new and higher- priority project. Indonesia, for example, cut petroleum subsidies in 2005 and used some of the proceeds to provide a cash transfer program to low-income families.

2. *Revenue increases*: a government can raise revenue to finance a new program or increase spending for an existing one. In 2006, for example, the Philippines raised the rate of its value-added tax (VAT) by 2 percentage points and used the resulting revenue to boost education expenditure.

3. *Expanding borrowing in a low-debt environment*: where the government's debt-to-GDP ratio is sufficiently small, a modest increase in the deficit could be used to provide fiscal space for a desired program. In 2009, for example, the People's Republic of China (PRC) raised its budget deficit by about 2 percentage points of GDP to finance fiscal stimulus, to limit the adverse effects of the global financial crisis on the economy. Because the central government's debt-to-GDP ratio was less than 30 percent of GDP, this increase in the deficit did not threaten the sustainability of the government's fiscal position.

4.3.6. *Revenue analysis*

When considering the revenue side of the government budget, three broad characteristics of revenue are worth noting. First is the structure of the tax system and other revenues. Second is the revenue system's performance: how well revenues keep up with the economy and with the growth in expenditures. Third is the effectiveness of tax administration, which can be assessed by the presence or absence of common problems.

4.3.6.1. *The structure of the tax system*

As noted earlier, all revenue systems include both taxes and non-tax revenue, and those of low-income countries may also include grants. However, the division of revenues between tax and non-tax sources and the percentage of revenue raised from different sources can vary tremendously across countries. This reflects both differences in the structure of national economies and the country's (or electorate's) views about the appropriate size of government relative to GDP and the composition of GDP itself.

On average, more advanced economies rely more heavily on consumption, income, and payroll taxes (or their equivalent). Higher income countries typically have many large employers, and from these firms it is relatively easy to receive payments of corporate, value added, and the withheld portions of employees' salaries or a payroll (social insurance) tax. Among Anglophone countries, income and profits taxes tend to predominate. Among lower income countries, where it may be harder to administer more complex tax regimes, governments often rely more heavily on import (customs) duties and excise taxes on alcoholic beverages, petroleum products, and tobacco, which are often easier to collect. Among oil producers, which include many Middle Eastern countries, non-tax revenues in the form of lease fees and royalty payments can represent half or more of all revenues. Table 4.4 provides a good description of the composition of taxation in different types of countries as of the early 2000s.

Another key difference among the revenue systems of different countries is the sheer size of revenues relative to the economy. Countries with higher per capita incomes tend to have relatively higher shares of revenue in GDP, in part because they can collect revenue more easily and thus "afford" a greater volume of government services. The same is true for small island economies, the reason being that these economies need to fund a complete array of public services, from education and infrastructure to military services and foreign poverty. By comparison, lower income countries tend to have smaller shares of

Table 4.4. *Composition of taxation*: Central government revenues, early 2000s, (percent of total tax revenues).

	Taxes on income, profit & capital gains	Social security & payroll taxes	Domestic taxes on goods & services	International trade taxes	Property taxes
Developing countries	**25.1**	**14.4**	**39.4**	**18.3**	**1.4**
Americas	23.9	14.8	48.3	11.7	1.9
Sub-Saharan Africa	29.5	2.0	31.2	34.8	1.3
Central Europe & Former Soviet Union	15.3	34.9	44.7	4.9	0.3
N. Africa & Middle East	32.4	6.0	34.6	19.4	3.1
Asia & Pacific	35.1	4.0	40.5	15.9	1.5
Small islands	19.5	11.4	26.0	39.7	1.4
High-income countries	**32.6**	**27.9**	**33.0**	**4.9**	**2.5**

Source: Keen and Simone (2004)

revenue in GDP, because revenue is harder to collect and their citizens do not expect the same array of extensive services available to residents of higher income countries.

4.3.6.2. *Measures of revenue performance*

Governments typically measure revenue performance in several ways. One involves ratios of total revenue and tax revenue to GDP. A second examines the elasticity of total revenue to GDP, while a third looks for inefficiencies in the structure of revenues and tax administration.

(a) *Key revenue ratios*: Ratios of *total revenue to GDP* and *tax revenue to GDP* indicate the government's ability to raise revenue to finance expenditure. Ratios of revenue to GDP are usually closely related to the ratio of total expenditure to GDP, since governments need to limit budget deficits (the shortfall of revenue from expenditure) to a few percentage points of GDP, to avoid accumulating a high and rising ratio of public debt to GDP. High revenue to GDP ratios are not necessarily a good thing: only a few countries with large expenditure burdens, traditionally in Scandinavia, boast ratios of total revenue to GDP above 50%. Moreover, it is hard to define a single, appropriate ratio of revenue to GDP. Countries differ in their taste for public services, and countries with a tradition of a larger public sector (e.g., France, Austria) need higher revenue to GDP ratios than do countries with a tradition of a smaller public sector (e.g., the United States). However, very low ratios — under 15% — often present problems, because countries in this position usually find it very hard to finance a basic set of goods and services. Countries with low ratios of revenue to GDP include a number of very low-income countries in Asia, such as Bangladesh.

Even if the ratio of revenue to GDP is above 15%, some countries with relatively low tax-to-GDP ratios typically rely heavily on non-tax revenue from mineral exports (e.g., oil producers and countries with extensive mining operations). Countries in this position, such as the Russian Federation, may find it hard providing steady financing for public services when commodity prices fluctuate significantly. When prices are high, revenues are abundant, and these countries may be tempted to spend them in not-always productive ways. When commodity prices collapse, as they did during the second half of 2008 and the second half of 2014, these countries may find themselves struggling for revenue to maintain services, while deficits soar. Thus, it is worth monitoring not only the ratio of total revenue to GDP but also tax revenue and the ratio of non-mineral (e.g., non-oil, or non-metal) revenue to GDP, to identify the relatively steady level of revenue likely to be available to finance expenditure in the event of a commodity price collapse. Finally, the levels of key tax rates, such as the marginal rates of personal and corporate income tax, can be compared to those in other countries as one indicator of the attractiveness of doing business.

(b) *Revenue elasticity*: The *elasticity of revenue to GDP*, which indicates the percent change in total or tax revenue for a 1 percentage point change in nominal GDP, is a particularly useful indicator, since it shows how total revenue and tax revenue respond to changes in GDP. Revenue is compared with nominal GDP because revenue is a nominal item.

Where the elasticity of revenue is 1 or larger, revenues grow at least as fast as GDP, meaning that they "keep up" with GDP. This, in turn, makes it easier for the government to undertake its activities, because revenues rise in tandem with the economy, and the government can afford to maintain the existing ratio of expenditure to GDP.

A revenue elasticity less than one is problematic, because fiscal measures are needed to keep the government's budget balance from deteriorating. To avoid a worsening of the budget deficit, either taxes must be rise or expenditures must be reduced. Moreover, the problem will continue so long as the revenue elasticity remains less than one. Thus, governments faced with an inelastic revenue structure would do well to consider policy changes that will raise the elasticity of revenue to GDP to at least 1.

(c) *Revenue structure and administration*: The *"Tanzi diagnostic test."* A third indicator of revenue performance examines the structure of revenues and the quality of tax administration, using a list of eight qualitative indices developed by Dr. Vito Tanzi, a renowned public finance economist who for many years headed the International Monetary Fund's Fiscal Affairs Department. Together, these indices are called the "Tanzi Diagnostic Test." The eight indices are as follows[11]:

(1) **Concentration index:** Do a relatively few taxes and tax rates provide a large share of revenue?
(2) **Dispersion index:** Are there few low-yielding, "nuisance" taxes?
(3) **Erosion index:** Are actual tax bases very close to potential bases (few major exemptions, exclusions)?

---

[11]This wording comes from Ouanes, A., and S. Thakur (1997), *Macroeconomic Analysis and Accounting in Transition Economies* (Washington: International Monetary Fund), Box 3.5, p. 70.

(4) **Collection lag index:** Are tax payments made with short lags and close to their due dates?

(5) **Specificity index:** Does the tax system depend on as few taxes as possible, and with specific rates?

(6) **Objectivity index:** Are most taxes imposed on objectively measured tax bases?

(7) **Enforcement index:** Is the tax system enforced fully and effectively?

(8) **Cost of collection index:** Is the cost of collecting taxes as low as possible?

A tax system with positive answers to all eight questions can be considered to have high productivity.

4.3.7. *Expenditure analysis*

As with revenues, certain indicators can be used to assess expenditures. The most common are measures of expenditure structure and composition, including ratios of total expenditure and various expenditure components to GDP; estimates of the effects on expenditure of changes in interest and exchange rates; and an assessment of expenditure productivity.

(1) **Measures of expenditure structure and composition, including ratios to GDP:** Fiscal analysts usually like to examine not only the level but also the structure and composition of government expenditure. Governments that devote only a small percentage of outlays to capital expenditure may be hampering growth, by shortchanging investments in infrastructure. Governments where a large percentage of expenditure goes toward interest payments often have difficulty funding more productive spending. Governments in which mandated social programs, such as subsidy payments, state pensions, or health care services, account for a large fraction of total outlays often have little flexibility to address new demands for public services, unless the budget as a whole

tends toward surpluses. Similarly, governments in which the wage bill (outlays for wages and salaries of government employees) is a high share of total outlays may find it hard allocating enough funds for operations and maintenance or capital expenditure. Hence, it is useful to analyze the shares of expenditure allocated to current and capital spending, and the allocation of current expenditure among wages and salaries, other goods and services (which include operations and maintenance), subsidies, transfers, and interest payments. It is also useful to assess the composition of public debt and the breakdown of interest payments between foreign and domestic debts.

(2) **The impact of interest and exchange rate changes on expenditure:** It can also be useful to assess how changes in key macroeconomic variables affect expenditures. Changes in domestic interest rates, for example, affect interest due on domestic debt. Similarly, changes in exchange rates can have a profound effect on interest payments if a significant share of government debt is denominated in foreign currency. As noted earlier, foreign-denominated debt exposes a government to exchange rate (currency) risk, so knowing the impact of exchange rate changes (in particular, depreciations) on the domestic cost of interest payments is important. Similarly, developing countries with major capital projects that rely heavily on imported inputs or foreign technical assistance will find capital outlays quite sensitive to exchange rate changes.

(3) **Assessment of expenditure productivity:** Although not easily quantified, it is useful to review the government budget for the extent of so-called "unproductive expenditure," meaning outlays with relatively low productivity. Many kinds of expenditure, both current and capital, fall into this category. They include unnecessarily high military expenditures, poorly targeted subsidies and transfers, capital projects whose benefits compare poorly with anticipated costs, and heavy spending on low-skilled and temporary employees. Reducing such outlays frees resources for more productive spending. Thus, it is useful to review periodically different expenditure programs, to identify relatively unproductive

activities that could be eliminated with little cost to the overall quality of public services.

4.4. Fiscal Forecasting

Forecasting the government budget depends not only on the specific elements of revenue and expenditure policy but also on the state of the national economy. Revenue, for example, depends heavily on the forecast level of household income, corporate profits, consumption, and imports. At the local level, where governments rely particularly on property taxes, forecast levels of property prices are important. Budget expenditure chiefly depends on forecasts of prices and inflation and on indicators of employment, since recession and slow growth may lead to increasing demands for subsidies and transfers to low-income households and unemployed workers. Thus, *forecasting the government budget requires a consistent set of macroeconomic assumptions (projections) for key indicators, such as GDP, inflation, and the balance of payments.* At the same time, the macroeconomic aggregates themselves depend on the budget, since revenue affects after-tax income, while outlays affect various components of aggregate demand. Thus, budget forecasts should be consistent with the macroeconomic forecast.

In general, budget revenue depends more than expenditure on existing policies and on the macroeconomic environment, since in most countries taxes provide the bulk of revenue, and tax rates and provisions are usually codified in law. Expenditure depends more on the policy decisions of government. Nevertheless, a large portion of budget expenditure can often be forecast in advance, because many important outlays depend on long-term programs or are linked to government programs whose level of activity changes only modestly from year to year. This is particularly true in advanced economies with large "entitlement" programs, in which outlays are linked to the number of citizens or residents meeting certain eligibility criteria and anticipated benefit levels or service costs. Thus, it is often possible to make a good "initial" forecast of expenditure, subject to revision for policy changes introduced by the government.

Before deciding how to forecast the budget, analysts must first decide at what level of detail (or aggregation) to forecast. Forecasting at too aggregate a level — for example, forecasting total revenue or total expenditure in the aggregate, without regard to detailed categories — is likely to create errors. The totals cannot take into account the many factors determining the expected levels of particular taxes or spending programs. Thus, they may fall wide of the mark. At the same time, limited data may make it impossible to forecast at too fine a level of detail. For example, it may be hard to forecast VAT collections on each of many kinds of food and beverages, although it may be possible to develop forecasts of VAT collections at various large retailers and then make estimates of collections from small retailers. To minimize errors, analysts generally recommend forecasting at the most disaggregated level the data will allow. Because data will vary from country to country, this may mean that forecasts can be made at more disaggregated levels in some countries (often the more advanced economies, where data may be more readily available), than in others.

4.4.1. *Forecasting revenues*

There are three basic ways to forecast budget revenues. One involves using a *computer model*, either a large macroeconomic model that includes a section for the fiscal sector or a "simulation" model that draws on a representative set of taxpaying units and uses forecast changes in key macroeconomic variables to simulate the effect on the tax base and tax liabilities of these households. Economists in the United States, for example, often use the second type of model to simulate the effects of various tax policy changes on different types of households, including households at different income levels.

The second method, called the *effective tax rate approach*, forecasts revenues by applying an effective tax rate — the ratio of anticipated revenues to the tax base — to a forecast tax base. The tax base is chosen so that it can be easily forecast in response to changes in macroeconomic indicators.

The third technique, called the *tax elasticity or buoyancy approach*, forecasts the *percentage change* in different elements of revenue as a function of *percentage changes* in key macroeconomic indicators. In this case, revenue items can rise faster or more slowly than the underlying macroeconomic indicators, depending on the observed elasticity. This technique is similar to the second one, although it allows for changes in the "effective tax rate," depending on the elasticity of revenues to changes in the relevant tax base.

Because the model-based approach depends on the nature of the model used, the discussion in this chapter focuses on the effective tax rate and elasticity/buoyancy approaches.

4.4.1.1. *The effective tax rate approach*

The effective tax rate approach involves calculating the components of revenue as fixed percentages of measurable tax bases. In each case, an element of revenue, such as the revenue from a personal or household income tax, is forecast as the product of an effective tax rate and an appropriate tax base

$$\text{Rev}_i = \text{Effective tax rate}_i^* \text{ Tax base}_i,$$

where Rev_i is the "ith" element of revenue, Effective tax rate$_i$ is the relevant effective tax rate, and Tax base$_i$ is a measurable tax base that appears reasonably well related to Rev_i.

The effective tax rate approach requires determining the effective tax rate and selecting an appropriate tax base to use in forecasting the amount of revenue to be collected. The effective tax rate represents the *ratio of revenue actually collected to the tax base*. Its value lies in relating the tax base used (which is usually an aggregate variable, such as household income, corporate profits, imports f.o.b., or imports c.i.f.) to revenues collected from various taxes and non-tax items. Since revenue laws are highly complex, it is virtually impossible to measure, let alone forecast, the true revenue base of a tax or non-tax item. Instead, one must use an approximation of the revenue base called a *proxy tax base*.

Because revenue laws often include exemptions, preferential treatment of certain items, and multiple tax rates and because tax and non-tax items are subject to different degrees of enforcement and evasion, revenue collections will rarely equal the product of the statutory (legal) tax rate and the approximate revenue base. Instead, an "effective" tax rate, meaning the ratio of actual collections to the proxy tax base, must be determined. This rate can be significantly less than the statutory rate (or weighted average of statutory rates), because of exemptions, exclusions, evasion, and problems with enforcement and administration.

The validity of the effective tax rate approach depends on two main factors. One involves identifying an appropriate, measurable, and forecastable proxy tax base. The other is the assumption that the effective tax rate is stable over time. The stability of the effective tax rate, in turn, depends on the stability of the tax base structure (the composition of tax units — for example, the share of imports subject to tax at each of several tax rates — should not change); the stability of the revenue system (no changes in revenue laws); and the stability of compliance with the law, meaning no significant changes in tax administration or tax evasion. While it is often possible to identify appropriate and measurable proxy tax bases, the stability conditions are harder to satisfy. Thus, the effective tax rate approach can lead to errors in revenue forecasting, unless appropriate adjustments are made to allow for changes in the revenue base, revenue law, compliance, and administration.

a. *Proxy tax bases*: As noted, the effective tax rate approach relies on having readily available and easily forecasted "proxy" tax bases for the main components of revenue. Thus, proxy bases are needed for the personal income tax, corporate profits tax, value added tax, excise taxes, property taxes, wage or social security taxes, export and import taxes, and miscellaneous taxes. Proxy bases are also required for such non-tax items as profits of state enterprises and the central bank, revenues from the lease or rental of government-owned property (which can include royalties from oil or mineral extraction), earnings from a state lottery, and revenues from fees and charges, including fines and penalties. In many developing and emerging market countries, data are not available for the closest proxy tax bases, such as household income (in the case of a personal income tax) or total corporate profits (for a corporate profits tax). In these countries, revenue forecasters must use other, more readily available data that are expected to move in the same way as the more desirable proxy base. Following are examples of revenue items and the proxy tax bases often used to estimate them:

Revenue Item	Proxy Taxbase
• Individual Income Tax	Personal income or nominal GDP
• Corporate Income Tax	Corporate profits or nominal GDP
• VAT, Excise Taxes	Nominal private consumption
• Import Duties	Imports, c.i.f.
• Export Duties	Exports
• Other Taxes	Nominal GDP (at factor prices)
• Non-tax Revenue	Nominal GDP; may disaggregate into various components

b. *Using effective tax rates to forecast revenues*: As noted earlier, if a proxy tax base is identified, the effective tax rate method forecasts revenue as the product of the effective tax rate and the proxy tax base. The following example, using import (customs) duties, illustrates the approach.

Suppose history shows the following information about total import duties and total imports, c.i.f.:

	2014	2015	2016	2017	2018	2019
Import duties	100	120	140	150	160	170
Imports, c.i.f.	1000	1200	1400	1500	1600	1700

If the composition of imports, the tax law, and tax administration have all remained unchanged during this period, one can estimate the effective tax rate for import duties as 10% of imports, c.i.f., since in every year from 2014 to 2019 total import duties collected equaled 10% of the proxy tax base, imports, c.i.f. Thus, 10%, which represents the ratio of actual collections to the proxy tax base, is the effective tax rate, regardless of the statutory rate, which could well have been higher (e.g., a single rate of 20% applicable to all taxable imports, or perhaps a weighted average rate of 15% on all imports subject to tax).

If, in 2020, imports, c.i.f. are forecast at 1,800, the effective tax rate approach would forecast import duties at 180:

$$\text{Import duties} = \text{effective tax rate} * \text{proxy tax base}$$

$$= 0.10 * 1,800 = 180.$$

On the assumption that the import forecast is reasonable, the effective tax rate approach would yield a plausible forecast of revenues, so long as the composition of imports remained the same and the tax law, tax administration, and compliance with the law did not change.

4.4.1.2. The tax elasticity/buoyancy approach

A second way of forecasting revenues is the *tax elasticity or buoyancy approach.* This method involves linking the change in a revenue item to the change in a proxy tax base through a scaling factor (an elasticity or buoyancy) that indicates how fast the revenue item increases (or decreases) when the proxy tax base grows (or contracts) by 1%. Thus, the revenue item is estimated using a two-step approach. First, the percent change in the revenue item is estimated, calculating the change as the product of two factors: (1) the percent change in the proxy tax base and (2) the scaling factor indicating how much the revenue item changes for each 1% change in the proxy tax base:

$$\text{Pct. chg. revenue}_t = e * \text{ percent change in the proxy tax base,}$$

where e is the scaling factor.

Second, the calculated percent change in revenue is applied to last period's amount to get the revenue forecast for the present or future period:

$$\text{Rev}_t = \text{Rev}_{t-1} * (1 + \text{Pct. chg. in revenue}_t/100).$$

Thus, the elasticity/buoyancy approach requires two steps to forecast a revenue item, while the effective tax rate approach involves only one step (forecasting revenue directly, as a stated percentage of the proxy tax base).

In most areas of economics, the scaling factor used in the elasticity/buoyancy approach is called an elasticity. In revenue estimation, the term *elasticity* is applied when the factor measures the "built-in" responsiveness of the revenue item to the tax base, meaning by how much revenues grow (or decline) in the absence of any change in tax law or policy. When it is impossible to estimate this "built-in" or inherent response of revenues to a change in the proxy tax base, because the tax law has changed during the period during which the coefficient is estimated, the coefficient is called a *buoyancy*. Thus, the buoyancy of a revenue item *vis-à-vis* a macroeconomic variable can always be estimated. However, an elasticity can only be estimated over a period of relatively unchanged tax law, or by adjusting actual revenues for the effect of tax law changes, to create "consistent" set of revenues over which the built-in responsiveness can be estimated.

Year	Actual Tax Adjusted Collections Receipts T	Discretionary Measure DS	Tax Collection Excluding New Measure T-DS	Share of Measure in Revenue T/(T-DS)	Tax T*Col 5
1	100	0			132.6
2	140	20	120	1.167	159.1
3	170				193.2
4	250	30	220	1.136	250.0
5	300				300.0

Figure 4.2.　An example of the proportional adjustment method.

One way of adjusting revenues is to assume that revenues in previous periods would have changed by the same percentage as the percentage change resulting from a tax measure in the current period. For example, if a tax change is estimated to raise revenues by 10% in the current period, past revenues are assumed also to have been increased by 10%, to get a consistent series of revenue values. One can then use this adjusted series of revenues to estimate the "true" elasticity of revenues to the proxy tax base. If the tax change raised revenues, the adjusted series will have higher than actual values in past periods, and the estimated elasticity will be smaller than the observed buoyancy. Figure 4.2 shows an example of using the proportional adjustment method to adjust revenues as a way of calculating the elasticity of revenues. Note that revenues in years before a tax increase (here, years 1–3) are adjusted by the percent increases in all subsequent tax increases. In particular, revenues in year 1 are adjusted by a total of 32.6%, reflecting the combined impact of tax increases in years 2 and 4.

The elasticity of a revenue item depends on the structure of the revenue item or system and on tax administration and compliance. If the revenue item is progressive and compliance is high, the elasticity (and the buoyancy) can be greater than one. In this case, the revenue item is called *elastic*. If the structure is regressive, if consumers are gradually shifting from the taxed item to other items, or if compliance is low, the elasticity can be less than one, and the revenue item is called *inelastic*. In this case, the revenue item grows more slowly than the tax base. As with individual revenue items, one can assess the elasticity of the tax system or the entire revenue system (tax and non-tax items) by comparing the rate of growth of total taxes or total revenues with the rate of growth of a country's GDP or gross national income (GNI). Tax or revenue systems that in which revenues grow at least as fast as GDP or GNI are considered *elastic*. Those in which revenues grow more slowly are called *inelastic*. By comparison, the effective tax rate approach, by fixing the ratio of revenues to a proxy tax base, requires revenues to grow as fast as the base. Thus, the effective tax rate approach is equivalent to setting the elasticity (or buoyancy) of a revenue item to its base to one.

Because estimating the true elasticity of a revenue item can be hard, this approach often requires using the buoyancy. This can create problems if revenues have typically been adjusted only in one direction. For example, if tax rates have been raised frequently, forecasts made using the buoyancy approach may overestimate revenues, because the observed buoyancy reflects many discretionary increases. Without these increases, revenues would have risen more slowly. In this case, the buoyancy will over-estimate the true elasticity (built-in responsiveness of revenues) to the tax base.

Where estimates of the revenue impact of tax changes are unavailable or unreliable, the buoyancy approach poses risks. If no other approach is available, one option is to estimate revenues using a conservative set of buoyancies, i.e., buoyancies toward the lower end of the estimated range. Alternatively, another forecasting approach may be preferable. If the observed buoyancies fluctuate considerably from year to year, it may be better to estimate revenues using the effective tax rate approach, possibly incorporating a trend if effective tax rates have been rising or falling steadily over the last few years. For small revenue items that have shown a fairly steady ratio to GDP, it may be sufficient to forecast the items as the same share of GDP as observed in recent years.

4.4.2. Forecasting expenditures

For purposes of forecasting, expenditures can be categorized as either *discretionary* or *non-discretionary*. *Discretionary expenditures* are those set by government as a matter of policy — for example, outlays for education. *Non-discretionary expenditures*, by comparison, are established by contract, such as interest payments, or mandates, such as government pension outlays. Although governments in principle set the levels of discretionary expenditures, in practice many of these items are affected by changes in key macroeconomic variables, such as the inflation rate. Thus, many outlays can be forecast by taking into account developments in real growth and inflation. In addition, expenditures for entitlement programs, such as public pension programs, depend on the number of eligible beneficiaries and factors affecting the average payment or benefit provided.

4.4.2.1. Forecasting discretionary expenditures

Forecasting outlays for specific categories of discretionary expenditure requires detailed knowledge of each program. Nevertheless, rough estimates of the main elements of discretionary expenditure can be made by estimating the outlays for non-interest spending, categorized by the economic classification.

a. *Wage and salary expenditure*: Government wage and salary outlays, for example, can be estimated by taking into account the number of government employees and the average wage or salary paid to each. In countries where civil service wages are increased by a uniform factor, one can adjust the previous year's expenditure by (1) the anticipated rise in average wages and (2) the expected change in the number of government employees. Different variables — for example, the expected rise in private sector wages, or perhaps the rise in the consumer price index plus some allotment for productivity growth — can be used to forecast the rise in average wages. Past experience may provide a guide to the growth in the number of employees. The resulting estimates can then be adjusted upward for wage drift (the rise in wages resulting from promotions) and downwards for retirements (the replacement of older, higher paid employees by younger, lower paid staff).

b. *Purchases of other goods and services*: Purchases of other goods and services, including equipment and spending for operations and maintenance, will depend on the level of government activity and the cost of inputs. Unless the government is downsizing operations, real levels of government purchases may tend to keep pace with some measure of real economic growth — real GDP, or perhaps real growth in private expenditure. Nominal outlays will depend on both the real growth rate and the inflation rate, and inflation must be forecast using an inflation index that moves in line with government spending. Because it is linked to consumer purchases, the consumer price index (CPI) may not always be the best index for this purpose. If there is no price index for government consumption, other price indices, such as a wholesale price index or the GDP deflator, may be appropriate.

c. *Subsidies and transfers*: Subsidies and transfers can be particularly hard to forecast, because their expenditures depend not only on inflation but also on the size of the eligible population and on the terms of individual programs. For example, a food or petroleum subsidy program depends on the underlying cost of the item, the price at which it is to be sold, and the number of units sold. Underlying costs can be forecast from projections of the market price of the item (e.g., crude petroleum or refined gasoline), while the price — and, thus, the amount of subsidy per unit — depends on government policy. The number of units sold may move in line with the level of real economic activity. However, actual sales may also depend on the price and availability of substitute products and any anticipation that the official price will change (anticipated price increases may cause a temporary jump in sales). A government transfer program, such as a state pension program, will depend on the number and composition of beneficiaries and the benefits paid to each class or recipients. Thus, forecasts should, if possible, be made by aggregating the expected benefits to each class of beneficiaries over all such groups of recipients.

d. *Capital expenditures*: Capital outlays typically depend on the number and nature of different projects. Forecasts should ideally be aggregated over individual projects, taking into account the timing of outlays for each project, since projects often take more than a year to complete. As with current expenditure, outlays will also vary with inflation, in particular the rates of inflation on labor and capital inputs. Where capital projects depend heavily on imports, changes in the exchange rate also matter.

4.4.2.2. *Forecasting interest payments*

Interest payments pose a challenge, for two reasons. First, for countries that issue debt both in their own currency and in foreign currency, interest payments should be estimated separately for domestic and external currency debt. Interest rates on the two will typically differ. In addition, interest due on foreign currency debt must reflect changes in exchange rates. Second, interest due on debt acquired during the year will typically be less than a full year's interest payments, as opposed to interest due on debt held at the start of a year. Thus, within both domestic and foreign currency debt, it is useful to estimate interest payments on existing and newly acquired debt obligations separately. This last point requires some elaboration.

Interest due on existing debt obligations will depend on the terms of these obligations — the maturity date and interest rate and whether the interest rate is fixed or floating. Ideally, interest due should be calculated for each security and then aggregated over all existing debt. If this is not possible, one can make a rough forecast by applying to the stock of debt at the end of the last fiscal year an interest rate that takes into account (1) the average interest rate on all debt expiring in more than 1 year and (2) some measure of the change in interest rates on debt that will expire and be replaced. For example, if the average rate on expiring debt is 10%, and interest rates on new government debt are expected to average about 8%, one could attach an interest rate of 8% on that fraction of debt expiring during the fiscal year and the average interest rate on non-expiring debt to the rest of the existing debt stock. If non-expiring debt were 80% of the total stock at the start of the fiscal year, and the average rate of interest on that debt was 10%, then the forecast interest rate on the existing debt could be estimated at $0.8 \times 10\% + 0.2 \times 8\%$, or about 9.6%.

Interest due on new borrowing will depend on the terms of the debt — the amount of the new debt, the interest rate, and when interest payments are due. Because the debt incurred as a result of a budget deficit (or the debt retired, if there is a surplus) will usually be issued at various points during the fiscal year, only part of a year's interest will generally fall due during that fiscal year. While the most accurate estimate will draw on the specific terms of each security issued, the interest payable can be estimated by assuming that the debt is issued at a uniform pace during the year. In this case, one can assume that about 1/4 of the debt is issued during the first three months, half during the first half of the year, and so forth. Under this assumption, the equivalent of about half the debt issued during the year will be outstanding for a full year. If interest is payable as soon as the debt is issued, the interest due on the new debt issued (or the interest saved on the debt retired) during the year can be estimated as the following product:

Interest due $= 1/2*$ amount of new debt issued (or retired) $*$ average interest rate on the relevant debt.

Under this assumption, if the new debt issued is 100, and the interest rate is 8%, the interest due on the debt needed to cover the current year's deficit is 4: $1/2 \times 100 \times 0.08 = 50 \times 0.08 = 4$.

Because interest due on new debt adds to the budget deficit, and thus the amount of new debt and the interest payments due on it, this part of interest should be forecast so as to take account of the iterative nature of the estimate. Fortunately, the rise in interest due to the additional borrowing needed by interest on new debt is typically small compared to the existing deficit, so a few iterations should yield a reasonable forecast of interest payments and, in turn, total expenditures. Spreadsheet programs such as EXCEL make it easy to handle these feedback loops, using features like automatic iteration or goal-seek.

4.4.2.3. *Forecasting budget financing*

Once revenue and expenditure have been forecast, the estimates can be combined to project the overall budget balance, which will have the same absolute value, but opposite sign, as the required financing. The amount of net foreign financing will often be known, since foreign drawings will be tied to certain outlays for development projects, while amortization (principal payments) will be stipulated in existing debt obligations. Domestic financing will thus be the difference between total and foreign financing. Because of the role of bank financing on money expansion, bank and non-bank financing should be forecast separately. Where nonbank financing traditionally has been limited, one should not overestimate how much new debt can be sold to the non-bank market, because this will produce an underestimate of the required bank financing. Underestimating bank financing could, in turn, understate the crowding out of private borrowing in the banking system, if commercial banks are the main buyers of government debt, or the resulting money expansion, if the monetary authority is the main purchaser.

4.5. Fiscal Analysis Case Study: Singapore

Singapore presents an intriguing country for fiscal analysis for several reasons. First, it is among the few advanced economies regularly to attain fiscal surpluses, at least according to the accounting used in the IMF's government finance statistics manuals. As noted in Table 4.5, based on data from the IMF's World Economic Outlook database, Singapore has rarely had a fiscal deficit since 2008. Even in 2009, when the Global Financial Crisis hit Singapore, the budget deficit was only

Table 4.5. Singapore: Key fiscal indicators, 2008–2019, in percent of GDP.

	2008	2009	2010	2011	2012	2013	2014	2015	2016	2017	2018	2019
Revenue	17.6	15.8	15.9	17.6	17.2	16.9	17.2	17.3	18.9	19.0	17.7	18.2
Expenditure	14.0	15.9	10.2	9.7	9.8	10.9	12.6	14.4	15.2	13.7	14.0	14.3
Fiscal Balance[a]	3.6	−0.1	5.7	8.0	7.3	6.0	4.6	2.9	3.7	5.3	3.7	3.8
Gross Debt	97.9	101.7	98.7	103.1	106.7	98.2	97.8	102.3	106.5	104.8	110.4	111.8

Note: [a]Net lending to (positive) or borrowing from (negative) outside the budgetary sector.
Source: International Monetary Fund, World Economic Outlook Databases, October 2019 and April 2020.

0.1% of GDP. The structural (cyclically adjusted) balance showed a small surplus of 0.2% of the estimated potential output.[12]

While Singapore normally attains a fiscal surplus, it has substantial gross public debt, currently equivalent to more than 100 percent of GDP (Table 4.5). Much of this debt has been issued in the form of non-tradable bonds called Special Singapore Government Securities, to provide assets in which the Central Provident Fund can invest. As of December 2019, total CPF balances were S$425.1 billion,[13] equal to about 83.7% of Singapore's 2019 GDP.[14] Most of the remaining debt comprises tradable Singapore Government Securities, used to develop the domestic debt market and provide a risk-free benchmark that can be used in pricing other debt securities. In addition, the government has issued non-tradable Singapore Savings Bonds to give individual investors a long-term asset for saving. Because all debt proceeds are invested in assets and cannot be used for government spending, net public debt is arguably zero.[15]

---

[12]See International Monetary Fund (2018), *Fiscal Monitor, October 2019*, Table A3, p. 59.
[13]Central Provident Fund Board (2019), "CPF Statistics — Balances," https://www.cpf.gov.sg/Members/AboutUs/about-us-info/cpf-statistics.
[14]Singapore's GDP in 2019 was estimated at S$507.6 billion, according to Singapore's Department of Statistics (Singstat).
[15]See Singapore Government (2012), "Is it fiscally sustainable for Singapore to have such a high level of debt?" (August), https://www.gov.sg/factually/content/is-it-fiscally-sustainable-for-singapore-to-have-such-a-high-level-of-debt.

Official government statistics typically show much smaller revenues and a less positive fiscal balance. The reason is that Singapore's Constitution bars counting as revenue proceeds from land sales and includes only a portion of the investment returns on government assets. Thus, the authorities' accounts showed an overall deficit equal to 1.0% of GDP for the 2015/2016 fiscal year, compared to a 2.9% surplus based on the presentation in the IMF's 2014 *Government Finance Statistics Manual* (Table 4.6).

In addition to the differences in fiscal accounting, Singapore's fiscal situation differs from that of other advanced economies in other respects. Because old-age pensions are provided through a Central Provident Fund, with benefits drawn from individual accounts funded by contributions from employees and employers, contributions and payments for these and certain medical benefits occur off-budget, thereby reducing both budget revenue and expenditure as a share of GDP. In addition, Singapore receives a sizable proportion of its revenues from land sales and profits from government-owned or government-linked corporations. This, along with large revenues from a value added tax, excises on tobacco and alcohol products, and substantial fees for car ownership and use, enables income and profits tax rates to be substantially lower than in most other advanced economies. The top personal income tax rate, for example, is 22%, and the corporate tax rate is 17%. On the expenditure side of the budget, the lack of unemployment benefits and a more discretionary approach to most social benefits help keep expenditure low, allowing Singapore to allocate a relatively high share of outlays to capital spending, including infrastructure. Thus, in recent years such spending has averaged 4–6% of GDP, well above levels in most other advanced economies. At the same time, the fiscal situation has provided the fiscal space for the government to provide periodic "top-ups" to benefits for the elderly and other social programs, all on a discretionary basis.

Table 4.6.　Singapore: Selected fiscal indicators, 2014/2015–2018/2019, in percent of GDP.

	2015/16	2016/17	2017/18	2018/19	2017/19	2019/20	2019/20
IMF Approach				Budget	Prelim.	Budget	Projected
Revenue	17.3	18.9	19.2	17.9	18.2	18.0	18.1
Taxes	13.1	13.1	14.1	12.8	13.5	13.2	13.2
Other	4.3	5.8	5.1	5.1	4.7	4.8	4.9
Expense	13.2	13.1	12.9	12.8	13.0	13.0	13.0
Gross Operating Bal.	4.1	5.8	6.2	5.1	5.2	4.9	5.1
Net acquis. of non-fin. assets[a]	4.9	4.6	4.2	5.0	4.6	4.3	4.3
O/w: Devel. Exp.	4.5	4.2	3.8	4.5	4.1	3.8	3.8
Net Lending/ Borrowing, excl. non- produced assets	−0.8	1.2	2.1	0.0	0.6	0.7	0.8
Net acquisition of non-produced assets	−3.6	−2.5	−3.3	−2.5	−3.0	−3.3	−3.3
Net lending/borrow'g	2.9	3.7	5.4	2.5	3.6	4.0	4.1
Memorandum item							
Primary balance[b]	−2.9	−2.4	−1.1	−3.2	−2.7	−2.7	−2.7
Authorities' budget accounts							
Operating rev.	15.2	15.4	16.1	14.7	14.9	14.6	—
Total expenditure	15.8	15.8	15.6	16.2	16.0	15.7	—
Primary fiscal bal.	−0.6	−0.5	0.5	−1.5	−1.1	−1.0	—
Special transfers (excl. endow. funds)	1.0	0.6	0.6	0.4	0.3	0.3	—
Basic balance	−1.6	−1.1	0.0	−1.9	−1.4	−1.4	—
Transfers to endowment funds	1.4	0.8	0.8	1.5	1.5	2.6	—
Net investment returns contrib.	2.1	3.3	3.1	3.2	3.3	3.4	—
Overall balance	−1.0	1.4	2.3	−0.1	0.4	−0.7	—

Notes: [a] Excluding non-produced assets (land).
[b] Net lending/borrowing excluding non-produced assets and net investment returns contribution.
Source: International Monetary Fund (2019), *Singapore: 2019 Article IV Consultation — Press Release; Staff Report; and Statement by the Executive Director for Singapore* (July), Country Report 12/233, Table 6, p. 41.

4.6. Summary

Understanding fiscal accounts is critical for analyzing fiscal policy. Accurate analysis requires as comprehensive a view of the public sector as possible. Ideally, this should include the general government sector (comprising the central government, state or provincial governments, and local governments), plus the operations of state-owned enterprises. Fiscal accounts typically record revenue, expenditure, a measure of the fiscal balance, and budget financing. Revenue includes both tax and non-tax items, plus grants in those countries receiving them. Expenditure can be classified by economic or functional categories.

Under the more traditional 1986 *Manual on Government Finance Statistics* (*GFS*), current and capital outlays and net lending comprise the main economic categories of expenditure. The 2001 and 2014 *GFS* manuals treat net lending as part of budget financing. From an economic perspective, foreign financing, domestic bank financing, and domestic non-bank financing represent the main forms of budget finance. Each has its own consequences. Foreign financing creates exchange rate (currency) risk, while domestic non-bank financing tends to crowd out private sector borrowing. Domestic bank financing can lead either to crowding out or to money expansion, if the monetary authority buys the new debt.

The government's budget balance can be measured in different ways, depending on the objective. The conventional or overall cash balance, which shows the budget's financing requirement, is the most often used measure. However, other balances can also be calculated, including the primary balance, which shows the budget balance once interest payments are excluded from expenditures; and the public sector borrowing requirement, which shows the borrowing needs of the entire public sector. Fiscal balances under the 2001 and 2014 *GFS* manuals differ slightly from the foregoing, which are based on the 1986 *GFS* manual.

Revenue and expenditure performance can be analyzed in various ways, looking at the composition of revenue and expenditure and the elasticity of revenue and expenditure with respect to GDP — how fast they grow when GDP expands. An inelastic revenue system, in which the elasticity of total revenue to GDP is less than one, is problematic, because the budget balance will tend to worsen over time unless new revenue measures are enacted periodically or expenditures are regularly limited.

Revenue and expenditure forecasts depend on the macroeconomic outlook. Revenues are typically forecast on the basis of anticipated changes in proxy tax bases — macroeconomic indicators that move in line with the true tax base. The effective tax rate and elasticity/ buoyancy approaches are two ways to use this information. Although many outlays are discretionary, a significant part of expenditures can be forecast using forecasts of real growth and inflation.

Chapter Five: Fiscal (Public Debt) Sustainability

Fiscal sustainability, a term sometimes used interchangeably with *public debt sustainability*, has become a major concern in recent years, as many developing and emerging market countries have experienced capital outflows or currency crises as a result of heavy public debt burdens. Consequently, countries are paying closer attention to this issue, and agencies such as the International Monetary Fund are devoting more attention to public debt sustainability in their periodic assessments of national economies.

Fiscal sustainability means the ability of a country to maintain its current fiscal operations without the threat of a crisis that would require a drastic change in policy. Although sustainability can depend on the government's short-term liquidity, sustainability assessments are typically based on the outlook for the ratio of public debt to GDP. Governments with high ratios of public debt to GDP that seem likely to rise without limit over time are considered to have unsustainable fiscal positions. What qualifies as "high" can depend on the country's income level and history. However, even high-income countries like the United States, where the public debt-to-GDP ratio jumped by more than 10 percentage points between 2007 and 2009 and threatens to rise much further over the coming decades without a major adjustment in fiscal policy, have had their fiscal policy being called unsustainable.[1]

Fiscal sustainability implicitly involves several related concepts. One is *solvency:* in principle, whether a government could repay all its

---

[1] See Auerbach, A., and W. Gale, 2009, "The Economic Crisis and the Fiscal Crisis: 2009 and Beyond," *Tax Notes*, October 5, pp. 101–130 http://econ.berkeley.edu/auerbach/fiscal_future. pdf. Gale, W. (2019), *Fiscal Therapy* (New York: Oxford University Press), has noted the steady upward trajectory of US federal debt without calling it unsustainable, at least in the near term.

debt by running appropriate surpluses. Another is *liquidity:* having the resources needed to meet payment obligations as they mature. Similarly, one can compare the notion of an *unsustainable fiscal position* to the following concepts: *insolvency* (the inability to repay one's debts); *illiquidity* (lacking the resources needed to meet maturing debt service obligations); and *vulnerability:* weaknesses in revenue structure or expenditure policy and management that can lead to an unsustainable fiscal situation. Until recently, 50% of GDP represented a critical level of public debt, in that few countries whose public debt to GDP ratio exceeded 50% had managed to reduce the ratio significantly below that level.[2] Since the mid-1990s, however, several countries, including Indonesia, have succeeded in doing so. Although there appears to be no particular debt-to-GDP ratio above which growth plummets, the growth trajectory matters.[3] Countries with high but declining debt appear to grow no more slowly than other countries with lower debt levels. However, high and *rising* growth appears to have a negative effect on output growth.[4]

5.1. Assessing Sustainability: Basic Considerations

Economists normally assess fiscal sustainability using mathematical formulas relating the change in the public debt-to-GDP ratio to certain macroeconomic indicators. The key indicators are as follows:

- The average level of real interest rates on total public debt
- The real rate of GDP growth

---

[2]International Monetary Fund (2003), "Public Debt in Emerging Markets: Is It Too High?" in *World Economic Outlook*, September 2003 (Washington: IMF), Chapter III, pp. 113–152, http://www.imf.org/external/pubs/ft/weo/2003/02/pdf/chapter3.pdf.

[3]Pescatori, A. *et al.* (2014), "Debt and Growth: Is There a Magic Threshold?" IMF Working Paper No. 14/34 (Washington: International Monetary Fund, February), https://www.imf.org/external/pubs/ft/wp/2014/wp1434.pdf. This paper is among several refuting earlier research by Reinhart and Rogoff suggesting that growth rates were particularly affected once the public debt to GDP ratio reached 90%.

[4]Chudik, A. *et al.* (2015), "Is there a Debt Threshold Effect on Output Growth?" IMF Working Paper No. 15/197 (Washington: International Monetary Fund, September), https://www.imf.org/external/pubs/ft/wp/2015/wp15197.pdf.

- The ratio of the primary fiscal balance to GDP
- The ratio of non-debt-creating flows, such as privatization proceeds, to GDP
- Where governments have issued debt in foreign currency, the relevant exchange rate and average rate of debt issued in foreign currency, as well as the average real interest rate on domestic currency debt

Deriving the key formulas related to fiscal (public debt) sustainability is worthwhile. For this purpose, the following definitions are useful[5]:

D_t = the stock of government debt at the end of year t;
B_t = the primary (non-interest) fiscal balance;
S_t = the amount of non-debt-creating flows to the budget during year t;
i_t = the average nominal interest rate on government debt (this presumes all debt is issued in domestic currency);
π_t = the inflation rate (using the GDP deflator);
r_t = the average real interest rate on government debt (again, this presumes all debt is issued in domestic currency); note that $(1 + r_t) = (1 + i_t)/(1 + \pi_t)$;
g_t = the real growth rate of gross domestic product (GDP).

To begin the derivations, note that the following budget constraint always holds:

$$D_t = (1 + i_t) * D_{t-1} - (B_t + S_t).$$

The level of public debt at the end of period t equals the sum of the debt at the end of the previous period, plus interest due on that debt, minus the primary surplus and any non-debt-creating flows.

---

[5]The derivation of this and related formulas is taken from Ley, E. (2009), "Fiscal (and external) Sustainability," unpublished (Munich Personal RePEc Archive, February 28), http://mpra.eub.uni-muenchen.de/13693/1/MPRA_paper_13693.pdf.

Now, divide both sides of the above equation by nominal GDP during time t, expressed as $P_t Y_t$

$$\frac{D_t}{P_t Y_t} = (1 + i_t) * \frac{D_{t-1}}{P_t Y_t} - \frac{B_t}{P_t Y_t} - \frac{S_t}{P_t Y_t}.$$

Because $P_t Y_t$ can also be expressed as $(1 + g_t) * (1 + p_t) * P_{t-1} Y_{t-1}$, the above expression can be rewritten as

$$\frac{D_t}{P_t Y_t} = (1 + i_t)/[(1 + g_t) * (1 + p_t)] * \frac{D_{t-1}}{P_{t-1} Y_{t-1}} - \frac{B_t}{P_t Y_t} - \frac{S_t}{P_t Y_t}.$$

Since $1 + r_t = \frac{1+i_t}{1+p_t}$, the above expression can be expressed as

$$\frac{D_t}{P_t Y_t} = \frac{1 + r_t}{1 + g_t} * \frac{D_{t-1}}{P_{t-1} Y_{t-1}} - \frac{B_t}{P_t Y_t} - \frac{S_t}{P_t Y_t}.$$

If lowercase letters are used to represent ratios to GDP (e.g., $d_t = \frac{D_t}{P_t Y_t}$), the above becomes

$$d_t = \frac{1 + r_t}{1 + g_t} * d_{t-1} - b_t - s_t.$$

Next, if β_t represents $\frac{1+r_t}{1+g_t}$, the following becomes the basic "law of motion" for the government's debt-to-GDP ratio:

$$d_t = \beta_t * d_{t-1} - b_t - s_t. \tag{5.1}$$

In other words, the debt-to-GDP ratio at the end of the current period depends on the real interest rate, real GDP growth rate, the debt-to-GDP ratio at the start of the period, the primary fiscal balance, b_t, and any non-debt creating flows to the budget, s_t. A higher initial debt-to-GDP ratio and a higher real interest rate increase the final debt-to-GDP ratio, while higher values for real GDP growth, the primary balance, and non-debt-creating inflows reduce the final debt-to-GDP ratio.

The above equation can be used to determine another useful expression, the *change* in the debt-to-GDP ratio, as a function of the above variables.

Let $\lambda_t = \frac{r_t - g_t}{1 + g_t}$.

Then $1 + \lambda_t = \frac{r_t - g_t}{1 + g_t} + \frac{1 + g_t}{1 + g_t}$. Rearranging this expression yields

$$1 + \lambda_t = \frac{1 + r_t - g_t + g_t}{1 + g_t} = \frac{1 + r_t}{1 + g_t}.$$

Equation (5.1) can then be rewritten as follows:

$$d_t = (1 + \lambda_t) * d_{t-1} - b_t - s_t.$$

Subtracting d_{t-1} from both sides of the equation yields an expression for $\dot{d}_t$, the *change* in the government's debt-to-GDP ratio during period t:

$$\dot{d}_t = \lambda_t * d_{t-1} - b_t - s_t, \quad \text{or} \quad \dot{d}_t = \frac{r_t - g_t}{1 + g_t} * d_{t-1} - b_t - s_t.$$

$$(5.2)$$

Equations (5.1) and (5.2) are used for many types of fiscal sustainability exercises. For example, suppose the initial debt-to-GDP ratio is 60%, the average real interest rate on government debt is 2%, the average real GDP growth rate is 4%, the government budget has a primary surplus of 1%, and there are no non-debt-creating inflows to the budget. Equation (5.1) then predicts that the debt-to-GDP ratio at the end of the period will be

$$d_t = (1 + 0.02)/(1 + 0.04) * 0.6 - 0.01 = 0.981 * 0.6 - 0.01$$

$$= 0.588 - 0.01 = 0.578 \quad \text{or} \quad 57.8\%.$$

Indeed, Equation (5.1) can be used to show the path of the debt-to-GDP ratio over time, as in the example contained in Figure 5.1, which assumes a primary deficit, rather than a surplus, each year.

Equation (5.2) can identify the primary balance needed to stabilize the debt-to-GDP ratio. Note that an unchanging debt-to-GDP ratio

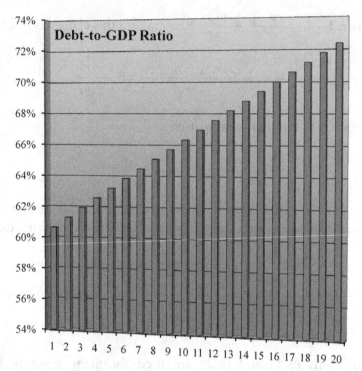

Figure 5.1. Implications of assumed parameters for the government's debt-to-GDP ratio over time.

requires the following:

$$\dot{d}_t = 0 = \frac{r_t - g_t}{1 + g_t} * d_{t-1} - b_t - s_t.$$

Thus, the debt-stabilizing primary balance is

$$b_t = \frac{r_t - g_t}{1 + g_t} * d_{t-1} - s_t. \tag{5.3}$$

Using the same values for the real interest and growth rates and the initial debt-to-GDP ratio as in the previous example, the required primary balance is calculated as follows:

$$b_t = (0.02 - 0.04)/(1 + 0.04) * 0.6 = -0.0192 * 0.6$$

$$= -0.0115 = -1.15\% \text{ of GDP.}$$

Thus, with the assumed values for r_t, g_t, and d_{t-1}, the budget can have a primary deficit of about 1.1% of GDP without raising the government's debt-to-GDP ratio.

When calculating the required primary balance to stabilize the debt-to-GDP ratio, it is worth noting that the corresponding overall budget balance can be far more negative than the required primary balance. Suppose in the previous example that the forecast inflation rate is 3%, in which case the average nominal interest rate on government debt is just under 5.1%.[6] Then the overall balance corresponding to the above primary balance is a deficit of about 4.2% of GDP:

$$\text{Overall balance} = b_t - (i_t * d_{t-1}) = -0.0115 - (0.0506 * 0.6)$$

$$= -0.0115 - 0.03036 = -0.042 = -4.2\%.$$

Equations (5.1) and (5.2) also show that the stability of the debt-to-GDP ratio ultimately depends on the relative size of the real interest and growth rates. If the real interest rate steadily exceeds the growth rate of real GDP, the government's debt-to-GDP ratio is likely to grow without limit unless the government consistently achieves a sufficiently large primary surplus each period, which can be difficult.

In addition to Equations (5.1) and (5.2), an equation can be developed to show the primary balance needed each period to achieve a target debt-to-GDP ratio after a certain passage of time, given an initial debt-to-GDP ratio. Recall that

$$\beta = \frac{1 + r_t}{1 + g_t}.$$

If β is constant over the various periods, the expression becomes

$$b = \frac{(\beta - 1) * (\sigma - \beta^n)}{(1 - \beta^n)} * d_0, \tag{5.4}$$

---

[6]$(1 + i/100) = (1 + r/100) * (1 + \pi/100)$. Thus $(1 + i/100) = (1 + 0.02) * (1 + 0.03) = 1.0506$; $i/100 = 0.0506$, so $i = 5.06\%$.

where σ is the target debt-to-GDP ratio divided by the initial ratio; n is the number of periods to achieve the targeted ratio; and d_0 is the initial debt-to-GDP ratio.

For example, suppose the initial debt-to-GDP ratio is 65%, the target ratio is 45%, the average real interest rate on government debt is 2%, the average real growth rate for GDP is 4%, and the goal is to arrive at the target ratio over a 10-year period. In this case, $d_0 = 0.65$, $n = 10$, $\beta = \frac{1.02}{1.04} = 0.981$, $\sigma = \frac{0.45}{0.65} = 0.692$. Thus,

$$b = \frac{(0.981 - 1) * (0.692 - 0.981^{10})}{(1 - 0.981^{10})} * 0.65$$

$$= \frac{(-0.019) * (0.692 - 0.8254)}{(1 - 0.8254)} * 0.65$$

$$= \frac{(-0.019) * (-0.1334)}{0.1746} = 0.0093,$$

or about 0.9% of GDP.

To verify the above result, note that, because of the debt dynamics, the debt-to-GDP ratio declines steadily, by about 2.1% of GDP during the first year and to slightly smaller amounts in each of the subsequent years, reaching 45% at the end of the 10th year (see Table 5.1).

Equations (5.4) and (5.3) can be combined to show the required fiscal balance needed to maintain a targeted debt-to-GDP ratio once it is achieved. For example, once the 45% debt-to-GDP ratio is attained, the government can maintain this debt-to-GDP ratio with a small primary *deficit* of just under 0.9% of GDP. From Equation (5.3), we have

$$b_t = \frac{r_t - g_t}{1 + g_t} * d_{t-1} - s_t.$$

Assume that r in every period is 2%, g is 4%, s is zero, and $d_{t-1} = 0.45$. Then the required primary balance is

$$b_t = \frac{0.02 - 0.04}{1 + 0.04} * 0.45 = \frac{-0.02}{1.04} * 0.45 = -0.00865,$$

or about −0.865% of GDP.

Table 5.1. Constant primary balance for 65% of GDP, different real growth and interest rates.

Initial level of public debt/GDP	65.00%	Years							10		
Nominal interest rate on domestic currency debt	2.00%										
Inflation	0.00%	Target debt/GDP							45.00%		
Real interest rate on domestic currency debt	2.00%	Initial debt/GDP							65.00%		
Share of domestic currency debt in total	100.00%	Sigma							0.692		
Real growth rate	4.00%	Required Pr. Surpl. $= ((B-1)*(\text{sigma}-B^{10})/(1-B^{10}))*.65$, where $B = $ beta									

Year	0	1	2	3	4	5	6	7	8	9	10
$dt+k$	65.0%	62.8%	60.7%	58.6%	56.5%	54.5%	52.5%	50.6%	48.7%	46.8%	45.0%
β	0.981	0.981	0.981	0.981	0.981	0.981	0.981	0.981	0.981	0.981	0.981
g	4.0%	4.0%	4.0%	4.0%	4.0%	4.0%	4.0%	4.0%	4.0%	4.0%	4.0%
r	2.0%	2.0%	2.0%	2.0%	2.0%	2.0%	2.0%	2.0%	2.0%	2.0%	2.0%
b	0.9%	0.9%	0.9%	0.9%	0.9%	0.9%	0.9%	0.9%	0.9%	0.9%	0.9%
Actual											

5.1.1. *Extensions of the basic formulas*

5.1.1.1. *Impact of non-debt-creating inflows*

If a government receives receipts from privatization or other non-debt-creating inflows not already accounted for in the budget, these inflows reduce the primary surplus required to achieve a given debt-to-GDP ratio. For example, recall from Equation (5.3) that the amount of such inflows, s_t, is subtracted directly from the required primary balance to keep the debt-to-GDP ratio unchanged:

$$b_t = \frac{r_t - g_t}{1 + g_t} * d_{t-1} - s_t.$$

If, as assumed earlier, the initial debt-to-GDP ratio is 60%, the average real interest rate on government debt is 2%, the average real GDP growth rate is 4%, but newly found privatization proceeds equal 0.5% of GDP, the debt stabilizing primary balance is now -1.65% of GDP, rather than -1.15%:

$$b_t = (0.02 - 0.04)/(1 + 0.04) * 0.6 - 0.005$$

$$= -0.0192 * 0.6 - 0.005 = -0.0165 = -1.65\% \text{ of GDP.}$$

The problem is that any government-owned asset can only be privatized once. In addition, assets once privatized can no longer provide profit transfers to the budget. Thus, governments should beware of using privatization to delay fiscal adjustment.

5.1.1.2. *Taking account of uncertainty in forecasts*

When there is considerable uncertainty about the forecast of real interest and growth rates over the coming year, probabilities can be attached to the various forecasts, so as to determine a primary balance reflecting the mean forecast for each variable. For example, suppose the initial debt-to-GDP ratio is 40%; there is a 20% probability for each of the following real interest rates: 1%, 1.5%, 2%, 2.5%, and 3%; and a 20% probability for each of the following real growth rates: 1%, 2.5%, 3.5%, 4%, and 5%. In this case, the mean forecast for the real interest rate is $(1 + 1.5 + 2 + 2.5 + 3)/5 = 2\%$, while the mean forecast for the real growth rate is $(1 + 2.5 + 3.5 + 4 + 5)/5 = 3.2\%$. Applying Equation (5.3) and using these means gives the following result for the debt-stabilizing primary balance:

$$b_t = (0.02 - 0.032)/(1 + 0.032) * 0.4 = -0.0116 * 0.4$$

$$= -0.00465 = -0.46\% \text{ of GDP.}$$

5.1.2. Other factors to consider when assessing sustainability

When assessing sustainability, it is also useful to consider the following factors:

1. **The feasibility of attaining the revenue and expenditure forecasts in the government budget:** Sustainability analysis presumes that the key budget aggregates are attainable. It is hard to assess sustainability if the budget presumes unrealistic forecasts of revenue or expenditure.
2. **The affordability of key programs:** The ability to finance significant programs, including large development projects, depends on the government's revenue-raising capabilities and the "fiscal space" in the budget to accommodate these programs. If revenues are insufficient, or if project costs are underestimated, key programs may be "unaffordable," thereby undermining fiscal sustainability.
3. **The structure of public debt:** The structure of public debt can also affect fiscal sustainability. Too much short-term debt subjects the budget to *rollover risk* (the difficulty of refunding debt when it falls due). A similar problem arises if debt is "bunched," meaning that large segments of debt fall due at the same time. In either case, the government may face liquidity problems. Alternatively, the large amounts of debt falling due may raise interest rates, possibly crowding out some private investment.
4. **Fiscal contingencies:** Government guarantees of state enterprise or private sector borrowing can cause public debt levels to jump if the

underlying entity cannot meet its obligations and the government must assume the debt. Public debt levels may also rise if, as has occurred in many countries during periods of financial crisis, the government has had to recapitalize banks. In each of these cases, the rise in public debt may force a reconsideration of the sustainability of fiscal policy. This, in turn, may require governments to adopt adjustment measures, to reduce the public debt-to-GDP ratio to a more appropriate level.

5.2. Analysis of Fiscal Solvency

Although most governments are able to issue new debt to cover retiring government securities, on occasion it is useful to consider the solvency issue: what primary fiscal balance would be needed for government to repay its existing debt over a given time period. To determine this amount, note that, with solvency, the current value of debt equals the sum of all future primary balances, properly discounted:

$$D_t = \frac{b_{t+1}}{1+i} + \frac{b_{t+2}}{(1+i)^2} + \cdots + \frac{b_{t+n}}{(1+i)^n}.$$

Thus,

$$D_t = \frac{\sum_{j=1}^{n}(1+i)^{n-j}b_{t+j}}{(1+i)^n},$$

and the primary balance, b, needed each period to repay the debt is

$$b = \frac{D_t * (1+i)^n}{\sum_{j=1}^{n}(1+i)^{n-j}},$$

in present value terms.

The following example illustrates the above formula. Suppose the initial value of the debt is 65, the required payoff period is 3 years, and the average nominal interest rate on government debt is assumed to be a steady 5% over this period. Note that the debt at the end of the period would be

$$D_{t+3} = 65 * (1.05)^3 = 65 * 1.158 = 75.25.$$

To solve for the constant primary balance, in present value terms, to retire the above debt, note that

$$b * (1.05)^0 + b * (1.05)^1 + b * (1.05)^2 = 75.25,$$

so

$$b * (1 + 1.05 + 1.1025) = 3.1525b = 75.25.$$

Thus,

$$b = 75.25/3.1525 = 23.87,$$

or about 23.9, *in present value terms.*

The actual b needed would be 23.87 * 1 in year 1, 23.87 * 1.05 in year 2 (i.e., 25.06), and 23.87 * 1.1025 (26.32) in year 3. Note that the three terms sum to 75.25 : 23.87 + 25.06 + 26.32 = 75.25.

5.3. Sustainability: Going Beyond the Basics

Besides the basic elements of sustainability assessment, several other issues are important to consider. These include "stress testing" pubic debt, analyzing fiscal vulnerability, and recognizing the links between financial sector vulnerability and the fiscal sector.

5.3.1. *"Stress testing" public debt*

Because the assessment of fiscal sustainability entails projecting debt and GDP levels over the future, it is useful to test the sensitivity of public debt forecasts to changes in key macroeconomic indicators. This type of sensitivity analysis is called *stress testing,* and it resembles the stress testing that many banks are asked to perform on their portfolios of financial assets. Stress testing public debt involves subjecting forecast values for variables such as real GDP growth, inflation, the average interest rate on public debt, and the exchange rate to adverse shocks, either alone or jointly, and seeing how these shocks affect the forecast ratio of public debt to GDP. If plausible adverse movements in any of these variables trigger a significant rise in the forecast ratio of public debt to GDP, in particular a continuing increase over time, one can argue that fiscal sustainability is fragile and depends on a favorable macroeconomic outcome.

The International Monetary Fund (IMF) regularly performs stress tests on public and external debt as part of its periodic economic surveillance of member countries, and the results are made public when governments authorize the IMF to post the Article IV Staff Report for their country on the IMF's public website. The IMF's debt sustainability analysis is based on a more complex variant of the sustainability formulas presented earlier that takes into account the separate contributions of domestic debt and external debt issued in foreign currency on public debt levels.[7] If i_t is defined as the weighted average nominal interest rate on all government debt, whether issued in domestic or foreign currency, ε_t as the percentage depreciation in the national currency relative to a reference foreign currency such as the US dollar, and a^f as the share of foreign-currency denominated debt in total public debt, then the change in the debt-to-GDP ratio can be expressed as follows:

$$\dot{d}_t = \frac{i_t - \pi_t * (1 + g_t) - g_t + \varepsilon_t * [a^f(1 + i_t)]}{(1 + \pi_t) * (1 + g_t)} * d_{t-1} - b_t - s_t.$$

(5.5)

Equation (5.5) can be used to identify the contributions to the change in the debt-to-GDP ratio from changes in the real interest rate, real growth rate, and nominal exchange rate, and thus from shocks to each of these variables. These contributions are as follows:

---

[7] For a derivation of Equation (5.5) and the following formulas, see Ley, Eduardo (2003), "Fiscal (and External) Sustainability." An updated version of this paper is available at http://mpra.ub. unimuenchen.de/13693/.

From changes in the real interest rate:

$$\frac{i_t - \pi_t * (1 + g_t)}{(1 + \pi_t) * (1 + g_t)} * d_{t-1}.$$

From changes in the real growth rate:

$$\frac{-g_t}{(1 + \pi_t) * (1 + g_t)} * d_{t-1}.$$

From a depreciation in the nominal exchange rate of ε_t:

$$\frac{\varepsilon_t * [a^f (1 + i_t)]}{(1 + \pi_t) * (1 + g_t)} * d_{t-1}.$$

Since 2011, the IMF has used a multi-pronged approach to public debt sustainability analysis (DSA). Economies are divided into "market access" (emerging market (EM) and advanced (AE) economies) and low-income economies. Market access economies are further subdivided into "Lower Scrutiny" and "Higher Scrutiny" entities, with Higher Scrutiny economies having one or more of the following characteristics: (1) current or projected public debt exceeds 50% (EMs) or 60% of GDP (AEs); (2) current or projected public gross financing requirements exceed 10% (EMs) or 15% (AEs) of GDP; or (3) country has or seeks exceptional access to IMF resources. Countries may also be considered for Higher Scrutiny in cases of large projected fiscal adjustment, volatile growth, large spreads over US or German bond rates or the Emerging Market Bond Index, high external financing requirements, a high share of public debt held by non-residents, a rapid increase in short-term debt, or a high share of debt in foreign currency (for EMs).[8]

For "Lower Scrutiny" market access economies, DSA involves preparing a baseline scenario using the most likely (baseline) projections for real growth, inflation (measured by the GDP deflator),

---

[8]See International Monetary Fund (2013), "Staff Guidance Note for Public Debt Sustainability Analysis in Market Access Countries," Washington, July, p. 7, https://www.imf.org/external/np/pp/eng/2013/050913.pdf.

government revenue and grants, non-interest government expenditure, the current stock of gross public debt, the interest rate and other key characteristics such as currency composition of debt, and other debt-creating or reducing flows, such as anticipated bank recapitalization or privatization of state assets. In addition, two alternative scenarios are prepared. One, termed an *historical scenario*, has real growth, the primary fiscal balance, and interest rates set at their historical average values. A second, called the *constant primary balance* scenario, fixes the primary fiscal balance at its value during the first year of the projection but keeps other variables at their baseline values. As noted in the Staff Guidance Note, the basic DSA presentation includes the following information: "(i) selected economic indicators under the baseline scenario, including the evolution of debt burden indicators; (ii) latest relevant market indicators, such as risk rating, EMBI and CDS spreads (or spreads over US or German bonds, for AEs); (iii) the debt dynamics under the baseline scenario, which presents the contribution of different factors to the evolution of the debt-to-GDP ratio; (iv) the debt-stabilizing primary balance; (v) the maturity structure (short-term vs. medium- and long-term debt) as well as the currency composition of public debt (domestic vs. foreign currency-denominated debt); and (vi) a comparison of the evolution of debt burden indicators under the baseline, historical, constant primary balance, and, where relevant, contingent liabilities and customized scenarios."[9] Figure 5.2, reproduced from the Staff Guidance Note, provides an example of a basic DSA for a lower scrutiny market access economy.[10] Where appropriate, the impact of contingent liabilities on the DSA would be included.

For "higher scrutiny" economies, the DSA also includes risk identification and analysis, including assessments of the realism of the baseline scenario, vulnerability of the debt profile, sensitivity to macro-fiscal risks, and contingent liabilities. The output includes a "heat map" of various risks, relevant fan charts, and a requirement that the DSA

---

[9] *Id.*, p. 14.
[10] *Id.*, p. 16–17.

Figure 2. Example of a Basic DSA
Country Public Sector Debt Sustainability Analysis (DSA) - Baseline Scenario
(in percent of GDP unless otherwise indicated)

Debt, Economic and Market Indicators [1]

	Actual			Projections						As of March 26, 2013		
	2002-2010	2011	2012	2013	2014	2015	2016	2017	2018	Sovereign Spreads		
Nominal gross public debt	39.4	55.4	62.3	71.9	76.4	77.2	77.1	76.7	76.3	Spread (bp) [2]		550
Public gross financing needs	-0.8	4.8	4.5	20.3	20.1	20.2	27.4	32.2	19.2	CDS (bp)		575
Real GDP growth (in percent)	1.3	-2.9	1.4	-1.5	-3.3	0.3	2.1	1.9	1.9	Ratings	Foreign	Local
Inflation (GDP deflator, in percent)	2.9	0.9	1.0	1.0	1.0	1.3	1.3	1.4	1.6	Moody's	Aa3	Aa3
Nominal GDP growth (in percent)	4.2	-2.0	2.4	-0.5	-2.3	1.7	3.4	3.4	3.6	S&Ps	AA	AA-
Effective interest rate (in percent) [3]	5.1	4.0	3.7	5.4	5.2	5.2	5.4	5.6	5.8	Fitch	AA	A

Contribution to Changes in Public Debt

	Actual			Projections							
	2002-2010	2011	2012	2013	2014	2015	2016	2017	2018	cumulative	debt-stabilizing
Change in gross public sector debt	1.6	7.65	6.93	9.6	4.5	0.9	-0.1	-0.4	-0.4	14.0	primary
Identified debt-creating flows	-0.4	7.71	5.28	9.6	4.5	0.8	-0.1	-0.4	-0.5	14.0	balance [7]
Primary deficit	-0.8	4.8	4.5	-1.8	-1.1	-1.8	-1.7	-2.1	-2.2	-10.6	1.7
Revenue and grants	26.6	26.5	27.7	29.8	28.5	28.4	28.1	28.0	27.9	170.8	
Primary (noninterest) expenditure	25.9	31.3	32.3	28.0	27.4	26.6	26.5	26.0	25.8	160.2	
Automatic debt dynamics [4]	0.3	2.9	0.8	3.7	5.6	2.7	1.5	1.7	1.7	16.8	
Interest rate/growth differential [5]	0.3	2.9	0.7	3.7	5.5	2.6	1.5	1.6	1.6	16.6	
Of which: real interest rate	0.8	1.5	1.4	2.8	3.1	2.9	3.0	3.1	3.0	18.0	
Of which: real GDP growth	-0.5	1.4	-0.7	0.9	2.4	-0.3	-1.6	-1.4	-1.4	-1.3	
Other identified debt-creating flows	0.0	0.0	0.0	7.8	0.0	0.0	0.0	0.0	0.0	7.8	
Privatization receipts (negative)	0.0	0.0	0.0	0.0	0.0	0.0	0.0	0.0	0.0	0.0	
Contingent liabilities	0.0	0.0	0.0	0.0	0.0	0.0	0.0	0.0	0.0	0.0	
Other debt-creating flows (specify)	0.0	0.0	0.0	7.8	0.0	0.0	0.0	0.0	0.0	7.8	
Residual [6]	2.1	-0.1	1.7	-0.1	0.1	0.0	0.1	0.0	0.1	0.2	

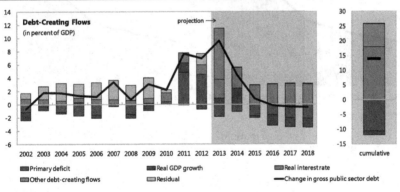

Source: IMF staff.
1/ Public sector is defined as general government.
2/ Bond Spread over U.S. Bonds.
3/ Defined as interest payments divided by debt stock at the end of previous year.
4/ Derived as [(r - p(1+g) - g + ae(1+r)]/(1+g+p+gp)) times previous period debt ratio, with r = interest rate; p = growth rate of GDP deflator; g = real GDP growth rate; a = share of foreign-currency denominated debt; and e = nominal exchange rate depreciation (measured by increase in local currency value of U.S. dollar).
5/ The real interest rate contribution is derived from the denominator in footnote 2/ as r - π (1+g) and the real growth contribution as -g.
6/ Including asset and exchange rate changes.
7/ Assumes that key variables (real GDP growth, real interest rate, and other identified debt-creating flows) remain at the level of the last projection year.

Figure 5.2.   Sample of IMF basic debt sustainability analysis.

Source: Reproduced with permission from International Monetary Fund (2013)," Staff Guidance Note for Public Debt Sustainability Analysis in Market Access Countries" Washington, July, pp. 16–17. https://www.imf.org/external/np/pp/eng/2013/050913.pdf.

Figure 2. Example of a Basic DSA (continued)

Country Public DSA – Alternative Scenarios and Composition of Public Debt

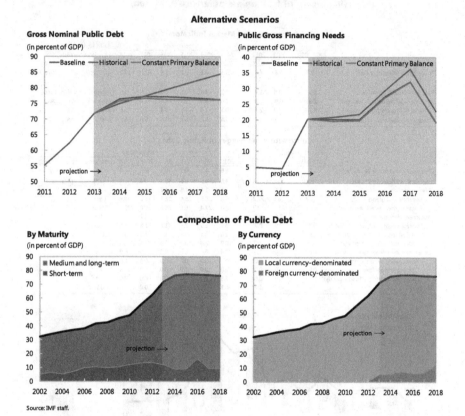

Figure 5.2. (*Continued*)

appear in the staff report. Details can be found in the Staff Guidance Note.[11] An online template is available to facilitate developing the various DSA reports.[12]

---

[11] *Id.*, p. 6 and 17–34.

[12] See International Monetary Fund (2018), "Debt Sustainability Analysis for Market Access Countries", https://www.imf.org/external/pubs/ft/dsa/mac.htm.

For low-income economies, the IMF has developed a single template for assessing both public and external debt sustainability.[13] Debt sustainability is assessed using the calculated present value of debt obligations and an assumed 5% discount rate. Debt burden indicators are developed in comparison to various thresholds over the projection period, with the thresholds set depending on an assessment of the country's ability to handle debt. This assessment is based on a "composite indicator" that draws on the following information: "the country's historical performance and outlook for real growth, reserves coverage, remittance inflows, and the state of the global environment in addition to the World Bank's Country Policy and Institutional Assessment (CPIA) index." Countries receive one of four ratings for the risk of debt distress, drawing on baseline projections and stress tests for debt: *low risk* (when indicators are below the various thresholds); *moderate risk* (when indicators are below the thresholds in the baseline scenario but stress tests show that the thresholds could be exceeded in the event of shocks or a sudden change in macroeconomic policies); *high risk* (when one or more thresholds are breached in the baseline scenario but no debt servicing problems are evident); and *debt distress* (when a country is experiencing repayment difficulties). Table 5.2, reproduced from the sustainability framework document, shows the various debt burden thresholds.[14] An online template is available for developing the debt sustainability assessment.[15]

---

[13]See International Monetary Fund (2019), "Joint World Bank-IMF Debt Sustainability Framework for Low-Income Countries," March, https://www.imf.org/en/About/Factsheets/Sheets/2016/08/01/16/39/Debt-Sustainability-Framework-for-Low-Income-Countries; and International Monetary Fund (2018), "Debt Sustainability Framework for Low-Income Countries," July, https://www.imf.org/external/pubs/ft/dsa/lic.htm. The discussion here follows closely the text in the first reference mentioned here.

[14]See International Monetary Fund (2019), "Joint World Bank-IMF Debt Sustainability Framework for Low-Income Countries," March.

[15]The framework can be accessed from a link at International Monetary Fund (2018), "Debt Sustainability Framework for Low-Income Countries," July, https://www.imf.org/external/pubs/ft/dsa/lic.htm.

Table 5.2.　Debt burden thresholds and benchmarks under the DSF.

Debt Burden Thresholds and Benchmarks Under the DSF

	PV of external debt in percent of		External Debt service in percent of		PV of total public debt in percent of
	GDP	Exports	Export	Revenue	GDP
Weak	30	140	10	14	35
Medium	40	180	15	18	55
Strong	50	240	21	23	70

5.3.2. Fiscal vulnerability

Fiscal vulnerability describes a situation where a government may be unable to meet its key fiscal policy objectives, not because of inappropriate policies, but because of underlying weaknesses in budgeting, accounting, revenue structure, expenditure control, or fiscal institutions. These factors can make it hard for government to attain future fiscal objectives. They may also limit the government's ability to respond to future fiscal policy challenges, such as the need for fiscal consolidation as part of a coordinated response to an external shock.

Fiscal vulnerability involves four different aspects:

(1) incorrect specification of the initial fiscal position;
(2) sensitivity of short-term fiscal outcomes to risk;
(3) threats to longer term fiscal sustainability; and
(4) structural or institutional weaknesses that affect the design and implementation of fiscal policy.

Each of these will be addressed in turn.

5.3.2.1. Incorrect specification of the initial fiscal position

Assessment of the fiscal position is closely related to the quantity and quality of available information. The less information is available about the extent of fiscal activities, the more vulnerable is the fiscal position. The reason is that the government becomes less able to plan a solid and flexible medium-term fiscal framework and to respond to short- and medium-term shocks. *Incomplete or inconsistent coverage of fiscal activity* often contributes to the problem. Where there are significant extrabudgetary activities or large quasi-fiscal operations,[16] the authorities may be unaware of the true scope of fiscal activity. In countries with large trust funds that operate outside the regular budget, failing to consolidate these activities with the formal budget will give too narrow a picture of fiscal operations. In addition, it may obscure potential problems, if the trust funds themselves are running short of funds to cover their expenses. Similarly, quasi-fiscal operations at central banks, including massive sales of government securities or central bank bills to banks to limit liquidity in the face of large capital inflows, may have a noticeable effect on the budget, by reducing the profits that central banks can remit to the budget as non-tax revenue.

Budgeting can also suffer from a *poor accounting and control system*. The budget may be based on unreliable revenue or expenditure data. Poor accounts may also obscure the true budget outcome and make it hard to control expenditure effectively. Problems can emerge if the government is unaware of the full extent of contingent liabilities, such as loan guarantees. Poor accounting can also lead to inconsistencies between the budget balance, measured as the difference between revenue and expenditure, and budget financing, again leading to an inaccurate view of the overall budget position.

5.3.2.2. Short-term fiscal risks

The assessment of fiscal risk should take into account not only the initial fiscal position but also a *short-term forecast* that looks *at least two*

---

[16] *Quasi-fiscal operations*, as noted in Chapter Four, are activities that look like regular budgetary activities but take place outside the budget, usually without government control or scrutiny. Examples include exchange rate guarantees and subsidized lending by central banks, which provide budget-like subsidies without legislative oversight, but have the effect of reducing budget revenue by reducing central bank profits that can be transferred to the budget.

years ahead. This forecast should be fairly detailed, assuming no change in policies, and exclude any temporary measures affecting the initial fiscal position. The risk analysis should examine a range of possible short-term macro-fiscal outcomes, focusing on variations in underlying assumptions and other parameters to which a likelihood of different events can be attached. Situations that cannot easily be accommodated in the current budget framework, or that would require significant policy adjustment, would provide indications of vulnerability.

Short-term fiscal risks can include the following:

a. **Unanticipated changes in macroeconomic variables or other sources of economic risk:** A change in the macroeconomic environment resulting from an external shock, such as a jump in oil prices or a sudden recession in major trading partners, can undermine revenue or create pressure for new expenditure to bolster aggregate demand. The financial crisis of 2007–2009 represented such a change for many countries, weakening revenues and creating demands for new spending that increased deficits and, in many cases, public debt-to-GDP levels.

b. **The exercise of contingent liabilities when no budgetary provisions have been made:** The failure to set aside funds in the event that state enterprises default on government-guaranteed loans can add significantly to government expenditure and debt when such defaults occur. Government budgets can also be strained if a major bank fails and deposit insurance is lacking or the available funds cannot cover the losses of depositors.

c. **Lack of clarity about the size of specific expenditure commitments:** Cost overruns, which are common for infrastructure projects, or the failure to anticipate operating and maintenance costs for newly constructed capital projects, can pose risks for the budget in the form of unanticipated expenditure.

d. **Inappropriate debt structure:** Too much short-term debt, or a bunching of debt falling due, can pose liquidity problems for the government or require the government to refund debt at higher interest rates, adding to expenditures.

5.3.2.3. *Threats to long-term fiscal sustainability*

Even if the initial budget or the short-term fiscal position appears sustainable, important structural changes in demographics or the economy can create threats to fiscal sustainability over the long run. Oil- and mineral-exporting countries whose resources are likely to be exhausted over the medium term face long-term fiscal problems, if revenues rely too heavily on earnings from these sectors and measures are not taken to raise non-oil or non-mineral revenues to offset the shortfall. Similarly, countries with aging populations are vulnerable to long-term fiscal problems if generous public pension programs are not adjusted by increasing revenues, cutting benefits, or raising the age for receiving benefits.

5.3.2.4. *Weaknesses in the structure of revenue or expenditure, or in institutional capacity*

Vulnerability can also arise if the structure of revenue or expenditure is weak, or if key fiscal institutions, such as the budget process or expenditure control mechanism, have serious problems.

a. Weaknesses in revenue structure

As will be discussed at length in the next chapter, a good tax structure is one where revenue comes from a range of taxes with broad bases, ideally related to large macroeconomic aggregates. Such a structure allows the rates for any one tax to be reasonable, thereby reducing the incentives for evasion. It can also make the tax system relatively elastic, allowing revenue to keep up with economic growth and facilitating countercyclical fiscal policy, as revenue automatically rises in good times and contracts during recessions.

A *revenue structure dominated by a very few large taxes*, especially if these taxes have narrow bases, creates vulnerability. Revenue from these taxes is likely to be volatile. In addition, the small number of significant revenue producers limits the capacity of government to respond to new demands for government activity, because tax rates may have to be raised to high levels.

Frequent tax law changes make it harder for taxpayers to comply, because of unfamiliarity. They also complicate the job of tax administration. In addition, frequent changes in exemptions and the creation of tax holidays and similar measures can undermine the tax base and reduce the yield of key revenue items. This is especially problematic if revenues depend on a very few large taxes.

Extensive earmarking limits the scope for discretionary tax changes, because taxes are already dedicated to funding specific expenditure activities, and tax rates cannot be raised to provide revenue for new activities or to cover revenue shortfalls arising from weaknesses in general taxes. In addition, *heavy reliance on nontax revenues*, such as oil leases, may also increase vulnerability, as these revenues may not be stable, and it may be hard to adjust revenues through policy measures (for example, if lease fees are fixed on outstanding oil fields).

b. Weaknesses in the structure of expenditure

On the expenditure side of the budget, having a *high share of non-discretionary spending* is a key source of vulnerability. This situation limits the government's flexibility to cut spending when necessary and makes it hard for the budget to adjust to new demands or spending priorities. The most notable examples of non-discretionary spending are interest payments, formula-based transfers to lower levels of government, and public pensions. In many countries, public health programs and other so-called entitlement programs are also an important component of non-discretionary spending. In countries with long-standing security concerns and ongoing civil war, military spending may also be hard to limit.

Besides non-discretionary programs, certain types of discretionary expenditure can be a source of vulnerability because the powerful interest groups they serve make them difficult to adjust. Examples include military expenditures in countries with powerful armed forces, and large government wage bills where public sector unions are strong or the government serves as an employer of last resort for unskilled laborers. In other countries, expensive and poorly targeted subsidies for oil are hard to curb because cutbacks could affect the earnings of truckers and manufacturers. Similarly, subsidies for religious institutions may be hard to reduce if the country's political structure gives such groups inordinate influence in determining the structure of the government.

There may also be *latent expenditure needs* that become apparent only after a shock or discontinuity of some kind. For example, the need for a social safety net may become apparent only following an economic crisis. Once in place, however, it may become permanent, adding to the total expenditure.

c. Weaknesses in institutional capacity

The fiscal position can also be vulnerable if serious institutional problems hobble the government sector. These include problems regarding the roles and responsibilities of government; inadequate public availability of information; weaknesses in the budget process; questions about the integrity of fiscal information; weak revenue or expenditure management; and corruption.

Inappropriate roles and responsibilities of government can be a major source of vulnerability if they impose heavy expenditure burdens that outstrip the ability of revenues to support them. For example, guaranteeing jobs to university graduates may lead to a bloated civil service and provide incorrect signals to students, encouraging many to choose easier but less marketable fields of study in place of more rigorous studies in science and engineering that could lead to a more capable national workforce and promote foreign direct investment.

Problems with the public availability of information may make it difficult for legislators and the public to assess fiscal problems and develop reasonable responses to fiscal challenges. Hidden costs and the difficulty of anticipating performance problems may make it hard to assess public–private partnerships as a way of providing expensive public services, such as new highways or electrical power plants. Similarly, the classified nature of many military programs may make it difficult for legislators and the public to undertake a reasonable assessment of benefits in relation to costs.

Weaknesses with the budget process can be a particularly difficult source of fiscal problems. Finance ministries that cannot make macroeconomic forecasts or that lack ready access to new forecasts made by other agencies will have trouble adjusting the budget for sudden changes in the macroeconomic environment, for example. Similarly, legal rules requiring super-majorities to enact revenue increases or other major changes may make it hard for a legislature to complete work on the budget in time for the next fiscal year.

Problems with the integrity of fiscal information can make it hard to develop reasonable budgets, or to track spending effectively. As a result, the government may be plagued with chronic overestimates of revenue or underestimates of expenditure, requiring disruptive expenditure cutbacks that reduce the effectiveness of public services.

Weaknesses in revenue or expenditure administration are also important sources of fiscal vulnerability. A poor system of tax administration makes it hard for the government to collect sufficient revenue, contributing to budget shortfalls and requiring higher tax rates from those who do pay to fund public services. Weak expenditure management allows cost overruns that can also add to budget deficits and public debt.

Finally, *corruption* can contribute to fiscal vulnerability where it leads to cost overruns or weak enforcement of the tax laws. Corrupt practices make it difficult to execute public programs efficiently, adding to public expenditure and reducing the quality of public services.

5.3.3. *Interactions with the financial sector*

Interactions between the government and the financial sector can also make the fiscal position more vulnerable, particularly in the case of a fragile banking system. An unsustainable fiscal position in an economy with a poor secondary market in government securities can mean that government bonds absorb a high percentage of bank resources. This, in turn, can lead to financial instability if fiscal overruns lead to a sizable increase in government debt. By comparison, a heavy external debt exposure among the banks could trigger a currency crisis, subsequent bank failures, and the need for heavy government outlays to recapitalize the banking system, as in the Asian crisis of 1997–98 or the Turkish banking crises of 1994 and 2000–2001. More generally, a fragile banking system, whether from nonperforming loans or the acquisition of highly risky financial assets, as in the 2007–2009 financial crisis, can lead to widespread bank failures and the need for massive government expenditure to prevent a systemic collapse.

5.4. Fiscal Sustainability and the Financial Crisis of 2007–2009

The massive efforts by advanced and emerging market economies to stabilize demand in response to the financial crisis of 2007–2009 have highlighted the relevance of fiscal sustainability to macroeconomic management. An interesting consequence of this crisis is that advanced economies, because of high initial levels of public debt and the much larger exposure of their banks to toxic assets, faced much greater sustainability problems than did most emerging market countries. As shown in Table 5.3, taken from an IMF Staff Position Note issued in 2009, large fiscal adjustments would be needed for some time to restore public debt-to-GDP ratios to more sustainable levels, e.g., closer to 60%. By comparison, in many emerging market countries, the required fiscal adjustments were smaller. Subsequent IMF reports have estimated that even larger adjustments would be needed in many of the advanced economies.

Table 5.3. Forecasts made in 2009 of public debt and debt-stabilizing primary balances in selected countries; data are in percent of GDP.

| | Pre-crisis WEO projections 1/ | | | | Current WEO projections | | | | Debt-stabilizing PB or PB needed to bring debt to benchmark level (shaded) 2/ |
| | Debt | | PB | | Debt | | PB | | |
	2009	2012	2009	2012	2009	2014	2009	2014	
Advanced countries									
Australia	7.8	6.0	0.9	0.6	13.7	25.9	-4.3	-0.4	0.3
Austria	56.8	51.5	2.2	2.0	70.0	83.7	-1.5	-1.2	2.3
Belgium	79.2	71.2	3.7	3.5	98.1	111.1	-0.5	-1.3	4.3
Canada	61.0	51.3	1.2	0.5	75.6	65.4	-3.5	-0.4	1.0
Denmark	16.1	6.6	3.5	2.3	26.1	30.0	-2.2	-0.7	0.3
Finland	29.6	26.8	3.2	1.8	40.6	54.4	-2.5	-3.0	0.5
France	63.0	60.5	-0.3	0.8	77.4	96.5	-5.3	-2.1	3.1
Germany	61.1	59.4	2.1	2.0	79.8	91.4	-2.3	1.9	2.8
Greece 3/	75.0	70.1	1.5	1.7	108.8	133.7	-1.5	-3.1	5.9
Iceland	28.8	27.4	-1.6	-0.6	139.9	134.1	-7.7	7.6	5.9
Ireland	23.6	23.2	0.5	0.4	59.9	82.2	-10.3	1.6	2.2
Italy	104.1	102.0	2.5	2.6	117.3	132.2	-0.9	0.5	5.8
Japan	194.2	189.6	-1.8	-0.2	217.4	239.2	-9.0	-6.1	9.8
Korea	32.6	31.8	4.3	4.3	35.8	39.4	-1.6	3.8	0.4
Netherlands	42.4	33.1	2.8	2.9	66.2	80.9	-3.1	0.2	2.1
New Zealand 4/	20.8	20.7	2.3	2.1	23.4	53.9	-2.1	-4.6	0.5
Norway	43.8	43.8	13.0	9.6	67.2	67.2	4.9	8.4	1.1
Portugal	63.6	57.0	1.3	2.1	73.3	87.5	-3.3	0.8	2.6
Spain	32.4	29.7	1.6	1.5	54.7	81.2	-8.5	-4.0	2.1
Sweden	33.6	21.1	2.1	2.7	43.5	49.4	-4.8	-0.6	0.5
United Kingdom	42.9	42.5	-0.5	0.2	68.6	99.7	-10.0	-3.8	3.4
United States	63.4	65.8	-0.8	-0.3	88.8	112.0	-12.3	0.3	4.3
PPP-weighted average	74.8	73.6	0.3	0.7	95.8	114.7	-8.0	-0.7	4.2
G-20	79.5	78.9	-0.1	0.5	100.6	119.7	-8.6	-0.6	4.5
High debt	79.4	78.4	0.1	0.5	101.8	121.7	-8.5	-0.9	4.5
Low debt	24.3	21.3	2.9	2.8	30.0	37.8	-2.8	1.1	0.4
Emerging market economies									
Argentina	51.0	39.6	2.8	2.4	50.4	48.4	0.5	2.2	1.0
Brazil	67.7	62.7	3.4	3.4	70.1	62.2	1.5	3.3	2.0
Bulgaria	20.8	15.6	3.1	1.1	20.4	17.6	0.2	0.3	0.2
Chile	3.8	2.8	4.4	3.1	5.1	2.9	-3.6	1.3	0.0
China	13.4	11.2	-0.4	-0.6	20.9	21.3	-3.8	-0.4	0.2
Hungary	66.0	65.6	0.3	0.2	77.4	66.9	1.0	3.9	2.3
India	69.8	61.6	0.2	0.5	83.7	73.4	-4.1	0.7	2.8
Indonesia	32.8	27.7	0.1	0.6	31.1	28.4	-0.6	0.2	0.3
Malaysia	40.7	35.8	-1.1	-1.6	39.0	50.0	-3.3	-5.2	1.1
Mexico	40.9	41.3	0.9	0.2	49.2	44.5	-1.1	-0.4	0.7
Nigeria	11.1	8.9	8.1	4.2	13.5	9.6	-6.8	3.0	0.1
Pakistan	48.9	43.2	0.7	0.5	55.2	55.1	0.7	0.1	1.5
Philippines	46.1	42.7	2.2	1.9	52.1	45.1	1.2	3.1	0.7
Poland	45.6	44.6	-0.7	-0.2	50.5	50.2	-1.9	0.5	1.1
Russia	3.9	2.3	1.7	1.5	7.3	7.3	-4.9	2.4	0.1
Saudi Arabia	14.8	11.4	19.2	16.8	14.6	9.4	4.6	14.0	0.1
South Africa	24.0	18.1	2.5	1.9	29.0	29.5	-0.5	0.0	0.3
Turkey 3/	48.7	37.3	6.3	6.3	46.9	58.1	-0.2	1.1	1.7
Ukraine	13.5	12.1	-1.7	-1.6	16.5	24.2	-4.4	-0.1	0.2
PPP-weighted average	32.9	29.0	1.4	1.2	38.9	36.8	-2.4	1.0	0.9
G-20	32.5	28.4	1.4	1.3	38.8	36.4	-2.5	1.1	0.9
High debt	57.8	52.1	1.6	1.5	64.7	60.0	-1.3	1.0	1.8
Low debt	13.4	10.9	1.3	0.9	18.7	18.6	-3.3	0.9	0.2

Sources: IMF, World Economic Outlook, July 2009 Update and IMF staff calculations.

1/ IMF, World Economic Outlook, October 2007.
2/ Average primary balance needed to stabilize debt at end-2014 level if the respective debt-to-GDP ratio is less than 60 percent for advanced economies or 40 percent for emerging market economies (no shading); or to bring debt ratio to 60 percent (halve for Japan and reduce to 40 percent for emerging market economies) in 2029 (shaded entries). The analysis is illustrative and makes some simplifying assumptions: in particular, beyond 2014, an interest rate–growth rate differential of 1 percent is assumed, regardless of country-specific circumstances; moreover, the projections are "passive" scenarios based on constant policies.
3/ Pre-crisis WEO projections are not fully comparable to current WEO projections for Greece and Turkey, owing to substantial revisions in their GDP series in late 2007 and early 2008, respectively. For Turkey, fiscal projections reflect staff's estimates given the authorities' policy intentions as stated in the EU Pre-Accession Program document but they do not include measures taken by the government in July 2009 to improve the fiscal position.
4/ Does not include the impact of debt-reducing measures announced in the recent Economic and Fiscal Update.

Source: Reproduced with permission from IMF, Staff Team Led by Mark Horton, Manmohan Kumar, and Paulo Maruo (2009), "The State of Public Finances: A Cross-Country Fiscal Monitor" (July), Staff Position Note 09/25 (Washington), Appendix Table 5, p. 30.

5.5. Case Studies of Fiscal Sustainability

5.5.1. Greece

Greece is probably the best known recent example of an economy that has encountered difficulties with fiscal (public debt) sustainability. Central government debt in Greece has exceeded 60 percent of GDP since the late 1980s, reaching nearly 105 percent by 2000. The Global Financial Crisis pushed Greece into a serious recession in 2009, with declines in real GDP of 5.5% in 2010 and 9.1% in 2011 raising the debt ratio above 180 percent of GDP at the end of 2011 (Table 5.3). With a budget deficit of more than 10 percent of GDP causing interest rates on new government debt to skyrocket, in 2010 the Greek government entered into the first of a series of economic support programs with the IMF and the European Union (EU) to secure financing in return for fiscal adjustment. In 2011, after further negotiations, the IMF and EU agreed to a new support package that included the restructuring of much of the private lending to government in return for further adjustment. In 2012, the IMF and EU agreed to yet another support package, involving a 53.5 percent write-off of private debt to the government and further financing, with the goal of reducing government debt to 120 percent of GDP by 2020, in return for even more adjustment. The 2012 program was modified late in the year, and

Table 5.4.   Greece: Selected economic indicators in percent.

	2000	2010	2011	2012	2013	2014	2015	2016	2017	2018
Government debt/GDP	104.9	146.2	180.6	159.6	177.9	180.2	177.8	181.1	179.3	183.3
Real GDP growth	3.9	−5.5	−9.1	−7.3	−3.2	0.7	−0.4	−0.2	1.5	2.1
Overall fiscal balance	−4.1	−11.2	−10.3	−6.6	−3.6	−4.0	−2.8	0.6	1.0	0.4
Primary fiscal balance	2.8	−5.3	−3.0	−1.5	0.4	−0.1	0.8	3.8	4.1	3.8

Sources: IMF, October 2016 and April 2019 WEO databases; IMF *Fiscal Monitor*, April 2019.

Greece was able to draw funds during 2013 and 2014. The election early in 2015 of a new government pledged to reverse some fiscal reforms halted further drawings on the IMF arrangement, although Greece and the EU agreed to a new arrangement that eventually disbursed about €62 billion of the authorized €86 billion by the end of the arrangement in August 2018. The IMF never activated a further arrangement with Greece.

As of March 2019 Greece had no borrowing arrangement with the IMF.[17] In November, after receiving EU approval, Greece repaid in advance about €2.7 billion of its outstanding IMF debt.[18] While Greek government debt exceeded 183% of GDP at the end of 2018, the IMF forecast the government's debt ratio falling to about 143% of GDP by 2024, well above projections made in 2012 but still a substantial decline from its peak level during 2018.[19]

5.5.2. *United States*

The United States has seen considerable variation in its public debt levels over its history. US federal (central government) debt held by the public, meaning debt outside of US government trust funds, did not exceed 40% of GDP until the Great Depression of the 1930s. The debt ratio surged during World War II, exceeding 100% of GDP, before declining to 30% or below in the 1970s.[20] Tax cuts and high military outlays during the 1980s raised the debt ratio above 40% of GDP, although fiscal tightening and favorable growth reduced it during the last half of the 1990s to just over 30% of GDP. The debt ratio then rose to about 35% of GDP in 2008 before doubling as a result of the Great Recession to more than 70% of GDP after 2010 (Figure 5.3).

---

[17]IMF (2019), IMF Country Focus, "Greece: Economy Improves, Key Reforms Still Needed (March), https://www.imf.org/en/News/Articles/2019/03/11/na031119-greece-economy-improves-key-reforms-still-needed.

[18]Reuters, "Greece Concludes Early Repayment of IMF Loans," https://www.reuters.com/article/us-greece-economy-imf/greece-concludes-early-repayment-of-imf-loans-idUSKBN1XZ23V.

[19]IMF (2019), *Fiscal Monitor*, April 2019, Table A7, p. 89.

[20]Congressional Budget Office (2019), *2019 Long-Term Budget Outlook*, June, p. 1.

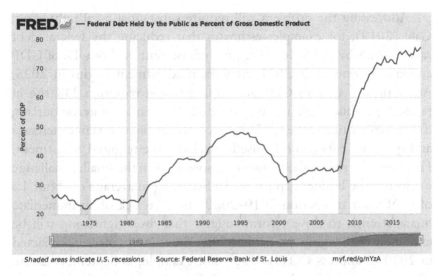

Figure 5.3.   US Federal debt held by the public, 1970–2018.

Continued large deficits, augmented by the Tax Cut and Jobs Act of 2017 and an expansion of federal spending in 2018 raised the debt ratio to nearly 78% of GDP at the end of 2018. In mid-2019, the Congressional Budget Office (CBO) projected that federal debt held by the public will reach 144% of GDP by 2049.[21]

The debt ratio is projected to rise substantially over the coming decades, due largely to rising costs for Social Security (old age pensions and disability benefits for the population), the main federal health care programs, and interest payments. With federal revenues projected to grow slowly, from 16.5% in 2019 to 19.5% in 2049 under current policies, in mid-2019 CBO projected federal deficits would expand from 4.2% of GDP in 2019 to 8.7% in 2049, raising federal debt held by the public to the above-mentioned 144% of GDP.[22] Other analysts have projected even higher ratios. For example, in 2019 William Gale projected that the debt ratio could approach 180% of GDP by 2050 if current policies remained in force.[23]

---

[21] *Ibid.*
[22] *Ibid.*
[23] Gale, W. G. (2019), *Fiscal Therapy* (New York: Oxford Univ. Press), Figure 3.1, p. 56.

Addressing the problem will require substantial fiscal tightening. Gale (2019), for example, estimates that reducing the federal debt ratio to 60% by 2050 would require adjustment of about 4% of GDP annually beginning in 2021, or 4.6% if adjustment begins in 2025. Attaining the 4.0% of GDP adjustment would require a 24% rise in taxes, if spending is left untouched, or a 21% cut in non-interest outlays, if revenues are unchanged.[24] Various combinations of revenue increases and spending cuts could be used to achieve the required adjustment. However, the political difficulty of resolving even the smaller challenge of closing the budget gap for Social Security (an average of about 1% of GDP over the period 2019–2050) and the lack of an immediate financial crisis to drive reform suggest that fiscal tightening will be extremely challenging, particularly after the stimulus measures enacted in 2020 to address COVID-19.[25] For example, in September 2020, after one round of such measures, CBO substantially raised its long-term projections for U.S. federal debt and deficits, with debt forecast to reach 195% of GDP in 2050.[26]

5.6. Summary

The frequency of fiscally induced financial crises has made assessing fiscal sustainability an important part of fiscal policy management. Sustainability assessments generally turn on the present and forecast level of the ratio of government or public debt to GDP. The formulas introduced in this chapter show that the average level of real interest rates on total public debt, the real rate of GDP growth, the ratio of the primary fiscal balance to GDP, and the ratio of non-debt-creating flows, such as privatization proceeds, to GDP all affect the path of the government's debt to GDP ratio. In addition, the relevant exchange rate and average rate of debt issued in foreign currency, as well as the average real interest rate on domestic currency debt, also matter

---

[24] *Id.*, Table 3.1, p. 61.

[25] *Id.* offers one example of a combination of revenue and spending proposals to attain the 60% objective.

[26] Congressional Budget Office (2020), *2020 Long-Term Budget Outlook*, September, p. 8.

when governments have issued debt in foreign currency. Stress tests can show the sensitivity of debt forecasts to changes in key macroeconomic assumptions.

Besides debt sustainability, governments can also review the fiscal sector for short-term fiscal risks and vulnerabilities in revenue, expenditure, and institutional structure, including risks from the financial sector. Moreover, the responses of countries to the financial crisis of 2007–2009 and the impact of these responses on government debt ratios underscore the value of public debt sustainability analysis.

Chapter Six: Revenue Policy

All governments need revenue to fund their operations. In most countries, the revenue comes mainly from *taxes:* compulsory and unrequited (non-repayable) receipts collected by governments for public purposes. Taxes are levied on a wide variety of items, including household income, corporate and enterprise profits, sales or value added from the production and sale of goods and services, imports, exports, and the value of different kinds of property and other assets, including land and buildings, estates, and assets transferred by gift or bequest. In addition, governments obtain revenue from *non-tax items.* These include the profits of public enterprises; central bank profits; income from government-owned property; and administrative fees, charges, and fines. In oil- and mineral-producing countries, non-tax revenue from land leases or fees tied to the value of petroleum or minerals extracted from land represent a substantial part of all revenue. Finally, a few national governments, mainly in low-income countries, receive *grants:* transfers from international institutions or other governments. Grants or transfers are more common among sub-national (provincial, state, regional, or local) governments, which typically receive them from national governments, often to carry out specific programs or in return for fulfilling certain conditions.

6.1. Selected Data on Government Revenue

Revenue levels vary considerably across countries by region and income level. As indicated in Table 6.1, revenue levels for general government,

Table 6.1. General government revenue in percent of GDP.

	2009	2014	2019
Low-income countries	**16.1**	**16.5**	**14.7**
Emerging market and middle-income countries	**26.9**	**28.5**	**27.1**
Asia	21.9	25.5	25.2
Europe	34.1	34.3	35.1
Latin America	28.9	29.2	28.1
Middle East, North Africa, and Pakistan	31.1	32.6	27.5
G20 emerging market countries	26.0	28.1	27.1
Advanced economies	**35.0**	**36.8**	**36.2**
Euro Area	44.4	46.7	46.5
G7 countries	34.2	36.3	35.8

Source: IMF, *Fiscal Monitor*, April 2018 and April 2020, Statistical Tables A5, A13, and A19.

as a share of GDP, tend to be higher in advanced (higher income) economies than in emerging market and low-income countries. In 2009, 2014, and 2019, general government revenue averaged 15–16% of GDP in low-income countries, 27–28% of GDP in emerging market and middle-income countries, and 35–37% of GDP in advanced economies.

Even within major country groups, revenue levels differ significantly. Among developing and emerging market countries, general government revenues averaged about 34–35% in European countries, in part reflecting large social insurance taxes, and somewhat lower levels elsewhere. Average revenues rose in Asia during 2009–2019 but fell in the Middle East, North Africa, and Pakistan, as oil prices declined sharply after 2014. Among advanced economies, average revenues were much higher as a percent of GDP in the Euro area (44–47% of GDP) than among the G7 countries (34–36% of GDP).

Among non-advanced Asian and Pacific economies, Table 6.2 shows that general government revenue ranged from about 10–11% of GDP in Bangladesh and 12–13% in Sri Lanka to nearly 28% of GDP in the People's Republic of China during 2019, with considerable

Table 6.2.   General government revenue in selected Asian countries, in percent of GDP.

	2009	2014	2019
Bangladesh	9.5	10.9	9.9
Cambodia	15.8	19.8	24.3
People's Republic of China	23.8	28.1	27.6
India	18.5	19.2	19.7
Indonesia	15.4	16.5	14.2
Lao P.D.R.	15.0	21.1	15.1
Malaysia	24.8	23.7	20.7
Philippines	17.4	19.0	20.8
Sri Lanka	13.1	11.6	12.6
Thailand	19.5	21.4	21.1
Vietnam	25.6	22.2	19.0

Source: IMF, *Fiscal Monitor*, April 2018 and April 2020, Statistical Tables A13 and A19.

variation across countries and over time. Between 2009 and 2019 revenue generally rose as a percent of GDP in Cambodia, China, India, Philippines, and Thailand. It declined in Indonesia, Malaysia (in part because of policy changes implemented by a new government), and Vietnam (reflecting lower petroleum prices). Revenue levels also differ considerably across advanced economies, as noted in Table 6.3, with average revenues in 2019 ranging from less than 20% in Hong Kong SAR and Singapore and the low- to mid-20% levels in Ireland and the Republic of Korea, to the low- to mid-30% range in Australia, Japan, Switzerland, and the United States, and more than 50% of GDP in Denmark, Finland, and Norway.

Like the level of revenue, the composition of revenue varies considerably across countries. As shown in Table 6.4, during the early part of the 2000–2009 decade, developing and emerging market countries received, on average, nearly 40% of all tax revenue from taxes on domestic goods and services (sales or value-added taxes and excise taxes). Taxes on income and profits, particularly corporate

Table 6.3. General government revenue in selected advanced economies in percent of GDP.

	2009	2014	2019
Australia	33.3	33.9	34.6
Austria	48.8	49.6	48.5
Belgium	48.8	52.2	50.3
Canada	39.5	38.5	40.8
Denmark	53.7	56.4	53.6
Finland	52.2	54.9	51.8
France	50.0	53.3	52.8
Germany	44.3	44.9	46.8
Greece	38.9	46.1	48.3
Hong Kong SAR	18.8	20.8	19.4
Iceland	37.9	43.7	40.9
Ireland	33.2	33.9	25.7
Israel	35.6	36.5	35.2
Italy	45.9	47.9	47.1
Japan	29.3	33.3	34.8
Republic of Korea	21.3	20.2	23.2
Netherlands	41.7	42.8	43.8
New Zealand	38.5	37.2	36.7
Norway	55.7	53.9	57.8
Portugal	40.4	44.6	43.3
Singapore	15.8	17.2	18.2
Spain	34.8	38.9	39.3
Sweden	50.9	48.0	48.7
Switzerland	32.7	32.4	33.6
United Kingdom	34.0	35.2	36.6
United States	28.4	31.4	30.3

Source: International Monetary Fund, World Economic Outlook Database April 2019 and *Fiscal Monitor, April 2020*, Table A5.

profits taxes, contributed about 25% of all tax revenue, while taxes on international transactions (mainly import duties) represented the third largest source, about 18%. Social security and payroll taxes were the fourth largest source, mainly because of high shares of revenue in Central Europe and the former Soviet Union, where the share of international trade taxes was very small. Relatively little tax revenue came from taxes on property — generally less than 2%.

Table 6.4. Composition of taxation, in percent of total central government revenues, early 2000s.

	Taxes on income, profit & capital gains	Social security & payroll taxes	Domestic taxes on goods & services	International trade taxes	Property taxes
Developing countries	25.1	14.4	39.4	18.3	1.4
Americas	23.9	14.8	48.3	11.7	1.9
Sub-Saharan Africa	29.5	2.0	31.2	34.8	1.3
Central Europe & former Soviet Union	15.3	34.9	44.7	4.9	0.3
Soviet Union	32.4	6.0	34.6	19.4	3.1
N. Africa & Middle East					
Asia & Pacific	35.1	4.0	40.5	15.9	1.5
Small islands	19.5	11.4	26.0	39.7	1.4
High income countries	32.6	27.9	33.0	4.9	2.5

Source: Keen and Simone (2004).

In advanced economies, by comparison, taxes on incomes and profits, and on domestic goods and services, were about equally important, each contributing roughly 33% of total tax revenue. Another 28% came from social security and payroll taxes, reflecting the prevalence of economy-wide public pension programs in many of these countries. Less than 5% of all tax revenue came from taxes on international trade, as revenue systems are more developed and import duty rates are generally lower than in non-advanced economies. Property taxes, more commonly levied at the sub-national level, represented only about 2.5% of total tax revenue. Table 6.5 shows more recent data for the level and composition of tax revenue among OECD countries.

Table 6.5. Levels and composition of tax revenue in OECD countries.

1.1 Revenue Statistics: overview

(1)	Tax revenue as % of GDP				Tax revenue as % of total tax revenue in 2017						
	2018p	2017	2016	2000	1100 Taxes on income, individuals (PIT)	1200 Taxes on income, corporates (CIT)	2000 Social security contributions (SSC)	4000 Taxes on property	5111 Value added taxes	Other consumption taxes (6)	All other taxes (7)
OECD - Average (1)	34.3	34.2	34.4	33.8	23.9	9.3	26.0	5.8	20.2	12.2	2.6
Australia		28.5	27.6	30.5	40.3	18.5	0.0	10.3	12.2	13.9	4.8
Austria	42.2	41.8	41.9	42.3	21.7	5.9	34.9	1.3	18.3	9.8	8.1
Belgium	44.8	44.5	43.9	43.5	27.2	9.3	30.5	7.9	15.2	9.0	0.9
Canada	33.0	32.8	33.2	34.7	35.7	11.4	14.1	12.0	13.7	9.9	3.2
Chile	21.1	20.1	20.1	18.8	9.7	21.1	7.3	5.4	41.6	13.2	1.8
Czech Republic	35.3	34.9	34.2	32.4	11.5	10.7	43.0	1.4	22.0	10.9	0.5
Denmark (2)	44.9	45.7	45.7	46.9	52.9	7.2	0.1	3.9	20.7	11.1	4.1
Estonia	33.2	32.8	33.5	31.1	17.4	4.7	34.1	0.7	27.8	14.8	0.5
Finland	42.7	43.3	44.0	45.8	29.2	6.3	27.8	3.6	21.0	11.8	0.2
France (2)	46.1	46.1	45.4	43.4	18.6	5.1	36.4	9.5	15.3	9.2	6.0
Germany (3)	38.2	37.6	37.4	38.2	27.1	5.0	37.9	2.7	18.4	7.9	0.6
Greece (2)	38.7	38.9	38.7	33.4	16.0	5.0	29.6	7.9	20.9	18.5	2.1
Hungary	38.6	38.2	39.1	38.5	14.2	5.5	32.1	2.8	24.8	18.2	2.5
Iceland	38.7	37.5	50.8	36.0	38.0	8.2	9.1	5.5	23.8	9.9	5.5
Ireland	22.3	22.5	23.4	30.8	31.2	12.3	17.1	5.7	19.6	12.8	1.3
Israel (4)	31.1	32.5	31.1	34.9	20.7	10.1	16.2	10.0	22.9	11.8	8.4
Italy	42.1	42.1	42.3	40.6	25.7	5.0	30.3	6.2	14.8	13.6	4.4
Japan		31.4	30.7	25.8	18.8	11.8	39.9	8.2	13.0	8.0	0.2
Korea	28.4	26.9	26.2	21.5	17.9	14.2	25.7	11.7	16.0	11.8	2.8
Latvia	30.7	31.1	31.2	29.1	21.1	5.1	26.9	3.3	25.7	17.3	0.6
Lithuania	30.3	29.5	29.7	30.8	13.1	5.1	41.5	1.0	26.8	12.0	0.8
Luxembourg	40.1	38.7	37.9	36.9	23.6	13.6	28.6	9.6	15.9	8.4	0.3
Mexico (5)	16.1	16.1	16.6	11.5	21.4	21.8	13.3	1.9	23.1	13.2	5.3
Netherlands	38.8	38.7	38.4	36.9	21.6	8.5	35.7	4.0	17.4	11.7	1.1
New Zealand	32.7	32.1	31.7	32.5	37.8	14.7	0.0	6.0	30.2	8.3	3.1
Norway	39.0	38.8	38.7	41.9	26.5	12.5	26.8	3.3	22.1	8.8	0.1
Poland	35.0	34.1	33.5	32.9	14.6	5.6	37.5	4.0	22.8	14.1	1.3
Portugal	35.4	34.4	34.1	31.1	18.8	9.4	26.8	3.9	25.1	14.9	1.1
Slovak Republic	33.1	33.1	32.3	33.6	10.2	10.4	43.9	1.3	21.1	12.1	1.1
Slovenia	36.4	36.3	36.5	36.6	14.2	4.9	40.0	1.8	22.3	16.3	0.5
Spain (2)	34.4	33.7	33.3	33.2	21.8	6.8	34.0	7.5	19.1	10.2	0.5
Sweden	43.9	44.4	44.2	48.9	29.9	6.3	21.8	2.2	20.9	6.9	11.9
Switzerland	27.9	28.4	27.7	27.6	30.3	10.7	23.6	7.6	12.0	9.1	6.8
Turkey	24.4	24.9	25.3	23.6	14.5	6.8	29.3	4.5	20.1	23.3	1.3
United Kingdom	33.5	33.3	32.7	32.9	27.2	8.5	19.2	12.5	20.7	11.1	0.8
United States	24.3	26.8	25.9	28.3	38.7	6.5	23.0	16.0	0.0	15.7	0.0

Disclaimer: http://oe.cd/disclaimer

1. 2018 provisional average calculated by applying the unweighted average percentage change for 2018 in the 34 countries providing data for that year to the overall average tax to GDP ratio in 2017. The 2016
2. The total tax revenue has been reduced by the amount of any capital transfer that represents uncollected taxes.
3. From 1991 the figures relate to the united Germany.
4. The data for Israel are supplied by and under the responsibility of the relevant Israeli authorities. The use of such data by the OECD is without prejudice to the status of the Golan Heights, East Jerusalem
5. 2018 provisional: Secretariat estimate, including expected revenues collected by state and local governments.
6. Calculated as 5000 Taxes on goods and services less 5111 Value added taxes.
7. Includes 1300 Unallocable between personal and corporate income tax, 3000 Taxes on payroll and workforce and 6000 Other taxes.

Source: Reproduced from OECD (2019), *Revenue Statistics 1965–2018*, Table 1.1, http://dx.doi.org/10.1787/888934054645.

6.2. Purposes of Taxation

Taxation serves a variety of purposes. These include the following:

- **Raising revenue:** Arguably the main purpose of taxation is raising revenue to finance government activities. Revenue raised from tax and non-tax sources reduces the need for government borrowing to finance pubic services. Although some government activities can be funded through user charges, charges for specific public services are generally too low to finance more than a small share of total government expenditure.
- **Encouraging or discouraging specific activities:** Taxation can be used to promote or discourage specific activities. Within an existing tax structure, tax subsidies — credits, exemptions, or deductions for spending or contributions to specified activities — can promote behavior by making it financially more attractive. Many countries, for example, encourage saving or contributions to charitable activity by offering tax credits or deductions from taxable corporate profits or household income for sums contributed to approved savings accounts or charitable organizations. In recent years, many governments have also promoted conservation by offering tax benefits for purchasing fuel-efficient vehicles or retrofitting buildings with energy-saving devices. Similarly, most countries discourage certain activities by imposing disproportionately high tax rates on them. Many governments, for example, impose high taxes on tobacco products to discourage smoking. Singapore levies high taxes on automobiles to discourage car ownership.
- **Redistributing income and wealth:** Many countries try to moderate the wide disparity in pre-tax income and wealth by levying progressive income taxes, in which higher portions of household income are subject to progressively higher marginal tax rates, along with taxes on large estates and inheritances. For example, in the United States, during 2019 the first US$19,050 of taxable household income was taxed at a rate of 10%, for married couples, while amounts above that were subject to rates ranging from 12% to 37%. Estates valued at more than US$11.18 million per person

were subject to the federal estate tax. In addition, some states taxed inheritances (amounts received from estates).

• **Addressing externalities:** Taxes can also be used to address externalities, using subsidies (credits, deductions, or exemptions) to make activities with positive externalities less expensive and imposing taxes or charges to make activities with negative externalities more expensive. A number of countries, for example, provide tax subsidies for basic research, which has positive externalities. By contrast, many countries impose pollution charges, such as effluent fees, and some impose carbon taxes, to make the use of heavily polluting fuels such as coal more expensive. In addition, Singapore imposes special fees (non-tax revenues) for entering crowded business and shopping districts during peak periods, to reduce congestion.

6.3. Challenges of Taxation

Taxation poses challenges because the imposition of a tax changes the price of a product or the return received from labor or an investment, which in turn affects the demand for or supply of the good or service on which it is levied. With normal goods and services, meaning goods with downward-sloping demand and upward-sloping supply curves, imposing a tax on the purchase price will reduce the demand for the product, while levying a tax on labor, profit, or the cost of supplying the item will reduce the supply. Figures 6.1(a) and 6.1(b) illustrate the general effects.

In Figure 6.1(a), levying a tax on buyers reduces demand for the item, shifting the demand curve down from D^0 to D^1. Because of the tax, the price rises from P^0 to P^1, while the amount that sellers receive declines from P^0 to P^{1*}. With a downward-sloping demand curve, the amount sold declines from Q^0 to Q^1. The precise changes depend on the slopes of the demand and supply curves, which in turn affect the *incidence* of the tax: what shares consumers and sellers bear. This point is discussed further in the discussion surrounding Figure 6.3. In Figure 6.1(b), the effect of taxing labor is to reduce labor supply, because the tax reduces earnings from labor. In this case, the supply

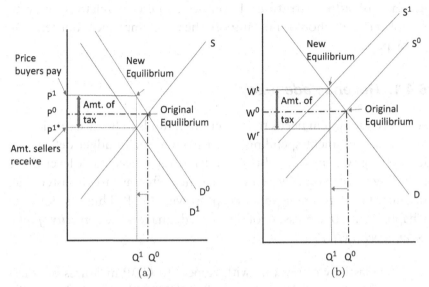

Figure 6.1. (a) Effect of imposing a tax on buyers. (b) Effect of imposing a tax on labor.

curve shifts back, from S^0 to S^1, and the quantity of labor supplied declines from Q^0 to Q^1. With a downward-sloping labor demand curve, the wage including tax payment rises to W^t, while the after-tax wage that workers receive declines from W^0 to W^r. Again, the slopes of the demand and supply curves determine the incidence of the tax as between employers and workers.

6.4. Principles for an Effective Revenue System

An effective revenue system should satisfy at least four basic criteria:

1. **Revenue adequacy:** The system should generate enough revenue to finance the preponderance of government expenditure during normal times, so as to minimize the need for deficit finance.
2. **Economic efficiency:** The system should raise revenue with minimal distortion to incentives and economic activity.
3. **Fairness:** The revenue system should be perceived as "fair," meaning that comparable taxpayers are treated similarly. Many would add that tax burdens should rise with income.

4. **Ease of administration:** Revenues should be relatively easy to collect and should not impose heavy compliance burdens on taxpayers.

6.4.1. *Revenue adequacy*

Any revenue system needs to raise enough funds to finance the desired level of government spending, apart from a small budget deficit that leaves the government's debt-to-GDP ratio at an acceptable level. Since spending needs typically grow over time, often as fast or faster than nominal GDP, revenues must keep up with GDP. Thus, as noted in Chapter Four, one measure of revenue adequacy is the *elasticity of total revenue with GDP.*

The elasticity of revenue with respect to GDP measures how fast revenue rises for each 1% rise in nominal GDP. This is equivalent to the percent change in revenue divided by the percent change in nominal GDP

$$\varepsilon_{rev,GDP} = (\Delta\ \text{Revenue}/\text{Revenue})/(\Delta\ \text{GDP}/\text{GDP}).$$

A revenue system whose elasticity with respect to nominal GDP equals one or more is considered *elastic*, meaning that total revenue rises as least as rapidly as nominal GDP. One indication of an elastic revenue system is that the ratio of total revenue to GDP is at least constant, if not rising over time.

Elastic revenue systems usually depend on taxes that have traditionally proved to be "good" revenue generators: taxes on personal or household income, corporate profits, and value added (or goods and services). The economic bases on which these taxes rely represent significant shares of total economic activity and are likely to move closely with GDP. Personal or household income and corporate profits, together, should represent the bulk of national income. Similarly, value added or the value of goods and services should be close to the value of total private consumption. In most economies, total private consumption represents a large share of GDP and should also move in line with GDP. So long as the legal bases for these taxes are not significantly narrowed by exemptions or exclusions and so long as evasion and weaknesses in tax administration are limited, revenues from these taxes should keep pace with GDP. Indeed, if the personal income tax has a progressive rate structure, meaning that marginal rates rise with income, revenues from this source may rise somewhat faster than GDP.

Although taxes on personal or household income, corporate profits, and value added (or goods and services) are the main sources of revenue elasticity, an elastic revenue system can benefit from including elements of non-tax revenue that are likely to increase with GDP. Such elements include profits from efficiently run state-owned enterprises and income from administrative services, fees, and charges. Keeping fees and charges current with inflation and increases in the cost of government services will help maintain the real level of these revenues and make total revenue more elastic.

6.4.2. Economic efficiency

Taxes distort economic behavior, by introducing a wedge between before- and after-tax prices or wages. An effective tax system minimizes the distortion, limiting the unwanted impact of taxation on incentives.

A useful concept for assessing the efficiency of a tax or the tax system is to measure the *excess burden*, or deadweight loss, of the tax or tax system. Excess burden represents the pure loss of welfare that results from imposing a tax. Figure 6.2 illustrates the concept. In Figure 6.2, before a tax is imposed, the supply and demand curves intersect so that the equilibrium price is P^*, and the equilibrium quantity sold is Q^*. At this intersection, consumers willing to pay at least P^* for the item are satisfied, and those willing to pay more are better off. The extent to which consumers as a whole are better off can be represented by the area bounded by P^* at the base, the vertical axis, and the demand curve.

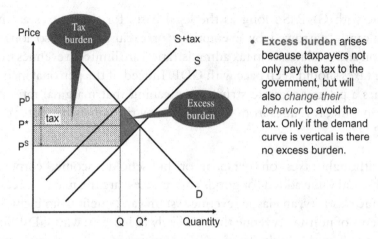

Figure 6.2.   Excess burden and efficiency of a tax.

When a tax is imposed on the item — in this case, a tax on suppliers — the supply curve shifts to the left, and the new supply curve intersects with the demand schedule at a point above and to the left of the original intersection. Thus, the amount sold decreases — here, from Q^* to Q. At the new equilibrium, the government obtains revenue equal to the difference between the new and the original supply schedules, multiplied by the number of units sold (Q). However, consumer and producer surplus each decline by more than this amount, and the difference between the loss in consumer plus producer surplus and the revenue that the government obtains, represented by the shaded triangle, is the *excess burden of the tax*. The excess burden is a pure loss of welfare. It occurs because taxation reduces the amount of goods sold below what would be sold without the tax. Only if the demand curve is vertical — meaning that a change in price does not affect the quantity of the product demanded — is there no excess burden from the tax.

The excess burden from taxation can be reduced by taxing mainly goods and services for which demand is highly inelastic, i.e., largely insensitive to price changes. Another option is to apply what is called *lump sum taxation*, meaning that individuals pay a fixed sum, regardless of their behavior or activity. Lump sum taxation avoids distorting incentives, because individuals cannot avoid paying the tax. Such taxes are often considered inequitable, however, because everyone pays the same amount, regardless of wealth or income. Thus, many governments avoid using lump sum taxes, except when imposed at very low levels. In this case, however, the tax may raise little money and may have high collection costs.

In the 1920s, the British economist James Ramsey observed that the distorting effects of a tax system can be minimized if the relative tax rates imposed on any pair of items are set in inverse proportion to their price elasticities of demand

$$t_1/t_2 = \text{elasticity}_2/\text{elasticity}_1.$$

According to the Ramsey rule, the tax rate for a good whose price elasticity of demand is 1 should be half that of a good whose price elasticity of demand is 0.5

$$0.5 t_2/t_2 = 0.5/1.$$

While the above rule might satisfy efficiency concerns, concerns about equity might argue against using this criterion as the sole, or even the primary, guide to taxation. For example, the price elasticity of demand for tobacco products is relatively low. However, in many countries lower income individuals are the main consumers of tobacco. Thus, imposing high taxes on cigarettes and other tobacco products will disproportionately affect the less affluent. It could also encourage smuggling, if neighboring jurisdictions have much lower tax rates. Of course, a government could decide to tax tobacco products heavily as a way to discourage smoking. If so, the authorities must be aware of the various implications of doing so.

Another aspect of efficiency involves the *neutrality* of a tax — whether it creates distortion by taxing similar items differently. If two items that are close substitutes are taxed differently, the tax system will encourage consumers to purchase the item taxed more lightly. The differing tax treatment distorts whatever preferences consumers might have if the items were not taxed, or were taxed in the same way.

For example, if import duties tax new automobiles at a higher rate than used vehicles, consumers may work with foreign dealers to have new cars driven for a few miles, so that they can be imported as used autos at a lower customs duty. Similarly, more favorable depreciation allowances may cause firms to invest in tax-favored equipment, or to shift their investments to industries with more favorable tax treatment. This happened in the United States during the early 1980s, when tax legislation promoted by the Reagan Administration provided more favorable tax treatment to certain industries and, for a time, encouraged investment in money-losing activities offering large tax deductions.

Large differences in tax treatment can sometimes prompt major changes in behavior. For example, some years ago, when Canadian taxes on cigarettes were far above tax rates in the United States, many Canadians drove into the United States to buy cigarettes and bring them back to Canada. The Canadian authorities tried to stop this behavior by limiting cigarette imports. In the end, however, the authorities had to lower the tax rate on cigarettes, to reduce the incentives for smuggling. This experience shows that differential tax treatment can have international implications. Indeed, countries with high marginal tax rates on personal income may find that some high-income individuals leave the country, or plan their activities to earn income in lower tax countries, so as to minimize their total tax liability. The same applies to firms deciding where to earn their profits.

6.4.3. Fairness

An effective tax system is perceived to be *fair*. This means that the tax system satisfies certain criteria.

1. *Horizontal equity. Horizontal equity* is much like neutrality. It means that taxpayers in similar circumstances are taxed alike. A tax system in which taxpayers with similar incomes are subject to similar tax rates exhibits horizontal equity. By comparison, one in which certain types of income, such as capital gains, are taxed at lower rates than

wages, salaries, or interest income violates horizontal equity. From the perspective of equity, legislators need strong justification for taxing some types of income more lightly than others. Otherwise, the tax laws may be perceived as being biased toward certain taxpayers or certain industries. This can undermine the legitimacy of the system and encourage evasion.

2. *Vertical equity.* *Vertical equity* implies that taxpayers with higher incomes should be subject to higher marginal tax rates, because they are presumed better able to afford taxation. Most countries accept the notion of vertical equity, insofar as they have introduced a progressive income tax (with marginal tax rates that rise as taxable income increases). However, the concept remains controversial, because it rests on an assumption of declining marginal utility of income. This means that the value of consumption falls as income rises, so that the loss in utility from taxation is smaller, the higher is a person's (or household's) income. Progressive taxation has also been justified by the claim that people need a smaller share of their incomes to finance consumption as their incomes rise.[1] Many politically right-of-center commentators, not to mention high-income individuals, reject this assumption and instead promote a "flat" income tax, in which all income is taxed at the same rate. Indeed, a few countries, such as Romania and Russia, have eliminated progressivity and adopted a single, "flat" marginal tax rate, to simplify the tax system and promote consumption by leaving the bulk of all income with consumers.

3. *No arbitrary treatment.* A fair tax system is one in which people believe that the authorities do not subject taxpayers to inappropriate treatment. Systems in which some taxpayers feel harassed, or where people in general believe that a particular industry or interest group receives special tax privileges, generate resentment, possibly leading taxpayers to evade taxation they consider unjust.

---

[1]The classic analysis is Blum, W. J., and H. Kalven, Jr. (1953), *The Uneasy Case for Progressive Taxation* (Chicago: University of Chicago Press). For a more recent discussion, see Lawsky, S. B. (2011), "On the Edge: Declining Marginal Utility and Tax Policy," *Minnesota Law Review*, vol. 95, pp. 904–952.

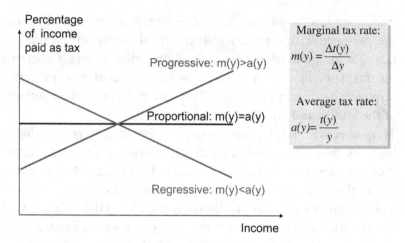

Figure 6.3.   Progressive, proportional, and regressive taxes.
Source: L. Tan.

4. *No worsening of income or wealth inequality.* A few analysts assess
   tax systems by their impact on income and wealth inequality.
   Some would argue that a "fair" tax system does not add to
   inequality, for example, by raising revenue mainly from taxes on
   consumption, which impose heavier burdens on lower and middle-
   income households because they save less than do more affluent
   households.

When assessing the fairness of a tax or a tax system, determining
whether that tax or the tax system generally is progressive, neutral,
or regressive can be useful. As shown in Figure 6.3, a tax in which
the marginal tax rate rises with income is called *progressive*, while
one in which the marginal rate is constant at all incomes is termed
proportional. A tax in which the marginal rate declines with income is
labeled *regressive*. Consumption taxes are typically considered regressive, because higher income households often spend a smaller share
of their incomes, thereby paying proportionately less of their incomes
in tax. The same applies to payroll taxes in which income above a
certain level, or types of income typically received only by high-income
households, such as dividends and capital gains, are not taxed. Because

higher income families are often presumed better able to bear the cost of taxation, regressive taxes are often considered "unfair." In addition, the existence of regressive taxes may mean that a country's tax system is at best proportional, even if there is a progressive income tax.

6.4.4. Simplicity

A fourth property of a sound and effective tax system is *simplicity*. The tax code should be relatively simple, with special provisions (exemptions, exclusions, deductions, and preferential rates) limited, to promote understanding and compliance with the law. Simplicity also facilitates tax administration, because tax officials have fewer complex provisions to enforce. A simpler tax code, with fewer exemptions and other special provisions, can also broaden the tax base, allowing the same amount of revenue to be raised with lower tax rates. Lower tax rates, in turn, encourage compliance, because the benefits from tax evasion are smaller.

The costs to taxpayers and governments from complex tax provisions can be staggering. Joel Slemrod, of the University of Michigan's Business School, has estimated that, in the United States, the costs of collecting income taxes, including both administrative and compliance costs, amount to about 10% of revenues collected.[2] Much of the expense involves the huge number of hours required to amass the information needed to complete tax forms, even if taxpayers hire professionals to prepare their tax returns. The cost to the government, though less, is also significant — an estimated 1% of tax revenues. In other countries, the complexity of many tax laws causes tax administration agencies to focus their resources on a more limited number of taxpayers or on taxes considered easier to collect. Indeed, complexity and compliance problems help explain why the elasticity

---

[2] See Slemrod, J. (2009), "Old George Orwell Got it Backward: Some Thoughts on Behavioral Tax Economics," CESifo Working Paper No. 2777, p. 2, http://www.ifo.de/portal/pls/portal/docs/1/1186062.pdf.

of some revenue systems is less than one, despite having a number of taxes that should, in principle, be good revenue producers.

Besides detailed studies by technical experts, several tools can be used to get an idea of the complexity, or inefficiency, in a tax system. One tool involves assessing the extent of *tax expenditures* in the tax system. Tax expenditures are revenue losses that result from special provisions that grant exemptions, exclusions, deductions, credits, or preferential rates in a tax code. These provisions include both tax subsidies, representing deviations from general tax principles, and "tax-induced structural distortions," provisions of the tax code that grant preferential treatment. The size of the tax expenditure is estimated by calculating the difference in revenue between actual collections and what could, in theory, be collected without the special provision. Tax expenditures can involve huge amounts of money. For example, the US Joint Committee on Taxation identifies many tens of billions of US dollars in revenue lost each year — a substantial percentage of total federal revenues collected — from individual tax expenditures.[3]

Another way of judging the simplicity of the tax system is to apply the *Tanzi Diagnostic Test* introduced in Chapter Four. This is a set of questions designed to assess the administrative efficiency of the system. The Tanzi Diagnostic test asks the following questions about a tax system, referring to eight specific indices[4]:

(1) *Concentration index*: Do a relatively few taxes and tax rates provide a large share of revenue?
(2) *Dispersion index*: Are there few low-yielding, "nuisance" taxes?
(3) *Erosion index*: Are actual tax bases very close to potential bases (few major exemptions, exclusions)?

---

[3]See, for example, Joint Committee on Taxation (2018), "Estimates of Federal Tax Expenditures for Fiscal Years 2018–22" (Washington: U.S. Government Printing Office, October), https://www.jct.gov/publications.html?id=5148&func=startdown.

[4]This wording comes from Ouanes, A., and S. Thakur (1997), *Macroeconomic Analysis and Accounting in Transition Economies* (Washington: International Monetary Fund), Box 3.5, p. 70.

(4) *Collection lag index*: Are tax payments made with short lags and close to when they fall due?

(5) *Specificity index*: Does the tax system depend on as few taxes as possible, and with specific rates?

(6) *Objectivity index*: Are most taxes imposed on objectively measured tax bases?

(7) *Enforcement index*: Is the tax system enforced fully and effectively?

(8) *Cost of collection index*: Is the cost of collecting taxes as low as possible?

A tax system with positive answers to all eight questions can be considered to have high productivity.

Achieving simplicity in the tax code depends heavily on removing special provisions that create significant deviations from a "clean" tax law. In particular, streamlining the number of exemptions and allowances, and taxing broad classes of income, goods, and services at a single rate, rather than creating multiple rates, will greatly simplify the tax system, making revenue easier to collect and facilitating compliance with the law.

6.4.5. *Conflicts among objectives*

Achieving all four goals simultaneously can be difficult. For example, a flat tax on corporate receipts is vastly simpler than a corporate profits tax. However, such a tax makes no allowance for differences in the cost of earning those receipts. It can thus subject true corporate profits to very different effective rates, thereby violating both fairness (horizontal equity) and efficiency (by distorting investment incentives). Similarly, a personal income tax without deductions or allowances scores well on simplicity, but could impose heavy tax burdens on some people with limited ability to pay (for example, those who have suffered heavy casualty losses or incurred large medical expenses). Sometimes the proper approach to measuring income involves unavoidable complexity — for example, calculating depreciation allowances in a corporate profits tax. As noted earlier, some attempts to increase efficiency, such as taxing mainly goods such as alcohol and tobacco products whose demand is not that price sensitive, can provoke objections on grounds of fairness, because the taxes impose particularly heavy burdens on less-affluent households. Finally, efforts to increase the "fairness" of a tax by introducing special provisions, such as lower tax rates on medicines and medical devices, inevitably increase complexity and reduce total revenues. Thus, policymakers sometimes must choose which objective to emphasize when designing a tax system or considering alternative approaches to taxing a particular revenue source.

6.4.6. *Special issues regarding exemptions*

Tax exemptions raise a variety of issues that require attention.

(1) Tax exemptions shrink the tax base and reduce revenues unless tax rates are increased to offset the shrinkage.

(2) Exemptions often result from efforts by special interest groups. The resulting politicization of the tax code may undermine perceptions of fairness.

(3) Letting exemptions proliferate not only reduces revenue but also makes tax administration and compliance more difficult and costly.

(4) In a progressive income or profits tax, tax exemptions provide proportionately larger benefits to those facing higher marginal tax rates, because the exemption shields income from tax at the highest marginal rate. Thus, exemptions provide disproportionate savings to those with higher levels of income or profit, worsening income inequality. If the goal is to provide uniform rates of subsidy, a flat rate tax credit, which reduces tax liabilities by the same percentage at all levels of income or profit, is preferable.

(5) Exemptions can be used in an otherwise "flat" or single-rate tax to introduce progressivity. The reason is that the exemption reduces the effective rate of tax, since no tax is paid on the lowest slab of income.

6.4.7. *Balancing the objectives*

Because tax provisions cannot always satisfy all four goals, it is usually necessary to "balance the objectives" when designing or reforming the tax system. Following is one way to do so:

- Using broad tax bases, so that tax rates can be kept low while still achieving good revenue yields
- Relying on several good revenue-producing levies, rather than just one, which also allows rates to be set relatively low for each tax
- Limiting exemptions to fairness objectives (e.g., casualty losses), to avoid shrinking the tax base
- Avoiding special interest provisions, which shrink the tax base and make taxes appear unfair
- Promoting fairness in personal income taxes through a combination of personal exemptions (which exclude the bottom tier of income from tax) and rising marginal tax rates as incomes increase
- Avoiding multiple tax rates for value-added taxes and complex sets of tariff and excise rates, which add complexity and can distort taxpayers' decision-making
- Avoiding small ("nuisance") taxes that raise little revenue but impose high administrative costs
- Avoiding the use of the tax system to provide subsidies, except where there is a clear administrative gain from providing the benefit by cutting taxes rather than providing a subsidy or cash transfer, to improve transparency and simplify the tax system

The above approach should allow the tax system to raise revenues relatively easily, in a way that limits distortion and minimizes the incentive for evasion, because rates for each tax are kept modest. It also means that income can be taxed more than once, however. For example, in a tax system with both a personal income tax and a tax on sales or value added, income is taxed first when received and again when after-tax income is used for consumption.

6.5. Major Revenue Sources

Most countries rely on a variety of revenue sources. The most important of these are taxes on personal income and corporate profits; taxes on value added or sales of goods and services; selective sales taxes (excises) on goods with relatively low price elasticity of demand; taxes on international trade; taxes on property and other assets; special taxes on wage income (payroll taxes); and certain non-tax revenues, including fees and charges for public services or the use of public property, penalties and fines, and profit transfers from state-owned enterprises and the central bank or monetary authority. In addition, a few governments levy minimum taxes and/or presumptive taxes. Each of these revenue sources involves special issues.

Before addressing these issues, it is worthwhile introducing the terms "direct" and "indirect" taxation, since many countries use these terms. *Direct taxes* are taxes that fall directly on the income or assets of physical or legal persons (corporations and foundations). Direct taxes include taxes on personal income and corporate profits; taxes levied on payrolls or wages, usually to help fund social insurance activities; and taxes on wealth and property, including taxes on estates and assets passed by gift or through inheritance. *Indirect taxes* are taxes that fall indirectly on income or assets, because they are levied on their *use*. Thus, indirect taxes are levied mainly on production, consumption, exports, and imports. Indirect taxes include taxes on goods and services, sales, or value added, including excise taxes. They also include taxes on imports and exports. Special taxes linked to consumption or production, such as taxes imposed on utility bills or computer service contracts or levies on oil or gas production (as opposed to the profits of oil and gas exporters), are also indirect taxes.

6.5.1. *Personal income tax*

The personal income tax is a tax levied on income received by physical persons. The tax can be assessed either on a household basis or separately, on each individual in a household. Personal income taxes are generally levied on all or most types of income that people receive, including wages and salaries, consulting fees and other income from personal businesses, interest, dividends, rental income, various government benefits, prizes and gambling profits, and, in many countries, capital gains from the sale of assets such as real estate and shares of stock. Under a "global" income tax, all forms of income are combined to determine taxable income and then taxed according to a common set of tax rates. Under a "schedular" system, different kinds of income are taxed at different rates. For example, capital gains, which raise a variety of issues, may be taxed more lightly than wages, salaries, and interest earnings.

Tax analysts have traditionally argued that tax burdens under an income tax should reflect the "ability to pay." Ability to pay typically reflects a variety of factors.

First, taxpayers are assumed to need a certain minimum income for subsistence. Thus, only income above this level should be taxed. This argument explains the use of personal exemptions, which exclude the lowest slab of income from tax. The subsistence argument also explains why many personal income taxes differentiate tax liability based on household size. In many countries, separate exemptions are given for the taxpayer, his or her spouse, and each dependent child.

Second, taxpayers can exclude from taxable income certain unusual and unavoidable expenses deemed to reduce their ability to pay tax. These can include casualty losses and high medical expenses. If taxpayers are subject to separate national, state or provincial, and local income taxes, the national income tax may allow taxpayers to reduce their taxable income by part or all of sub-national income tax payments.

Third, once taxable income is determined, the "ability to pay" argument is sometimes used to justify progressive taxation, subjecting progressively higher levels of income to higher marginal tax rates.[5]

---

[5]Blum and Kalven (1953), *op. cit.*

Most countries accept the argument and use a progressive rate structure in their personal income tax. A few countries, notably Romania and the Russian Federation, apply a single tax rate to taxable income. Thus, a key issue is how progressive the personal income tax should be.

The nature of the personal income tax raises a variety of issues.

6.5.1.1. *Double taxation of savings*

Taxes on personal income inevitably subject income used for savings to double taxation. When all forms of income are taxed, households pay an initial tax on the wage, salary, and profit income they receive and a subsequent tax on the earnings from any income saved. This double taxation discourages saving by reducing the return on income saved, arguably diminishing funds available for investment. Taxing consumption, rather than income, eliminates the double taxation; this can be achieved by allowing taxpayers to exclude from taxable income any income used for approved savings activities. Taxing consumption raises its own issues, however; these will be discussed later on.

6.5.1.2. *Double taxation of dividends*

Corporate profits paid as dividends, rather than retained by the firm, are subject to double taxation when households must include dividends in their taxable income. This double taxation introduces a distortion, encouraging firms to retain earnings rather than pay dividends. A few countries, such as Germany, address the problem by subjecting dividends to a lower tax rate under the personal income tax. Another option is to eliminate the corporate income tax and allocate all corporate profits to shareholders. However, this approach may prove difficult to administer, because of the need to monitor earnings attributed to each of thousands or millions of corporate shareholders. It may also reduce national tax collections, where foreign firms or individuals own a part of company shares.

6.5.1.3. *Taxing non-cash income*

Taxing income received in the form of in-kind benefits, such as food, lodging, employer contributions to health insurance, or free parking, can be difficult because the benefit is hard to value. Although market-provided goods and services can provide a basis for valuing some services (e.g., the cost of parking at nearby commercial lots), in other cases, such as the savings provided by access to an unsubsidized, employer-run cafeteria, no ready market alternative is available for valuation. Partly for administrative reasons, a number of countries, such as the United States, exempt non-cash benefits from the personal income tax. However, excluding non-cash income from tax provides a windfall to employees who receive such benefits. It can also distort the compensation process, encouraging firms and workers to replace a part of cash wages with non-cash benefits, to reduce taxation.

6.5.1.4. *The marriage penalty*

Under a progressive income tax in which the tax rate applies to total household income, two-earner households may pay more in tax as a married couple than if they were not married. The reason is that at least part of the income of the lesser earning spouse is subject to a higher marginal tax rate than would be true if each spouse were taxed as an individual. Partly for this reason, some jurisdictions, such as the state of Virginia in the United States, let married couples decide whether to be taxed on their total household income, or taxed separately on each of their incomes. Giving this option, however, means that an individual taxpayer whose income equaled the combined income of the two spouses will pay more in tax. So long as the tax is progressive, there is no way to avoid one of these inequities — the marriage penalty or imposing a higher tax rate on individuals than on a married couple with the same income.

6.5.1.5. *Taxing worldwide income*

As globalization leads growing numbers of people to work in countries outside their official homelands, the taxation of households on worldwide income has become a critical issue. Most countries have treaties that eliminate the double taxation of income. However, income tax rates vary from country to country. Thus, individuals whose homelands tax only income earned in the country are subject to the tax rates of the countries in which they earn their incomes. This can create inequities between those working at home and abroad.

Taxing individuals on their worldwide income eliminates this inequity. However, where many countries do not tax foreign earnings, citizens of countries that tax on worldwide incomes face a disadvantage, because they need higher pre-tax incomes to compensate for the higher tax rates of their home countries. As of 2019 five countries — China, Eritrea, North Korea, the Philippines, and the United States — taxed their citizens on their worldwide income. The United States, however, gives some tax relief on earnings and on housing expenses an employer pays for those with foreign earnings.

6.5.1.6. *Taxing capital gains*

Most economists consider that capital gains, the increase in value of assets held, should be included in taxable income, because they add to taxpayers' net worth. Nevertheless, taxing capital gains raises a variety of issues. These include the following:

a. *When to recognize the gain*: Although gains on paper assets increase net worth, the gains are only assured when realized, i.e., when the assets are sold. The United States and many other countries tax capital gains only on realization. This creates the possibility of a *lock-in effect*, whereby taxpayers delay selling assets with unrealized gains to avoid having to pay tax. The lock-in effect can work in the reverse direction, encouraging taxpayers to realize gains early if tax rates are scheduled to rise in the next year. Taxing only realized gains can also give a benefit to those holding unrealized gains for an extended period, because the discounted cost of deferred tax payments is less than if taxes were paid as soon as the gains materialized (even if the gains were not realized).

b. *How to value the gain*: The nominal value of many assets, such as real estate, rises with inflation. In this case, the "real" increase in asset values is less than the nominal gain, and many economists would argue that only the real increase should be taxed. The proper adjustment for inflation is not obvious, however. Consumer price indices reflect changes in a basket of consumer goods and services, while many other factors can affect asset prices. Perhaps for this reason, countries tend not to adjust nominal gains for inflation when figuring tax liability. However, in some countries the overstatement of real gains is used to justify taxing nominal capital gains at preferential rates.

c. *What can capital losses offset?* Since asset prices can decline as well as increase, some analysts have argued that capital losses as well as gains should be included in total taxable income. However, others have noted that allowing capital losses to offset regular income can create perverse incentives. For example, where marginal tax rates are high, some high-income taxpayers may find it attractive to invest in money-losing assets, to reduce taxable income. The resulting distortion can reduce economic welfare. For this reason, some countries, such as the United States, allow capital losses only to offset capital gains, although unused losses can be carried forward in the event that losses exceed gains during a year.

6.5.1.7. *Tax allowances to encourage behavior*

Many countries use the personal income tax to provide incentives for certain objectives. Some tax codes, for example, provide tax benefits for charitable contributions. A number of other tax codes also provide tax subsidies for contributing to authorized savings schemes. Certain countries provide tax allowances for education expenses. A growing number of countries offer incentives for buying more energy-efficient cars or improving the energy efficiency of houses and buildings.

Many countries consider the above to be worthwhile objectives. In addition, many countries prefer to give subsidies in the form of tax allowances, rather than budget expenditures, because taxpayers find it simpler to claim relief from their tax liabilities than to apply for a subsidy from a government agency. However, these allowances narrow the tax base and complicate the tax code. Thus, each claim for tax relief must be carefully reviewed, to avoid a proliferation of tax allowances and resulting shrinkage of the tax base.

It is also useful to consider the form in which the tax allowance is provided. In a graduated income tax, exemptions or deductions reduce the taxpayer's taxable income, so the amount of tax relief depends on the taxpayer's marginal tax rate. Taxpayers in higher tax brackets (typically those with higher incomes) get a larger percentage subsidy than those in lower brackets, while those with no tax liability get no tax relief whatsoever. If the tax allowance is intended to provide a subsidy for the activity, and the intention is to give taxpayers the same rate of subsidy, regardless of income level or marginal tax rate, the tax relief should be given in the form of a tax credit equal to a fixed percentage of the subsidized expenditure. With a tax credit, all taxpayers receive the same rate of subsidy. Moreover, if those without tax liability, or those whose tax liability is less than the amount of credit, are to receive the full amount of tax relief, the credit should be *refundable*. In that case, eligible taxpayers can file a return and receive the full credit (i.e., a cash payment from the government) even if their total tax liability is less than the amount of the credit.

6.5.1.8. *Reaching "hard-to-tax" incomes*

A key challenge facing any personal income tax is the difficulty of taxing certain kinds of income that can be easily hidden, because of limited record-keeping or the difficulty of monitoring and verifying taxpayer records. Good examples include the incomes of independent professionals and contractors, such as solo physicians and lawyers, or electricians, plumbers, and carpenters; the income from farmers; and the income and profits of sole proprietors and small businesses with limited assets. Some farmers and small shopkeepers, such as those who have stalls in traditional urban markets, may have minimal literacy and very limited records. Skilled independent contractors and professionals may be able to hide their income by receiving payments in cash or by keeping two sets of accounts. The same is true for household workers, although in many countries these employees earn less than the minimum income required to pay income tax.

Tax authorities have various ways of addressing these problems. One involves *presumptive taxation*, in which various indices are used to estimate the total receipts of a firm or independent operator, after which a small tax is imposed on the estimated receipts, because no allowance is made for costs. More will be said about this approach later in this chapter. Another is to subject higher earning contractors, such as doctors and lawyers, to monitoring and periodic auditing. For very small proprietors, the cost of collecting income or profits tax may not be worth the effort. Instead, some revenue can be obtained by imposing a license fee in lieu of a formal tax on income or profit. Finally, to avoid distorting the choice of whether to retain income in a business or pay it out in distributions or dividends, the same tax rates should apply to the corporate and personal income tax.

6.5.1.9. *The degree of progressivity*

As noted earlier, countries differ in the progressivity of their personal income tax. Most countries have progressive rate schedules, although the degree of progressivity has diminished considerably from the 1960s, when the top marginal rate exceeded 90% in some advanced economies (including the United States). Marginal tax rates typically range between zero and 40% or 50%, with the top marginal rate currently 37% in the United States and 22% in Singapore. Very high marginal tax rates may discourage work effort or lead to tax avoidance, as in cases where high-earning entertainers or sports professionals move across national borders to avoid being subject to high marginal tax rates. High marginal tax rates may have particularly strong effects on the work efforts of spouses in two-earner households with children. Where child care is expensive, high marginal rates may make it cheaper for the lower earning spouse to stay home and take care of the children, rather than earn income and use the much-reduced after-tax income to pay for child care and the costs of going to work outside the home. The impact of high marginal tax rates is magnified if earnings are also subject to payroll taxes for social insurance. In this case, the combined marginal tax rate may exceed 50%, making earnings after taxes and work-related expenses much smaller.

6.5.1.10. *Adjusting the income tax for inflation*

Because most tax laws define exemptions, exclusions, and tax brackets in specific amounts, the real value of these amounts declines with inflation. Thus, without adjustment, inflation will cause taxpayers to pay steadily larger shares of their income in a progressive income tax. To prevent this, many countries index the various fixed amounts in their tax codes for inflation, often raising the amounts by the observed rise in the consumer price index since the previous year. As noted earlier, adjusting capital gains for inflation is harder, and few countries attempt such an adjustment.

6.5.1.11. *Taxing income versus consumption*

As noted earlier, income taxation creates a double taxation of savings, because earnings from saved income are taxed, as well as the initial income itself. One way around the problem is to tax consumption, rather than savings, by allowing taxpayers to deduct from taxable income any contributions to approved savings vehicles, such as bank accounts, or purchases of financial assets. Taxing consumption rather than income provides more incentives for savings, thereby providing greater financing for investment and possibly inducing more economic growth. However, consumption taxation has its own problems. These include the following:

a. *Opportunities for windfall gains and losses*: Moving from an income to a consumption tax would provide gains for middle-aged households and those with high savings — typically, higher income families. However, many older households, which had previously been taxed on their entire incomes, might face higher taxes as they withdrew funds from their savings accounts or liquidated assets during retirement. Many would consider these changes inequitable.

b. *Changes in marginal tax rates*: Excluding savings from tax would narrow the tax base, requiring higher tax rates to collect the same amount of revenue. Not only might this encourage greater evasion, but it could also mean lower effective tax rates for high-income households that found it easier to save. Here, too, some observers might find these changes inequitable.

c. *Issues in tax administration*: Moving to a consumption tax could create administrative challenges. The tax law would have to define which savings qualified for tax relief. In addition, the authorities would have to be able to monitor reductions in savings or the liquidation of financial assets.

For these and other reasons, no country has yet replaced its income tax with a consumption tax. Nevertheless, some economists continue to advocate the change.[6]

6.5.1.12. *Administrative issues regarding a personal income tax*

Certain elements of tax administration greatly enhance the efficiency of a personal income tax. One is the extensive use of *withholding* tax as soon as income is earned. Many countries require personal income tax to be withheld from wage and salary payments. The United States, for example, has an elaborate set of rules to determine *withholding from paychecks*. Workers are required to complete a form whenever they begin work at an establishment with a minimum number of employees. A formula then determines how much to be withheld from each paycheck, taking account of the number of dependents

---

[6]For further discussion, see Pechman, J. A., ed. (1980), *What Should Be Taxed: Income or Expenditure?* (Washington: Brookings); U.S. Treasury Staff (1977), *Blueprints for Basic Tax Reform* (Washington: U.S.G.P.O), available at http://www.treasury.gov/offices/tax-policy/library/blueprints; and Congressional Budget Office (1997), *Economic Effects of Comprehensive Tax Reform* (Washington: July), http://www.cbo.gov/ftpdocs/0xx/doc36/taxrefor.pdf.

the worker has and other factors that can affect tax liability. Besides withholding tax from workers' salaries, some countries require that a *percentage of interest income paid by financial institutions be withheld* as an advance against ultimate tax liability. Studies have shown that withholding greatly increases the percentage of tax due that is actually received (see discussion in Section 6.6, on tax administration).

Requiring estimated or advanced payments of tax provides another way to improve the efficiency and yield of a personal income tax. In some countries, households for which taxes are not withheld on earned income, or for which withholding is insufficient to cover tax liabilities, are instructed to make estimated tax payments against final tax liabilities or face significant penalties and interest. In the United States, taxpayers are required to pay 90% of their ultimate tax liabilities through a combination of withholding and estimated tax payments to avoid penalties.

Estimated or advance payments help spread tax receipts over the fiscal year. They may also increase total yields, especially if taxpayers can anticipate fines or interest from non-compliance. Where inflation is significant, requiring advance payments increases the real value of revenues, by shortening the delay between the accrual of tax liability and the government's receipt of payments.

6.5.2. *The corporate income or profit tax*

The corporate income or profits tax is a major source of revenue in many countries. Nevertheless, average tax rates have fallen in most countries during the last several decades, and the contribution of corporate taxation to total revenue has fallen since the early 1990s. Between 1990 and 2002, the average corporate tax rate fell from 39% to less than 31% across a group of developing countries and from 34% to 28% across a number of advanced economies. In developing countries, average corporate tax revenues declined from 2.9% of GDP in 1990 to 2.3% in 2002, although in advanced economies, they rose from 1.9%

of GDP to 2.5% over the same period,[7] reflecting the sharp increase in corporate profits overall and a shift in the income distribution from labor to capital in many higher income countries. Among OECD countries, the trend continued after 2002, with profit taxes reaching 9.0% of total revenues and averaging 2.9% of GDP in 2016.[8] However, tax competition between jurisdictions has led to further reductions in corporate tax rates, particularly in Asia. For example, both Hong Kong SAR and Singapore reduced their corporate tax rates below 20% after 2007. Beginning in 2018, the United States reduced its federal corporate rate from 35% to 21%.

The corporate income tax has several points of interaction with the personal income tax. As noted earlier, taxing corporate profits leads to a double taxation of dividends when dividends received by households are subject to the personal income tax. Nevertheless, the corporate income tax can serve as a useful "backstop" to the personal income tax, to ensure that income earned by small businesses is subject to some taxation. Without a corporate income tax, owners of firms could avoid tax on their earnings by retaining income in their businesses indefinitely, and possibly pass the earnings onto heirs without tax if estates below a certain size are exempt from estate or inheritance taxes.

1. *Incidence.* A perennial issue facing the corporate income tax is who bears the burden of the tax. Although the tax is nominally imposed on corporate profits, under some circumstances a corporation can shift the tax forward, onto consumers (by raising product prices), or backward onto its employees (by paying lower wages). Figure 6.4 illustrates how forward shifting, onto prices, can occur.

---

[7] Keen, M., and A. Simone (2004), "Tax Policy in Developing Countries: Some Lessons from the 1990s and Some Challenges Ahead," in Gupta, S. *et al.*, eds., *Helping Countries Develop: The Role of Fiscal Policy* (Washington: International Monetary Fund).

[8] Data from OECD (2018), *Revenue Statistics 1965–2017, 2018 Edition*, Table 3.9, https://read. oecd-ilibrary.org/taxation/revenue-statistics-2018_rev_stats-2018-en\#page71.

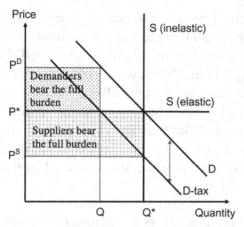

Figure 6.4.   What determines the incidence of the corporate income tax?

Suppose the demand curve for a good or service is downward sloping, as in Figure 6.4 — neither perfectly inelastic (consumers want only a fixed amount, regardless of price) nor perfectly elastic (demand disappears if the price goes above a specific level). As the producer's supply curve becomes more elastic, a steadily larger share of the tax is shifted onto consumers. At the limit, when supply is perfectly elastic (the case of the horizontal supply curve), producers can shift all the tax onto consumers. By comparison, as supply becomes less elastic, a larger share of the tax falls on suppliers. At the limit, when supply is perfectly inelastic and the supply curve is vertical, suppliers bear the full burden of the tax. Recent research has suggested that shareholders bear at least some portion of the tax, because they have difficulty shifting the tax in the short run and may be unable in the long run to shift taxes on rents, taxes attributable to a "discount" on old capital, and taxes that reduce the advantages of corporate ownership. The Urban Institute–Brookings Tax Policy Center assumes that investors bear 80% of the burden of the corporate income tax when making revenue estimates, with labor income bearing the remaining 20%.[9] Nevertheless, there

---

[9]Auerbach, A. (2005), "Who Bears the Corporate Income Tax: A Review of What We Know," paper presented at the *NBER Tax Policy and the Economy Conference*, http://www.econ.berkeley. edu/~auerbach/bearstax.pdf. See also Tax Policy Center (2019), "Briefing Book — Who Bears

may be situations — for example, in a highly monopolistic economy, where firms threaten to leave if they are not granted tax concessions — where the effective burden of the tax could be shifted onto consumers.

2. Issues of complexity and equity. Taxing corporate profits typically makes a country's tax system more complex, because the proper definition of corporate income involves allowing deductions for the *depreciation* of plant and equipment, the *depletion* of mineral assets, and *changes in inventories* (stocks) of unsold goods. Determining the useful life of different corporate assets is difficult, although tax codes often try to simplify matters by offering standard "useful" lives for various types of assets, such as computers and warehouse buildings. In addition, many tax systems compound the difficulty by offering *accelerated depreciation* (a faster write-off of assets than justified by their normal economic life) as a way of stimulating investment or reducing the effective rate of corporate tax. Allowances for the depletion of oil and minerals also create problems, because firms sometimes find new oil or mineral resources in a site or need to change the valuation of existing resources as market prices change. Valuing inventory raises issues similar to depletion allowances, because the market prices of goods not yet sold can change. Applying a "first in — first out" ("FIFO") rule may undervalue inventory changes if goods produced earlier can be sold for higher prices today. On the contrary, a "last in — first out" ("LIFO") approach may allow firms to overvalue the cost of producing older items, thereby understating true corporate profits.

Depreciation allowances can also create equity problems, if the rules favor certain types of assets that are more common to certain industries than to others. For example, the so-called "Reagan" tax cut that the United States introduced in 1981 reportedly provided much faster acceleration for equipment than for structures. Thus, it

---

the Burden of the Corporate Income Tax?" https://www.taxpolicycenter.org/briefing-book/who-bears-burden-corporate-income-tax.

was thought to favor newer industries and activities less reliant on large production facilities, as compared with traditional manufacturing industries in which factory buildings represented a high share of production costs.

3. *Creating a bias toward debt finance.* The corporate income tax is often considered to distort how firms choose to finance investment, because interest payments are normally a deductible business expense, but dividend payments are not. Because dividends are not only not deductible but may also be subject to double taxation (when received by households), firms have an incentive to retain earnings rather than paying dividends and to issue bonds or borrow from banks rather than sell stock (issue equity) to finance expansion. Various policy measures can address the bias. These include the following:

a. integrating the corporate and personal income tax, or exempting dividend payments from tax, to address the double taxation of dividends;
b. taxing corporate cash flow, rather than profits, in which case both dividend and interest payments qualify as deductions, since they both reduce corporate cash flow; and
c. providing a special tax allowance for the dividends associated with issuing equity.

Taxing corporate cash flow raises its own problems, since it involves granting a full and immediate deduction for all investment expenses. Doing so can bias investment in favor of long-lived assets and subject firms with sudden cash inflows (but small economic profits) to significant tax, while sparing those with large profits but huge investment expenditure. Transitioning to a cash flow tax could also create windfall losses for firms, if economic losses not yet recognized for tax purposes could not be considered in calculating taxable cash flow. For these and other reasons, few countries have shifted to a corporate cash flow tax. Accordingly, there may be a case for a special allowance for dividend payments.

4. *Taxing multinational firms.* Because tax rates and provisions vary across (and sometimes within) countries, multinational firms can minimize their corporate tax liabilities through the artful use of *transfer pricing*, which involves the pricing of good produced in one jurisdiction and then shipped to another for further processing or final sale. By charging artificially high prices for components, a multinational firm can minimize the profits earned in a high-tax jurisdiction. Likewise, a firm can shift profits to a low-tax jurisdiction by importing components at artificially low prices, inflating the measured profit. In principle, the problem can be addressed by requiring firms to value component parts using an "arm's length" standard, applying market prices to avoid artificial valuations. While this approach works for standard components, it may be hard to apply in the case of items unique to the firm, for which ready alternatives with market prices are not available.

A further issue can arise if firms attempt to shift profits to "thinly capitalized subsidiaries," such as shell corporations established in so-called *tax havens* (jurisdictions with unusually low profit tax rates). Some countries address this problem by re-computing the firm's profits, to increase the amount of taxable profit in places where the firm has a true presence (e.g., corporate headquarters or major production subsidiary). Accordingly, the firm is barred from shifting profits to the low-tax jurisdiction.

Minimizing corporate taxation through profit shifting creates major revenue losses for many countries. Saez and Zucman (2019) provide discussion of the issues, including estimated revenue losses.[10]

5. *Tax incentives.* To promote investment and make the business climate more competitive, countries often grant firms tax incentives,

---

[10]Saez, E., and G. Zucman (2019), *Triumph of Injustice* (New York: W.W. Norton & Co.), Chapter 4. See also OECD (2020), "International Collaboration to End Tax Avoidance," https://www.oecd.org/tax/beps/.

including accelerated depreciation or other allowances for investment, special rebates on other taxes, tax breaks for exporters, and the creation of free trade zones, or outright exclusion from tax for a specified period of time (so-called *tax holidays*), either on all profits or on profits resulting from specific activities or investments. Economists typically argue that tax holidays are inefficient, because they provide relief against all income, rather than targeting tax reductions on the earnings from new investment. Thus, more targeted incentives, such as tax credits or deductions for new investment, may be more efficient ways of encouraging new investment.

Unless tax relief can be carried forward for a number of years, however, tax credits, deductions, or even lower tax rates work better for well-established firms than for new firms or firms that expect losses during their first few years of operation. In addition, countries that provide targeted tax incentives may find themselves less attractive than other countries that provide more generous tax holidays. Thus, tax reform must be considered in the context of general tax practices of competing jurisdictions.

6.5.3. *Payroll taxes*

Payroll taxes are taxes imposed on wages and salaries. They are typically separate from personal income taxes, which are levied on a much broader set of income sources. In most countries, payroll taxes are used to fund social insurance programs, such as the various social funds in Eastern Europe and the Social Security program in the United States. In a few countries, such as Malaysia and Singapore, mandatory contributions equivalent to payroll taxes are imposed to accumulate balances in individual provident fund accounts that can be used to finance a pension, pay for housing or university tuition, or fund a portion of approved medical expenses. Although in most countries payroll taxes are levied both on employers and employees, research suggests that workers typically bear a large portion, if not all, of the burden of the tax. For the United States, empirical research during the 1970s suggested that social security taxes were fully shifted onto wages.[11] For Europe, more recent empirical work suggests that at least half of such taxes are shifted onto wages.[12]

Payroll taxes offer the advantage of simplicity. Levied on payrolls, they are typically easy to collect, at least at large establishments, although in some countries enforcement at smaller firms has sometimes proved difficult.[13] Because they are levied only on wages and salaries, they are typically regressive, since non-wage income, which forms a larger share of the incomes of higher income households, is exempt from the tax. Where the tax is levied only on income up to a ceiling, as in the United States, the tax is even more regressive, since households with earnings above the ceiling pay no more in tax than those at the ceiling. Such taxes can thus increase income inequality.

Where payroll taxes are levied only on wages up to a ceiling amount, the tax may discourage employment, because firms pay no more tax on an employee once his or her wage has reached the ceiling. Thus, a payroll tax may encourage some firms to limit the number of employees and instead impose overtime on their workers, to minimize total labor costs. For this reason, countries such as Singapore sometimes vary the employer's rate of social insurance contributions, lowering the rate during recessions to discourage layoffs and then restoring it when the economy becomes stronger.

Payroll taxes may also discourage employment if, together with the personal income tax, they result in a high effective tax rate on labor. In the Ukraine during the early 1990s, for example, the combined impact of the personal income tax and social insurance levy was a marginal

---

[11] See, for example, Brittain, J. (1971), "Incidence of Social Security Payroll Taxes," *American Economic Review*, vol. 61, pp. 110–125, http://profluming.com/Article/UploadFiles/201008/2010081807331083.pdf.

[12] See, for example, Sendlhofer, R. (2001), "Incidence of Social Security Contributions and Taxes, Evidence from Austria," Institute of Public Economics, University of Innsbruck, Discussion paper 2001/1, http://homepage.uibk.ac.at/c40414/fiwidp200101.pdf.

[13] In Turkey during the 1980s, for example, compliance at smaller firms was reputed to be low, making the tax in effect a tax on the payrolls of government agencies and a few large private companies.

tax rate on labor exceeding 50%. For firms seeking unusually qualified employees, the resulting high marginal rate meant that gross wages had to be very high to yield a particular level of after-tax income. Similarly, in the United States, highly paid independent contractors, who are liable for both the employer's and employee's shares of Social Security, can face a marginal tax rate of more than 50%: up to 37% from the federal income tax, 11.7% from the Social Security tax (after taking into account deductions from taxable income),[14] plus as much as 6.5% or more from state and local income taxes. (The net rate is 6.5% if the combined marginal rate for state and local income is 10% and the income tax payments are fully deductible; as of 2019, only the first US$10,000 of state and local taxes are deductible on the federal income tax.)

6.5.4. *Taxes on property and other assets*

Property taxes are taxes levied on fixed and movable property, or as sometimes called, real and personal assets. The tax liability typically depends on both the value of the property and the tax rate, although in many jurisdictions the taxable ("assessed") value of the property is set at a level other than the estimated market value.

Because property taxes are levied particularly on fixed property, they are especially useful for local jurisdictions, which have trouble imposing taxes on more mobile bases such as income and profits. Thus, in many countries property taxes are more common at the local or regional level than for central governments. The main exceptions are taxes on estates or inheritances, which represent property transferred at death, and taxes on gifts, which are transfers of property by living donors.

---

[14]Only 92.35% of contractor income is subject to tax. In addition, half the tax is deductible from taxable income. Using a marginal income tax rate of 35%, the effective tax rate can equal 11.66%: $15.3*0.9235*(1 - 0.35*15.35*0.9235/2) = 11.66$.

Probably the main challenge facing property taxes is the accurate valuation of taxable property. Although a few advanced economies maintain extensive records of property valuation, in many countries, governments have difficulty maintaining or estimating current market values for taxed property. With property often assessed well below market value, property tax collections can fall quite short of potential. One response to the problem, implemented in Colombia, has been to ask taxpayers to assess the value of their property but require that taxpayers be willing to sell their property for the assessed valuation, plus a small percentage. In this case, property owners have a strong incentive not to under-assess their property, less they be forced to sell at well below market value.

In 2019 and 2020, several US presidential candidates advocated a new federal wealth tax on very high wealth individuals as a way to raise revenue and reduce wealth inequality. Economists have debated the likely effects of such taxes, in some cases suggesting that higher income, estate, and gift taxes could yield the same results.[15]

6.5.5. *Taxes on general consumption*

Taxes on general consumption are a major revenue source in most countries. Among OECD nations, for example, value-added and other consumption taxes averaged nearly 33% of total revenues in 2016, with value-added taxes alone representing 20%, the third largest source behind personal income and social insurance taxes.[16] Consumption taxes are relatively easy to levy on large firms. In advanced economies, they can also be imposed effectively on smaller firms, including retail establishments.

---

[15] See, for example, Saez, E., and G. Zucman, *op. cit.*; Viard, A. A., "Wealth Taxation: An Overview of the Issues," in *Maintaining the Strength of American Capitalism* (Aspen Institute Economic Strategy Group, 2019), M. S. Kearney and A. Ganz; and E. N. Wolff, eds., "Wealth Taxation in the United States," National Bureau of Economic Research Working Paper No. 26555 (Cambridge, MA: December).

[16] OECD (2019), *op. cit.*, Table 1, reproduced in Table 6.5.

General consumption taxes have four main forms:

- *turnover taxes*, which typically levy a fixed percentage tax on total company sales, applicable to all firms;
- *manufacturers' sales taxes*, which levy a percentage of tax only on the sales of manufacturers;
- *retail sales taxes*, in which a tax of a specified percentage is levied on sales at retail firms; and
- *value-added taxes*, which levy a tax of a specified rate on the difference between revenues and costs (the "value added") of firms at all points in the distribution chain.

Value-added taxes (VATs) represent the most common type of general consumption tax. Retail sales taxes occur mainly in the United States and Canada. Manufacturers' sales taxes were common in India until recently, when most states replaced them with VATs, which in turn were replaced by the central goods and services tax (GST) in July 2017. Few countries today have turnover taxes.

Value-added and retail sales taxes have an advantage over turnover and manufacturers' sales taxes in that they avoid *cascading* — a distortion that can arise when goods are produced and sold through a series of firms, each of which is responsible for a single stage of production and distribution. Figure 6.5 illustrates the issue.

Consider a product involving four separate stages from production to final sale: primary production, manufacturing, wholesaling, and retailing. Suppose that each stage adds US$100 of value, so that, without taxes, the final product would retail for US$400. Now assume that the authorities impose a turnover tax, a retail sales tax, or a value added tax, each levied at 10%.

With a *turnover tax*, sales at each stage of production bear a tax equal to 10% of the sales price. A primary producer, for example, pays a tax of 10%, or US$10, on sales of US$100. If the tax is passed on, a manufacturer buys the unprocessed item for US$110, adds US$100 of value, and sells a manufactured item for US$210, paying a tax of

US$21. A wholesaler buys the manufactured good for US$231, adds US$100 of value through distribution services, and sells it to a retailer for US$331, plus a tax of 10 percent, or US$33.10. The retailer, having paid US$364.10, adds US$100 in marketing value and can sell the good to consumers for US$464.10, on which a further 10 percent tax of US$46.41 is paid. From start to finish, a total of US$110.51 in taxes is collected on a total of US$400 in value added: US$10 from the producer, US$21 from the manufacturer, US$33.10 from the distributor, and US$46.41 from the retailer. Because the process involves four separate firms, the effective tax rate on US$400 in value added is more than 27% (110.51/400). If a single firm undertook all four steps in the operation — primary production, manufacturing, distributing, and retailing — and sold the final good for its value added of US$400 plus tax, the total tax collected would be only US$40 (10% of US$400) and the final price US$440, rather than US$510.51. Thus, the turnover tax encourages the private sector to consolidate the

	Primary producer	Manu-facturer	Whole-saler	Retailer
10% multistage turnover tax				
Sales (excluding tax at current stage)	*$100.00*	$210.00	$331.00	$464.10
Purchases (including tax)	*$0.00*	$110.00	$231.00	$364.10
VA	*$100.00*	$100.00	$100.00	$100.00
Tax	*$10.00*	$21.00	$33.10	$46.41
10% single stage retail sales tax				
Sales (excluding tax at current stage)	*$100.00*	$200.00	$300.00	$400.00
Purchases (including tax)	*$0.00*	$100.00	$200.00	$300.00
VA	*$100.00*	$100.00	$100.00	$100.00
Tax	*$0.00*	$0.00	$0.00	$40.00
10% VAT				
Sales (excluding tax at current stage)	*$100.00*	$210.00	$320.00	$430.00
Purchases (including tax)	*$0.00*	$110.00	$220.00	$330.00
VA	*$100.00*	$100.00	$100.00	$100.00
Tax	*$10.00*	$10.00	$10.00	$10.00

Figure 6.5. Cascading: Comparison of turnover, retail sales, and value added taxes. *Source*: L. Tan.

separate stages of production into single, multi-stage enterprises, which may not be optimal from the perspective of production efficiency.

If instead a 10%, *single-stage retail sales tax* is levied, only US$40 in taxes are collected. The primary producer sells output of US$100 to a manufacturer, who sells the processed item to a wholesaler for US$200, who in turn sells it to a retailer for US$300, who then sells the item to a consumer for US$400 plus a 10% tax, or US$440. In this case, the tax is collected at one time, at the retail stage. Unlike the turnover tax, the retail sales tax avoids the cascading problem and creates no incentive for firms to consolidate production, wholesaling, and retailing.

If a 10% VAT is levied, the total tax collection also equals US$40. However, part of the tax is collected at each stage. As in with the turnover tax, the primary producer sells output for US$100 and pays a tax of US$10. The manufacturer buys the good, paying US$110. However, after adding US$100 in value, the manufacturer pays only US$10 in tax on selling it to a wholesaler, because the tax is levied on *only the value added*, not on the manufacturer's total sales. Thus, the manufacturer can sell the finished item to a wholesaler for US$220 (US$210 plus US$10). The wholesaler, in turn, after adding US$100 in value, again pays only US$10 in tax and sells the good to a retailer for US$330 (US$320 plus US$10). Finally, the retailer, after adding US$100 in value, can sell the item to a consumer for US$440 (US$430 plus US$10). Like the retail sales tax, VAT avoids the cascading problem.

6.5.5.1. Retail sales tax

A retail sales tax is a single-stage tax, imposed at the retail level. The main countries with retail sales taxes are the United States, where 45 states have such taxes, and Canada, where three provinces maintain traditional sales taxes in addition to the federal goods and services (value added) tax.

Retail sales taxes have the advantage of relative simplicity. The tax is levied directly on the value of sales, and governments need only collect revenues from retail establishments. However, sales taxes have several disadvantages:

a. *Exempting services.* Many sales taxes, particularly those in the United States, tax only goods and exempt services. This excludes a tremendous amount of commerce from the tax base. Because services represent a growing share of economic activity in most advanced economies, exempting services means consigning the sales tax to a diminishing share of total consumption.

b. *Hard to impose in many developing countries.* A large share of retail trade in many developing countries takes place in small shops and market stalls. Many retailers are small family firms with limited records. The large number of such establishments and the difficulty of bringing them into the tax net make it hard for many developing countries to introduce retail sales taxes. As a result, most developing and emerging market countries that tax consumption do so using a value-added tax, where most of the revenues can be collected from a more limited number of large manufacturers and wholesalers.

c. *Cascading, exemptions, and the risk of evasion.* Because the entire tax is collected at the retail level, intermediate producers need to be exempted to avoid cascading, i.e., imposing the tax on producers or wholesalers and then having the final good taxed again. Providing exemptions can give rise to evasion, however, since firms may allow favored employees to use the "firm's account" to purchase goods for private use. More generally, having the tax collected at a single stage means that a substantial amount of tax is collected at the time of retail sale. If the tax rate becomes sufficiently high, purchasers may have incentives to try to avoid taxation, using artful schemes or finding ways to collude with retailers.

d. *Difficulty in taxing e-commerce.* Administrative, and sometimes legal, issues make it hard to levy sales taxes on goods sold online. A growing number of states in the United States impose sales taxes on large Internet retailers, and many websites impose sales taxes for purchasers living in states where the retailer has offices or a minimum volume of sales. However, with US states prohibited from taxing goods sold in other states, because of the interstate commerce clause of the US constitution, the growth of Internet sales means that a significant share of commerce escapes sales tax. Indeed, on occasion the US Congress has voted to prohibit levying sales tax on goods purchased from online websites.

6.5.5.2. *Value-added tax*

The VAT is a tax levied at each stage in producing a good or service, from raw material to retail sale. Unlike the turnover tax, a VAT is levied only on the value added at that stage of production. Thus, a VAT avoids the cascading that can arise from turnover taxes. Indeed, because a VAT taxes only the value added at a specific point in the production process, both national and sub-national governments can apply VATs without cascading, as is done in the Canadian province of Quebec.

The VAT is currently the main type of general consumption tax. As of 2019, more than 160 countries had enacted VATs.[17] Every advanced economy except the United States (which has retail sales taxes), and almost all other countries, have VATs. In 2019, VAT rates ranged from 5% in Bahrain, Saudi Arabia, and Canada (federal rate, to which provincial taxes are added) to 27% in Hungary.[18]

Table 6.6 shows the range of VAT rates among OECD countries.

VATs typically are levied on both goods and services, thereby avoiding the exclusion of services in most conventional retail sales taxes. At the same time, they are easily designed to exempt exports,

---

[17]Kagan, J. (2019), "Value-Added Tax — Tax Definition," Investopedia, https://www.investopedia.com/terms/v/valueaddedtax.asp (April).

[18]PriceWaterhouseCoopers (2019), "Value-Added Tax (VAT) Rates," http://taxsummaries.pwc.com/ID/Value-added-tax-(VAT)-rates.

Table 6.6.   VAT rates in OECD countries as of
January 2019.

	Basic rate	Reduced rates
Australia	10.0	0.0
Austria*	20.0	10.0/13.0
Belgium	21.0	0.0/6.0/12.0
Canada*	5.0–15.0	0.0
Chile	19.0	—
Czech Republic	21.0	10.0/15.0
Denmark	25.0	0.0
Estonia	20.0	0.0/9.0
Finland	24.0	0.0/10.0/14.0
France*	20.0	2.1/5.5/10.0
Germany	19.0	7.0
Greece*	24.0	6.0/13.0
Hungary	27.0	5.0/18.0
Iceland	24.0	0.0/11.0
Ireland	23.0	0.0/4.8/9.0/13.5
Israel*	17.0	0.0
Italy	22.0	4.0/5.0/10.0
Japan*	8.0	—
Korea	10.0	0.0
Latvia	21.0	5.0/12.0
Lithuania	21.0	5.9/9.0
Luxembourg	17.0	3.0/8.0/14.0
Mexico*	16.0	0.0
Netherlands	21.0	9.0
New Zealand	15.0	0.0
Norway	25.0	0.0/12.0/15.0
Poland	23.0	5.0/8.0
Portugal*	23.0	6.0/13.0
Slovak Republic	20.0	10.0
Slovenia	22.0	9.5
Spain*	21.0	4.0/10.0
Sweden	25.0	0.0/6.0/12.0
Switzerland	7.7	0.0/2.5/3.7
Turkey	18.0	1.0/8.0
United Kingdom	20.0	0.0/5.0

Source: OECD (2019), "VAT–GST Rates and Trends,"
Table 2.A2.1, available on the Internet.

and most countries provide a rebate or exemption for VAT paid on exported goods. Many countries that have adopted VATs have done so by converting from earlier sales or turnover taxes. Empirical research suggests that the conversion has increased revenues in most countries, particularly in more advanced economies, where the ability to administer and comply with a VAT may be greater.[19]

a. *VAT formats.* VATs are typically imposed in one of three ways: the credit invoice, deduction, and addition approaches.

(1) In the *credit invoice* approach, firms calculate the tax owed on the amount of their sales but claim as a credit against the tax paid on all inputs, using the tax payments shown on all invoices for purchases of inputs. This "credit invoice" method, which most countries use,[20] has the advantage of encouraging firms to seek suppliers who will provide invoices showing the VAT paid. Thus, it encourages compliance, unless firms at every stage of production operate without invoices, i.e., all firms pay in cash.

(2) In the *subtraction approach,* companies calculate the difference between their taxable sales and the cost of most inputs from sales and apply the tax rate to this difference. In this approach, wages are excluded from deductible amounts, since wages are part of the value added. Interest income and expenses, together with certain taxes, are typically also excluded. Japan has applied a variant of this approach, allowing those purchasing goods from small retail shops exempt from VAT to claim the cost of these purchases when figuring their own VAT liabilities.[21] When only the cost of taxable inputs can be excluded in figuring value added, the

---

[19] See Keen, M., and Ben, L. (2007), "Value-Added Tax: Its Causes and Consequences," Working Paper No. 07/183 (Washington: International Monetary Fund, July), p. 27, http://www.imf.org/external/pubs/ft/wp/2007/wp07183.pdf.

[20] See Grinberg, I. (2009), "Where Credit Is Due: Advantages of the Credit-Invoice Method for a Partial Replacement VAT," paper prepared for the American Tax Policy Institute Conference, Washington, DC (February 18–19), Note 2, p. 2, http://www.americantaxpolicyinstitute.org/pdf/VAT/Grinberg.pdf.

[21] See Sunley, E. (2009), "Comments on Itai Grinberg's Paper," p. 2, http://www.americantaxpolicyinstitute.org/pdf/VAT/Sunley.pdf.

subtraction approach yields about the same result as the credit invoice approach. As of 2019, only Japan used this approach.

(3) In the *addition approach*, the firm calculates its value added as the sum of wages plus certain taxes paid, plus owner profits, and applies the tax to that amount. This method effectively calculates tax due in the inverse way as the subtraction approach. As of 2015, no country used the addition approach for its VAT.[22]

b. *Current issues.* Despite its attractiveness, the VAT also raises certain issues.

(1) **Single vs. multiple rates.** As with sales taxes, governments are sometimes tempted to levy VATs at more than one rate, to give preference to certain goods, such as basic foods, arguably to help the poor. As Table 6.5 indicates, in addition to exempting exports, virtually every OECD country provides zero or reduced rates on certain items. Eight countries have at least three separate VAT rates. While multiple rates may make the VAT less regressive, they also complicate its administration and create incentives for taxpayers to classify their goods as qualifying for lower rates. Thus, economists often recommend minimizing the number of rates and adopting a single rate, if politically feasible. For similar reasons, economists recommend being very selective on granting exemptions, to avoid narrowing the tax base and requiring higher rates to obtain the desired revenue yield.

(2) **Taxing small traders.** Because a VAT is relatively complex to administer and comply with, many countries have chosen to exclude small retailers from VAT. This greatly simplifies the work of tax administrators, since imports, plus a small number of large manufacturers, distributors, and retailers, usually provide most of the revenues. In some countries such as Japan, the system has been designed so that the excluded retailers are not disadvantaged by being unable to provide invoices showing VAT payments. The

---

[22] Schenk, A., *et al.* (2015), *Value Added Tax: A Comparative Approach, Second Edition*, Ch. 3, p. 33.

main problem from excluding small retailers arises in countries with high VAT rates and systematic tax avoidance, where the exclusion of small retailers may give them a price advantage over larger stores.

(3) **Rebates and fraud.** The normal practice of granting rebates for exports opens the possibility of fraud, if goods are classified as being exported when, in fact, they are sold and consumer domestically. However, in the case of one country (Ukraine), the opposite problem has sometimes occurred: a delay in processing and sending valid rebates to exporters, as a result of administrative problems. Similarly, the credit invoice approach to the VAT creates incentives for firms to claim rebates for taxes not paid, although auditing can presumably identify the fraud. More interesting is the case of "missing trader" fraud, where a firm invoices, but fails to pay, VAT on imported goods, and a firm further down the line gets to claim a rebate for this VAT payment when it exports the goods that use the imported items. This situation can arise when a firm need only pay VAT on imports at the time of its regular VAT filing, rather than at the point of importation.[23]

6.5.6. *Excise taxes*

Excise taxes are consumption taxes on specific goods. Along with import duties, excise taxes are among the oldest of all government levies. In ancient times, governments often imposed excises on goods such as salt, for which the demand was not especially sensitive to changes in price. Today, excise taxes are typically levied on alcoholic beverages, tobacco products, and petroleum, for which the price elasticity of demand is relatively low, at least in the short run. Many countries also impose excises on hotel occupancy and air tickets, and some impose excises on expensive vehicles and other luxury goods.

---

[23]For details on this "carousel" operation, see Keen, M., and S. Smith, "VAT Fraud and Evasion: What Do We Know, and What Can Be Done?" Working Paper No. 07/31 (Washington: International Monetary Fund, February), pp. 13–15, 18, http://www.imf.org/external/pubs/ft/wp/2007/wp0731.pdf.

Excise taxes are generally imposed at the retail level. Like more general retail sales taxes, excises are relatively easy to administer. In addition, by imposing them on luxuries and goods with negative externalities, such as alcohol and tobacco products, excises may be politically more palatable than income taxes or more general consumption levies. Because excises are often imposed at a high rate — taxes of 50% or more on alcohol and cigarettes are not unusual — imposing excise taxes often creates strong incentives for tax evasion. Literature is filled with stories of people producing "moonshine" — homemade gin, whiskey, and brandy — to escape paying alcohol taxes. Similarly, high-tax jurisdictions often uncover elaborate schemes to smuggle cigarettes or alcoholic beverages into a country to avoid paying the necessary excises. Even ordinary consumers can become involved if excises make the price of these products across the border substantially less. As noted earlier, Canada, for example, has periodically had difficulty with large numbers of citizens crossing the border into the United States to purchase less expensive cigarettes.

Excise taxes typically are either *specific*, meaning that a flat fee is imposed on each unit of the taxed item, or *ad valorem*, in which case the tax is levied as a percentage of the price. With *ad valorem* rates, revenues rise with the price of the product. *Ad valorem* rates can thus keep up better with inflation. The one risk with *ad valorem* taxes is that revenues will be suppressed if traders fraudulently undervalue the product when declaring their tax liability. For this reason, some countries establish excises at an *ad valorem* rate, but with a minimum amount per unit. In addition, a few countries set their excises using a combination of specific and *ad valorem* rates. For example, in September 2005, Thailand set its excise on whiskey and similar alcoholic beverages at a high level of 40% to 50% of the pre-tax price or 400 baht per liter of alcohol content.[24]

Despite their popularity, excise taxes on products other than alcohol, tobacco, and petroleum tend to generate relatively little

---

[24] *The Nation* (2005), "Excise Tax Raised for Hard Liquor" (September 7), http://www.phuket-info.com/forums/news-articles/9077-nation-excise-tax-raised-hard-liquor.html.

revenue. Thus, governments may not always find them a productive use of scare administrative resources. Moreover, to maximize revenue yields, the taxes need to be imposed on goods with relatively little price sensitivity, and for which the cost of administration is low. This argues for limiting these other excises to goods on which the tax can be easily collected (such as airport service charges) and for which levying a modest excise, such as on air tickets, will not significantly affect the volume sold. In addition, to avoid giving incentives to imported items, excises should apply equally to domestic and imported goods, particularly in an environment of declining import duties.

6.5.7. Taxes on international trade

Taxes on international trade, like excises, are among the oldest kinds of tax instruments. The ability of governments to stop and search goods entering or leaving their borders makes the administration of import and export duties relatively straightforward, and many developing countries and small island economies rely heavily on taxing international trade to finance government activity. The importance of these taxes has also made customs subject to bribery, and many countries have had great difficulty with "corruption at the port."

Governments have learned that export duties discourage exports, so most countries avoid them, except in the form of "windfall" taxes, which tax the amount by which the price of an exported item such as crude oil or unprocessed minerals exceeds a standard reference price. Thus, most taxes on international trade involve imports. However, import duties also have adverse effects on welfare. They discourage trade, reduce competition for domestically produced goods, and diminish consumption opportunities for consumers. Thus, economists typically advise countries to minimize the use of import duties and keep rates relatively low and simple, with at most a very few rates of duty, each of which applies to a broad category of goods.

As with excises, import duties raise the maximum revenue when levied on goods with relatively low price elasticity of demand, for example, goods for which domestic substitutes are unavailable or limited in supply. In addition, countries must be aware of World Trade Organization (WTO) rules, which typically restrict the ability of countries that belong to the WTO to increase rates of duty. Indeed, the trend over time has been for countries to reduce their reliance on import duties, as a result of bilateral and global trade agreements. Thus, countries that maintain high import duties may want to plan for a transition to relying more on other taxes, such as an increase in VAT rates to accompany a reduction in duty rates.

6.5.8. Minimum taxes and presumptive levies

Minimum taxes are levies designed to secure payment from small taxpayers, often small proprietors with poor records or limited ability to file tax returns. Small firms typically generate little revenue individually but require major investments of resources from tax authorities to collect revenue. Thus, it can be worthwhile to exempt such establishments from complex levies like the VAT, and many countries do so for firms whose annual revenues fall below a stipulated amount. To ensure that these firms contribute something to government revenues and avoid giving them a financial advantage over larger firms, countries can impose much simpler levies, such as a quarterly or annual license fee for the right to operate a business. Fees such as this require a minimum of paperwork, and the authorities can easily check whether someone has paid by verifying that the proprietor has a current and valid license.

Presumptive levies offer another way for countries to raise revenue from hard-to-tax proprietors. With a presumptive levy, the tax authority uses readily available information to estimate the revenue that an establishment could be expected to earn during a period (usually a year) and then imposes a small tax on the estimated gross receipts. In so doing, the authorities eliminate the need for the taxpayer to report income, expenses, and profit. Instead, the authorities simply submit a bill based on the presumed revenues of the firm.[25]

The following example illustrates how a presumptive levy could work in the agricultural sector. Suppose a farmer owns and operates a small farm for growing wheat. The tax authorities could determine the average wheat yields for farms in that vicinity and, knowing the size of the farm, estimate how much wheat could be harvested during a normal crop year. The authorities would also have access to farm prices and could use that information to estimate the value realized from the crop. Thus, if a farmer owns 5 hectares of land, raises 40 bushels of wheat per hectare, and wheat sells at 200 rupees per bushel, the authorities could presume that the farmer realized 40,000 rupees from farming activities. The presumptive levy could then impose a tax, say, of 3%, which would yield a tax liability of 1,200 rupees.

One drawback with the presumptive levy is that is does not distinguish between high- and low-cost operators. A farmer who works the land using only family labor, presumably at minimal cost, pays the same tax as another farmer who hires outside labor. In the previous example, a farmer who incurs expenses of 10,000 rupees pays a tax of 120 rupees on implicit profits of 30,000 rupees, or an effective profit tax rate of 4%. Another farmer with costs of 30,000 rupees would pay the same 120 rupees in tax on implicit profits of only 10,000 rupees, an effective profit tax rate of 12%. Thus, a presumptive levy can impose very different effective tax rates on enterprise profits, a disadvantage from the standpoint of fairness (horizontal equity).

To address this problem, countries can offer small proprietors the option of submitting a profit tax return, with data on revenues, costs,

---

[25]This type of presumptive taxation differs from its use in some countries, such as Pakistan, which have used presumptive taxation more widely as an alternative to formal profit or income taxation. For details on presumptive taxation in Pakistan, see Alm, J. and M. Ahmad Khan (2008), "Assessing Enterprise Taxation and the Investment Climate in Pakistan," International Studies Program, Working Paper No. 08-10 (Atlanta: Georgia State University), pp. 19–21, http://aysps.gsu.edu/isp/files/ispwp0810(2).pdf.

and profits, as an alternative to paying the presumptive tax. Doing so would give small firms an incentive to begin compiling the type of information needed for regular corporate filing. It would also help in bringing these enterprises into the formal tax system.

6.5.9. *User fees*

User fees are charges that governments impose for the use of certain public services. User fees include tolls for highways, bridges, and tunnels; charges for admission to publicly owned parks and museums; and payments for government publications. Governments impose these charges to help defer the costs of these services. The justification is an application of the "fairness" criterion called the *benefit principle:* those who benefit significantly from a government service should pay for it, so long as the charge does not create serious, adverse consequences. From this perspective, imposing modest tolls for highway use can help defer the cost of highway construction. However, governments should avoid imposing tuition or other substantial charges for primary and secondary education, since these could lessen the ability of children from low-income families to attend primary or secondary school.[26]

Besides helping to fund certain government services, user fees can have other advantages. Highway tolls, for example, can reduce congestion, particularly if tolls can vary with the time of day and day of the week. As noted in Chapter One, Singapore uses such tolls to regulate traffic in congested areas, helping reduce traffic during busy periods by setting tolls relatively high and then reducing them once peak periods have passed. When setting fees, governments should be aware of the potential problems arising from cross-subsidization. For example, charging all customers a flat fee for trash service may provide a huge subsidy to large firms that provide substantially more refuse.

---

[26]An interesting issue that has arisen in some developing countries is whether localities should be able to impose charges for books or school uniforms. Doing so could reduce enrollment among low-income children. However, if central governments cannot provide enough funds to cover all the costs of public education, local school districts may feel compelled to impose such charges to ensure the availability of enough uniforms or teaching materials.

A fee based on the quantity of refuse will better match costs to use and convey more accurately the cost of trash services to different users.

6.6. Other Tax Policy Issues

Revenue policy also raises special issues that deserve mention. These include tax expenditures, the challenge of taxing the financial sector, tax treaties and harmonization, and the impact of globalization on tax policy.

6.6.1. *Tax expenditures*

As mentioned earlier, *tax expenditures* are special benefits provided to individuals, households, or firms through the tax code, rather than legislated outlays. Tax expenditures are equivalent to budgetary expenditures, in that they benefit specific firms or groups of people and reduce the government's overall budget balance. Unlike expenditures, they do not appear in the official government budget. Instead, they reduce revenue from what it would otherwise be.

Tax expenditures can take many forms. They include the exclusion, or exemption of income or receipts from taxable income; the deduction of certain expenses from taxable income or profit; the deferral of tax liability until future periods; granting a credit against tax liability for incurring certain expenses; and taxing certain income at preferential rates.[27] All these measures have the effect of reducing tax liability as a result of incurring certain expenditures or receiving certain types of income. They also complicate the tax law and cause it to deviate from what might be considered a relatively "clean" tax code.

---

[27]This definition closely follows that in section 3(3) of the U.S. Congressional Budget and Impoundment Control Act of 1974 (Pub. Law 93-334), which defines tax expenditures as "revenue losses attributable to provisions of the Federal tax laws which allow a special exclusion, exemption, or deduction from gross income or which provide a special credit, a preferential rate of tax, or a deferral of tax liability."

Tax expenditures are hard to quantify, monitor, and control. The various deductions, exemptions, exclusions, deferrals, credits, and preferential rates are usually permanent elements of the tax code. Unless created with "sunset" provisions (expiration dates), they do not require reauthorization by the legislature. In addition, the revenue losses are open ended, in that they turn only on the extent to which taxpayers receive preferential income or incur authorized expenditures and make use of the tax provisions. Thus, tax expenditures differ in many ways from formal expenditures, which usually require explicit authorization and whose amounts the legislature can control, with the exception of entitlement programs such as state-provided pensions.

Nevertheless, tax expenditures can be very costly. In the United States, the Joint Committee on Taxation annually publishes estimates of the revenues the US federal government loses from tax expenditures. The report issued in October 2018 identified hundreds of tax expenditures in the US individual income and corporate income taxes and estimated the revenues lost from each, along with estimates of the distribution of revenue losses for the individual income tax by taxpayer income. Although aggregating the various revenue losses is complex, these tax expenditures clearly reduce US federal revenues by many hundreds of billions of US dollars.[28] The Joint Committee on Taxation estimated that tax expenditures as a whole cost the US federal government more than US$1.3 trillion dollars in 2018, equivalent to almost 80% of federal income tax revenue that year.[29] Other countries have also reported estimates of the cost of their tax expenditures. In 2010, for example, Poland published its first report on

---

[28] Joint Committee on Taxation (2018), "Estimates of Federal Tax Expenditures for Fiscal Years 2018–2022" (Washington: U.S. Government Printing Office, October), JCX-81-18, https://www.jct.gov/publications.html?func=startdown&id=5148.

[29] Gale, W. (2019), *Fiscal Therapy*, (New York: Oxford University Press), p. 210, citing Joint Committee on Taxation (2018), "Estimates of Federal Tax Expenditures for Fiscal Years 2017–2021," JCX-34-18 (Washington: U.S. Government Printing Office, May), https://www.jct.gov/publications.html?func=startdown&id=5095.

tax expenditures, estimating total revenue losses from tax expenditures at 4.9% of GDP.[30]

Because of their cost, limited visibility, and problems with controllability, economists and public finance authorities have frequently proposed that various tax expenditures be trimmed or eliminated. In the United States, the US Congressional Budget Office has listed cutbacks in a number of tax expenditures as measures to consider in its periodic reports on options to reduce the US federal budget deficit.[31] In addition, during 2010 several commissions on options to reduce the long-term federal budget deficit proposed cutbacks in tax expenditures. The President's Commission on Fiscal Responsibility and Reform suggested that cuts in tax expenditures, offset partly by lower tax rates, provide about 19% of the savings in its proposed US$4.1 trillion in budget cuts during the period 2011–2020.[32] The Bipartisan Policy Center's Debt Commission Task Force recommended that 35–38% of all budget savings come from removing tax expenditures and proposed eliminating virtually all such provisions in the US individual income and corporate income taxes, except for a small set of provisions listed in an appendix.[33]

6.6.2. *Taxing financial transactions*

Many countries impose stamp duties and other taxes on real estate transactions, such as the recording of deeds following the sale of housing or buildings. In addition, some nations have periodically taxed

---

[30]See Republic of Poland, Ministry of Finance (2010), *Tax Expenditures in Poland* (Warsaw: November), p. 5, http://www.mofnet.gov.pl/_files_/english/fiscal_system/tax/report_tax_expenditures_in_poland_english_version.pdf.

[31]For early examples, see U.S. Congressional Budget Office (1982), *Reducing the Federal Budget: Strategies and Examples, Fiscal Years 1982–1986* (Washington: U.S. Government Printing Office), http://www.cbo.gov/doc.cfm?index=11171.

[32]Commission on Fiscal Responsibility and Reform (2010), *Moment of Truth* (Washington), Figure 17, p. 65, http://www.fiscalcommission.gov/sites/fiscalcommission.gov/files/documents/TheMomentofTruth12_1_2010.pdf.

[33]See Bipartisan Policy Center, Debt Reduction Task Force (2010), *Restoring America's Future* (Washington), pp. 15 and 130, http://www.bipartisanpolicy.org/sites/default/files/FINAL{\%}20DRTF{\%}20REPORT{\%}2011.16.10.pdf.

financial transactions, such as sales and purchases of equity (stock) or the use of bank checks. Although in recent years countries have been phasing out the use of taxes on securities transactions, the financial crisis of 2007–2009 revived interest in these taxes as a way of funding future bank recapitalizations and discouraging financial speculation that could lead to new crises. The IMF, for example, has explored this issue in response to a request from the G20 countries.[34]

Because of the volume of financial transactions, financial sector taxes have appeared to some countries as a potential source of substantial revenue. Although taxes on securities transactions typically raised less than 0.2% of GDP in several European countries that eliminated then since 1990, these taxes have generated 0.2–0.7% of GDP in countries such as South Africa, South Korea, Switzerland, and the UK since 2001. Hong Kong SAR and Taiwan, P.O.C. have raised substantially more, 0.8–2% of GDP, since 2007, the amounts varying with the financial cycle. Bank transactions taxes have also been attractive, because large financial institutions can easily withhold and remit these levies from customers' accounts. In Latin America, taxes imposed at relatively low rates (0.15–1.5%) raised 0.3–1.9% of GDP in revenues during 2009.[35]

Although these taxes have considerable appeal, the experience of bank transactions taxes shows that revenues from these levies can decline over time, as customers shift to using cash payments and other activities to avoid taxation. In addition, banks collecting transactions taxes typically impose higher interest spreads, discouraging investment and making government borrowing more expensive. The resulting disintermediation reduces saving and impedes economic growth. In several Latin American countries, bank transactions taxes were estimated to reduce financial transactions through the banking system by

---

[34] See Claessens, S. *et al.*, eds. (2010), *Financial Sector Taxation — The IMF's Report to the G-20 and Background Material* (Washington: September), http://www.imf.org/external/np/seminars/eng/2010/paris/pdf/090110.pdf.

[35] Matheson, T. (2010), "Taxing Financial Transactions: Issues and Evidence," in Claessens, *op. cit.*, Ch. 8, pp. 151–152.

more than 25%. In addition, because fees are paid on each financial transaction, these levies have a cascading effect, much like turnover taxes.[36] As a result, the IMF and many public finance economists have typically discouraged countries from taxing bank transactions.

Although securities transactions often involve much larger sums of money and can therefore raise significant revenue from very small rates of tax (e.g., 0.01–0.5%), research indicates that even small taxes on securities transactions can make many short-term trades unprofitable, lower share prices, and reduce trading volume. One reason is that technological improvements and the elimination of fixed-price commissions have significantly reduced trading margins in many markets. Thus, even small securities taxes could significantly increase effective spreads between bid and asked rates on stocks, bonds, and foreign exchange, thereby reducing the efficiency of financial markets.

Because of these many drawbacks, IMF staff economists suggest that countries consider alternatives to financial transactions taxes that create fewer distortions as a way of addressing financial sector difficulties. Options could include imposing a financial stability contribution levy on financial institutions' balance sheet debt (net of equity and deposits), possibly scaled to impose higher charges on larger institutions whose failure would pose greater systemic risks to the economy; extending the VAT to at least some financial sector transactions; and imposing a financial activities tax based on the value added (e.g., compensation and profits) at financial institutions.[37]

6.6.3. *Tax treaties and harmonization*

Most countries enter into tax treaties with other nations, as a way of securing treatment comparable to that of other countries regarding the taxation of imports and other international transactions of their

---

[36] *Ibid.*

[37] IMF Staff, "A Fair and Substantial Contribution by the Financial Sector," in Claessens *et al.* eds., (2010), *op. cit.*, p. 21, and Matheson (2010), *op. cit.*, pp. 167–168.

citizens and firms. Tax treaties typically include provisions against double taxation, so that citizens and firms engaging in international commerce pay tax only once on their incomes and other transactions. In addition, countries often enter into bilateral and multilateral trade agreements, to reduce restrictions and tariffs on their exports.

Besides these treaties, many countries enter into agreements to harmonize taxes on sales, value added, and corporate profits. Tax harmonization agreements aim to create common rules for assessing tax liability among member states or countries. In Canada, for example, harmonization has led several provinces to make their provincial sales taxes consistent with the federal goods and services tax, effectively converting the provincial taxes into VATs to avoid cascading. Harmonization can also lead to more uniform tax rates. When harmonization in Canada first took effect, in 1996, the combined federal and sales tax rates in these provinces moved to 15% and later declined to 14% and then 13%, when the federal GST rate was reduced. One of the provinces later increased its provincial rate, returning the combined (harmonized) rate to 15%. Tax harmonization can also lead to more uniform rates of tax among signatories to an agreement. For example, the European Union requires that all member countries maintain VATs with a minimum general rate of at least 15%.[38]

An interesting application of tax harmonization involves the use of treaties to address troublesome aspects of tax competition. Many countries, for example, maintain tax holidays as a way of promoting foreign investment because other countries offer similar benefits, despite their relative inefficiency. Tax treaties can provide a way for countries to agree mutually to eliminate such measures. Similarly, G20 countries have agreed on a common definition and classification of tax havens, in an effort to encourage countries to adopt an "internationally agreed tax standard" that includes "exchange of information on request

---

[38] Stults, T. (2004), "Tax Harmonization versus Tax Competition: A Review of the Literature," entry to the 2004 Moffatt Prize in Economics, http://economics.about.com/cs/moffattentries/a/harmonization.htm.

in all tax matters for the administration and enforcement of domestic tax law without regard to a domestic tax interest requirement or bank secrecy for tax purposes. It also provides for extensive safeguards to protect the confidentiality of the information exchanged."[39] As a result of this effort, several countries that had initially been sanctioned as tax havens agreed to adjust their policies on exchanging information, in order to meet the OECD standard.[40]

6.6.4. *Implications of globalization for tax policy*

Globalization — the increasing connectivity and interdependence of people, firms, and economies across international boundaries — has had important implications for tax policy. The greater willingness of firms to operate outside their home countries has encouraged countries to compete more vigorously for new investment. As noted earlier, this has led many countries to reduce their corporate tax rates. To a lesser extent, tax competition has also encouraged countries to review their personal income taxes, with a view toward attracting high-income individuals. Globalization and the setting up of plants in different countries to assemble products have also created more opportunities for firms to use transfer pricing to minimize tax liabilities, through the strategic allocation of costs worldwide. This trend may also encourage countries to reduce corporate tax rates, possibly triggering a "race to the bottom" as jurisdictions compete to retain firms and investment. Together, these developments have encouraged jurisdictions to rely less on direct taxes and more on indirect taxes, such as the VAT.

However, globalization also poses risks for value-added and retail sales taxes. The growth in commerce across national and international boundaries, as a result of the Internet, has created difficulties for tax authorities. In some countries, legal or constitutional provisions limit

---

[39] OECD (2009), "Following G20 OECD delivers on tax pledge," http://www.oecd.org/document/57/0,3343,en_2649_34487_42496569_1_1_1_1,00.html.
[40] For more information on the OECD/G20 project to address base erosion and profit shifting, see OECD (2020), "International Collaboration to End Tax Avoidance," https://www.oecd.org/tax/beps/.

the ability of state or provincial authorities to impose sales or VATs on goods purchased from other states or provinces. In the United States, for example, states may only tax goods sold by firms that have a presence within their borders or sufficient sales into the state. Thus, firms can only be required to charge sales tax on Internet sales to customers from states in which they have a minimum amount of sales to the state, with the amount varying by state.[41] As regards purchases by Internet from overseas locations, countries must use their customs facilities to impose VAT or sales tax. Although this may be straightforward for traditional products, it will be harder for purchases of downloadable items, such as electronic books and music.[42]

As a result of these and other developments, globalization may well reduce tax revenues in a number of jurisdictions, both national and sub-national. This, in turn, will put downward pressure on government expenditure unless governments can find substitute revenue sources or improve collections from the remaining sources through better tax administration.

6.6.5. Tax policy and fiscal federalism

Although Chapter Ten discusses this matter at greater length, it is worth noting that fiscal federalism — using multiple levels of government to deliver public services — has implications for revenue policy. Each level of government needs sufficient resources to finance the activities it undertakes, particularly if, as is common for sub-national governments in many countries, fiscal rules limit or prohibit borrowing. Every jurisdiction thus needs its own revenue sources, supplemented in the case of sub-national governments by transfers from higher level

---

[41]For further information, see National Conference of State Legislatures (2020), "Remote Sales Tax Collection," https://www.ncsl.org/reserach/fiscal-policy/e-fairness-legislation-overview.aspx (March).

[42]For a discussion of these and other tax challenges arising from globalization, see Tanzi, V. (2000), "Globalization, Technological Developments, and Fiscal Termites," Working Paper No. 00/181 (Washington: International Monetary Fund, November), http://www.imf.org/external/pubs/ft/wp/2000/.pdf.

governments when local tax bases are insufficient to finance locally provided public services.

Because some tax bases are more mobile than others, governments at different levels need to rely on bases most appropriate for their circumstances. Central governments can best tap relatively mobile tax bases, such as personal and corporate income, and impose taxes such as import duties, which involve the passage of goods across national borders. State and provincial governments can draw on tax bases that are relatively immobile at the state or provincial level. These will likely include sales, value-added, and excise taxes. Personal and, to a lesser extent, corporate income may also be relatively immobile, unless major employment centers are located near borders and commuting to work from another state or province is relatively simple. In this case, the jurisdiction of residence, rather than employment, will probably be best able to levy a personal income tax. Localities will most likely need to rely on the least mobile tax bases. Thus, property taxes, business licenses, and fees for local services are likely to provide most of the revenue for local governments.

6.7. Tax Administration

Although this chapter focuses on revenue policy, it is important to say something about tax administration. Revenue policy creates the structure of a government's tax system. However, the administrative system produces the revenues on which government activities rely. Collections may fall far short of potential as a result of evasion, poor record keeping, weak enforcement, and a lack of current payment practices. Thus, countries need effective tax administrative systems to achieve their revenue objectives. Reforms in tax administration can also be a central component of improving revenue performance, as the experience of Indonesia since 2001 demonstrates.[43]

---

[43] See Brondolo, J. *et al.* (2008), "Tax Administration Reform and Fiscal Adjustment: The Case of Indonesia (2001–07)," Working Paper No. 08/129 (Washington: International Monetary Fund), http://www.imf.org/external/pubs/ft/wp/2008/wp08129.pdf.

6.7.1. *Basic considerations*

Effective tax administration requires certain elements.

1. *Simplicity.* Tax laws inevitably have some complexity. However, the simpler is the underlying tax — fewer rate categories, fewer exemptions, fewer special provisions — the easier it will be for administrators to enforce the law. Simpler laws also facilitate compliance, allowing administrators to focus on more challenging enforcement cases.

2. *Resource needs.* An effective tax administration requires sufficient staff and physical resources. The authorities need skilled, dedicated, honest, and knowledgeable employees. The employees, in turn, need appropriate equipment and facilities to perform their responsibilities. This includes adequate computers and telecommunications equipment. The tax authority also needs an effective Internet presence and the ability to post and update important information quickly. In addition, the tax authority requires sufficient judicial support. Whether in special tax courts or in the general justice system, tax administrators should be able to bring cases and have them adjudicated promptly and impartially. In addition, laws should be written that grant tax administrators the necessary legal powers to support their work, without having to engage in extra-legal and arguably improper means.

3. *Structure needs.* Effective tax administration also requires a supportive cultural and legal context. Taxpayers and the authorities need to have common accounting traditions, whether they be "Generally Accepted Accounting Practices" (GAAP) or other widely recognized systems. Taxpayers must also have a tradition of maintaining accurate written records, including bank records, and the authorities need to be able to access these records to verify the information provided on tax returns and the underlying financial transactions. Perhaps most important, effective tax administration requires a culture of compliance by taxpayers. Even with contemporary computers, tax

authorities cannot expect to review and audit every taxpayer and every tax return in detail. However, effective systems for identifying taxpayers — for example, requiring that every taxpaying unit have a unique and verifiable identification number — and tools such as tax withholding can contribute importantly to the overall structure of tax administration.

4. *Establishing a framework that promotes compliance.* The integrity of a tax system relies ultimately on the willingness of most taxpayers to comply with the law. However, certain elements can establish a framework that promotes compliance. These elements include the following:

- relatively simple and stable tax laws;
- withholding and estimated payments for major taxes (see below);
- an effective taxpayer information and education service, including the timely dissemination of tax information through the Internet and other readily accessible means;
- procedures that create a perceptible likelihood that non-compliance will be detected;
- appropriate penalties and interest charges; and
- access to a fair and timely appeals system.

In many countries, large numbers of taxpayers remain to be registered. In others, ignorance of legal requirements is a major problem. Thus, tax authorities need to invest significant resources in taxpayer education, since a large base of knowledgeable taxpayers is essential for an effective tax system.

6.7.2. Administrative tools

Certain administrative tools have proved to be valuable components of an effective tax administration.

1. *Withholding at source.* Experience has shown that withholding tax at the time wages, salaries, and other payments are received can be an extremely effective way of securing secure compliance with the law. For the United States, as noted earlier, research shows that misreporting on wage and salary income, where tax is typically withheld at source, is only about 1%, compared to an estimated 4.5% of misreporting for items such as interest earnings, for which extensive information is sent to the Internal Revenue Service but tax is not withheld at source.[44] For this reason, most countries withhold income and social insurance taxes on wages and salaries at source, and many also withhold tax on interest and dividend payments.

2. *Estimated tax payments.* For categories of income and receipts on which tax is not withheld, most countries require periodic payments of estimated tax toward the eventual tax liability during the year. These estimated payments, which are sometimes called "progress payments," ensure that taxpayers remain roughly current on their tax liabilities. This reduces collection obligations at the end of the year and can preserve the real value of tax receipts in countries with noticeable rates of inflation, because inflation erodes the real value of taxes paid on income received earlier. Depending on the country and type of income, estimated tax payments are required quarterly or monthly and are based on the taxpayer's estimates of annual taxable income or profits. Appropriate penalties and interest for substantial underreporting of income can help keep estimated tax payments from falling significantly behind actual liabilities.

3. *Penalties and asset seizures.* Tax administrators need sanctions to enforce compliance with the tax laws. These include a variety of penalties ranging from interest and fines to the ability to seize taxpayer assets in satisfaction of legal judgments. Penalties should be scaled in

---

[44] OECD, Forum on Tax Administration, Compliance Sub-Group (2009), "Information Note — Withholding & Information Reporting Regimes for Small/Medium-Sized Businesses & Self-Employed Taxpayers," (Paris: August), Box 1, p. 13, information drawn from U.S. Internal Revenue Service, *Reducing the Federal Tax Gap — A Report on Improving Voluntary Compliance, IRS (08/ 2007)*, http://www.oecd.org/dataoecd/49/16/43728416.pdf.

accordance with the severity of noncompliance. The smallest penalties should be for lateness, with greater penalties for underreporting. The largest penalties should apply to the most serious problems: non-reporting and fraud.

4. *Bounties for information*. Besides penalties, tax authorities can benefit from offering bounties (rewards) for information leading to the apprehension of tax violators. These rewards can provide incentives for private parties to inform the tax authorities of alleged illegality. Bounty programs should include provisions to keep so-called "whistle-blowers" from unjustly accusing or harassing others. In the United States, the Tax Relief and Health Care Act of 2006 established bounties of 15–30% of the ultimate recovery of tax claims totaling US$2 million or more, when certain conditions are satisfied.[45]

5. *Concentrating resources on taxpayers who generate the most revenues*. Revenue authorities will have the greatest success if they focus their resources on the taxpayers most likely to provide substantial revenue. In some developing and emerging market countries, 1% of the taxpaying units — in some cases, fewer than 1,000 firms and individuals — provide 70% or more of total revenues. In the United States, the top 1% of individual income tax filers paid about 37% of all individual income taxes in 2016, and the top half paid 97%.[46]

Many countries have established special administrative units for large taxpayers. In addition, audit resources can be stratified, so that audits focus on the highest income taxpayers and the largest firms. At the same time, all taxpayers should face a genuine possibility of being audited. Where large numbers of very small taxpayers make auditing infeasible, the authorities may want to exempt small taxpayers from

---

[45]For details, see Loevy and Loevy (2007), "Tax Fraud," http://www.loevy.com/Whistleblower-Claims/Tax-Fraud.shtml.

[46]Bellafiore, R. (2018), "Summary of the Latest Federal Income Tax Data, 2018 Update," Tax Foundation, Fiscal Fact No. 622 (Washington: November), https://files.tax foundation.org/20181113134559/Summary-of-the-Latest-Federal-Income-Tax-Data-2018-Update-FF-622.pdf.

tax liability, as many countries do with small firms under the value-added tax. Another option is to use presumptive taxation, where audit requirements are smaller. Presumptive taxation can also provide a useful auditing device. For example, tax authorities are said to have checked doctors' incomes by (1) using the number of chairs in the waiting room, the average length of a consultation, and the number of days the office is open to estimate the number of patient visits in a period and then multiplying this figure by (2) the average cost of a visit.

6.7.3. Trends in tax administration

Two trends have characterized tax administration during the past two decades. One involves integrating most domestic tax collections into a single administration, while keeping customs administration separate. The other has been a move away from having separate units for different types of taxes and instead organizing administration around the size of the taxpaying unit. Increasingly, countries are developing separate units for large, medium, and small taxpayers, generally starting with the creation of a large taxpayer unit (LTU). LTUs are expected to reduce non-compliance among large taxpayers while providing them with better service. LTUs can also serve as pilot organizations to introduce major administrative changes, such as self-assessment procedures in countries where these have not traditionally been used. In addition, LTUs can serve to spearhead major administrative initiatives, such as efforts to establish a VAT or reforms in existing taxes. In some countries, creating an LTU can signal to the taxpaying community the government's commitment to enforcing the tax laws.

6.7.4. Dealing with tax evasion

Governments have traditionally addressed tax evasion using a combination of audits, investigations, and penalties. Some countries even have special tax police, such as the Financial Guard in Italy and Romania. However, experience shows that a more effective approach involves combining these resources with policy and administrative changes that reduce the incentives for tax evasion. Such changes can include broadening the tax base to allow lower tax rates, reducing exemptions, and simplifying compliance. Reducing collection lags and requiring estimated payments can also help.

Penalties and sanctions remain an important part of the arsenal that authorities can use to enforce compliance. However, tax authorities should be careful about implementing tax amnesties. Although amnesties can generate revenue, they may also lead taxpayers to anticipate future amnesties, thereby undermining the incentive to comply with tax laws. Thus, many tax experts do not recommend them.

6.8. Summary

Revenue policy represents a critical component of a government's fiscal activities. Although revenue levels, as a percentage of GDP, and the composition of revenue vary considerably across countries, generating enough revenue to meet expenditure needs with limited recourse to debt finance remains an objective toward which all governments strive. In developing revenue policy, governments should keep in mind four key principles for an effective revenue system: revenue adequacy, economic efficiency, fairness, and administrative simplicity. Besides generating sufficient revenues, revenue systems should do so with a minimum of interference with economic decision-making, in a way that taxpayers perceive as equitable, and in a manner that is simple to administer and promotes compliance. Occasionally, these objectives will conflict, so governments must seek an appropriate balance among them — for example, knowing when attempts at fairness may create heavy burdens on compliance and administration.

Governments relay on a variety of different revenue sources. Among these, taxes on household and company income and profits and taxes on general consumption, in particular VATs, have proved to be strong revenue generators. Most countries also rely, to a lesser extent, on import duties, excise taxes, non-tax revenues such as user fees and charges, and property taxes, the latter being especially important for local governments. Many also use payroll taxes or mandatory contributions to fund social insurance programs. Each of these revenue sources raise specific issues regarding implementation and administration. Some revenue sources appear better suited for certain levels of government than others. As a general rule, national governments can best tap the most mobile revenue bases, such as taxes on income and profits, as well as customs duties. Some also have VATs. Many state and provincial governments have had success with value added, sales, and excise taxes. Many also rely on income and profits taxes. Local governments need to rely on the least mobile revenue bases, such as property taxes, license fees, and charges for public services.

Governments must keep in mind certain issues when designing revenue systems. These include the risks associated with tax expenditures, i.e., using the tax code to provide special allowances, exemptions, or exclusions that are equivalent to budgetary expenditures; the adverse effects of taxing financial transactions directly, as opposed to more indirect methods to raise revenue from the financial sector; the value of tax treaties and harmonization; and the consequences of globalization for revenue policy.

A strong revenue system depends on effective tax administration, which in turn requires adequate resources, a well-trained and honest staff, and a framework that encourages compliance, including relatively simple tax laws and ensuring that all taxpayers have identification numbers. Tools such as withholding at source, the use of estimated tax payments, appropriate penalties, and concentrating resources on the largest taxpayer units are also important. While audits, investigations, and penalties combat tax evasion, policy and administrative changes that reduce the incentives for evasion also help.

Chapter Seven: Expenditure Policy and Reform

Government expenditure comprises the outlays for everything that government undertakes. While government involves a broad array of activities, from spending programs to regulation, expenditure policy has traditionally focused on spending programs that affect aggregate demand and, over time, aggregate supply.

This chapter begins with a brief review of the main rationales for government activity presented in Chapter One. The next section reviews information on the levels and composition of government expenditure across countries at different income levels and in different regions. The third section reviews the main types of expenditure, by economic and functional classification, while the fourth discusses specific issues pertaining to particular types of expenditure. The fifth section addresses expenditure issues that cut across specific types of spending, including unproductive expenditures, quasi-fiscal outlays, mandatory expenditures and entitlements, and contingent outlays. The final section discusses various tools that governments have developed for expenditure control.

7.1. Rationales for Government Expenditure: A Brief Review

As noted in Chapter One, the main economic rationale for government activity is to provide goods and services that private firms and households cannot be expected to provide efficiently or in amounts commensurate with public demand. Thus, a case can be made for governments to do the following:

Allocate public goods. Public goods are goods and services that, by definition, are available to everyone if anyone has them and whose consumption by one person does not diminish consumption opportunities for others. Typical examples include general security, an efficient and effective legal system, and effective governance (lack of corruption and effective government services).

Stabilize the economy. Because private firms rarely benefit from acting contrary to current trends in economic activity, only government can effectively implement countercyclical monetary and fiscal policies.

Establish a sound framework within which private markets can operate. Because of the inherent conflicts of interest between private parties, only a disinterested third party, such as government, can establish "rules of the game" to encourage optimal levels of commerce. This includes the provision of effective means for dispute resolution, such as courts and arbitration systems, and measures to ensure effective competition, including the regulation of natural monopolies.

Address problems of information asymmetry. Because the financial sector, health care, and some other activities exhibit adverse selection, moral hazard, and other market imperfections arising from asymmetric information, it is essential that the government (as a party charged with representing the "public interest") address the consequent market failures through appropriate regulation of the financial sector, health care, and other activities, such as food safety.

Address concerns about the distribution of income. Because markets inevitably lead to wide variances in income, a case can be made to create a social safety net for the poor, elderly, and disabled. Progressive income taxation, additional income support, and taxing large inheritances and gifts can be added, if desired, to address further distributional inequities.

The above concerns help justify a wide array of government activities, ranging from monetary, fiscal, and regulatory policies to many specific expenditure programs. The following sections discuss these in further detail.

7.2. Expenditure Levels and Composition — An International Comparison

To indicate the relative size of government activity in an economy, government expenditure is typically measured as a share of gross domestic product (GDP). However, it can also be measured as a share of gross national income (GNI), which includes net (factor) income from abroad and can be useful for countries with large earnings from overseas investments.

Whether measured as a percentage of GDP or GNI, government expenditure varies considerably among countries. In general, government expenditure in higher income economies exceeds that in economies with lower per capita incomes. One reason is that higher income countries have generally proved more successful in raising revenue, particularly for social welfare programs such as state-provided health insurance and pensions. Nevertheless, expenditure levels differ considerably among high-income countries. For example, during 2019, the total government expenditure at all levels in selected advanced economies ranged from 14% of GDP in Singapore and 22% in the Republic of Korea to 33–39% of GDP in Switzerland, the United States, Japan, Australia, and the United Kingdom and more than 50% of GDP in Denmark and France (Table 7.1). Total expenditures in most of these economies rose by several percentage points of GDP in 2009, as governments responded to the financial crisis by increasing spending even as GDP fell. As the crisis waned, spending diminished by varying amounts across countries. In comparison, government expenditure

Table 7.1. General government outlays in selected advanced economies (in percent of GDP).

	2005	2009	2014	2019
Australia	34.7	37.8	36.8	38.4
Canada	38.5	43.4	38.4	41.2
Denmark	51.2	56.5	55.2	51.1
France	53.3	57.2	57.2	55.8
Germany	46.2	47.6	44.0	45.4
Greece	45.6	54.1	50.2	47.9
Italy	47.1	51.2	50.9	48.7
Japan	34.6	39.5	38.9	37.6
Korea, Rep. of	19.6	21.3	20.8	22.4
Netherlands	41.4	46.7	44.9	42.2
Norway	41.5	45.4	45.1	49.9
Singapore	14.2	17.3	15.7	14.3
Spain	38.3	45.8	44.8	41.9
Sweden	51.3	51.7	50.1	48.3
Switzerland	32.9	32.2	32.7	32.7
United Kingdom	38.2	44.1	40.5	38.7
United States	33.6	41.1	35.0	36.1

Source: IMF (2019), World Economic Outlook Database, April 2019, and IMF (2020), *Fiscal Monitor, April 2020*, Table A6.

ranged from 15 to 36% of GDP in many emerging market and low-income countries, partly reflecting lower ratios of revenue to GDP (Table 7.2).

The composition of government expenditure also differs considerably across countries, even within the same region. For example, during 2015–2016, the share of government expenditure devoted to investment (net acquisition of non-financial assets) ranged from about 16% in Malaysia to 38% in Cambodia (Table 7.3). By comparison, only 13% of central government outlays went for wage and salary payments in Timor-Leste, versus 30–31% in the Philippines and Thailand. Countries also differed in the extent of their subsidy programs. Malaysia, Nepal, and the Philippines, for example, each allocated more than 20% of all central government outlays to subsidies and transfers, compared with less than 10% in Cambodia, Thailand, and Timor-Leste. Finally, high

Table 7.2. General government expenditure in selected countries (in percent of GDP; data for 2019).

High-income countries	
Canada	41.2
Denmark	51.1
France	55.8
Germany	45.4
United States	36.1
Emerging market and developing countries	
Bangladesh	15.1
Cambodia	23.9
China	34.0
Ecuador	36.2
India	27.1
Malaysia	23.9
Lao P.D.R.	20.3
Peru	21.3
South Africa	35.3
Thailand	21.8

Source: IMF (2020), *Fiscal Monitor, April 2020.*

Table 7.3. Composition of expenditure in selected Asian countries, 2015* (in percent of total central government expenditure).

	Wages & Salaries	Other Goods & Services	Interest	Subsidies & Transfers	Social Benefits & Other Exp.	Net Acquisition of Non-Financial Assets
Cambodia	27.1	14.9	1.6	6.9	11.2	38.3
Indonesia	28.0	18.0	7.4	14.8	10.6	21.2
Malaysia	27.6	14.0	9.5	25.3	7.7	15.8
Nepal	18.5	9.3	1.9	35.2	11.6	23.6
Philippines	29.9	18.0	14.4	21.0	1.2	16.8
Thailand	30.8	28.5	4.7	5.1	14	16.8
Timor-Leste	13.1	31.9	0.0	0.0	33.2	21.8

Note: *For Nepal, 2016.
Source: International Monetary Fund (2016), *Government Finance Statistics Yearbook 2016.*

government debt required the Philippines to use more than 14% of outlays for interest payments.

Research offers no advice on the optimum size of government expenditure as a percentage of GDP. The size of government depends heavily on the ability and willingness of countries to finance the government through tax and non-tax revenues. Taxpayers in European countries such as Denmark, France, and Sweden have been willing to bear higher levels of taxation to finance more extensive government activities, in particular social benefits, than taxpayers in other high-income countries, such as Japan and the United States. Tanzi and Schuknecht (1997), comparing economies in Europe and the United States during the period through the mid-1990s, found that economic growth rates were no higher, and often lower, in countries with higher ratios of government expenditure to GDP than in countries with lower ratios. In low-income countries, by comparison, greater spending on health care and education, relative to GDP, often correlates with better human development indicators for health and education.[1]

However, governments must ensure that higher spending during emergencies, such as wars and severe economic recession, does not lead to permanently higher outlays. During periods like the Global Financial Crisis of 2007–2009 many governments increased expenditures to combat the fall in aggregate demand. As noted in Table 7.1, government expenditure rose by an average of about 3% of GDP in the OECD and about 4% of GDP in the Euro area, between 2005 and 2009. By late 2010, countries were grappling with when and how to reduce spending, with some countries such as the United Kingdom opting to move sooner, and others waiting because of the uncertainty of economic recovery.

---

[1]Gupta, S. *et al.* (2002), "The Effectiveness of Government Spending on Health Care and Education in Developing and Transition Economies," *European Journal of Political Economy*, vol. 18, pp. 717–737, http://www.appg-popdevrh.org.uk/Publications/Population% 20Hearings/Evidence/IMF%20report%206.pdf.

When considering government expenditure, less visible forms of spending must also be considered. For example, as noted in Chapter Six, the tax codes of many countries contain vast amounts of *tax expenditures* — provisions that provide benefits to taxpayers that are comparable to budget subsidies or transfers, except that they are paid on the tax side of the budget, thereby reducing revenue.[2] Tax expenditures include exemptions or lower rates for certain types of income, such as capital gains. Other tax expenditures provide subsidies, in the form of deductions from taxable income or credits against tax liability, for spending on certain items. Tax expenditures are popular, because they allow governments to provide benefits in a form readily available to qualifying taxpayers. However, they complicate the tax code and making filing and paying taxes more difficult. Being off-budget, tax expenditures are less visible than budgetary outlays and harder to control, because they serve as entitlements. Thus, their cost is harder to estimate than comparable budget expenditures. Nevertheless, many analysts believe that tax expenditures cost governments huge amounts of revenue. As noted in Chapter Six, some analysts estimate that tax expenditures reduce federal revenues in the United States by more than US$1.3 trillion annually.[3]

Quasi-fiscal expenditures represent still another form of hidden government outlays. Quasi-fiscal expenditures are expenditures by off-budget public agencies that look and function like regular budgetary outlays. Examples include bank recapitalizations and the cost of exchange rate guarantees made by central banks; compensation to depositors under deposit insurance provided by central banks; and losses imposed on state enterprises as a result of price ceilings,

---

[2]For the United States, the Congressional Budget Act of 1974 defines tax expenditures as "revenue losses attributable to provisions of the Federal tax laws which allow a special exclusion, exemption, or deduction from gross income or which provide a special credit, a preferential rate of tax, or a deferral of tax liability." Congressional Budget and Impoundment Control Act of 1974 (Pub. L. No. 93-344), Sec. 3(3).

[3]Gale, W. (2019), *Fiscal Therapy* (New York: Oxford University Press), p. 210, citing Joint Committee on Taxation (2018), "Estimates of Federal Tax Expenditures for Fiscal Years 2017–2021," JCX-34-18 (Washington: U.S. Government Printing Office, May), https://www.jct.gov/publications.html?func=startdown&id=5095.

government-mandated inefficiencies, and the inability (or unwilling-ness) to collect legitimate income. As with tax expenditures, some governments create quasi-fiscal expenditures as a way of providing benefits off-budget. Thus, these outlays are less visible and controllable than regular budget outlays, since they are not subject to the regular budget process. Nevertheless, the amounts involved can be substantial. For example, in several republics of the former Soviet Union, quasi-fiscal activities in the energy sector were estimated to range from about 3 to more than 20 percent of GDP during 1999 or 2000.[4]

Government tax laws, expenditure programs, and regulation all impose costs, often substantial, on the private sector. These costs do not count as government expenditures. Yet, they represent part of the "burden" of government on an economy. Government building codes impose additional costs on contractors, businesses, and home-owners, for example. Paying taxes and complying with tax regulations also involve substantial amounts of time and expense for firms and households. These amounts should be remembered when figuring the "true" cost of government.

Finally, many expenditure programs contain hidden taxes, in the form of reducing benefits as income rises. In some countries, subsidy rates and benefit payments for certain programs decline as income rises. For example, in the United States, an "earnings test" causes social security benefits for those younger than "full retirement age" (the age at which benefits are no longer reduced for early retirement) to be reduced by US$1 for every US$2 in earnings. Before 2000, benefits were reduced by this amount for those aged 65–69; before 1983, it applied to those younger than 72.[5]

---

[4]Petri, M. *et al.* (2002), "Energy Sector Quasi-Fiscal Activities in the Countries of the Former Soviet Union," Working Paper No. 02/60 (Washington: International Monetary Fund), Figure 1, http://www.imf.org/external/pubs/ft/wp/2002/wp0260.pdf.

[5]McGill, D. M. *et al.* (2010), *Fundamentals of Private Pensions*, Ninth Edition (New York: Oxford University Press), p. 261.

7.3. Main Categories of Government Expenditure

As noted in Chapter Four, the main components of government expenditure can be classified in two ways: economically and by function. Under the 1986 *Manual on Government Finance Statistics*, which most countries still use, the economic classification of government expenditure identifies three broad types of outlays: current expenditure, capital expenditure, and net lending (which represents net outlays — loans minus the repayment of principal — for government lending programs that serve policy purposes). Current expenditure comprises outlays for wages and salaries (compensation of employees), purchases of other goods and services (non-wage outlays for operations and maintenance), interest payments, and subsidies and transfers. Military outlays are usually included in current expenditure, except for identified outlays for military bases. Capital expenditure comprises all outlays for long-term projects, such as infrastructure, and spending for military installations (but not weapons or armaments). The 2001 *Government Finance Statistics Manual* classifies most government outlays as either part of "Expense" or as "Net Acquisition of Nonfinancial Assets." The main categories of Expense, which resembles current expenditure under the 1986 classification, comprise compensation of employees, the use of goods and services, interest, subsidies, grants, social benefits (which together were similar to "transfers" under the 1986 classification), and other expense. In addition, Expense includes the depreciation of government assets, called "consumption of fixed capital." The net acquisition of non-financial assets is very close to capital expenditure under the 1986 classification, although it excludes capital transfers. In the 2001 Manual, net lending is considered part of the net acquisition of financial assets rather than expenditure. Thus, the 2001 classification combines net lending with more traditional budget financing.

The functional classification of government expenditure represents the breakdown of government spending across program areas. Most government budgets report planned and historical expenditure by function. A functional classification of expenditure typically includes outlays divided among categories[6] such as general public services (or public administration), defense, public order and safety (or police and fire services at the sub-national level), economic affairs, environmental protection, energy, commerce, agriculture, transportation, housing and community amenities, health, education, social protection, foreign affairs, and recreation, culture, and religion. Functional classifications will differ across countries, depending on the nature of government programs and how their purposes are viewed in the country.

7.4. Issues Affecting Specific Categories of Expenditure

7.4.1. *Wages and salaries*

In many countries, long-standing rules about tenure and the desire to make government an employer of last resort have led to *serious inefficiencies in the government workforce.* In some countries such as India, a non-trivial part of the government's employment budget goes to hire short-term employees (sometimes called "day workers") for menial and low-skilled positions. Although individual wage payments are small, the large number of such workers causes a significant fraction of the government's wage bill to be spent on such employees, adding expense and constraining the government's ability to hire more expensive, highly skilled workers for analytical, regulatory, and policy positions. Some other countries, such as Mauritania during the early to mid-1980s, have occasionally guaranteed government jobs to university graduates. Doing so has filled government payrolls with highly educated but not always useful employees, as many university graduates had degrees in the humanities that did not equip them with the quantitative and technical skills needed for high-level government positions.

---

[6]Most of these categories are taken from IMF (2006), *Government Finance Statistics Yearbook 2006*, Table W6.

Besides job guarantee programs, many countries suffer from rigid employment structures and limited wage scales that make it hard for governments to attract and retain highly skilled workers for positions in which the government competes with the private sector. Frequently, government wage scales limit salaries for such positions as tax attorneys and bank examiners, making it hard for government to retain talented and experienced workers. In many developing and emerging market countries, bank regulatory agencies routinely train bank examiners, only to find that many of those trained are hired away by private sector banks offering several times their government salaries. Similarly, in the United States many business economists start their careers at the Federal Reserve Board and are then hired away, at much higher salaries, by investment banks.

Low wage scales also create incentives for bribery among officials charged with law enforcement and regulation. In many countries, low salaries contribute to wholesale corruption in police departments, customs offices, and among high-level government officials. Partly for this reason and partly to ensure that pay levels do not discourage the most able from accepting senior government positions, Singapore has established unusually high salaries for ministers and senior civil servants. For example, salaries for ministers are typically set at a certain percentage of the average core earned income of the top four earners in six professions: accounting, banking, engineering, law, local manufacturing firms, and multinational corporations, following the recommendation in a White Paper issued in 1994.[7] Senior civil servants also receive unusually high salaries. To provide incentives to promote economic growth, ministers and civil servants receive bonuses during periods of strong economic growth and salary cuts (as bonuses and variable payments are deferred) during times of recession, such as 2009.

---

[7] See Government of Singapore (1994), *Competitive Salaries for Competent & Honest Government: Benchmarks for Ministers & Senior Public Officers: White Paper [Cmd. 13 of 1994]*, Singapore: Prime Minister's Office.

When considering programs, governments need to remember their staffing needs. Some flexibility in civil service arrangements will allow governments to reallocate employees across programs and even ministries as programs and policies change. In addition, governments must take into account the changing mix of skill needs among civil servants. For example, the Global Financial Crisis of 2007–2009 reinforced the importance of effective regulation and supervision of financial institutions. Accordingly, governments have had to adjust the composition of employees, expanding the number of bank examiners and skilled financial regulators while reducing positions for less essential staff.

7.4.2. Purchases of other goods and services

Fiscally constrained governments often target purchases of other goods and services for budget cuts, because of the difficulty of reducing government employment. As a result, spending for operations and maintenance has often been cut, at great cost to the quality of government services. Many developing countries have endured schools with teachers but too few textbooks and health centers with nurses but shortages of medicines and other equipment. Indeed, in some countries major reductions in malaria have resulted not from government programs, but from the massive distribution of mosquito nets by nongovernment organizations financed by foreign aid and charitable contributions from high-income countries. Thus, countries need to resist the urge to close fiscal gaps by cutting operations expenditure, as opposed to a more general review of outlays to identify unproductive spending.

Expenditures for maintenance pose similar challenges. Financially strapped governments often find it attractive to defer maintenance. As a result, government facilities deteriorate faster, and buildings and installations must be replaced more often, usually at greater expense over the long run. Many developing countries have sizable numbers of schools, highways, and hospitals that have deteriorated substantially as a result of deferred maintenance. However, similar problems plague some high-income countries, including the United States, where 7.6%

of all bridges were classified as structurally deficient in 2018, with some 38% overall needing repair, according to an analysis of US government data by the American Road & Transportation Builders Association.[8] Inadequate maintenance has led to dramatic events, such as the collapse of a major bridge spanning the Mississippi River in Minnesota during 2007 and the earlier collapse of a bridge along the Connecticut Turnpike in the Northeast.

Government procedures for purchasing present a third issue in this area. Despite calls for reform, many countries continue to allow sole-source contracts and select contractors without competitive bidding to provide goods and services, often raising costs and reducing quality. In addition, surveys suggest that bribery in public procurement and other interactions with government is widespread in many countries, especially in the developing world.[9] Ensuring that competitive bidding rules apply to government contracts can reduce opportunities for corruption, lower costs, and improve the effectiveness of services. The resulting decline in corruption may also allow a reallocation of funds to operations and maintenance, by reducing unproductive spending on public investment projects.[10]

7.4.3. Subsidies and transfers

Subsidies and transfers can be provided in many ways. One option is for government to produce and sell (or provide) goods and services directly, at a below-market price, through state-owned enterprises. Although the subsidy is clear if the state enterprise operates at a loss covered by the budget, a subsidy also occurs if the government provides the service at a cost-covering price lower than what a profit-making

---

[8] American Road & Transportation Builders Association (2019), "2019 Bridge Report," https://artbabridgereport.org/reports/2019-ARTBA-Bridge-Report.pdf.

[9] See, for example, OECD (2008), "Keeping Government Contracts Clean," Policy Brief, Figure 1, citing World Bank research by Kaufmann and others, http://www.oecd.org/dataoecd/63/21/41550528.pdf.

[10] See Tanzi, V. and H. Davoodi (1997), "Corruption, Public Investment, and Growth," Working Paper No. 97/39 (Washington: International Monetary Fund, October), http://www.imf.org/external/pubs/ft/wp/wp97139.pdf.

private firm would have to charge. Alternatively, governments can provide subsidies or transfers for beneficiaries to purchase goods and services produced by private firms. Subsidies can involve rebates to consumers when they purchase specific items; payments to firms, on condition that the items are sold at an approved price; and subsidies for loans, typically payments to financial institutions that allow them to lend at lower interest rates. Subsidies also result if the government provides funds to a public institution, such as a university, that charges lower fees as a result. Subsidies can also involve tax expenditures, in the form of deductions from taxable income or profits for specified expenditures or credits against tax liability set at a specific percentage of qualifying expenditures.

Subsidy and transfer programs can involve either one-time or continuing measures. Many countries, for example, provide continuing subsidies for selected food items or gasoline ("petrol") and tax subsidies for contributions made to approved charitable organizations. By comparison, countries sometimes limit the duration of certain subsidies, to contain their costs or provide incentives for firms and households to act within a specified time period. The United States, for example, enacted a tax credit for energy-saving home improvements set to expire at the end of 2010, which triggered extensive purchases of replacement windows and more energy-efficient furnaces and air conditioners during the last half of 2010.

Ongoing programs that provide benefits to households or individuals meeting certain conditions are called *entitlements*, because those meeting the requirements are automatically eligible to receive benefits, if they apply. Entitlement programs are an important part of the social safety net in many high-income countries and some formerly centrally planned economies. However, planned benefit levels and inadequate funding have made many of these entitlements a source of long-term fiscal concern. Staff of the International Monetary Fund, for example, have estimated that, between 2010 and 2030, forecast increases in health and pension benefits will add at least 4 percentage points of GDP to the structural deficits in the world's largest economies (the

G7 nations) and possibly 5.5% of GDP in the United States, where the expected rise in government-funded health care expenditures is even greater.[11] For the period from 2019 to 2049, the US Congressional Budget Office has estimated that rising benefits for Social Security (federal pension programs) and major federal health programs will add 5.4% of GDP to federal expenditures.[12]

7.4.3.1. Consumer versus producer subsidies

A key issue for subsidy programs is choosing between consumer and producer subsidies. *Consumer subsidies* benefit consumers directly, while *producer subsidies* do so indirectly, lowering production costs so that producers can sell an item more cheaply.

Consumer subsidies directly reduce the price of a good or service, making it more affordable. However, subsidies usually increase the demand for subsidized items. If additional supplies are available, either through domestic producers or through imports, more will be sold. Figure 7.1 illustrates the process, showing that the market price before subsidy may increase as a result (the price to the consumer after the subsidy, P_C, is less than the original price). Unless the subsidy is well targeted, the benefits may go to unintended recipients. Singaporean drivers, for example, have long benefited from the large fuel subsidies in neighboring Malaysia by driving across the Causeway or through the tunnel linking Singapore to the Malay Peninsula. Malaysia's government has tried various schemes to restrict purchases by non-citizens, for example, by requiring cars to enter the country with gas tanks at least three-quarters full. However, it is hard to prevent some spillover of benefits to foreigners.

Producer subsidies are designed to make goods more affordable by lowering costs to the producer, on the assumption that producers

---

[11] See Cottarelli, C. and A. Schaecter (2010), "Long-Term Trends in the Public Finances of the G-7 Economies," Staff Position Note 10/13 (Washington: International Monetary Fund, September), pp. 15–16, http://www.imf.org/external/pubs/ft/spn/2010/spn1013.pdf.

[12] Congressional Budget Office (2019), *2019 Long-Term Budget Outlook* (June), https://www.cbo.gov/publication/55331, p. 20.

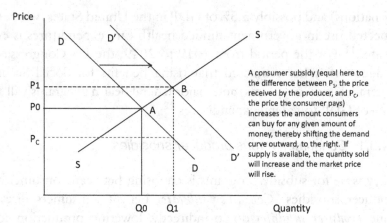

Figure 7.1. Impact of consumer subsidy.

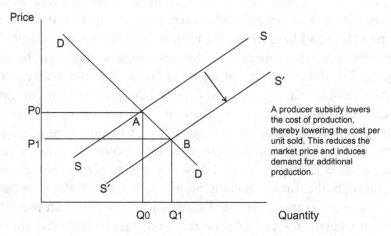

Figure 7.2. Impact of producer subsidy.

will pass their cost savings onto consumers. Figure 7.2 shows how producer subsidies are presumed to work. By shifting the supply curve for an item, a producer subsidy can ordinarily be expected to increase supply, and thus the quantity sold, as well as lowering the price (unless demand is perfectly inelastic and a monopolistic producer, or cartel of producers, knows and takes advantage of the situation). A producer subsidy can be useful if the subsidized item is in short supply. In this case, subsidizing consumers may only raise prices, rather than making the good more accessible. Such an argument has been used to support certain low-income housing programs in the United States, where some analysts have claimed that the supply of "acceptable" low-cost housing is limited. A producer subsidy may also be useful if the goal is to help specific producers, such as low-income farmers, provided that they can be identified and other producers excluded.

Unless aggregate demand rises as a result, however, the producer subsidy will likely lead to a reallocation of resources toward producing the subsidized item, and away from producing others. If the subsidized item is less efficient to produce than other goods and services, it may have the unintended result of causing producers to shift output from goods they can produce more efficiently. Indeed, the producer subsidy may even lead to excessive production of the subsidized item, creating pressure for the government to stabilize prices or develop new export markets, in which case part of the benefits will leak outside the country.

Although targeting subsidies is always difficult, it is probably easier to target consumer subsidies on the intended beneficiaries. Governments can limit access to those who are issued special identification cards or to households and individuals that can prove qualifying income. For example, during the mid-1990s the Ukrainian government established a subsidy program for utility charges that required consumers to prove that costs exceeded 15% of household income in order to receive benefits. By contrast, it is much harder to restrict access to goods benefitting from producer subsidies, since the items may be widely sold on domestic markets and, if additional production is exported, outside the country as well. For this and other reasons, it is usually more efficient for governments to use consumer rather than producer subsidies, if the goal is to benefit specific groups of consumers.

7.4.3.2. General issues in subsidy design

When developing subsidy programs, governments need to address the following issues:

a. *Whether to provide subsidies explicitly or implicitly* (for example, through government provision and supply). Explicit provision may make the subsidies more transparent and controllable, particularly because provision by a government agency can lead to a host of issues related to the creation and maintenance of state enterprises and the inefficiencies they can generate.

b. *Whether and how to target benefits.* Restricting eligibility to particular groups of people (such as low-income households or small firms) allows benefits to be focused on the intended beneficiaries. However, targeting may be hard, because of the difficulty of identifying beneficiaries or preventing fraud. At the same time, overly strict eligibility requirements will reduce a program's accessibility and, thus, its ability to reach the intended beneficiaries. Targeting may also reduce the popularity of the program and stigmatize beneficiaries, discouraging some of those eligible from applying and receiving benefits.

c. *How to set the duration of the program.* Entitlements provide assured benefits but are harder to control and limit total expenditures. Programs requiring annual renewal, or whose outlays can be set each year through the budget process, are easier to control and possibly easier to revise if conditions change. To provide the benefits of continuity without creating a permanent entitlement, programs can include a so-called *sunset clause*, whereby a program expires unless it is reauthorized by a specific date.

d. *How to finance the program.* Programs with dedicated sources of funding, such as a tax "earmarked" to fund the program or a trust fund financed from specific revenue sources, have assured financing but can make it harder for a government to meet broader fiscal objectives. In addition, having dedicated revenue sources does not ensure full program financing if benefits are set independent of revenues. For these reasons, economists often discourage "earmarked" taxes, although many citizens who are suspicious of government like them as a way to ensure that revenues are used for specific purposes.

e. *How to increase transparency and controllability.* Governments can increase the transparency and controllability of programs by financing them through regular budget appropriations, rather than tax expenditures (which are hard to quantify) or quasi-fiscal operations (which are typically off-budget and even less transparent). In addition, governments must watch that the creation of programs does not create new constituencies for their preservation, for example, workers and managers at state enterprises who are keen to keep their jobs.

f. *How to minimize distortions created by subsidies.* Governments must also be careful that subsidies do not create major economic distortions. For example, a food subsidy should not cause consumers to reduce their consumption of locally produced items in favor of imports. During the 1980s, a generous bread subsidy in Zambia led many consumers to reduce purchases of locally produced maize (corn) meal and increase purchases of bread, made from imported wheat, thereby raising imports and exacerbating an already worrisome trade deficit. Thus, the government had to scale back the bread subsidy.

Governments can reduce the distortions arising from subsidies by providing subsidies that apply to broad, rather than narrow, categories of goods and services. This allows consumers to choose from many qualifying goods and services, minimizing the risk that subsidy will distort consumer choice. A general subsidy on food products, perhaps with the exclusion of alcoholic beverages, for example, is less likely to create distortions than a subsidy just on a few items, such as bread, sugar, or cooking oil. A more general food subsidy may also enhance competition among food producers and retailers. Similarly, so long as adequate supplies of low-cost housing exist, a voucher that reduces the cost of housing generally will create fewer distortions than will building or subsidizing the construction of apartments and limiting the benefits to those residing in approved housing units.

7.4.4. Interest expenditure

Governments must ensure that interest on public debt is paid, to avoid default and keep financial markets willing to buy and hold government securities. Thus, it is important to maintain careful records on government debt, so that interest (and principal) payments can be anticipated and budgeted.

Special problems arise when debt is issued in foreign currency. Interest on such debt bears currency risk, meaning that interest payments in local currency can rise if the exchange rate depreciates. This is a recurring problem in developing and emerging market countries, which typically cannot sell debt denominated in local currency to foreign lenders. Foreign debt, including debt on concessional terms, must therefore be carefully monitored. In many countries ranging from Argentina to the Russian Federation, foreign currency debt has led to serious fiscal problems when economic shocks triggered a massive depreciation in the national currency.

7.4.5. Capital expenditure

Ideally, governments should reserve a substantial share of government spending for capital expenditure, to ensure adequate infrastructure and public facilities to support private sector activity. The Spence Commission on Growth observed that rapidly growing countries typically devote at least 25% of GDP to investment, with government investment in infrastructure, plus human capital development, representing about one-third of that amount.[13] The Commission also noted that many of the fastest growing Asian countries have typically devoted 5–7% of GDP, and sometimes more, just for infrastructure spending.[14]

---

[13]Commission on Growth and Development (2008), "Highlights of the Growth Report," p. 2, http://www.growthcommission.org/storage/cgdev/documents/Report/ReportHigh lights.pdf.

[14]*Ibid.*, *Growth Report* (Washington: World Bank), p. 35, http://cgd.s3.amazonaws.com/ GrowthReportComplete.pdf.

In practice, countries have varied tremendously in their capital expenditure. As noted in Table 7.3, even in Asia, as recently as 2015–2016 only four of seven emerging market and low-income countries with detailed data devoted at least 20% of all central government expenditure to capital outlays. Most high-income countries spend a much smaller share of their budgets on infrastructure and other capital spending, because of the heavy burden of social benefits, including transfers to persons under public pension programs. In the United States, for example, nondefense federal spending for investment totaled about 1.5% of GDP in 2018, of which about 41% (0.6% of GDP) went for physical infrastructure, according to the Congressional Budget Office.[15]

To maximize the productivity of public investment spending, projects should be selected using cost–benefit analysis to identify those with the greatest net present value. In practice, reliable cost–benefit estimates depend on a variety of uncertain parameters, such as costs of future maintenance, projections of obsolescence and project life, and the choice of interest rates to discount future benefits and costs. However, governments should beware of projects whose main value appears to be political, for example, costly projects providing limited benefits to a small group of people. To the extent possible, governments should avoid such projects, focusing instead on projects whose benefits exceed their economic costs, after reasonable discounting.

7.5. Special Expenditure Issues

Besides the issues outlined above, governments need to heed the following special expenditure issues.

7.5.1. Unproductive expenditure

Government budgets in many countries include sizable amounts of *unproductive expenditure*. The IMF has defined unproductive

---

[15]Congressional Budget Office (2019), *Federal Investment, 1962 to 2018* (June), https://www.cbo.gov/system/files/2019-06/55375-Federal_Investment.pdf, p.2.

expenditure as the difference between actual spending for a particular program, or category of good or service, and the reduced amount of spending that would yield the same social benefit with maximum cost-effectiveness.[16] Activities falling under this heading include the following:

- military expenditure that exceeds a reasonable cost estimate for maintaining national security;
- public investment projects with negative net present value;
- poorly targeted subsidy programs;
- prestige programs with few beneficiaries, such as a costly hospital in the capital city, that crowd out expenditures benefiting a much larger population (e.g., rural health centers).

Unproductive expenditure includes both capital and current outlays, and capital projects are not always more productive than current expenditure. For example, spending for expensive capital projects that benefit relatively few people can be far less productive than current expenditure that assures adequate maintenance of existing facilities. Similarly, broad categories of expenditure can include both productive and unproductive elements. Thus, wage and salary payments can simultaneously fund overstaffing in some ministries (for example, excess numbers of teachers, when student enrollments have declined) and critical employees in other agencies (for example, bank examiners and budget forecasters).

Unproductive expenditure can be very costly. Consider, for example, fuel subsidies. A recent IMF staff working paper estimated that subsidies for fossil fuels were equivalent to 6.3% of global GDP in 2015 and 6.5% in 2017, with coal and petroleum together accounting for more than 80% of all subsidies.[17] Since 2004, several countries

---

[16]International Monetary Fund (1995), "Unproductive Public Expenditures: A Pragmatic Approach to Policy Analysis," IMF Pamphlet No. 48, http://www.imf.org/external/pubs/ft/pam/pam48/pam4801.htm.

[17]See Coady, D. *et al.* (2019), "Global Fossil Fuel Subsidies Remain Large: An Update Based on Country-Level Estimates," Working Paper No. 19/89 (Washington, DC: International

have reduced fuel subsidies to improve the targeting of benefits on low-income households. For example, Indonesia reduced the cost of fuel subsidies to about 1.9% of GDP in 2006, compared with 3.4% in 2005, by raising petrol prices. At the same time, the government gave cash transfers worth about US$30 per month to some 16 million low-income families at a cost of 0.7% of GDP and used some of the budgetary savings from the subsidy reduction to raise outlays on health, education, and infrastructure projects benefiting low- and middle-income households.[18] The government also raised subsidies on electricity made from fossil fuel. Ghana and Jordan have also reduced fuel subsidies and used the budgetary savings to provide other benefits focused more on lower income households.

In addition to reducing poorly targeted subsidies, other strategies are available to reduce unproductive expenditure. These include the following:

- *Changing the mix of programs within a category of expenditure.* In many developing countries, reallocating funds from universities to primary education will likely increase the number of students benefited and do more to address illiteracy. In higher income countries, raising university tuitions and allocating the resulting savings to need-based scholarships will focus educational benefits more on low-income students.
- *Imposing appropriate user charges.* Imposing modest tolls for bridges, tunnels, and expressways will help allocate the costs for these infrastructure projects to their users. However, governments should avoid imposing charges that would preclude access to critical public services for low-income households. Thus, governments

---

Monetary Fund, May), https://www.imf.org/en/Publications/WP/Issues/2019/05/02/Global-Fossil-Fuel-Subsidies-Remain-Large-An-Update-Based-on-Country-Level-Estimates-46509, p. 5.

[18]See Baig, T. *et al.* (2007), "Domestic Petroleum Product Prices and Subsidies: Recent Developments and Reform Strategies," Working Paper No. 07/71 (Washington: International Monetary Fund, March), p. 15, http://www.imf.org/external/pubs/ft/wp/2007/wp0771.pdf.

should beware of levying significant fees or tuition for primary and secondary school (although in some countries school fees may be needed at the local level because funds from the central government are inadequate).

- *Ensuring an appropriate balance among complementary programs.* Where hunger and malnutrition are prevalent, school breakfast or lunch programs may be needed to ensure the effectiveness of public education. Similarly, public health programs may be important to limit school absences from contagions such as malaria and dengue fever.

- *Focusing expenditures on the intended population.* In most developing countries, a subsidy for bus fares will aid low-income households more than fuel subsidies, because high-income households represent the bulk of vehicle owners. Similarly, imposing tuition on university students and using the proceeds to fund need-based scholarships will focus education spending more effectively on those from low-income households.

7.5.2. *Quasi-fiscal expenditures*

As noted earlier, quasi-fiscal expenditures are expenditures by off-budget public agencies that look and function like regular budgetary outlays. Being off-budget, they are less transparent and far harder to control than regular budgetary outlays.

Many quasi-fiscal activities take place at monetary authorities, in particular central banks. Monetary authorities generally have funds available, because they earn profits from many of their core activities. These include rediscounting government securities for banks seeking capital, issuing central bank bills or trading government securities in open market operations, undertaking foreign exchange transactions, and investing foreign exchange reserves in interest-bearing securities. Thus, monetary authorities are an ideal place for governments to use in financing budget-like activities without having to show the expenditures on the government budget. Quasi-fiscal activities often imposed on monetary authorities include the following:

- *Lending to non-bank institutions.* Countries sometimes force monetary authorities to lend to specific sectors or borrowers, often at below-market interest rates. Such loans provide subsidies to the borrowers and typically reduce the authorities' profits. Thus, they diminish the funds that monetary authorities can transfer to the budget. By favoring sectors or groups that may be less productive or profitable than others in the economy, the loans may also distort the allocation of resources, promote unviable activities, and ultimately lead to non-performing assets. If so, they may also reduce the monetary authority's capital.

- *Providing exchange rate guarantees.* When the exchange rate depreciates, many importers who have ordered goods for domestic resale at fixed prices may incur losses if contracts are honored at market exchange rates. Thus, the monetary authority may face pressure to sell foreign exchange at a more favorable (less depreciated) rate. Doing so amounts to an off-budget, non-transparent subsidy to those participating in the program. If the authorities agree to provide unlimited amounts of foreign exchange at this rate, the subsidy is also incontrollable. Exchange rate guarantees generally create losses for the monetary authority, reducing its profits and thus the revenue it can transfer to the government budget. The guarantees can also have broader economic effects, diverting foreign exchange from regular markets and creating the possibility for black markets, if purchasers can resell to others the foreign exchange they receive at a higher (more depreciated) exchange rate.

- *Funding deposit guarantees.* If a country does not have a formal deposit insurance program, or if the program's resources are insufficient, a monetary authority may be asked to "bail out" depositors by covering their losses at failing banks. If it does, the monetary authority provides a non-transparent, hard-to-control subsidy to depositors that reduces its own profits and, thus, the revenues it can provide to the government budget. As with a program of unlimited deposit insurance, funding deposit guarantees, or serving as a back-up to an existing program, can create a moral hazard for the banking system, because bankers no longer fear the consequences of bad loans that can lead to bank failure. Under these circumstances, a system-wide banking collapse could decapitalize the monetary authority, requiring budgetary transfers to restore its financial viability.

- *Sterilizing capital inflows*. Many monetary authorities try to limit the impact of capital inflows on their economies through sterilization. Sterilization involves selling government securities, or the authority's own securities, to commercial banks, to offset the impact of additional foreign exchange on the money supply. Sterilization, while effective at reducing the so-called monetary base (the amount of high-powered money in an economy), generally reduces the monetary authority's profits and, thus, the revenues it provides for the budget. The reason is that interest rates on foreign exchange reserves are typically less than those on the government securities it sells (or the interest it must pay when issuing its own securities).[19] Thus, monetary authorities can usually engage in sterilization for only a limited time and typically turn to other actions as a response to capital inflows, unless the exchange rate is allowed to appreciate. Economically, sterilization creates distortions by allowing the exchange rate to remain more depreciated than market conditions would otherwise allow. This promotes exports and suppresses imports, while reducing budget revenues from import duties.

7.5.3. Mandatory vs. discretionary expenditures

Mandatory expenditures are outlays that are made automatically, as a matter of law, without the need for appropriation or legislative approval

---

[19] The People's Bank of China may be an exception to this rule, because interest rates on its securities have often been less than those on its foreign exchange reserves. See Ljungwall, S. *et al.* (2009), "Central Bank Financial Strength and the Cost of Sterilization in China," Stockholm School of Economics, http://swopec.hhs.se/hacerc/papers/hacerc2009-008.pdf. Monetary authorities in most other countries can only sell their own bills at interest rates well above those received from their foreign exchange reserves.

during the formal budget process. Entitlements represent the most common mandatory expenditure programs. Similar programs include pensions for prior government employees and certain subsidy programs that governments have committed to pay. Discretionary expenditures, by comparison, must be approved each year, allowing the government to set the level of spending as conditions warrant.

By definition, discretionary expenditures are easier to control than mandatory spending programs. Many mandatory programs are determined by formulas that allow steady spending increases from year to year, unless the legislature intervenes. Entitlements present a special problem in this regard. For example, unless subject to an explicit ceiling on total outlays, outlays for government-funded health insurance or national health services will automatically rise as new medical procedures are developed and approved and new drugs become available and are authorized. Similarly, expenditures for government-funded pension programs will rise over time as life expectancy increases and consumer prices rise, if benefits are indexed to inflation. The same problem need not arise with discretionary expenditures, because the government sets the overall spending limits through the budget process. Thus, the government can limit the rise in spending for education, highways, and other discretionary programs, although there may be pressure to increase outlays as a result of economic growth, the deterioration of existing infrastructure and facilities, and the effects of inflation. For this reason, governments should carefully monitor and consider limiting entitlement programs and other mandatory expenditures.

7.5.4. *Contingent expenditures*

Contingent expenditures represent spending obligations that arise if specific events happen. Contingent expenditures include the following:

- *Loan guarantees.* When a government guarantees a loan for a state enterprise or other institution, the government budget becomes liable for debt service payments if the agency with primary responsibility for the loan cannot meet these obligations.

- *Bank failures.* If the government has implicitly guaranteed some or all of the deposits in the country's banking system, it must reimburse depositors for any losses. The same applies if the government has underwritten a deposit insurance fund and the fund has exhausted its resources. To prevent banks from closing, the government may also have to recapitalize insolvent institutions, either by providing them with government debt in exchange for bad assets or by creating an asset management company with funds to purchase their bad assets.
- *Catastrophe-related expenditures.* Governments typically bear the burden of emergency relief and repairs in the event of natural disasters, such as earthquakes, floods, and hurricanes.

Contingent expenditures also include future outlays triggered by foreseeable events. For example, certain age-related expenditures, such as rising outlays for health care and public pension programs, can be considered contingent expenditures, because they will materialize as the population ages.

To maintain control over the budget, governments should anticipate contingent expenditures and constrain them where possible. For example:

- Loan guarantees should be limited to the most creditworthy borrowers and used only for projects with a clear public purpose. This could mean, for example, restricting loan guarantees to public enterprises, and then only for investments that the government has approved.
- Programs should avoid incentives for early retirement, which can impose long and costly expenditure obligations. Thus, programs allowing miners or military officers to retire after a fixed period of service, such as 20 years, regardless of age, deserve careful scrutiny.

- Retirement programs should not allow women to retire at a younger age than men. Because women typically live longer than men, such provisions inflate the cost of pension programs.
- Governments should avoid implicit guarantees for bank deposits and limit explicit insurance to the deposits of small savers, to avoid encouraging banks from undertaking risky behavior.

7.5.5. Public–private partnerships

Public–private partnerships (PPPs) involve the use of private firms to supply public infrastructure or infrastructure services. They offer benefits similar to privatization, if successful, and can be considered analogous, in the field of capital spending, to contracting out public services such as waste management.

PPPs appeal to many governments because they can reduce the cost for providing infrastructure. They may also bring better service delivery, if the private operator performs well. In many projects, a private contractor agrees to design, build, finance, and operate a public facility, such as a highway or electricity plant, in return for receiving operating income, although the government may contribute to project financing. Often the contractor owns the facility for a specified period and transfers ownership to the government at the end of the contract, although sometimes the contractor only leases the facility. While the government does not operate the facility, it bears ultimate responsibility for substandard service. Thus, the government faces financial risks from poor performance and from cost overruns, unless the agreement clearly imposes these risks on the private operator and the agreement can be enforced.

Research indicates that PPPs can prove beneficial under certain conditions. These include the following:[20]

---

[20] The following points are drawn from Michel, F. (2008), "A Primer on Public–Private Partnerships," Public Financial Management Blog (Washington: International Monetary Fund, February), http://blog-pfm.imf.org/pfmblog/2008/02/a-primer-on-pub.html.

1. the ability to contract for service quality;
2. the ability to transfer a significant share of risks to the private operator;
3. the existence of incentive-based regulations or competition;
4. a strong institutional and legal framework;
5. sufficient technical expertise in government to oversee such contracts; and
6. satisfactory disclosure of PPP commitments and any related government guarantees, in government financial statements (and in debt sustainability analyses).

PPPs can also be advantageous if they allow the government to benefit from the resources, technology, managerial skills, and access to credit that a private contractor can offer. This may be especially valuable in a developing or emerging market country, where the private contractor has considerable experience in building and operating relevant facilities and the government has limited skills in the field.[21]

PPPs have risks. For the public sector, these include the government's ability to use a PPP to bypass spending controls and move spending off budget; problems with accounting for PPP spending; and the difficulty of developing and maintaining adequate control procedures over PPP decision-making and PPP projects, because of their technical nature.[22] Thus, PPPs need considerable oversight, by skilled professionals, to be successful. For the private contractor, a variety of political, economic, and financial risks can arise. Moreover, in developing and emerging market countries, contractors may face greater risk of disruption stemming from substandard power supplies and the problems that can arise from weak governance and a difficult local political and institutional environment.[23]

---

[21] Koveos, P. and P. Yourougou (2009), "Public–Private Partnerships in Emerging Markets," *QFinance*, p. 2, http://www.qfinance.com/contentFiles/QF02/gjbkw9a0/17/0/publicprivate-partnerships-in-emerging-markets.pdf.
[22] Michel (2008), *op. cit.*
[23] Koveos and Yourougou (2009), *op. cit.*, p. 3.

For these reasons, governments should recognize that PPPs, rather than being a panacea, raise many challenging issues. Adequate risk transfer, though essential, can be hard to assess, given the complexity of PPP projects and the many risks they face. Experience in countries such as Brazil, Chile, and Ireland underscores the importance of a strong institutional environment and proper, transparent accounting, among other factors.[24]

7.6. Tools for Controlling Expenditure

Governments have many resources to help control expenditure and achieve fiscal objectives. These include general management tools, practical rules of thumb, and measures that can be adopted quickly to address spending issues in the short run.

7.6.1. *General management tools*

Governments can control spending more effectively with more comprehensive information about fiscal activities. Thus, governments should *consolidate fiscal accounts* to the extent possible. This includes monitoring off-budget as well as regular budgetary operations; including in the budget the activities of any special funds, such as trust funds for road construction and public pension programs; and maintaining estimates of tax expenditures, quasi-fiscal operations, and contingent liabilities.

Governments should also *use effective budgeting procedures and expenditure control systems.* Governments need formal budget procedures. In addition, many countries have found that fiscal rules limiting the size of the budget deficit or "pay go" rules that require the cost of new programs to be covered by offsetting revenue increases or cuts in other spending help contain total expenditures. Some countries, notably Chile and the United Kingdom, have had success

---

[24]See Fiscal Affairs Department (2004), "Public-Private Partnerships," especially Appendix I, pp. 30–41, http://www.imf.org/external/np/fad/2004/pifp/eng/031204.pdf

with *performance budgeting*, which involves setting broad goals and assessing how well particular programs achieve them. However, this approach works only when policy-makers view the budget in terms of broad policy objectives, have tools to identify ineffective and low-priority programs, and are willing to change or abandon them in favor of other programs that better meet spending priorities. *Zero-based budgeting*, under which spending for each program must be "justified anew" in the budget cycle, rather than simply reviewing requests for additional outlays, can also be useful if policy-makers are willing to terminate programs that are shown to be unproductive. *Having a budget office with evaluation capability* and some control over the spending of other agencies can also help restrain expenditure.

7.6.2. *"Rules of thumb" that can help control expenditure; fiscal space*

Certain "rules of thumb" can also help with expenditure control. For example, governments should avoid converting discretionary spending into mandatory programs. This will help maintain adaptability and allow outdated programs to be phased out in favor of new activities better attuned to current priorities. If expenditure commitments do not rise over time, the natural tendency for revenues to rise in a growing economy will provide room for the government to finance new activities. This, in turn, underscores the importance of maintaining *fiscal space* in the budget.

Fiscal space has been defined as the "availability of budget resources to finance worthwhile activities without prejudicing the government's financial position."[25] Assessing fiscal space requires reviewing the budget, to see what room is available for new programs. This involves taking account of their medium-term, as well as immediate, costs and consequences. Fiscal space can be created through a combination

---

[25] Heller, P. (2005), "Understanding Fiscal Space," IMF Policy Discussion Paper 05/4 (Washington: International Monetary Fund, March), http://www.imf.org/external/pubs/ft/pdp/2005/pdp04.pdf.

of revenue increases, cuts in existing, low-priority programs, and borrowing, if debt ratios are low. Debt relief can also provide fiscal space, and many low-income countries have obtained fiscal space for new health care, education, and infrastructure programs by using debt relief from bilateral donors and international organizations.

7.6.3. *Short-term measures to improve expenditure control*

In the short-term, governments have several ways to curb spending and improve control over outlays.

1. *Marginal services can be cut*, to protect core functions of an expenditure program. In education, for example, governments can look closely at the set of supportive services, such as supplementary teachers' aides, pre-school programs to boost fluency in the main national language, and little-used programs for students with disabilities, to see if economizing can free resources for core activities to boost competence in reading, writing, mathematics, and science.

2. *Similar programs can be consolidated*, to achieve economies of scale. For example, separate health care programs, each with different claim forms, might be combined if eligibility requirements and benefit levels are similar. Other candidates for savings could include parallel programs funded by the central and sub-national governments, or multiple programs designed to assist low-income households.

3. *Appropriate fees can be imposed* for activities that are currently free, or for which fees have not kept pace with inflation. Good candidates could include imposing tuition for public universities, coupled with offering scholarships for low-income students, and charging reasonable admission fees for museums and public recreation facilities. Modest fees for medical services may also lead consumers to use them more carefully. For example, Thailand's 30 baht per consultation program, now called Universal Health Care, provides coverage to a large share

of the population, using a modest charge as a way to discourage unnecessary use of medical services.

4. The government can *require co-financing for certain activities*, to help reduce budget outlays. In the United States, for example, the federal (central) government has many programs requiring contributions from state or local governments to obtain federal funds. Examples include the federal Medicaid program, providing health benefits for low-income households, and funds for certain infrastructure improvements. Particularly for the latter program, the co-financing requirement may encourage units of government to think carefully before seeking federal support for infrastructure projects. However, co-financing requirements can sometimes cause a financially constrained unit of government to cancel a seemingly worthwhile program, such as New Jersey's decision in 2010 to cancel a tunnel that might have doubled the capacity for commuter train travel to New York City.[26]

5. The government can *improve the targeting of benefits* for specific programs, where feasible. For example, child care or tuition subsidies can be limited to low-income households. Similarly, Singapore has reduced budgetary outlays for hospital care by focusing subsidies on those using the least expensive hospital wards. Subsidies are substantial for those using multi-bed class C and B2 wards, while subsidies are limited to 20 percent for those using four-bedded class B1 rooms and not at all for those using A class (private) rooms. To limit subsidizing wealthy patients using lower class hospital rooms, subsidies were cut for users with relatively high incomes or assessed housing values.[27]

6. Governments can *postpone less essential capital projects while preserving spending to maintain existing facilities*. It is easiest to defer spending for projects not yet started, or only in the design stage, rather

---

[26]See, for example, Frassinelli, M. (2010), "Governor Christie Cancels ARC Tunnel for Second Time," *Newark Star-Ledger* (October 27), http://www.nj.com/news/index.ssf/2010/10/gov_christie_cancels_arc_tunne.html.

[27]See Ministry of Health (2010), "Singapore Healthcare System," http://www.ahp.mohh.com.sg/singapore_healthcare_system.html.

than postponing or canceling projects already under construction. Moreover, spending for maintenance, which is often cheaper than new construction, can extend the useful life of public institutions and reduce the need for replacement facilities.

7.6.4. More fundamental expenditure reforms

Besides the above measures, more fundamental reforms can be used to improve expenditure control.

1. *Adopting a medium-term budgeting framework.* One strategy many countries have taken involves *adopting a medium-term budget framework* (MTBF). An MBFT establishes medium-term objectives for fiscal policy and uses those as a way of guiding annual budgets and the choice of specific spending programs. A recent World Bank study has noted that an MBFT involves setting an overall envelope for budget resources and a "bottom up estimation of current and medium-term costs of existing policies," with an annual update to reflect changes in overall policies. The government then applies this technique when preparing the annual budget.[28]

Pakistan's experience is illustrative. The agency responsible for its MTBF, for example, has noted that

> *The main feature of a MTBF is that annual budget preparation is carried out within a framework which takes into account the resources expected to be available to the government over the medium term. The main objectives of the MTBF are to:*
>
> - *Strengthen fiscal discipline, by creating an orderly framework for management of the annual budget over the medium term;*

---

[28] Kasek, L. and D. Webber, eds. (2009), *Performance-Based Budgeting and Medium Term Expenditure Frameworks in Emerging Europe* (World Bank), http://siteresources.worldbank. org/INTECA/Resources/WBperformanceBudgetingTEF.pdf, p. 38.

- *Strengthen the allocation of federal resources to the government's strategic priorities;*
- *Improve operational efficiency, by strengthening the capacity of federal line ministries to prepare and manage their budgets effectively.*"[29]

A well-designed MTBF can provide a strategy for improving fiscal performance over a several year period. If honored, it can also deflect last-minute requests for non-emergency spending that might derail efforts to achieve medium-term objectives.

2. *Privatizing certain activities.* A second strategy involves *privatizing activities for which government management or operation offers no comparative advantage.* Many governments routinely subcontract certain activities, such as cleaning services or trash collection, to private companies that can provide the service at lower cost. Provided that the contractors are chosen through competitive bidding, without corruption, this type of contracting reduces the size of the government workforce. It also allows governments to shift contractors if services deteriorate or new entrants offering comparable quality at lower cost enter the market, avoiding problems that could arise from having to fire permanent employees. If there is an extensive public enterprise sector, appropriate privatization may enable the government to terminate money-losing activities and secure more effective service through private management. Chapter Eight, on state enterprises, explores privatizing state enterprises in greater detail.

3. *Reviewing pay and employment policy.* A third strategy involves a *more thorough review of government pay and employment policy.* Measures can include providing incentive pay and appropriate bonuses for exceptional performance; rethinking political staffing in ministries; giving civil servants more managerial authority; and reviewing the

---

[29]Government of Pakistan, Finance Division (MTBF Secretariat), "Medium Term Budgetary Framework: Frequently Asked Questions," http://www.mtbfpakistan.gov.pk/pdf/MTBF %20FAQs-FINAL.pdf.

balance between short-term, low-skilled workers and higher skilled, permanent employees. A civil service review may also offer a way of addressing corruption. Anti-corruption measures could include providing more competitive salaries, offering rewards for reporting corrupt activities, and creating an environment that supports clean government. In some cases, it may require firing corrupt officials and officers. Measures to establish or strengthen competitive bidding for goods and services by government would support these efforts.

7.7. Summary

Government expenditure can provide useful support for the private sector while providing goods and services that the private sector cannot be expected to provide efficiently or in optimal amounts. Nevertheless, each of the main economic categories of expenditure poses specific issues, and governments need to be aware of these when setting policy and developing budgets. In reviewing spending, governments need to monitor potentially unproductive expenditure and take measures to relocate spending toward more productive programs. They should also look closely at entitlements and other mandatory expenditure programs and watch efforts to create new ones.

Besides on-budget activities, governments must also monitor off-budget spending, including quasi-fiscal activities, and beware the proliferation of tax expenditures as alternatives to formal spending programs. They also need to monitor contingent expenditures and be aware of the risks of public-private partnerships before undertaking such projects. Finally, governments can apply a variety of techniques to improve expenditure control over the short and medium term, including the development of a medium-term budget framework to ensure that annual spending programs are consistent with longer term fiscal targets.

Chapter Eight: State Enterprises

State enterprises are government-owned entities that operate like independent organizations or institutions, with their own mandates, revenues, and budgets. Although central banks and other state-owned financial institutions operate in the financial sector, most state enterprises represent non-financial entities. Typical state enterprises include state-owned airlines, airport authorities, public universities, publicly owned electric and telephone companies, and deposit insurance agencies. Many countries also have state-owned banks, and some have state-owned companies that produce more conventional goods and services, such as automobiles (Malaysia's Proton carmaker) and food products (Romania's earlier chain of state-owned bread factories and retail shops, which existed through the mid-1990s).

Governments have offered a variety of reasons to justify owning and operating state enterprises. However, government ownership has important implications for the efficiency and productivity of these entities. This chapter analyzes these issues in detail. It also explores the arguments and consequences for privatizing state enterprises and discusses measures governments can take to improve the efficiency of those enterprises that government wants to remain in the public sector.

8.1. Justifications for State Enterprises

Various arguments have been offered to justify government ownership of different enterprises. Many of these follow from the claim that private operation is impossible. Each argument requires careful scrutiny.

8.1.1. *Natural monopoly*

Probably the most common justification for government ownership of an enterprise is that the good or service provided represents a *natural monopoly*. As discussed in Chapter One, natural monopolies arise when a good or service can be provided at declining average costs. With declining average costs, it is cheaper for a single enterprise to provide the good or service, rather than having competing suppliers. Thus, the largest producer will tend to eliminate all its competitors, because the producer can efficiently undersell any smaller supplier. This situation may arise, for example, with an electricity distributor or a provider of landline telephone service.

The tendency for a single producer to dominate the market can be expected to result in monopoly, with all the attendant economic problems. Figure 8.1 illustrates the situation. A monopolist will maximize profits by choosing to produce at the point where marginal revenue equals marginal cost. At this point, the retail price (on the average revenue curve) exceeds marginal revenue, so the producer will

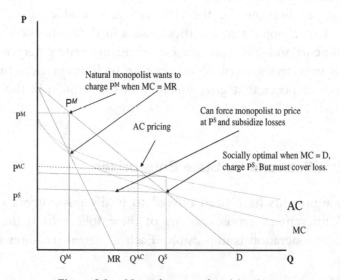

Figure 8.1.   Natural monopoly pricing issues.

earn a profit indicated by the area between P_M and the average cost curve for all sales. At the high price P_M, however, consumers will want to buy relatively few units.

If the government intervenes and acquires the monopoly supplier, it need not try to maximize profits. Instead, it can set the price at the socially efficient level, where price (the point on the demand curve) equals marginal cost. At this point, P_S, consumers will want to purchase substantially more units (Q_S). However, at P_S the price covers only the marginal cost of production, not the overhead or fixed costs incurred. Thus, the government loses an amount equal to the difference between the average cost and the marginal cost at output Q_S for each unit sold. The government must cover this loss in some way, either by allocating funds from general revenues or by having the state-owned enterprise borrow or issue bonds to offset the loss.

If the government lacks the resources to cover the loss or prefers to allocate its funds to other activities, the price can be set at a level where it covers the average production costs (P_{AC}). In this case, the state enterprise covers all of its costs and needs no budget support from government. At this price, which is somewhat less efficient from the standpoint of the market (because the price exceeds marginal cost), consumers will want to purchase somewhat fewer units (Q_{AC}).

8.1.2. *Externalities require public management*

A second argument sometimes offered for public ownership is that the good or service involved has *important externalities requiring a public entity* to secure. For example, an airport authority has the responsibility of maintaining clean and reliable service, which includes allocating gate assignments among competing airlines. Under private ownership, a profit-maximizing manager might choose to limit cleaning services and other amenities, in order to maximize net revenue. Alternatively, gate assignments might be priced at a high level, possibly reducing the number of airlines willing to use the airport. If the airlines determined the choice of manager, the airport might be managed so as to maximize benefits for the airlines, rather than consumers. In particular, airlines with existing landing rights might collude to make it difficult for new entrants to obtain convenient landing slots.

With public ownership, an impartial manager not subject to side payments could assess the benefits and costs associated with different levels of service and chose a level that maximized the net public value of the facility. Not constrained to maximize profits, a public authority could increase spending on maintenance and set gate fees at levels sufficient to finance an acceptable level of airport amenities. In addition, the public manager could allocate gate assignments and landing slots through competitive bidding, avoiding collusion, and allow any airline willing to pay the price to obtain a desired slot.

Similar arguments have been raised about public management of postal facilities. Because of the high costs associated with serving remote and sparsely populated areas, a private postal service might provide only limited service to such regions or impose high fees to provide service. A public manager, not constrained to maximize profits, could ensure service to all regions, setting rates at a level to cover all costs and using profits from more densely populated areas to offset losses in remote areas.

8.1.3. *High risk or capital scarcity precludes private entry*

On occasion, governments will claim that *high risk or a shortage of capital* makes it impossible for the private sector to undertake a project with clear public benefits. For example, until public agencies demonstrated the feasibility of launching satellites, private firms hesitated to do so. More recently, however, firms have been willing to launch satellites to facilitate telephone service. In the United States, until the U.S. government's Federal Housing Administration demonstrated in the 1930s that consumers would repay loans covering a high fraction of home value, private lenders rarely provided mortgages to cover much more than half the value of a home.

Once firms observed that consumers would honor their commitments, private firms became willing to offer high loan-to-value mortgages. Indeed, the private sector has since developed instruments, such as private mortgage insurance, to reduce the risk of default so that private firms will lend more than 80% of a home's assessed value.

As regards capital scarcity, many developing countries claim that private entities lack the capital or access to financing to undertake large infrastructure projects. The Chinese government, for example, could argue that no private firm would have undertaken the gigantic, more than US$1 billion Three Gorges Project on the Yangtze River. The Egyptian government could make a similar claim regarding the Aswan Dam, for which Egypt received considerable assistance from the Soviet Union and the United Nations Economic and Social Council (UNESCO).

8.1.4. *The service is essential but users cannot pay*

Still another claim offered for state ownership or operation is that an entity provides *an essential service for which users cannot pay*. For example, primary and secondary education are very costly. In many developing countries, independent private schools must charge the equivalent of many thousands of US dollars per student yearly to cover the costs of teachers, facilities, books, supplies, and administration. Few private citizens have the wealth or income to afford such costs or even the significantly lower costs (several hundreds of US dollars per student each year) for schooling at much simpler facilities. To ensure that children receive enough schooling to attain literacy and basic skills in mathematics and writing, governments create and operate public schools, using public funds to make schooling accessible to children of all incomes. A similar argument could be offered for maintaining some public health centers. In some countries, governments offer this argument to help justify public ownership of electrical distribution services, to ensure that power can be provided to low-income households.

8.1.5. The public sector can manage the operation better

Governments have argued that public ownership will likely yield better results in providing certain critical services, such as national security and the courts. Having the private sector manage the military could result in unequal security or favoritism toward certain areas or groups of citizens. The same might apply even more strongly to police protection, where local groups sometimes hire at great expense security services that protect themselves and their property, but not others. In the legal realm, public management might be considered important to ensure the impartiality of trials, although private parties in many countries have willingly engaged private arbitration services to resolve commercial disputes.

8.2. Economic Implications of State Ownership

State ownership has important implications for how public enterprises operate. State ownership affects the incentives for production and management, with important consequences for consumers. It also influences pricing decisions and can have important ramifications for enterprise financing. State ownership can also affect innovation and how enterprises undertake planning.

8.2.1. Incentives for production and management

State ownership has consequences for production and management at public enterprises. Managers are expected to meet certain performance objectives, which typically involve levels of production, standards of service, and covering costs or minimizing losses. Apart from the unusual enterprise for which the government requires a certain level of earnings, however, *state enterprise managers rarely face the same profit pressures that managers in private firms confront*. State enterprise managers need not meet periodically with investors or the financial media to discuss company performance, nor do they face calls from boards of directors or major stockholders to achieve certain levels of earnings per share. Thus, they are shielded from a major concern that drives the activity of the typical private sector executive.

State enterprise *managers also face much less pressure from consumers* regarding the price or quality of goods and services their enterprises provide. Unlike private firms, which typically have to compete for sales, state enterprises often have a privileged market position — either a monopoly or a dominance that results from government support or other unique factors, such as a nationwide branch network that postal savings banks automatically enjoy. Because of this special position, and because consumers usually lack alternative sources of supply, state enterprises rarely need worry about consumer dissatisfaction. When dissatisfied, consumers are more likely to complain to the government, or vote to change their public officials, than abandon the public enterprises. For example, few consumers can afford to withdraw their children from public school systems if they are dissatisfied. However, they can and do approach their public officials to address school problems. In the United States, many school districts have responded to public dissatisfaction by providing some choice of schools that students may attend, including charter schools with special mandates and greater flexibility in setting curriculum and hiring and firing teachers.

Because of their special status and advantaged position in the market place, *state enterprises also tend to be shielded from the pressures to innovate* that private firms face from competing producers or suppliers of services. For example, few airports face much competition from other airport authorities, although the quality of air travel affects a region's or a nation's competitiveness. Even in localities with multiple airports, competition between them is rare, and a single public agency (such as the Port Authority of New York and New Jersey) often manages all the facilities in the immediate region. At most, government officials, observing service levels in other countries, may press for their own public institutions to match these. Competition has led airports in Singapore and in Seoul, Korea to offer state-of-the-art facilities with free Internet terminals. However, such innovations have yet to induce changes at airports in many other countries. School systems in many US cities and regions closely monitor the performance of their students using standardized tests, and local governments compete in attracting residents by advertising the average test scores that students in their schools achieve. Indeed, a few school districts in the United States, aware of Singapore's success with teaching mathematics to primary school students, have ordered textbooks used in Singaporean public schools.[1]

Still another factor affecting performance at state enterprises is that the *financial incentives enterprises can offer managers are usually limited*. Salaries at public enterprises are often based on a scale similar to that for civil servants. In many countries, laws and regulations restrict the opportunities to provide financial rewards to high-performing executives. In addition, political pressure makes it hard to grant high salaries, give bonuses, or provide large incentive payments to many enterprise managers. Citizens who rarely complain about high salaries paid to private executives often protest when managers at state enterprises receive competitive salaries or significant bonuses. In addition, because state enterprises are publicly owned, these entities cannot grant their executives stock options. Perhaps more importantly, managers at state enterprises often receive little or no reward for achieving cost control. Instead, managers may be attacked if they pursue normal management goals too aggressively. For example, Michelle Rhee, the Chancellor of Schools for Washington, DC from 2007 to 2010, attracted widespread criticism after closing more than 20 schools said to have excess capacity and firing more than 200 teachers claimed to be seriously deficient. Public opposition to her decisions contributed to the defeat of Washington's then mayor and to Ms. Rhee's decision, in October 2010, to resign.

---

[1] See, for example, Jacobs, J. (2010), "U.S. Schools Adopt Singapore Math" (October 10), http://www.joannejacobs.com/2010/10/u-s-schools-adopt-singapore-math.

8.2.2. *Factors contributing to management problems*

Managerial problems at state enterprises reflect not only the lack of competition and limited financial incentives for performance but also more structural problems. These include issues related to the manager's role as an agent for the public and various bureaucratic failures.

1. *Principal-agent problems.* In many state enterprises, managers worry that revealing problems will only cause their political masters to criticize them, since politicians want evidence that enterprises are performing well. Perhaps more important, managers face powerful incentives to use their positions for private gain, rather than to provide public service. Where salaries are low and the enterprise has considerable power, enterprise managers can use their positions to extract rents, in the form of bribes or other side payments. In many countries, enterprise managers at state monopolies are notorious for extracting such payments from contractors, much as tax inspectors in some countries demand payments from taxpayers to avoid harassment. In some public health services, medical officers routinely receive bribes from patients. The author has even heard of school principals in one transition country demanding payment to allow children to transfer to a particular school.

2. *Bureaucratic failures.* In many state enterprises, *managers are chosen for political reasons, rather than competence.* International agencies, for example, are notorious for using nationality as a criterion for selecting their chief executives. Sometimes this principle also affects senior managers. In many countries, managers of certain enterprises must belong to a favored political party or have the support of important members of parliament. Although school superintendents in some school districts are chosen by competition, using executive search systems, others are selected because they are close friends or allies of the local mayor or regional government executive.

Another bureaucratic problem that plagues public enterprises is *political interference*. Politicians frequently intervene in state enterprise activity to ensure that jobs are created in their home areas or to steer the awarding of contracts to political allies. Political interference can also result when political leaders have ideological views that may conflict with the judgment of managers about how to run the enterprise efficiently. David Gunn, for example, a highly regarded manager of transit systems in Toronto and New York City, was fired as the director of Amtrak, the US rail passenger system, when he refused to implement certain Presidential directives aimed at decentralizing rail operations.[2] As a result of political interference, enterprise managers lack the managerial discretion typically available to their private sector counterparts. For example, managers in many state enterprises must consult with the government on price increases or major changes in strategy, because providing certain services at "acceptable" prices is a matter of public policy in many units of government.

Finally, the same lack of financial incentives for good performance also encourages many enterprise managers to *avoid risk*. When addressing inefficiency threatens important political interests and offers few financial rewards, many managers find it preferable simply to sit back and allow current policies to continue. Thus, the incentives at many state enterprises encourage managers to *pursue the quiet life*, keeping the enterprise running smoothly but avoiding reforms that could upset workers or politicians.

8.2.3. *Consequences for efficiency*

The various incentives affecting the management of state enterprises can mean that operating and administrative costs exceed norms in the private sector. Wages may exceed those in private firms, and pressures to provide jobs to those who might otherwise be unemployed can lead

---

[2] See Hughes, J. (2005), "Amtrak Fires David Gunn as Railroad's Chief Executive (Update Five)," *Bloomberg* (November 9), http://www.bloomberg.com/apps/news?pid=newsarchive&sid=a7O0SxbxAgos.

to overstaffing and low employee productivity. Enterprise managers may be unable to select the lowest cost contractors and suppliers of materials. In addition, rents may exceed those in the private sector, because managers have no incentive (and may face disincentives) to bargain hard with potential suppliers.

Financial advantages provided to state enterprises may also subsidize operations and provide special advantages in competing with private firms. For example, government loan guarantees may enable state enterprises to borrow at below-market costs or obtain financing more easily than can private companies. As a result of these advantages, state enterprises may crowd out private investment. It may also be hard to compare costs at private firms and state enterprises and assess the relative efficiency of each.

Many of the cost advantages provided to state enterprises result from their facing a *soft budget constraint.* This can include ready access to transfers from the government budget to cover losses and an ability to pressure banks into granting softer lending terms and deferring or rescheduling overdue loan payments. Greater access to loans, lower borrowing costs, less pressure to repay loans, and, when needed, recourse to the government budget all make it easier for state enterprises to offer their goods and services at super-competitive prices. Thus, state enterprises can undercut private competitors, particularly if the enterprises have a dominant share in the market. Alternatively, state enterprises can use their advantages to operate less efficiently than private competitors while remaining in business.

Empirical work has shown that, on average, provision by private firms has been more efficient than by state enterprises, even in noncompetitive markets. For example, Shirley and Walsh (2001) found that private firms did better, not only in competitive markets but even in monopolistic ones because of inefficiencies that governments in practice do not overcome, even in advanced economies. Only five of the 52 studies they surveyed showed that public ownership was superior. Most showed either a better private sector performance (32) or no difference (15). In addition, of 21 empirical studies cited in their paper, 14 showed that most firms perform better after privatization. Not one performed worse.[3]

Despite the averages, a determined government, bent on promoting efficiency at state-owned firms, can have a positive impact. For example, Singapore's DBS Bank regularly wins awards for excellent service and innovation, despite the government being a dominant shareholder. The same applies to Singapore Airlines, which typically earns profits while winning awards as one of the world's top airlines.

8.2.4. *Consequences for consumers*

As noted earlier, the dominant position of many state enterprises means that they have less need to address the needs of consumers, unless the government (as owner) requires it. Consumers typically have few choices when one firm has a monopoly or is the dominant service provider. Thus, consumer power alone generally cannot compel dominant state enterprises to change. Where the state enterprise uses its monopoly to charge high prices or provide inferior service, consumers may buy fewer units, seek other products as substitutes, or simply do without. Indeed, under central planning, the poor output of many state enterprises led many consumers either to amass unwanted savings (because they found too little worth buying) or to smuggle in better quality consumer goods from abroad.

8.2.5. *Pricing at state enterprises*

In general, pricing goods at marginal cost gives consumers the best information about the relative costs of different products. This is one reason why monopolies misallocate resources and why governments argue for a role in owning or setting prices at monopoly suppliers.

---

[3]*Shirley, M. and P. Walsh (2001), "Private vs. Public Ownership: The Current State of the Debate," World Bank Research Paper No. 2420, http://papers.ssrn.com/sol3/papers.cfm?abstract_id=261854.

However, pricing at state enterprises often reflects cross-subsidization, partial cost recovery, and political interference. For example, in countries where state-owned electric firms charge consumers much lower prices than private firms, business customers are forced to subsidize private households. Similarly, when a national airline is forced to service far-flung, sparsely populated regions at low prices, passengers living in major population centers may be charged high fares to cover losses elsewhere in the network. This cross-subsidization may create incentives for new private airlines to enter the market and offer cheaper flights between major cities. Similarly, in the United States, high fares between New York City and Washington, DC on the publicly owned rail system (which must cover losses incurred in serving more remote parts of the US) have led to the introduction of much cheaper bus service between these cities.

Where state enterprises have a monopoly and strong support from their government shareholder, they face no immediate penalty from charging high prices and losing sales. At the same time, so long as they have access to budget support, they can afford to set prices below average, and even below marginal, cost. However, pricing below marginal cost creates deficits and demands for budget assistance. Either way, pricing far from marginal cost creates difficulties.

8.2.6. *Financing issues*

As noted earlier, soft budget constraints, in the form of easy access to budget subsidies, may allow state enterprises to hide losses. Thus, it can be hard determining whether the enterprise is covering its costs. Access to the government's capital budget may give state enterprises a competitive advantage or cause expenses to be underestimated. It may also crowd out other investments that only the budget can finance, such as additional expenditures for school or road construction. For this reason, all budgetary financing for state enterprises, whether for current expenses or capital projects, deserves careful review.

Not so long ago, many countries provided substantial support to state enterprises. In some cases, budgetary transfers exceeded central government funding for health and education, as reported in the World Bank study entitled *Bureaucrats in Business*.[4] Efforts by many governments to reduce fiscal deficits have helped curb state enterprise deficits in more recent years.

8.3. Reforming State Enterprises

With state enterprises facing strong incentives to perform inefficiently, many countries have moved to reform their publicly owned entities. When deciding to do so, governments should first decide on the desired size and structure of the state enterprise sector. Once they have decided which enterprises should remain publicly owned, the authorities should move to reform and restructure these entities. The remaining enterprises should be privatized — sold to private buyers — or closed.

8.3.1. *Whether to divest or reform*

Figure 8.2 provides a useful "decision tree" of how to address the issue. After determining that the country is ready for state enterprise reform, the first question is whether the enterprises are potentially competitive. If yes, the next question is whether the enterprises can be divested. If divestiture is possible, the authorities should introduce competition in the relevant markets and then use a method for divestiture that ensures transparency and allows for competitive bidding. If divestiture is not possible, the authorities should determine if contractual arrangements with the private sector for managing the enterprise can be established. Management contracts, where possible, can be useful, so long as the production and delivery technology and consumer

---

[4]See World Bank (1995), *Bureaucrats in Business: The Economics and Politics of Government Ownership* (New York: Oxford University Press), Figure 1.1, p. 48, http://www-wds.worldbank. org/external/default/woscontentserver/IW3P/IB/1995/09/01/000009265_39612191046 59/Rendered/PDF/multiopage.pdf.

Decision Tree: Divest or Reform?

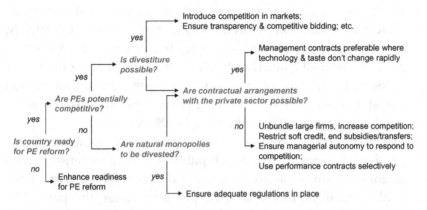

Figure 8.2.   Deciding whether to divest or reform a state enterprise.

Source: Reproduced from *Bureaucrats in Business: Summary* (1995, Figure 8.1).

tastes do not change often. If contractual arrangements cannot be implemented, the authorities should unbundle large enterprises and increase competition; restrict easy credit and end budgetary subsidies and transfers; ensure that enterprise management has the autonomy to respond to competition; and consider using performance contracts, but on a selective basis.

If the enterprises are not potentially competitive, enterprises that are natural monopolies will need to be subject to appropriate regulation before they are divested, to limit the possibilities for monopoly pricing. Enterprises that are not natural monopolies should probably be closed, unless a private entity feels that the franchise is valuable and is willing to purchase the entity and absorb its debt.

The following examples illustrate the kinds of alternatives authorities have in reforming or divesting state enterprises.

1. *Public utility*. Public utilities, such as electricity generating and distributing enterprises or landline telephone companies, are often publicly owned because they provide an essential service, have

large capital requirements, and may be natural monopolies, with declining average costs of service as the number of customers rises. Enterprise reform could lead to privatization, with the company subject to regulation regarding prices and service. Alternatively, the firm could remain a public utility but be charged with setting prices to cover all costs, thereby eliminating the need for budgetary support. In the case of telephone companies, the authorities can introduce competition by allowing private operators, as well as the state enterprise, to offer cellular telephone service.

2. *Postal service.* A government-owned postal service can be said to provide an essential service with public goods characteristics, such as ensuring universal access to mail delivery. Where part of the public lives in remote or sparsely populated areas, this portion of the customer base may entail losses. In addition, as with public utilities, the more densely populated regions of the country may exhibit declining average costs as the size of the mail network increases. Nevertheless, the government may authorize private firms to provide express mail and courier services, so that consumers can benefit from competition. A state enterprise could continue to provide regular mail service, so long as postal revenues cover all costs.

3. *State-owned airline.* A state-owned national airline can ensure that all regions of the country are served. It may also bring prestige and enhance tourism. If run profitably, the airline may generate earnings in hard currency. However, many state-owned airlines incur losses, because of poor management, overstaffing, or an inability to charge sufficient tariffs on profitable routes to offset losses on less trafficked routes. An alternative could be to privatize the airline, on condition that acceptable service is provided to outlying areas in return for a pre-specified subsidy.

8.3.2. *Enterprise restructuring: Key issues*

As a general matter, enterprises with decreasing average costs (or increasing returns to scale), such as railways, the electricity grid, landline telecommunications, and enterprises whose activities provide essential support for large parts of the economy, such as an airport or highway authority, are good candidates for restructuring, rather than privatization. Once the decision to restructure has been taken, the key issues become how to improve efficiency and increase responsiveness to consumer demand.

8.3.2.1. *Changing operating assumptions*

The first step toward enterprise restructuring involves making the organization operate in a commercial manner. Except for special operations, such as serving outlying areas, enterprises should be expected to cover their costs and avoid loss-making activities. Enterprise managers should undertake serious labor negotiations and be rewarded, not penalized, for efficiency-enhancing moves to streamline operations, while giving opportunities for existing workers to be trained and upgraded. Enterprises must be allowed to apply commercial purchasing standards, including competitive bidding and arm's-length negotiations with suppliers. Perhaps most important, enterprises should be forced to borrow at market interest rates and avoid recourse to the state budget for losses on regular operations. Soft budget constraints, which create inefficiencies and unfair competition with private firms, should end, as should special privileges. Moreover, underperforming firms should be allowed to close or go bankrupt. In 2001, for example, the Swiss government allowed Swissair, which incurred large losses after ill-fated expansion, to close the airline after refusing further capital injections. A successor private airline, Swiss, formed in 2002, absorbed many of Swissair's assets and was acquired in 2005 by Germany's Lufthansa airline.

8.3.2.2. *Organizational changes*

At many enterprises, separating commercial from public service objectives offers a way for the unit's regular activities to be performed in a commercial manner. At Singapore's DBS Bank, standard banking activities are expected to show a profit, much as in any privately owned institution. However, small savers linked to the bank through its acquisition of the previous Post Office Savings Bank (POSB) benefit from some special provisions. Children up to age 21 have a minimum deposit of only S$1, as against the regular minimum deposit of S$500. In addition, no monthly fees are levied on children with current (i.e., checking) accounts whose savings balances fall below S$1,500.

Besides establishing distinct commercial and public service objectives, enterprise oversight should be shielded from the political process. While the legislature should periodically review the basis for an enterprise's existence, regular supervision should be conducted at a technical level, much as a company's board of directors periodically reviews the performance of the firm's chief executive officer and stockholders have a chance to raise questions during the company's annual meeting. In particular, politicians should not be involved in day-to-day supervision of the enterprise, second-guessing management on matters related to implementing policy directives (as opposed to setting policy). In addition, the government's role as majority or sole owner of the enterprise should be separated from its regulatory duties. In a country with state-owned banks, the government unit that owns these banks should be separate from the agency performing bank regulation and supervision. Supervisory agencies should operate independently, so as to avoid conflicts of interest that could favor state-owned banks at the expense of private institutions.

8.3.2.3. *Reforming management*

Linking management compensation to enterprise performance represents a key step in enterprise restructuring. Managers should receive appropriate rewards if the enterprise performs well and face penalties if performance falls short of expectations. In addition, governments can consider various ways to change management, in order to improve performance. One option involves letting foreign investors share in the ownership of some enterprises, so as to encourage them to provide new management and technology to these institutions. Alternatively, performance or management contracts can be created for specific enterprises.

Performance contracts represent contracts that enterprises establish with in-house managers. These contracts specify particular objectives that managers must attain, such as the levels of profitability or reductions in losses. Performance contracts typically provide rewards for managers who achieve specified objectives. The rewards can include profit-sharing, if the enterprise achieves a stipulated level of profits. Under some contracts, managers who fail to reach certain targets can be penalized or fired.

State enterprises that use *management contracts*, by comparison, contract with outside individuals or firms to manage the enterprise, in return for specified compensation. Management contracts effectively privatize managing the enterprise, allowing outsiders to run it. In so doing, the enterprise can remain in the public sector while securing the benefits of new management.

Evidence from studies compiled in the World Bank's 1995 report, *Bureaucrats in Business*, suggest that performance contracts, on average, have yielded poorer results than management contracts. A study of 12 state enterprises in six countries that established performance contracts showed that none of the enterprises showed significantly better returns on assets, while three experienced lower returns. Only two of the 12 recorded better labor productivity. Perhaps more significant, as many enterprises recorded a decline in total factor productivity (TFP) as showed an improvement, and TFP showed no significant change in 6 of the 12 enterprises. By comparison, of 20 enterprises in 11 countries that used management contracts, 13 recorded improvements in both productivity and profitability, six had mixed results, and only two showed no significant improvement in either measure.[5] At least for the enterprises studied, securing new managers appeared to make a substantial difference in enterprise performance. Outside managers brought new ideas and were willing to address previously sacrosanct issues, allowing enterprises to reduce costs, improve productivity, and raise profits. Of course, new management does not always lead to

---

[5]World Bank (1995), *Bureaucrats in Business, op. cit.*, Ch. 3.

success. Managers need to understand the culture of the enterprise and obtain support from workers in order to succeed.

8.3.2.4. *Introducing competition*

Increasing competition can help in securing better enterprise performance. Allowing new competitors, or restructuring an enterprise so that private firms can compete on more even terms, can compel a state enterprise to respond, especially if the government makes clear that the enterprise will close if it cannot compete. Permitting competition from domestically owned private firms may be the most politically acceptable way to introduce competition. However, allowing foreign firms to enter the market may introduce new technology and strategies for serving the public, particularly in less advanced economies. Developing more effective capital markets can also support competition, by making it easier for private firms and individuals to raise the funds needed to establish viable competitors in the market.

8.3.2.5. *Risks from restructuring*

To be sure, restructuring may bring costs as well as benefits. Allowing or compelling enterprises to cover costs may lead to higher prices and corresponding consumer dissatisfaction, particularly from those accustomed to enjoying free or unsustainably cheap services. Enterprise closures usually lead to job losses, and communities dependent on enterprise establishments can suffer major losses of income and possibly revenue that support public services. Adverse consequences to regions and specific interest groups can lead to political outcries and pressure to reverse the reforms. Similarly, the public may protest the increases in salaries offered to successful managers.

Nevertheless, successful restructuring can bring about major improvements, not just for the enterprise but also for a region or, in some cases, a nation's economy. The recent *restructuring of India's state-owned railways* offers a useful case study. In 2001, Indian Railways failed to pay its customary dividend to the government and saw its cash reserves dwindle to 3.6 billion Rupees, equivalent to US$80 million at the time. Lalu Prasad Yadav, who became Railways Minister in 2004, introduced important reforms, such as having freight cars carry heavier loads and reducing the average turnaround time of trains from seven to five days. These measures led to substantial financial improvements, with Indian Railways achieving a surplus of 215 billion rupees (US$4.5 billion) during the 2006–2007 fiscal year. Minister Lalu Prasad Yadav attributed the reforms largely to greater efficiency. Indeed, the head of India's Federation of Chambers of Commerce and Industry was reported as saying that "The railways are now working like a private corporation."[6] Many business schools have studied the improvements at Indian Railways and have concluded that more businesslike methods succeeded in making the agency profitable. After several years of rising surpluses, however, net revenues fell sharply during 2008–2009, to about half their level during the previous fiscal year.[7] This underscores the importance of continuing the reform process.

8.4. Privatization

If an enterprise is performing poorly and there is no compelling reason to keep it in the public sector, privatization becomes an attractive alternative, and many governments have chosen this option. Kikeri and Nellis (2004) have estimated that, during the 1990s, receipts from privatization totaled about US$850 billion, with most revenues coming from sales of enterprises in Europe. Proceeds from privatization in non-OCED countries have been estimated at about US$250 billion during the 1990s, with Latin American and Caribbean countries representing about 55% of the total.[8] Figure 8.3 presents relevant data.

---

[6]See Padmanabhan, A. (2007), "Tracking the Indian Railways' Turnaround Saga" (*Business Times*, July 21), http://indiainteracts.in/columnist/2007/07/21/Tracking-the-Indian-Railways-turnaround-saga.

[7]See Government of India (2009), Economic Survey 2009–10, Table 2.15, "Financial Performance of Indian Railways," http://indiabudget.nic.in/es2009-10/chapt2010/tab215.pdf.

[8]See Kikeri, S. and J. Nellis (2004), "An Assessment of Privatization," *World Bank Research Observer*, vol. 19 (Spring), pp. 87–118.

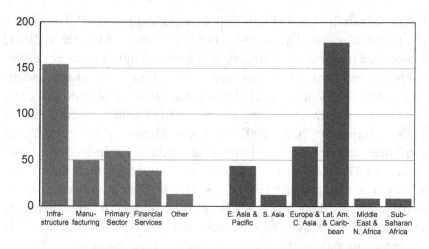

Figure 8.3.   Privatization by region and sector, 1990–1999.
Source: Kikeri and Nellis (2004).

To proceed with privatization, the government needs to prepare for the disposition of the enterprise, choose a method for privatization, and have plans to address the possible adverse consequences of privatization. The following materials address each of these issues.

8.4.1. *Preparing for privatization*

1. The first step in preparing for privatization involves *securing public support*. In many countries, particularly developing and emerging market nations, the public questions the wisdom of privatization. Customers may fear higher prices. Workers may worry about the loss of jobs. There may also be concerns that the newly privatized entity will focus only on maximizing profits, to the detriment of services to the public. Thus, the government needs to explain the reasons for privatization and discuss how possible consequences for prices, employment, and service standards will be met.
2. The second step involves *preparing the enterprise for disposition*. This may entail some legal work or clarification of ownership rights and responsibilities. Economists have debated the merits of restructuring enterprises before privatization, rather than selling

enterprises "as is" and letting purchasers decide on restructuring. Occasionally, however, governments may fear that the enterprise is in such poor shape that no one may want to acquire it as is. In this case, the government may decide to undertake some restructuring, or agree to absorb some of the enterprise's debt after privatization.

3. The third step involves *designing a regulatory contract*. If the enterprise is a natural monopoly, the government must develop an appropriate regulatory mechanism to ensure that the enterprise will price its goods and services at an appropriate level, with an eye to social welfare. Typically, the contract will allow for a certain rate of return and specify minimum standards of service, along with other operating criteria (such as ensuring that debt service obligations are honored).

8.4.2. *Methods of privatization*

Governments have many ways to privatize enterprises. These include public sales and auctions; direct sales to large (strategic) investors; management and/or employee buyouts; mass privatization; and restitution to previous owners. Each method has its advantages and disadvantages.

1. *Public sales and auctions.* Public sales and auctions include initial public offerings, public auctions of the enterprise or enterprise shares, sales of shares in enterprises that have already been "corporatized" (i.e., ordered to operate on a commercial bases), or sales of majority stakes in firms for which a portion of the shares are already publicly traded (typically on stock exchanges). In all these methods, the government makes available all or a controlling share of the enterprise in a way that allows relatively open bidding. Public sales and auctions provide the greatest opportunity for a "market" solution to privatizing an enterprise. This approach can be particularly attractive if the enterprise appears financially attractive and multiple parties have shown interest in becoming owners.

2. *Direct sales.* Direct sales represent negotiated sales of enterprises to strategic investors. Direct sales are less open than public sales, in that

the government pre-selects a particular individual or organization to which the enterprise is offered for sale. To that extent, direct sales are sometimes criticized as favoring particular investors and possibly leading to lower purchase prices than would result from public auctions. However, direct sales may be useful for selling a distressed enterprise, when it is not clear that a traditional auction or public sale would attract interested buyers.

3. *Management and/or employee buyouts.* In many countries, managers and employees of an enterprise, acting either individually or together, have had the chance to purchase the enterprise. Advocates of this approach sometimes argue that it allows those most knowledgeable about an enterprise to operate it, or that this approach can lead to management that is most sensitive about avoiding job losses. In some of the previously centrally planned economies, however, particularly Russia, many management and employee buyouts have been seen as letting previous managers and workers acquire valuable assets at cut-rate prices, in effect transferring the wealth of the society to a handful of well-placed individuals.

4. *Mass privatization.* Mass privatization is a technique developed during the early transition of the formerly centrally planned economies to capitalism. It involves distributing to the citizenry either shares in state enterprises or coupons that can be used to acquire shares in state enterprises. The developers of mass privatization hoped that, by allowing citizens to become owners of state enterprises, they would benefit from their privatization and support efforts to make these entities more efficient. Rationalization might cause some workers to lose their jobs, but the dividends from being shareholders would offset the loss of income and provide support as job losers sought work in new or expanding private firms. Mass privatization was also considered a way to help develop capital markets, as the need for shareholders to sell or exchange shares would encourage the formation of stock exchanges.

In practice, mass privatization largely failed to match the intentions of its founders. In countries such as the Czech and Slovak Republics, widespread unemployment, limited incomes, and inexperience drove many citizens to sell their shares or coupons to sharp-eyed entrepreneurs and investment funds that then used these coupons to amass large shareholdings in newly privatized firms.[9] Mass privatization has also been criticized for failing to create shareholder blocs sufficiently large to oversee management and compel reforms,[10] although in many cases the sale of individual shares to investment funds overcame that problem. Mass privatization did succeed, in countries such as Ukraine, in accelerating privatization, by transferring a large percentage of shares in state enterprises to the population in a comparatively short time, although the time varied considerably from one country to another.[11]

5. *Restitution.* Restitution involves the return of state enterprises to their original owners or heirs. This approach was used in a few countries to return companies that had been nationalized. In some cases, such as Bata Shoes, which started as a Czech company, the government approached former owners and agreed to allow them to reclaim part of their former assets.[12]

8.4.3. *Fiscal impact of privatization*

The fiscal consequences of privatization will depend on the terms on which state enterprises are privatized. Guarantees to undertake a certain volume of investment or maintain employment at a specified level typically reduce the selling price and the revenues to the government from privatization. Speed can also affect the fiscal impact, although the direction of impact can vary. In some cases, faster privatization will raise revenues, because of the purchaser's desire to take control

---

[9]See, for example, Shafik, N. (1995), "Making a Market: Mass Privatization in the Czech and Slovak Republics," *World Development*, vol. 23, pp. 1143–1156.

[10]Saving, J. L. (1998), "Privatization and the Transition to a Market Economy," *Federal Reserve Bank of Dallas Economic Review*, Fourth Quarter, http://www.dallasfed.org/research/er/1998/er9804b.pdf.

[11]See, for example, USAID and PriceWaterhouse Coopers (1998–99), "Final Report — Ukraine Mass Privatization Project," http://pdf.usaid.gov/pdf_docs/PDABR432.pdf.

[12]See Lank, A. G. (1997), "A Conversation with Tom Bata," *Family Business Review*, vol. 10 (Fall), pp. 211–220, http://www.decon.unipd.it/info/sid/materiale8/bel_bata.semiario-9-4.pdf.

and quickly begin restructuring. In others, speedy privatization may preclude interest from potentially strong buyers who want more time to consider a proposed offering. Imposing eligibility conditions on buyers will likely reduce the proceeds, by excluding some potential customers from bidding or entering negotiations. Often, privatization programs have been overloaded with inconsistent objectives, such as seeking to maximize the sales price while requiring investment or employment guarantees from the new owners. Thus, governments should clarify their objectives and be willing, for example, to compromise on the sales price if maintaining employment or obtaining certain levels of investment are key goals.

Despite the above difficulties, privatization has reduced the need for budget support to state enterprises in many developing and emerging market countries. IMF staff found that enterprise privatizations between the mid-1980s and late 1990s substantially reduced the size of budget transfers and subsidies to state enterprises in 10 such countries, with reductions of more than 1% of GDP in six countries (Argentina, Czech Republic, Mexico, Mongolia, Mozambique, and Philippines). Moreover, privatization tended, on average, to reduce the budget needs for domestic financing by about 1% of GDP.[13]

8.4.4. *Impact of privatization on employment, the share of state enterprise activity in GDP, and revenue*

Reform policies have considerably affected employment at state enterprises in less affluent countries. Sheshinski and Lopez-Calva observed from the World Bank database on privatization that, in low-income countries, state enterprise employment fell from about 21% of total employment in 1980 to less than 10% in 1997.[14] Privatization had a more pronounced effect on the contribution of state enterprises to

---

[13]Davis, J. *et al.* (2000), *Fiscal and Macroeconomic Impact of Privatization*, Occasional Paper No. 194 (Washington: International Monetary Fund), Ch. 4, pp. 17, 19.
[14]Sheshinski, E. and L. F. Lopez-Calva (2003), "Privatization and Its Benefits," *CESifo Economic Studies*, vol. 49, pp. 429–459 at p. 447.

GDP during this period, with the share falling from 15% of GDP in 1980 to 2.5% in 1999. For middle-income countries, the decline was noticeable but smaller: from about 11% in 1980 to 4% in 1999.[15]

The decline in employment corresponds with a common concern about privatization: that it eliminates jobs. To the extent that state enterprises have excess employment, privatization (like restructuring) can be expected to lead to some job loss, as new private managers move to rationalize operations. Governments can address this issue by having an effective social safety net in place, providing unemployment benefits and job retraining during the period of restructuring, so that unemployed workers have support while seeking new work. If privatization takes place during a period of economic growth, an optimistic scenario would show job losses eventually reversed, as workers let go by privatized enterprises eventually find other work in the private sector (or at the original enterprise, if restructuring leads to additional sales and the need for more workers). Figure 8.4, drawn from work by Gupta and others (1999), illustrates the stylized outcome in the optimistic scenario described here.[16]

Evidence suggests that the degree of protection afforded to the enterprise and the method of privatization have a bearing on the employment consequences. According to research by Gupta and others (2001),[17] privatizing an enterprise that had previously operated in a competitive environment has either no impact or a positive impact on employment, with the least positive effect occurring with management and employee buyouts. If the enterprise had previously operated in a protected environment, however, employment typically declines, with the greatest job losses occurring in the case of public sales and

---

[15] *Id.*, p. 430.

[16] See Gupta, S. *et al.* (1999), "Privatization, Social Impact, and Social Safety Nets," Working Paper No. 99/68 (Washington: International Monetary Fund: May), http://www.imf.org/external/pubs/ft/wp/1999/wp9968.pdf.

[17] Gupta, S. *et al.* (2001), "Privatization, Labor, and Social Safety Nets," *Journal of Economic Surveys*, vol. 15 (December), pp. 647–670.

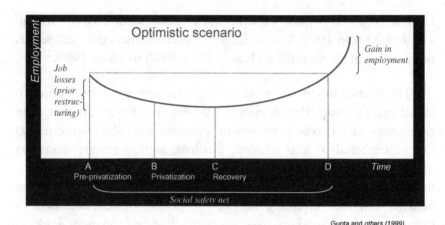

Figure 8.4.   Labor impact of privatization.

restitution. Management and employee buyouts represent the only exceptions. In these cases, job losses may be nil.

According to this study, the greatest increase in government revenue typically occurs with public sales, in line with the competitive nature of the process. Negotiated sales and management and employee buyouts also tend to generate net revenue for the budget, although the amounts are typically smaller. However, mass privatization and restitution generally yield no significant revenue, consistent with the nature of the process (distributing shares for free, in the first case, and returning enterprises to prior owners, in the second).

8.4.5. *Effect of privatization on enterprise performance and perceived welfare*

Megginson and Netter, reviewing studies of more than 200 privatized firms, have found that privatization generally improves their performance.[18] As summarized in Figure 8.5, relative to levels observed

---

[18]Megginson, W. L., and J. M. Netter (2001), "From State to Market: A Survey of Empirical Studies on Privatization," *Journal of Economic Literature*, vol. 39 (June), pp. 321–389, data drawn from Table 5, pp. 355–356.

Results of three studies covering over 200 firms

Indicator	Mean value before privati-zation	Mean value after privati-zation	Mean change due to privati-zation**	% change due to privati-zation		% of firms with improved performance
Profitability	9%	13%	+4%	46%	↑	68%
Efficiency*	97%	116%	+19%	19%	↑	82%
Investment	14%	19%	+5%	35%	↑	61%
Output*	94%	172%	+79%	84%	↑	80%
Employment	22,936	23,222	286	1%	↑	50%
Leverage	48%	44%	-5%	-10%	↓	67%
Dividends	3%	2%	+7%	231%	↑	80%

* Relative to year of privatization	** Change in percentage points.

Figure 8.5.   Effect of privatization on performance — cross-country evidence.
Source: Megginson and Netter (2001), Table 5, pp. 355–356.

under state ownership, privatization led to a 46% improvement in enter-prise profitability, a 19% gain in efficiency (real sales per employee), a 35% rise in investment, an 84% rise in output, and a more than doubling of enterprise dividends. Moreover, relative leverage declined by about 10%, suggesting that privatized firms were better capitalized or relied less heavily on debt financing. Improvements were observed in more than 60% of the firms surveyed. Interestingly, in the firms surveyed, average employment actually rose slightly. Sheshinski and Lopez-Calva (2003), summarizing the work of a number of studies, also found that privatization generally improves enterprise performance.

Research also suggests that privatization often increases general welfare, in the sense that most of the relevant groups benefit. According to a study by Galal *et al.*,[19] 11 of 12 major privatizations in four countries led to welfare gains, measured as a percentage of annual sales in the last year before the enterprise was privatized. In three cases, welfare gains were estimated at about half the annual sales in the year

---

[19] Galal, A. *et al.* (1994), *Welfare Consequences of Selling Public Enterprises: An Empirical Analysis* (New York: Oxford University Press).

before privatization. In one case, the privatization of Chile's Telecom, welfare gains were estimated to exceed total sales in the year before privatization. Another study, reviewing the privatization of public utilities in Argentina, found no net losers from privatization, with workers and buyers of the enterprises increasing their perceived surpluses. Privatization was estimated to raise GDP by about 0.9 percentage points, with a further 0.35 percent of GDP in gains if efficient regulation was also introduced.[20]

To summarize, the evidence indicates that privatization yields many benefits. Privatization has a positive effect on enterprise performance, particularly in competitive sectors. On average, privatization also improves the government budget. Privatization also contributes to developing a country's financial sector. Privatization does not, on average, reduce total employment (as opposed to employment at privatized enterprises). Moreover, there is some evidence suggesting that privatization improves welfare.

8.4.6. Public concerns about privatization and how governments can respond

Despite the evidence, the public often has a negative opinion of privatization, particularly in developing and emerging market countries. A World Bank report on reforming state enterprises found solid majorities of the public in seven Latin American countries in 2002 opposed to privatizing state enterprises involved with public utilities. Moreover, the objections had grown over time. Particularly high shares of the public — over 80% of Argentines and Chileans — were unhappy with privatization, despite clearly improved performance at the privatized firms. Layoffs, price increases, perceived lengthy delays

---

[20]Sheshinski and Lopez-Calva (2003), *op. cit.*, p. 446.

in receiving benefits, and the distributional effects of privatization help explain the dissatisfaction.[21]

This experience highlights the importance of building support for privatization before it takes place: explaining the goals and objectives, alerting the public to possible adverse effects, ensuring that privatized monopolies are subject to appropriate regulation, and providing a reasonable safety net for employees who may be laid off. It may also be important to offer financial support to low-income households that face price increases as a result of privatization.

Addressing the employment consequences of privatization is critical. Even if total employment in the economy remains unchanged or increases, privatization will likely cost at least some workers their jobs and lead to pay cuts or fewer hours of work for others. Thus, privatization plans should consider measures to help cushion the impact for the newly unemployed. Possible responses would include earmarking some of the proceeds of privatization to finance worker and consumer protection programs; advocating sequential, rather than all-at-once downsizing; and implementing other labor market policies, such as severance payments, job search assistance, training, and, if necessary, public works programs to provide temporary jobs and income to job losers.

Governments should also be aware of governance problems that can arise after privatization. For example, privatization may lead to the creation of private monopolies and private firms with negative externalities, such as tobacco manufacturers. In these cases, the government should be prepared to impose appropriate regulations, such as restricting cigarette advertising. Similarly, the privatization of mines or aluminum manufacturers should be accompanied by appropriate taxes and, if necessary, regulations to address the health hazards resulting

---

[21]World Bank (2004), Reforming *Infrastructure: Privatization, Regulation, and Competition* (Washington), p. 52.

from toxic waste products. Many countries with weak governance risk having corruption lead to inadequate regulation of newly privatized firms. Governance problems may explain many of the unfortunate experiences with privatizing public utilities in Latin America, where poorly conceived restructuring programs and hasty deregulation led to widespread public dissatisfaction.[22] For all these reasons, countries must guard against poorly designed programs.

8.5. Summary

Countries have offered many justifications for state enterprises. The most prominent include natural monopoly, externalities, high cost, and the risk associated with private operation of such entities. However, many factors create incentives for inefficiency at state enterprises, and experience shows that, on average, state enterprises run less efficiently than comparable private firms. Addressing these inefficiencies may require restructuring enterprises, establishing management contracts, privatization, and/or reviewing enterprise objectives and governance.

Restructuring can be beneficial for enterprises that the government believes should remain under public ownership. However, research shows that privatization often yields substantial benefits in the form of greater efficiency, higher profitability, and reduced financial risk. On average, privatization reduces budgetary costs and typically provides net revenues to the budget, particularly in the case of public sales and auctions. However, privatization can also have adverse consequences, including job losses, higher prices, and reductions in service for consumers as a byproduct of improving efficiency. Thus, governments should consider accompanying privatization with measures to address these consequences. These could include severance pay, job search and retraining, possibly short-term public works projects for laid off workers, and well-targeted subsidies to offset the costs of price increases for low-income households.

---

[22] *Ibid.*

Chapter Nine: Fiscal Aspects of Responding to Financial Crisis and Bank Restructuring

Financial crises have occurred regularly in recent decades. During the 1980s, countries in Latin America and Scandinavia, as well as the United States, all experienced bank failures and financial crises. The 1990s saw bank failures in Turkey (1994) and East Asia (1997) ignite macroeconomic crises and currency collapse. During the first decade of the 21st century a massive bubble in the housing market, fueled by lax monetary policy and regulatory failure, triggered a wave of financial losses that spread from the United States and United Kingdom to continental Europe, causing aggregate demand to plunge and triggering sharp declines in export demand around the world.

In each of these situations, national governments were asked to use their powers to stabilize the economy and remedy financial sector weaknesses. This led to massive increases in budget deficits, sometimes coupled with government takeovers of banks and financial institutions. This chapter reviews the circumstances that can trigger these developments, analyzing why and how governments respond to them and strategies that can make the responses less costly and more effective. Since this is a text on fiscal policy, the discussion focuses on the fiscal aspects of these issues.

9.1. Background: What Triggers Bank Failures and the Need for Restructuring

Before considering what role the public sector can play in addressing financial crises, it is useful to understand how banks can fail. Banks

313

ASSETS	LIABILITIES
Foreign Assets	Foreign Liabilities
Reserves: Required (Cen. Bk.) Excess Reserves	Deposits: Demand Time and savings Certificates (CDs)
Domestic Credit: Government securities Loans to private firms and HHs Less: Provision for Loan Losses Other assets	Other, less liquid liabilities Bank capital

Figure 9.1. Typical bank balance sheet.

are firms whose operation turns on financial leverage. Funds invested by bank owners allow banks to attract deposits, which in turn can be invested in loans and other assets, such as government bonds. Figure 9.1 offers a stylized presentation of a bank's balance sheet, with assets (loans and other assets) equaling liabilities (deposits, foreign and other liabilities, and bank capital). Banks typically hold some reserves against possible loan losses, and loans are recorded as a net asset item: the face value of each loan, minus any reserves held against potential losses.

If borrowers meet their loan obligations, the bank earns income, which increases its capital. The bank's capital also rises if the other assets that the bank holds increase in value. If borrowers cannot pay their loans, and loans must be written off, however, the bank must reflect the charge in its balance sheet. If the amount of the loan is less than the bank's reserves, net assets do not change. Instead, the bank reduces both the face value of loans outstanding and the offsetting value of loan loss reserves. If loan losses exceed the value of loan loss reserves, however, the bank must decrease its capital, to reflect the corresponding decline in bank assets. If loan losses become sufficiently large, the bank must write down its entire capital, becoming bankrupt. Thus, a bank's capitalization is extremely important. Many of the important reforms in bank regulation during recent decades have involved requiring banks to increase both the amount and the kind of capital they hold, with required capital typically measured as a percentage of assets weighted by risks.[1]

During financial crises, many banks incur loan losses, and losses typically overwhelm the existing loan loss reserves. In addition, the failure of a large bank may trigger asset write-downs at many other financial institutions, because banks often hold short-term obligations of other banks. If many banks become imperiled, a systemic financial crisis can emerge. In this case, even financially sound firms may have trouble getting or maintaining credit, and large depositors (those whose deposits exceed the amount of deposit insurance provided by national authorities) risk losing much or all of their deposits.

Special problems can arise in countries with state-owned banks. As discussed in Chapter Eight, political constraints can make it hard for these institutions to operate in a commercial manner. In countries that have recently emerged from central planning, many state-owned banks were compelled to lend to loss-making state enterprises that had trouble servicing their loans. Thus, many state-owned banks have large amounts of non-performing loans, requiring capital write-downs that may threaten bankruptcy. Poor creditor protection and weak bankruptcy laws have magnified the problems, although recourse against loss-making state enterprises may be politically impossible.

9.2. Justification for Public Sector Response to Bank Failure and Financial Crisis

Chapter One identified several aspects of the financial sector that create market failure through asymmetric information, including adverse selection, moral hazard, and the difficulty outsiders have in knowing

---

[1] The first Basel Accords, for example, required banks to hold capital equal to 8% of risk-weighted assets.

the true situation of financial institutions. These aspects help justify financial sector regulation. However, bank failures can have wider effects on the broader economy, because of the many other institutions that rely on them. A bank failure, or even a serious impairment of bank capital, reduces the ability of firms and households to obtain loans. Unless deposit insurance is available, bank failure can also wipe out the deposits of firms and individuals. In either case, firms and households will find themselves financially constrained, for no reason of their own. If a major financial institution fails, many other companies can suffer losses. Indeed, failure of a large bank or financial institution may impair many other financial organizations, because of inter-linkages among financial institutions. This, in turn, may imperil many non-financial companies, because of the adverse impact on numerous individual banks and other institutions.

Government intervention can thus be justified as part of its economic stabilization activities. Indeed, during the 2007–2009 Global Financial Crisis, many governments felt compelled to intervene in the financial system. Countries throughout Western Europe and North America created rescue packages for banks and financial institutions. In addition, central banks sharply lowered interest rates and liberalized rules to accept new collateral and provide help for institutions traditionally not eligible for lender of last resort assistance. Even outside the OECD, regulatory authorities in many countries raised the ceilings on deposits eligible for insurance. In Australia and parts of Asia, central banks extended a blanket guarantee for all deposits.

Even before the 2007–2009 Global Financial Crisis, however, many countries undertook reform measures to address financial sector weaknesses that threaten broader macroeconomic difficulties. Financial sector reform, for example, was a key element in the adjustment packages that Indonesia, South Korea, and Thailand implemented with support from the International Monetary Fund during 1997 and subsequent years. Malaysia also implemented major banking reforms as part of its self-financed adjustment strategy in 1998–1999. Financial sector reforms played a role in the Turkish adjustment program that began in 2001. Even China, whose economy has grown steadily since the early 1990s, acted to recapitalize key state-owned banks after many loans to state enterprises turned bad. Thus, government intervention to strengthen the financial system is hardly a new phenomenon.

9.3. Policy Options to Support Failing Banks

Aside from central bank activity, governments have several options for addressing current or potential bank failures. On the regulatory front, governments can strengthen the supervision of financial institutions, tightening prudential standards and monitoring institutions more closely. The authorities can also move to strengthen the performance at state-owned banks, changing management and adjusting rules so that these institutions can behave as commercial institutions. On the fiscal side, the authorities can move to recapitalize weak or failing institutions. To reduce the moral hazard associated with recapitalization, the authorities should condition capital injections on changes in bank management and require shareholders to bear at least some of the costs. Many analysts would also recommend requiring the creditors of financial institutions to accept losses, in the form of a write down of bank debts, although the United States largely avoided such measures in its response to the 2007–2009 Global Financial Crisis.

9.3.1. *Fiscal costs of addressing bank failure*

From a fiscal perspective, addressing bank failures involves several different activities, each of which has a cost to the government budget, even if undertaken by the monetary authority. These activities include the following:

1. *The cost of providing liquidity support to threatened institutions.* Serving as a lender of last resort requires the central bank to lend to and accept collateral from threatened financial institutions. Making these loans requires either expanding the money supply or selling

off government securities in return for less secure collateral from the borrowing institutions.

2. *Purchasing impaired assets.* In some countries, governments or special government agencies have been authorized to buy troubled assets from financial institutions. Doing so relieves the financial institutions of weak securities and bad debts. Buying the assets for cash or interest-bearing government securities will help recapitalize these institutions, preventing bankruptcy and enabling them to start lending again. However, purchasing troubled assets adds to government expenditure, while exchanging good assets for bad exposes the government to losses that can expand its own budget deficit.

3. *Recapitalizing financial institutions.* In many countries, the government has undertaken a formal recapitalization program. Typically, this involves establishing a bank recapitalization agency with funds to purchase troubled assets and the authority to try and realize money from them, either through their sale (usually at a loss) on financial markets or through arrangements with bad debtors to pay off at least part of their loans. To establish the recapitalization agency, the government generally must issue new debt of its own. Thus, establishing the recapitalization program becomes a direct budgetary expense.

4. *Payments to depositors, to honor guarantees or deposit insurance.* Addressing bank failure also involves reimbursing depositors for at least some of their losses. The cost to the public sector from bank failures includes the drawdown of funds from existing deposit insurance systems. In a systemic banking crisis, the official deposit insurance system's reserves may be exhausted, requiring the government to provide support from the budget.

IMF staff have estimated that, in percent of GDP, the gross fiscal costs of bank recapitalization in 14 systemic banking crises occurring between 1981 and 2003 ranged from 2.5% (Norway) to 56.8% (Indonesia), with net costs after asset recoveries ranging from 0% (Sweden) to 52.3% (Indonesia). Gross and net fiscal costs were estimated to have exceeded 20% of GDP in six cases (Chile, Ecuador,

Indonesia, South Korea, Thailand, and Turkey).[2] Research has shown that the less the liquidity support and the smaller the extent of deposit guarantees, the lower was the total cost of the operation. Similarly, costs were lower in countries that responded faster, because delaying the response resulted in larger losses to be absorbed. Honohan and Klingebiel argue that fiscal costs were highest in countries that provided open-ended liquidity support; offered unlimited deposit guarantees; and practiced regulatory forbearance, repeated recapitalizations, and debtor bailouts.[3] These authors' regressions suggest that, on average, pursuing strict policies in all five areas could limit the fiscal costs of responding to banking crises to perhaps 1% of GDP, while costs would be much higher with lax policies. With other variables assumed to be at their average values, adopting strict policies for any one of the variables was estimated to reduce the fiscal costs of resolution by 1–6% of GDP, depending on the variable involved. By comparison, pursing relaxed policies in all five areas was estimated to raise the average fiscal cost of crisis response to nearly 63% of GDP.

The net costs of responding to bank failure may be less than the gross costs. A bank recapitalization agency, for example, may be able to realize funds from the sale of non-performing loans and use the proceeds to reduce its own obligations to the government, allowing the government to withdraw some of the debt used to create the agency. Likewise, the government may realize funds from selling its stakes in recapitalized financial institutions, much as Sweden did after its banking crisis during the 1990s. Recapitalized financial institutions may also be able to repay loans received from the government. Together, these events can offset some or all of the gross costs of bank recapitalization. The events may take time to materialize, however, causing public debt to remain elevated for a while.

---

[2] See Staff Team led by Hoelscher, D. S., and M. Quintyn (2003), *Managing Systemic Banking Crises*, Occasional Paper No. 224 (Washington: International Monetary Fund, August), Table AI.1, p. 41.

[3] See Honohan, P., and D. Klingebiel (2000), "Controlling Fiscal Costs of Banking Crises," World Bank Policy Research Paper No. 2441 (Washington: May), http://elibrary.worldbank.org/content/workingpaper/10.1596/1813-9450-2441.

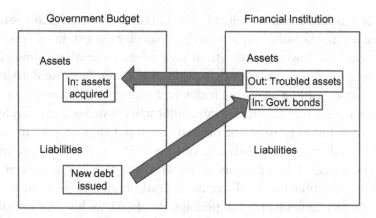

Impact of asset transfer: Financial institution receives government bonds in exchange for assets. Government receives assets in exchange for debt issued.

Figure 9.2.   Bank recapitalization via asset transfers.

9.3.2. *Accounting issues in bank recapitalization*

The budgetary consequences of bank recapitalization depend in part on the methods used. The following examples illustrate several of the more common approaches.

1. *Recapitalization through the exchange of assets.* If a government recapitalizes a financial institution by giving it good assets, such as government bonds, in exchange for troubled assets (Figure 9.2), the measured impact on the government's cash deficit could be small. The government will incur interest costs on the debt it issues and gives to the financial institution, less any interest or other earnings from the troubled assets it obtains. Unless the government recognizes a loss, estimated as the difference between the value of the debt it provides and the estimated value of the assets it receives, no further increase in the cash budget deficit will occur. In this case, the deficit would reflect only the rise in net interest payments. However, the level of public debt will rise by the amount of any debt issued to acquire the assets, plus the increase in the cash deficit resulting from higher interest payments.

Under the accounting rules of the 2001 *Government Finance Statistics Manual*, which record the change in the government's net worth, the government budget immediately reflects the change in the net value of the government's assets. If the market value of the assets acquired is less than that of the bonds issued to acquire the assets, the government's accrual balance worsens by that difference — plus the rise in net interest payments that the government incurs. If the assets have some value, the worsening in the balance will differ from the increase in public debt associated with the transaction. However, the discrepancy will likely be smaller than under the traditional, cash definition of the budget deficit.

2.Recapitalization using an asset management company. In response to the 1997–1998 Asian Crisis, many countries, including Indonesia and Malaysia, established asset management companies (AMCs) whose role was to purchase troubled assets from banks using cash, so that the banks could re-establish lending. If a government uses this approach for recapitalization (Figure 9.3), it must ordinarily issue debt to set up the AMC and give it the cash needed to purchase bank assets. The only exception is if the government has large net assets, in which case some of these assets can be used to finance the AMC. In the more typical case, the government records the establishment of the AMC as a budget expenditure, and the cash deficit rises by the full amount of the debt issued, plus the cost of any interest payments. Arguably, this approach is more transparent than that of exchanging assets, because it forces the government to recognize the costs associated with bank recapitalization "up front," rather than postponing them until the time that acquired bad assets must be written off.

Over time, if the AMC can sell or realize earnings from the troubled assets, the agency can remit dividends to the government. This will reduce the cash deficit and allow the government to withdraw some of the debt it initially issued to create the AMC.

Something like this occurred in Indonesia during 2002, when the AMC that the government established realized some funds from the

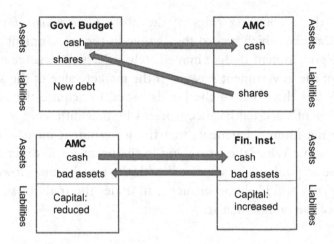

Impact of government action: Government issues debt to finance creation of AMC; AMC uses cash to acquire bad assets from one or more financial institutions. Replacing bad assets with cash increases the value of assets, and thus the capital, of the financial institution(s).

Figure 9.3.　Bank recapitalization via an asset management company (AMC).

sale of assets and remitted money to the budget. The government recorded this inflow as nonbank financing, and it allowed the government to reduce the amount of bonds outstanding to the banking sector, in effect allowing negative bank financing for the budget in that year.

Under the 2001 *Government Finance Statistics Manual*, the AMC approach to bank recapitalization yields less of a difference in budget accounting, compared to asset exchanges. In this case, the government incurs the expenses of establishing the AMC but acquires an asset (the value of the AMC) in return. Thus, the accrual deficit initially worsens only by the value of the additional interest payments incurred. As the AMC purchases troubled assets from the banks, its net worth — and, thus, the net worth of the government that owns it — deteriorates. The government's net lending/borrowing changes by the amount of the government debt issued. Over time, if the AMC realizes funds from the assets it acquires, its net worth increases, as does that of the government.

3. *Hypothetical example.* The following example may make the above distinctions clearer. Suppose the government wants to assist a bank with non-performing loans (NPLs) having a face value of 100 but an assumed market value of only 60 (because the assets are impaired). Assume that the government can issue bonds at 10% to finance recapitalization activities.

a. *Asset transfer.* In the first case, suppose that the government transfers 100 in 10% bonds to the bank in exchange for the 100 of NPLs. During the first year, the government incurs a cost of 10 for interest payments plus an implicit loss of 40 (100 less the market value of the NPLs) on the asset transfer. If the government recognizes the loss, its first-year cost is 50: 10 plus 40. Otherwise, the first-year cost is 10. If, in the second year, the government sells the NPLs for 55, its cost over the two-year period is 65: 20 in interest plus 45 for the loss on the NPLs. The government could use the 55 to reduce its outstanding debt, thereby cutting interest payments during the third and subsequent years.

b. *Recapitalization using an AMC.* In the second case, the government issues 110 in 10 percent bonds and uses the proceeds to establish an AMC, giving it cash worth 100. The AMC uses its cash to purchase 100 in NPLs from the bank. In the first year, the government incurs expenses of 121: 11 for interest plus an additional 110 to establish the AMC. In the second year, the AMC sells the NPLs for 75 (the AMC has more expertise than the government in handling troubled assets) and remits 70 of the 75 to the government. In this case, the two-year cost to the government is 62: 22 in interest plus 110 for the initial bond issuance, less 70 in funds remitted by the AMC. As in the previous case, the government could use the 70 to reduce its outstanding debt, cutting its interest obligations in subsequent years. Despite the higher initial cost of this approach, the government may find it worthwhile, because the responsibility of dealing with financial institutions is given to an agency with special skills in this area. This approach also makes the initial costs of recapitalization more transparent, since the main costs are incurred at the start.

9.3.3. Illustrative cases of responding to bank crisis in Asia: Indonesia and Malaysia

The following case studies from East Asia offer illustrations of the fiscal cost of addressing bank crises.

1. *Indonesia.* Indonesia's bank recapitalization in response to the Asian Crisis of 1997–1998 proved very costly. The initial expenditures were estimated at 51% of GDP. Gross costs, through the early 2000s, were almost 57% of GDP. Recoveries from asset sales and workouts totaled less than 5% of GDP, leaving a net cost of about 52% of GDP.

Of the initial costs, liquidity support for failing banks totaled 12% of GDP, for which the budget reimbursed Bank Indonesia. Bank recapitalization and the costs of reimbursing depositors for deposit guarantees cost another 23% of GDP. Purchases of non-performing loans and the cost of capital given to the asset management company set up to address bank failures absorbed a further 12% of GDP. Interest costs on the debt issued to support these operations added another 3% of GDP.

The high costs of Indonesia's operations reflected both the liberal nature of the guarantees and the relatively slow pace of the operation. After the initial closure of a few failing institutions triggered a run on many banks, halting the run by guaranteeing all deposits contributed to high total costs. In addition, it took the asset management company some time to acquire troubled assets and longer still to realize money from the assets it acquired. By 2002, the company had recovered about 4.6% of GDP: 2.4% of GDP in 2001 and slightly less in 2002.

2. *Malaysia.* The costs of Malaysia's response to its banking crisis were far less than Indonesia's. The fiscal costs of the Malaysian program, inaugurated in 1998, were only about 5% of GDP during 1999: about 2% of GDP for recapitalization and deposit guarantees, and another 3% of GDP for purchasing non-performing loans from financial institutions.

What kept the costs of Malaysia's program so much less? To begin, Malaysia had always maintained relatively tight banking supervision, so its banks did not experience the same difficulty as Indonesia's. Moreover, Malaysia did not suffer the same degree of cronyism in its financial sector as Indonesia, where several institutions initially slated for closing were owned by children of Indonesia's then leader, Suharto.

Malaysia also benefitted from experiencing less exchange rate depreciation than Indonesia. Although Malaysian banks also had foreign exchange exposure, Malaysia's currency, the ringgit, depreciated less than the Indonesian rupiah. From early 1997 through end-August 1998, the ringgit depreciated from about 2.5 per US dollar to about 4.1 per US dollar. The authorities then stabilized the exchange rate at 3.8 per US dollar in September 1998, an overall depreciation of about 34% relative to early 1997. By comparison, the Indonesian rupiah depreciated from less than 2,500 per US dollar during early 1997 to more than 10,000 per US dollar in late 1998, a depreciation of more than 75%. Indonesian banks that had borrowed in foreign currency thus suffered far greater losses and required substantially more money for recapitalization.

Finally, Malaysia benefitted from a much faster and stronger regulatory response. Although Malaysia's leaders stressed their independence from the IMF, as in Korea and Thailand the authorities moved quickly to address bank failures, in some cases forcing weak banks to merge. Together, these measures helped limit the fiscal costs of Malaysia's response to its 1997–1998 banking crisis.

9.4. Summary

Many countries have faced the need to restructure banks and address financial crises. The costs of restructuring have been substantial, in some cases exceeding 50% of GDP. Financial crises have also imposed heavy costs on government budgets. As noted in this chapter, governments have different ways to address these problems, and the accounting linked to different approaches can lead to different estimates of the costs for the government budget.

Whichever method is used, governments should be transparent about the costs, keeping track not only of the immediate budgetary implications but also the longer term effects, including the impact of recapitalization and restructuring on levels of government debt. In addition, governments should keep in mind policy options that can help contain the costs of responding to banking difficulties. These include limiting deposit guarantees, moving to strengthen bank supervision and regulation, and responding quickly rather than practicing forbearance.

Chapter Ten: Fiscal Federalism and Decentralization

Fiscal federalism involves the use of multiple levels of government to perform public sector activities. Most countries have at least some degree of fiscal federalism, since their public sectors are typically organized into localities, provincial (regional or state) governments, and a national government. However, the precise structures differ from country to country. In some, such as France, the central (national) government has substantial fiscal and administrative control over regional and local governments. In others, such as Brazil, India, and the United States, state governments have considerable authority and account for a large share of all government sector activity. In every nation, legal rules and history play a major role on the pattern of fiscal federalism.

As shown in Table 10.1, drawn from the work of Purfield,[1] the shares of fiscal revenue, expenditure, and the overall budget balance at the sub-national level vary considerably across countries. During the 1990–1997 period, average revenues collected at the sub-national level ranged from less than 10% of total government sector revenues in France and Romania to more than 50% of the total in Canada and China. The share of total government sector outlays spent at the sub-national level also varied considerably, from less than 20% of the total in France to more than 80% in China. For every country, however, the share of sub-national expenditures exceeded the share of own revenues at the sub-national level. Thus, in every country transfers from the central government financed at least some portion of expenditure at

---

[1]Purfield, C. (2004), "The Decentralization Dilemma in India," Working Paper No. 04/32 (Washington: International Monetary Fund, February), p. 22, http://www.imf.org/external/pubs/ft/wp/2004/wp0432.pdf.

Table 10.1. Percentage of government sector activity at the sub-national level, selected countries (averages for 1990–1997).

	Own revenues[a]	Total expenditure[b]	Budget deficit[c]
Austria	26.8	34.1	—
Finland	31.7	39.7	−3.0
France	9.2	18.7	7.7
Germany	33.8	38.8	43.8
Sweden	31.4	36.0	−8.1
Czech Republic	15.8	23.0	13.1
Hungary	12.7	26.9	−7.9
Romania	8.7	12.5	−7.3
China	59.7	81.5	−0.9
India	39.1	56.7	36.7
Argentina	39.1	45.6	177.4
Mexico	21.9	29.0	48.7
Australia	31.7	49.0	−75.7
Canada	53.0	58.8	3.8
United States	42.1	44.4	−48.2

Notes: [a] Percent of total government sector revenues collected by sub-national governments.
[b] Percent of total government sector expenditure spent by sub-national governments, including outlays funded by transfers from central government.
[c] Percent of total government sector deficit from sub-national governments. A negative number denotes a net budget surplus for the sub-national sector in that country.
Source: Purfield (2004), "The Decentralization Dilemma in India," IMF Working Paper No. 04/32, Table 3.

the sub-national level. Table 10.1 also shows an interesting pattern for budget balances at the sub-national level. In about half the countries shown, sub-national governments as a whole achieved budget balance or surplus, partly as a result of transfers from the central government. In only four of the countries surveyed did sub-national governments account for more than 30% of the total government sector deficit. However in one country (Argentina), combined deficits at sub-national units of government far exceeded the central government deficit.

The data in Table 10.1 reveal an important aspect of fiscal federalism: the challenge facing sub-national governments in collecting enough revenue to finance their expenditures. For a variety of reasons noted in this chapter, sub-national governments have difficulty raising enough money to fund their activities. Thus, these governments

Table 10.2. Percent of general government revenue and expenditure at the sub-national level in selected OECD countries, 2008 and 2016.

		Revenue		Expenditure	
Country	Level of government	2008	2016	2008	2016
Canada	Central	44.8	43.6	32.4	31.8
	Sub-national	55.2	56.4	67.6	68.2
Germany	Central	63.8	63.2	61.5	59.9
	Sub-national	36.2	36.8	38.5	40.1
Switzerland	Central	52.3	51.3	42.8	42.6
	Sub-national	47.7	48.7	57.2	57.4
United Kingdom	Central	90.8	91.4	72.5	75.9
	Sub-national	9.2	8.6	27.5	24.1
United States	Central	55.5	57.6	51.7	51.6
	Sub-national	44.5	42.4	48.3	48.4

Source: OECD, Fiscal Decentralization Database.

often depend on the central government for significant parts of their financing. This has important implications for developing budgets at state or provincial and local governments.

More recent data for selected OECD countries tell a similar story. As noted in Table 10.2, the shares of sub-national governments in general government revenue and expenditure differ considerably across countries. However, sub-national governments account for a larger share of general government expenditure than revenue.

Key issues in fiscal federalism

Fiscal federalism poses important issues for governments. These include the following:

1. Deciding which unit and level of government should be responsible for each category of expenditure.
2. Ensuring that each level of government has enough revenue, from its own and other sources, to finance its expenditure obligations.
3. Maintaining fiscal discipline across the entire sector, including sub-national units of government.

Maintaining fiscal discipline in a federal or decentralized government sector is much harder than doing so where only the central government manages fiscal and budget policy. The reason is that the central government must be able to control revenue and expenditure, both at the central and at the sub-national levels of government. Unless there is a long tradition of central government involvement in the budget activities of state (provincial) and local governments, heads of sub-national governments may challenge the central government's attempts to control their budgets. In some countries, dissension between central and state or regional government may be so powerful so as to create fiscal problems for the entire government sector. For example, the refusal by Minas Gerais state in Brazil to service its debt to the central government helped trigger Brazil's 1998 macroeconomic crisis. In Argentina, fiscal overruns and the issuance of parallel currency by provincial governments added to the difficulties that helped trigger Argentina's crisis towards the end of 2001.

10.1. Assigning Expenditure Responsibilities to Different Levels of Government — General Principles

Fiscal decentralization can improve well-being by allowing a closer match between government spending and the preferences of those residing in a specific locality or region. For example, city residents generally need a set of services appropriate for urban areas. These services may include mass transit, frequent trash collection, and more intensive police services, including traffic management. If big cities attract low-income residents, there may be a particular need for certain social services, ranging from income support to child care and public health clinics. In addition, residents may want cultural projects, whether government run or subsidized. The demand for extensive public services may require higher taxes. Thus, many cities have higher tax rates, or a broader tax base, than do less densely populated areas. In rural areas, the desired level and mix of public services may be quite different. For example, maintaining a scenic attraction may be more important than public transportation. There may also be greater need for school buses, because schools are located further apart. Fewer services, in turn, may allow lower taxes.

Decentralization also allows residents to select a level of public services commensurate with their preferences. In the United States, for example, citizens in Northeastern states such as Massachusetts and New York are accustomed to a relatively high level of public services, including extensive sanitation and maintenance activities, many cultural facilities, and a lot of social services, including facilities in the schools for students with special needs. Funding these public services requires a relatively high level of taxation. By comparison, residents of southern states like Florida and Texas have traditionally preferred a less extensive set of public services, including lower spending per pupil for education and smaller benefits for those receiving state-supported social services. Fewer services and lower benefits have allowed these states to have lower taxes.

Finally, decentralization allows different regions of a country to experiment with different approaches to providing public services. In the United States, the federal government's health care program for low-income persons, Medicaid, permits the states considerable latitude in deciding how to structure benefits. For example, the state of Oregon evaluates different medical procedures and decides which ones to cover under the program, providing relatively full coverage for those deemed essential and no coverage for those considered less important. Since the mid-1990s Oregon has periodically changed the set of insured medical procedures, to allow more flexibility in the set of people who can be covered under the program while operating within budget constraints.[2]

10.1.1. *Application of the "benefit principle"*

One of the classic concepts in public finance is the so-called *benefit principle*: the notion that people who benefit from a particular good or service provided by the public sector should bear its cost. The

---

[2]See, for example, Oregon Health Authority (2019), *Prioritized List of Services*, https://www.oregon.gov/oha/HSD/OHP/Pages/Prioritized-List.aspx.

benefit principle helps justify charging tolls for bridges, tunnels, and expressways. It also argues for charging admission to public parks and museums and levying fees to use public health services.

On the expenditure side of the budget, the benefit principle argues for having services provided by the level (or unit) of government that best represents the area benefitting from that service. From this perspective, local governments seem best able to deliver services such as police protection, sanitation services, preventive health care, and primary education, even if a higher level of government provides financial support or offers technical assistance to improve the quality of service (for example, a national educational assessment, so that localities can see how their schools compare with those in other areas). State or regional governments, by contrast, may do better at providing regional transit services, especially if a number of localities in an area share a common employment or shopping hub. If there are regional differences in commercial or legal norms, a state or provincial government may be appropriate to provide legal and judicial services. A central government, by comparison, can best provide public goods and services with national implications, major economies of scale, or that create perverse incentives for mobility if provided at the sub-national level. Thus, the national government would seem most appropriate for managing national defense, foreign affairs, stabilization, income and wealth redistribution, and infrastructure for inter-regional transportation and telecommunications. Involvement by the national government may also be useful if there is a consensus on national standards that should be observed in goods delivered by localities or regional governments. For example, in a country with national universities that students aspire to enter, having the central government develop a national entrance exam or national assessments of student progress in different states could be worthwhile.

Where regional variation has a value, the benefit principle would suggest having the appropriate sub-national government deliver the service. For example, if the authorities are not clear on the best way to teach mathematics, state or local governments could be given broad latitude on how to organize individual schools and what teaching methods are used, so long as students followed a general curriculum aimed at achieving certain standards.

10.1.2. *Factors supporting more central control*

Despite the foregoing arguments for decentralization, concerns about the quality of administration, governance, fiscal control, and equal access to high-quality services may argue for having the center deliver or control the delivery of public services.

1. *Administrative weaknesses at the sub-national level.* In many countries, the financial weakness or lesser prestige of state, provincial, or local governments can make it hard to attract civil servants comparable to those in the central government. As a result, some programs may not be administered as well as if managed at the sub-national, rather than national, level. Where the quality of program administration is critical, having the central government manage the program may be preferable.

2. *Concerns about governance.* In many countries, sub-national governments, particularly at the local level, may be more susceptible to corruption or control by dominant local interests. These groups may have more influence at the local or provincial level and thus find it easier to obtain more than their "fair" share of program benefits if programs are locally administered. In addition, in some countries local or provincial leaders are sometimes well-entrenched and less open to adjusting policy as preferences of the public change. If these characteristics apply, having the central government manage public sector programs may again be preferable.

3. *Concerns arising from major inequities in wealth or income across regions.* When different regions or localities have very different levels of wealth or income, allowing regional or local control of public programs may lead to sharp differences in the quality of services provided. In

China, for example, the much higher per capita incomes of citizens in many of the coastal provinces allow them to have much higher funding for schools, roads, and other public services than in the less affluent interior regions of the country. Grants from the central government can reduce the disparity of resources between regions and among different localities, but fully eliminating the disparity is very difficult. Thus, if an activity is important enough to make uniform service levels across the nation a priority, central administration and funding of the program can be valuable. This may be one reason why the central government has a dominant role in managing public education at the primary and secondary level in France, and why most countries administer anti-poverty programs at the national level.

4. *Concerns about maintaining fiscal control.* Decentralizing responsibility for government programs can make it harder for a country to achieve nation-wide fiscal objectives. It may be hard for the central government to achieve an overall fiscal target, such as limiting government sector debt to a certain percentage of GDP, if sub-national units of government can determine the spending levels for key public programs. Unless the borrowing capacity of states and localities is limited, these units of government may be able to expand outlays on programs for which they are responsible, thereby adding to the total public debt. Borrowing limits on state, provincial, regional, and local governments may thus be useful. The pros and cons of such restrictions are discussed in a later section of this chapter.

5. *Risks of increasing opportunities for corruption.* To the extent that decentralization increases the number of units of government that must agree for a particular public sector operation to occur, decentralization can increase the opportunities for corruption, particularly if local officials are politically powerful. Partly for this reason and partly to simplify governance, some countries have unified the process of obtaining permits for foreign direct investment by consolidating these activities into a single national office.

10.1.3. *Examples of how expenditure functions are allocated across levels of government*

The foregoing points suggest that particular expenditure functions may be more appropriate for some levels of government than others. Following are some examples.

1. *Social insurance.* In most countries, *old-age pensions and disability insurance*, both of which involve important elements of redistributing income, are usually administered at the national level. The same applies to *unemployment insurance.* In the United States, individual states administer their own unemployment insurance programs, setting benefit levels and the qualifications for receiving assistance. However, the federal (central) government often provides funding for additional weeks of assistance during serious recessions. Thus, the federal government funded an additional year of benefits for many recipients during the recession that began in 2008 and extended the program in late 2010.

2. *Social assistance programs,* such as income support for food, utilities, and housing, are often provided by local governments, with financial support and legal guidance from the central and, sometimes, state or provincial governments. Again, however, the modalities differ from country to country. In Ukraine, for example, the revised utility support program was administered through local offices that followed national guidelines about payment levels and eligibility. Similar rules apply to the Supplemental Nutritional Assistance (SNAP, formerly called the "Food Stamp") program in the United States, which provides uniform benefits through the country, although individuals usually apply through local social service agencies. However, the Earned Income (Tax) Credit program of the United States, which provides tax relief and cash payments to eligible low-income households, is run by the federal government, through the Internal Revenue Service.

3. *Education.* Countries differ in how they provide public-funded education. Many countries organize and implement *primary and*

secondary education at the local level, often with financial support and guidance from the central and/or state and provincial governments. In Cambodia, for example, localities have a major say in organizing pre-university education, although the Ministry of Education often issues textbooks, allocates teachers, and provides guidance on curriculum. In the United States, localities provide primary and secondary education under the supervision of state governments. Many states establish curricula for different subjects, and some determine what textbooks may be used for each course. At the same time, the federal (central) government provides supplementary funding to promote certain objectives, such as expanding resources for disabled students or improving student performance in key subjects such as reading. Often state and localities must satisfy certain conditions to receive funding.

University-level education, by comparison, often has more involvement from the central government. Many countries, such as Romania and South Korea, have nationally recognized public universities that receive most of their funding from the central government. Admission is determined on a national basis, and tuition is set in accord with provisions in the central government budget. In other countries, subnational governments play a greater role. In the United States, most state governments support a system of public colleges and universities, each of which sets its own fees and admissions requirements. In addition, New York City and a few other large municipalities also maintain their own public colleges and universities. At the same time, the federal (central) government provides some financial assistance to students, through grants, loans, and tax subsidies. The federal government also provides support for academic research and for training physicians, through supplementary payments to teaching hospitals.

4. *Health care.* Different levels of government often share responsibilities in delivering publicly funded health care. Many African countries, for example, have a network of nationally run public health centers, staffed by doctors and nurses. Other countries, such Romania, have a network of nationally funded but locally run health clinics and hospitals. The United Kingdom's National Health Service is a central

government program. In the United States, localities typically establish public health clinics and public hospitals. However, state governments are required to fund an important share of the federal government's Medicaid program, which provides health insurance for qualifying low-income households. In return, each state has a major say in determining the eligibility for its program, which services are covered, and the level of payments to doctors and other providers. The federal government covers a majority of the cost of Medicaid and is fully responsible for Medicare, the government's health insurance program for the elderly. The federal tax code also provides the bulk of subsidies for purchases of private health insurance, in the form of tax expenditures. For example, health insurance premiums paid by employers represent a deductible business expense but are not included in employees' taxable incomes.

10.2. Assigning Revenue Sources to Different Levels of Government — General Principles

As with expenditures, several principles help guide the assignment of revenue across different levels of government in a federal or decentralized fiscal system.

10.2.1. *Each level of government needs dedicated revenue sources*

A key principle underlying the assignment of revenue sources in a federal system is that *each unit of government needs its own revenue sources.* Many state and provincial governments obtain financial support from the central government, and many localities receive funding from both central and state or provincial governments. However, experience shows that sub-national governments fare best if they can rely mainly on their own sources of funds, supplemented if needed by transfers from higher levels of government. Having dedicated sources of revenue enables governments to budget more effectively. It also allows them to manage when political or other events disrupt funding from higher levels of government. The same applies when weak governance makes it hard for localities to receive their share of funds from the central, provincial, or regional government. In most cases, the challenge for sub-national governments is to find sufficient revenue to finance their activities. Difficulties in raising enough revenue often lead state or provincial governments to seek financial assistance from the center, while localities will approach both the central and state or provincial governments for support.

Different countries interpret the revenue mandate differently. Some countries, such as India, allocate separate kinds of taxes to different levels of government. India's constitution, for example, assigns the personal and corporate income tax, excises on goods other than alcohol, and customs duties to the central government, although much of the revenue so collected is shared by formula with the states. State governments, by comparison, were traditionally authorized to levy sales and value added taxes, excises on alcohol, and a variety of other taxes, including taxes on land and agriculture, motor vehicles, and professions. However, a 2016 amendment to the Indian constitution led to the creation in 2017 of a nationwide goods and services tax, administered by both the central and state governments, that incorporated a number of existing central and state government levies, including state-level value added taxes.[3] Some other countries, such as the Canada and the United States, allow different levels of government to levy the same taxes. Thus, both the federal (central) and state governments in the United States impose gasoline taxes, while the federal government, most state governments, and a few localities have personal income taxes. In Canada, many taxes are imposed at the provincial level but collected and distributed by the central government. Several countries, including China and India, also have "shared" taxes, in which revenues from certain levies are divided between the central government and state or provincial governments.

---

[3]Dhasmana, I. (2017), "What is GST, How is it Different from Now: Decoding the Indirect Tax Regime," *Business Standard* (17 April), https://www.business-standard.com /article/economy-policy/what-is-gst-how-is-it-different-from-now-decoding-the-indirect-tax-regime-117041700033_1.html.

Revenue sharing among different levels of government can create perverse incentives. For example, if the central government is required to share the proceeds of certain taxes, but not others, the national legislature may find it attractive to increase revenues only for those taxes that the central government fully retains. Thus, if revenue sharing is considered appropriate, establishing a rule to share a certain percentage of all central government revenues, regardless of source, avoids these incentives. At the same time, revenue sharing should not be allowed to reduce the revenue effort of sub-national governments. Assured revenue from the central government may encourage these other units of government to reduce taxes or be less vigilant in generating their own revenues.

To avoid this problem, revenue sharing can be conditioned on having recipient governments achieve certain revenue targets. Finally, governments should be aware of the risks involved in allowing other units of government to collect revenue for them. The greatest problems occur in countries where provinces collect at least some of the revenue destined for the central government. In Lao PDR, for example, until recently decentralization required the central government to depend on the provinces for revenue collection. Because they had little financial incentive to collect revenues for the center, collections remained relatively weak.[4] In the last few years, however, the government has moved to address this problem by taking steps to recentralize its revenue collection.

10.2.2. *Higher levels of government can best tap more mobile revenue sources*

A second principle governing the allocation of revenue sources reflects the recognition that *some tax bases are more mobile than others.* In general, households and firms can move more easily from one locality to

---

[4]See International Monetary Fund (2005), *Lao People's Democratic Republic: Selected Issues and Statistical Appendix*, IMF Country Report 05/09 (Washington), Ch. 2, p. 21, http://www.imf. org/external/pubs/ft/scr/2005/cr0509.pdf.

another than they can from one state or province to another. Similarly, they can more easily relocate from one state or province to another than they can to another country. For this reason, central governments can best tap the most mobile revenue sources, while localities should focus mainly on the least mobile types of revenues.[5] State or provincial governments occupy an intermediate position.

Tax base mobility has implications for the kinds of revenues that different levels of government can raise.

1. *Central governments.* Central governments can most easily tax company income and profits, the most mobile revenue sources. They are also best able to impose customs duties, since the central government usually supervises borders and allows entry of goods and services into the country. The risks from having different tax rates on similar transactions in different parts of the country also argue for letting the central government tax household income. In addition, where income levels differ significantly from one region to another, a case can be made for having the central government collect revenues for a variety of taxes at a uniform tax rate and distribute them to state or regional governments, using a formula that helps reduce the disparity in tax bases across the country. Alternatively, if state or provincial governments agree to harmonize their tax laws with those of the central government, they may benefit by having the central government's tax authority collect revenues for them, thereby reducing the cost of administration. Many of Canada's provinces use the Canada Revenue Agency, for example, to collect their sales or value added taxes, reducing the need for separate tax authorities to collect these revenues.

2. *State or provincial governments.* State and provincial governments often find that relying on sales or value added taxes can be useful, because sales may prove less mobile than income as a tax base. In

---

[5]Localities also need be aware that certain expenditures, such as social services, may also raise mobility issues. Although research is inconclusive, high income support payments may attract the poor to a state or locality.

Canada, for example, provinces typically have a provincial sales tax, in addition to the federal government's goods and services tax. In the United States, all but five states (Alaska, Delaware, Montana, New Hampshire, and Oregon) have sales taxes. State and provincial governments also impose certain excise taxes. For example, state governments in India and the United States impose excise taxes on alcohol, and most states in the United States also tax tobacco and petroleum products. Many states in the United States also impose excise taxes on vehicles, in the form of registration fees, and taxes on inheritances and the value of movable property (vehicles and boats).[6] In the United States, 41 of the 50 states also have their own taxes on personal income (two states, New Hampshire and Tennessee, tax only income from dividends and interest), and 47 tax corporate profits (all but Nevada, Washington, and Wyoming). In some states, such as Virginia, major parts of the personal income tax laws have been harmonized with the federal tax law, to reduce compliance burdens on individual taxpayers. Tax rates vary considerably from state to state, however, reflecting both the relative size of government in the state and whether the state has both an income and a sales tax, or only one of these.

3. *Local governments.* Local governments typically focus on the least mobile tax bases. Thus, taxes on real property (houses and buildings) and fees from business licenses often form the bulk of local revenues, along with fees for locally provided services and, in some cases, special taxes on tourist-related activities, such as excise taxes on hotels and supplementary sales or value added taxes on restaurant meals. In the United States, a few large cities, including New York, Philadelphia, and Washington, D.C., have their own income taxes (Washington's taxes reflect its being separate from any of the 50 states). Moreover, some counties in Maryland derive revenue from the state income tax by imposing an additional tax of a few percentage points, on top of the state levy (what economists sometimes call a "piggy-back"

---

[6]The ability to register a vehicle in one state and reside in another can make these taxes hard to enforce.

tax). The limited tax bases available to localities mean that they have trouble financing costly public services, such as primary and secondary education, without help. Thus, localities in most countries rely at least partly on revenue transfers from higher levels of government.

Administrative capability as well as mobility of the tax base should influence the assignment of taxes among different levels of government. Partly for this reason, in most countries the central government levies and administers value added taxes, even if revenues are shared with state, provincial, or local governments. In addition, as noted earlier, in Canada many provinces harmonize their sales or value added taxes with the federal goods and services tax, so that the Canada Revenue Agency can collect the tax for them.

10.3. Intergovernmental Transfers in Federal Systems

Because lower levels of government have narrower tax bases, decentralized fiscal systems usually incorporate revenue sharing from higher to lower levels of government. Various transfer mechanisms have been developed for this purpose.

10.3.1. *Different levels of government receive specified shares of certain tax revenue*

As noted earlier, some countries have allocated specific taxes to different levels of government. For example, India's constitution authorizes the central government to collect taxes on personal and corporate income, household wealth, imports, many types of sales, and a number of services, the latter two categories incorporated in 2017 into the goods and services tax. A Finance Commission appointed by the President recommends a percentage of central government taxes to be transferred to state governments, along with certain grants, and proposes the amount of shared taxes each state should receive. In recent years, the Finance Commission has recommended that the center give a flat percentage of its sharable revenues to the states (42 percent in 2013).[7] India's parliament generally approves the recommendations. However, the central government sometimes limits revenue sharing, for example, by imposing cesses or surcharges whose proceeds are not shared with the states.

In other countries, fundamental laws or constitutional provisions allocate certain revenues between the central government and subnational governments in fixed percentages. In China, for example, the central government generally receives 75 percent of the value added tax and 60 percent of corporate and personal income taxes, with the rest going to the provinces.

10.3.2. *Revenues may be apportioned on the basis of relative population, revenue effort, or other factors*

Countries use a variety of methods to apportion shared revenues. As noted above, in India the Finance Commission recommends the percentage of shared central government taxes that each state receives. Thus, in 2010 the Thirteenth Finance Commission recommended that individual states receive shares ranging from 0.239% to 19.677% of shared central taxes, excluding the Service Tax, and 0–19.987% of the Service Tax.[8] In the United States, many states allocate a portion of the revenue collected at the state level to supplement local government revenues, particularly for public education. Funds are allocated to different jurisdictions based on population and other factors, including relative income levels and the percentage of students in poverty.[9]

---

[7] See Mann, G. (2018), "Central Transfers to States: Role of the Finance Commission," *PRS Blog* (April 11), https://www.prsindia.org/theprsblog/central-transfers-states-role-finance-commission.

[8] Thirteenth Finance Commission, India (2010) "Report of the Thirteenth Finance Commission," Table 1.1, p. 4, http://fincomindia.nic.in/ShowContentOne.aspx?id=28&Section=1. The Fourteenth Finance Commission recommended somewhat different shares. See Mann (2018), *op. cit.*

[9] See Baker, B. D. *et al.* (2010), "Is School Funding Fair? A National Report Card" (Rutgers University), http://www.schoolfundingfairness.org/National_Report_Card.pdf.

In a number of states, these revenue transfers supplement formal sharing of sales tax revenues with the locality where the revenue is received. In some states, state law authorizes localities to receive a specific share of sales tax collected. Virginia, for example, grants localities 1 percentage point of all sales tax collected within their borders. Other states specify a state sales tax rate and allow localities to levy additional tax, up to a limit. California, for example, had a 7.25% state sales tax as of July 2019 and allowed localities to levy supplemental taxes, with some adding up to 3.25 percentage points of tax, for a maximum combined tax rate of 10.50%.[10] In New York, the basic state tax rate is lower (4%), but cities and counties may add up to 4.875 points of additional sales tax (for a maximum rate of 8.875%). Some states also mandate sharing revenue from other taxes. For example, New Jersey at one time had counties and municipalities each receive 25% of the state's Public Utilities Gross Receipts and Franchise Tax, to provide relief from local property taxes. In recent years, however, the state has not shared these revenues, because of its own heavy spending obligations.[11]

10.3.3. *Grants*

Besides revenue sharing, governments support activities at lower levels through a variety of grants or transfers. These include the following:

1. *General purpose grants.* General purpose grants are unrestricted transfers by one level of government to another. They allow the recipient government to use the funds as desired and, thus, represent pure revenue sharing. Receiving governments find these most useful, because they have no restrictions.

---

[10]California Department of Tax and Fee Administration, "California City & County Sales and Use Tax Rates," https://www.cdtfa.ca.gov/taxes-and-fees/sales-use-tax-rates.htm.
[11]New Jersey State League of Municipalities (2010), "A Short and Simple Glimpse at the Property Tax in New Jersey," http://www.njslom.org/tax_brochure.html.

2. *Block grants.* Block grants allow recipient governments to use the funds freely, within a broad subject area, such as education or health. Donor governments find these grants more appealing, because they ensure that the funds are used for a policy area considered important. In the United States, for example, the American Recovery and Investment Act of 2009, popularly known as the "Stimulus Bill," provided substantial grants to state governments, to help maintain existing services. Many of these grants went directly to local school districts, to preserve jobs for teachers.

3. *Program grants.* Program grants provide funds for recipient agencies and units of government to implement projects consistent with a program enacted by a higher level of government. Program grants include transfers to local governments for school lunch programs and funds to state, provincial, or local governments for highway construction and maintenance. In the United States, the American Recovery and Investment Act of 2009 provided many billions of dollars in funding for infrastructure projects, particularly at the state level. Program grants typically require the receiving governments to account for funds used and to satisfy specific program requirements, some of which may be controversial (e.g., using affirmative action rules to select contractors).

4. *Matching grants.* Governments in many countries require recipient agencies and governments to contribute to the cost of specific programs, as a condition of receiving transfers to support their cost. Such transfers are called *matching grants*. The required contribution reduces the cost to the donor government of implementing the program. It also demonstrates the commitment of the receiving government, since the recipient must contribute in order to receive funds. Matching grant programs are common in the United States. Among the most important are the federal Medicaid program, which requires states to contribute between 23% and 50% of the cost of the program, depending on the state's per capita income;[12] and the 20% match required for grants from the US government's

---

[12] See Rudowitz, R. *et al.* (2019), "Medicaid Financing: The Basics," kff.org, https://www.kff.org/report-section/medicaid-financing-the-basics-issue-brief/.

Major Capital Investments (New Starts) program involving new transit construction projects.[13] Many state and local governments complain that the required matching contributions, along with other conditions, impose substantial financial burdens on their own budgets.

10.4. Achieving Fiscal Control in Federal Systems

It can be hard achieving broad fiscal objectives in decentralized systems unless the budgets of sub-national, as well as national, governments can be constrained. Many nations address this issue by imposing borrowing constraints on sub-national governments. Although many countries allow state or provincial governments to incur debt, often, as in the case of India, these units of government may not borrow from abroad. Other countries have tighter constraints. In the United States, all but one of the 50 states require that revenues fully finance the budget for current expenditure. Borrowing for capital expenditure is allowed, however, although voters must often approve bond issues. Rules for local governments vary across countries. Indonesia, for example, prohibits local governments from incurring debt. In the United States, many large cities are permitted to incur deficits. However, repeated, large deficits have created difficulty for large cities such as New York and Washington, forcing them to adopt painful adjustment programs to reduce their debt.

Problems with fiscal control have contributed to macroeconomic difficulties in many countries with fiscal systems. Brazil's 1998 crisis, for example, was arguably triggered by the failure of Minas Gerais state to service its debt to the central government. The lack of cooperation by state governments worsened Argentina's crisis of 2001–2002. In India, the ability of enterprises owned by state governments to borrow has undermined fiscal control at the state level in the past. In the

---

[13]See US Department of Transportation, Federal Transit Administration, "Major Capital Investments (New Starts & Small Starts)," http://www.fta.dot.gov/funding/grants/grants_financing_3559.html.

United States, balanced budget rules have limited state government borrowing. During economic downturns, however, the inability of most states to run deficits in their current budgets exacerbates the economic contraction, as declines in revenue force states to reduce expenditures and lay off employees.

10.4.1. *Strategies to achieve fiscal control in federal systems*

Countries with federal systems can achieve fiscal control over sub-national governments in several ways.

1. *Imposing borrowing limits.* The most direct way to constrain sub-national governments involves constraints on borrowing. Sub-national governments can be prohibited from borrowing for current expenditures, as in the United States. Alternatively, they can have fixed limits on their debt, or, as in the case of India, be required to borrow only from the central government. The tightest restriction involves a total prohibition on incurring debt.

Borrowing limits can help in achieving overall limits on total government sector debt. Rigid limits, however, can prohibit sub-national governments from expanding or maintaining spending during recessions in countries where counter-cyclical fiscal policy can be implemented. Thus, it may be useful to allow some leeway in the application of borrowing limits, for example, to maintain spending during economic downturns, so long as debt is retired when the economy recovers. Doing so will promote the coordination of national and sub-national government budgets, from the perspective of fiscal policy.

2. *Imposing hard budget constraints.* As an alternative to outright debt ceilings, debt accumulation can be limited by imposing a "hard budget constraint" on sub-national governments. Expenditures can be limited to the sum of their own revenues plus well-defined, clearly anticipated transfers from higher levels of government. This approach will reduce

the chance that sub-national governments will need supplementary budget transfers or exceed approved debt limits. The success of this approach may depend on the relative power of the central government and sub-national governments. In India, for example, where central government leaders have often relied heavily on support from the heads of state governments, enforcing rules against supplementary transfers to the states has proved difficult. Brazil also had trouble imposing limits on state borrowing until its Fiscal Responsibility Law was enacted.

10.5. Fiscal Federalism in Practice

Each country has its own approach to fiscal decentralization. Thus, the issues arising from federalism differ from country to country. Because many sub-national governments lack hard budget constraints or effective limits on their borrowing, achieving fiscal control over the entire government sector has proved difficult. The proliferation of state enterprises, some of which have their own borrowing authority, has further complicated matters. The following descriptions illustrate many of the issues that fiscal federalism has raised.

10.5.1. *Brazil*

Brazil's state governments play an important role in the country's fiscal system. The Constitution does not assign specific expenditure responsibilities to the central and state governments. Instead, different levels of government can allocate funds freely across a wide range of program areas. On the revenue side, the central and state governments have, for the most part, different taxes. The central government collects an income tax, an industrial products tax, and rural property taxes, among others, while the states collect a sales tax on merchandise and services and, interestingly, a tax on exports (especially valuable to the most economically advanced states in the southeast region, which includes Sao Paulo). Substantial revenue transfers take place from the central government to sub-national governments, and from the states to municipalities. In 2005, the central government collected about 68% of all government sector revenues, with the states collecting 26%

and municipalities collecting 6%.[14] After revenue transfers, the central government retained about 58% of disposable revenue, with states keeping about 26% and the share for municipalities rising to about 16%.[15] In addition, revenue is transferred from the wealthier south and southeast regions to less developed areas. In 2005, disposable revenue for sub-national governments averaged about 12% of GDP across Brazil. In the wealthier southern and southeastern states, however, disposable revenue (revenue after transfers received from the central government) averaged only 10% of state GDP, while in the less affluent northern and central states it averaged nearly 18%. Moreover, revenue transfers from the center averaged about 18% of total disposable revenue in the more affluent states, compared with 48% in the less affluent regions.[16]

Brazil has experienced cycles of fiscal decentralization and recentralization, with decentralization characterizing the most recent period. Between 1988, when the current constitution (which promoted decentralization) became effective, and 2003, the central government's share of non-financial outlays in the general government sector fell from 44% to 26%, while that of municipalities rose from 17% to 35%. State and local governments have become responsible for well over half of most categories of public expenditure, with the central government maintaining a dominant role mainly for pensions and interest on public debt.[17]

Until recently, central government assumption of sub-national government debt was a recurring theme in Brazil, with the central government becoming a kind of lender of last resort to the states.

[14]In 2017, the shares of taxes were similar: about 65.2% for the central government, 27.5% for the states, and 7.3% for localities. See Fernandes, A. L. and P. Santana (2018), "Reforms of Fiscal Relations in Brazil," OECD (November), Graph 3, p. 4, https://www.oecd.org/tax/federalism/reforms-of-fiscal-relations-in-brazil.pdf.

[15]See Serra, J. and J. R. R. Afonso (2007), "Fiscal Federalism in Brazil: An Overview," *CEPAL Review* 91 (April), pp. 29–51, http://www.eclac.org/publicaciones/xml/8/29498/lcg2333iSerra.pdf.

[16]*Id.*, Table 4, p. 37.

[17]*Id.*, p. 35.

As recently as 1999, the central government assumed the entire debt of the states, to be repaid over a 30+ year period at high interest rates. In addition, just before implementation of the Fiscal Responsibility Law of 2000 (FRL), the center assumed debt from municipalities under similar terms. The FRL changed this practice, however. Subsequent federal financing of sub-national government was barred, and state and local governments were prohibited from further bank financing. In addition, many parts of the law helped curb spending. However, curbs on the net debt of state and local governments have proved less effective at curbing overall borrowing. Thus, sub-national government debt in Brazil rose from about 7% of GDP in 1991 to 20% in 2002 before declining to about 11% in 2013. Thereafter, debt levels rose again, reaching about 12% of GDP in 2017.[18]

Despite the trend toward decentralization, certain counter-trends have also occurred. For example, since the 1990s federal revenues from social contributions on income and sales, which are not shared with the states, rose from 2.7% of GDP in 1990 to 4.4% in 2005, while receipts from the federal industrial products tax fell from 2.2% in 1990 to 1.2% in 2005.[19] Brazil has also seen the emergence of inter-state rivalry in cutting the state sales tax, reducing revenues and forcing expenditure cutbacks. Nevertheless, the total net public debt fell from nearly 60% of GDP in 2002 to 30.5% at the end of 2013 before rising again to 55.7% at the end of 2019.[20]

10.5.2. United States

Fiscal federalism in the United States reflects the boundaries established in the US constitution, legal precedent, and tradition. The federal (central) government is responsible for foreign policy, defense, and matters affecting commerce between and among the various states. All other powers are, in principle, reserved to the states, which in turn determine

---

[18] *Id.*, p. 48; and Fernandes and Santana (2018), *op. cit.*, Graph 1, p. 3.
[19] Serra and Alfonso (2006), *op. cit.*, p. 46.
[20] International Monetary Fund (2020), April 2020 World Economic Outlook Database.

the rights and responsibilities of municipalities within their borders. In practice, interstate commerce has been defined quite broadly, allowing the federal government considerable scope to establish, finance, and regulate a wide range of economic activities. In many policy areas, however, the federal government has chosen to implement programs through agencies maintained by state and local governments, providing funding in return for complying with various program obligations and conditions. As a result, the federal government has more influence over public policy than the share of federal expenditures in total government sector outlays would suggest. Federal programs for health care and other policy areas impose major fiscal burdens on state governments, many of which also share a significant part of their revenues with municipalities, to support education and other local functions. Local governments provide many of the most tangible public services — primary and secondary education, police and fire protection, public health clinics, primary judicial services, parks and recreation, and water and sanitation services — although in many states regional bodies are responsible for public transportation. Because local revenue sources are limited — apart from a few large cities, most localities rely mainly on revenues from taxes on real property and various fees and licenses — localities depend heavily on transfers from their state government and, to a lesser extent, the federal government.

The contours of fiscal federalism in the US have changed over time. In general, the trend has been an expansion of federal government authority, with ratification of the sixteenth amendment to the US Constitution in 1913 making possible broad-based taxes on income and corporate profits. As shown in Table 10.3, government sector revenue rose from about 7% of GDP in the early 1900s to a high of 37% of GDP in 2000 and again in 2007, with major increases during the 1920s, the mid-1940s (reflecting World War II), the late 1960s (reflecting the Vietnamese War), and the late 1990s (the so-called Internet and dot-com boom). Through the mid-1940s, most of the growth in government sector revenue as a share of GDP came from rising federal receipts, although state government revenue also rose considerably, from about 1% of GDP in the early 1900s to about 4%

Table 10.3. United States: Government sector revenue, 1902–2018.

Year	(In percent of GDP)				(In percent of sector total)		
	Federal	State	Local	Total	Federal	State	Local
1902	2.7	0.8	3.6	7.1	38.0%	11.3%	50.7%
1913	2.5	0.9	4.2	7.6	32.9%	11.8%	55.3%
1922	5.8	1.7	5.2	12.7	45.7%	13.4%	40.9%
1927	4.7	2.1	6.0	12.8	36.7%	16.4%	46.9%
1932	4.5	3.9	9.2	17.6	25.6%	22.2%	52.3%
1942	9.9	3.7	3.9	17.5	56.6%	21.1%	22.3%
1944	23.4	3.1	3.0	29.5	79.3%	10.5%	10.2%
1950	14.8	3.9	4.0	22.7	65.2%	17.2%	17.6%
1952	20.0	4.0	3.9	27.9	71.7%	14.3%	14.0%
1960	19.0	5.0	5.2	29.2	65.1%	17.1%	17.8%
1965	16.2	5.4	5.3	26.9	60.2%	20.1%	19.7%
1970	18.6	6.6	5.7	30.9	60.2%	21.4%	18.4%
1975	17.0	7.1	6.0	30.1	56.5%	23.6%	19.9%
1980	18.6	7.6	5.6	31.8	58.5%	23.9%	17.6%
1985	17.4	8.3	6.3	32.0	54.4%	25.9%	19.7%
1990	17.8	8.7	6.7	33.2	53.6%	26.2%	20.2%
1995	18.2	9.7	6.7	34.6	52.6%	28.0%	19.4%
2000	20.4	10.2	6.7	37.3	54.7%	27.3%	18.0%
2005	17.0	10.3	6.8	34.1	49.9%	30.2%	19.9%
2006	18.0	10.7	6.9	35.6	50.6%	30.1%	19.4%
2007	18.2	11.7	7.3	37.2	48.9%	31.5%	19.6%
2008	17.5	8.6	7.0	33.1	52.9%	26.0%	21.1%
2010	14.4	9.8	7.3	31.5	45.8%	31.0%	23.1%
2012	15.1	8.4	6.6	30.2	50.1%	28.0%	22.0%
2015	17.8	8.5	6.6	33.0	54.1%	25.9%	20.1%
2018	16.2	9.7	6.7	32.6	49.9%	29.7%	20.4%

Source: US Bureau of Census, Statistical Abstract and Annual Census of State and Local Governments; and Budget of the United States Government, as presented in usgovernmentspending.com.

during the 1940s and early 1950s. Since then, most of the growth in government sector revenues has occurred at the sub-national level, with state government revenues rising to about 11% of GDP and local government revenues reaching about 7% of GDP during 2007, before declining in subsequent years. By comparison, federal revenues have generally ranged from 17% to 20% of GDP since the 1950s while falling to 16.2% in 2018.

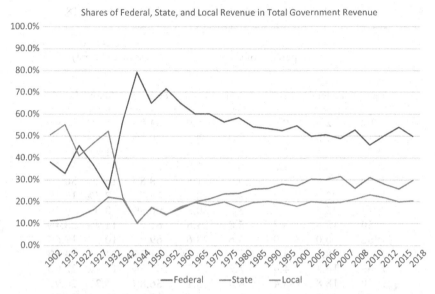

Figure 10.1. United States: Shares of federal, state, and local revenue in total government revenue, 1902–2008.

As shown in Table 10.3 and Figure 10.1, from the early 1900s through 1932, local governments comprised about half of all government sector revenues, with the federal government representing between 25% and 40%, and state governments comprising about 20%. The federal share jumped rapidly during the mid-1940s, reaching a peak of nearly 80% toward the end of World War II. Federal revenues subsequently declined, averaging about 55% of all sector revenues during the 1990s and about 50% from the mid-2000s, reflecting the Bush-era tax cuts. The share of local government revenue, after falling sharply during the 1940s, has stabilized at about 20% of the total government revenue. State government revenue, after falling to about 10% of total receipts in the mid-1940s, rose steadily from about 1960 through 2007. As of 2018, it comprised about 30% of total government receipts.

As Table 10.4 indicates, government expenditures have shown similar trends, rising sharply from about 7% of GDP in 1902 to 29% of GDP in 1942 before reaching a high of 50% of GDP during World War II (1944). After falling to about 24% of GDP in 1950,

Table 10.4.   US government sector expenditures, 1902–2018.

Year	(In percent of GDP)				(In percent of estimated total)		
	Federal	State	Local	Total	Est. Federal	State	Local
1902	2.4	0.6	4.0	6.9	34.8%	8.7%	58.0%
1913	2.5	0.8	5.0	8.3	30.1%	9.6%	60.2%
1922	5.1	1.5	6.2	12.8	39.8%	11.7%	48.4%
1927	3.7	1.5	6.7	11.9	31.1%	12.6%	56.3%
1932	7.3	3.5	10.9	21.6	33.8%	16.2%	50.5%
1942	22.0	2.2	4.5	28.7	76.7%	7.7%	15.7%
1944	45.7	1.5	3.3	50.5	90.5%	3.0%	6.5%
1950	15.3	3.7	5.8	24.8	61.7%	14.9%	23.4%
1952	20.0	3.0	5.6	28.6	69.9%	10.5%	19.6%
1960	18.5	4.2	7.4	30.1	61.5%	14.0%	24.6%
1965	16.4	4.4	7.7	28.5	57.5%	15.4%	27.0%
1970	18.8	5.4	8.9	33.1	56.8%	16.3%	26.9%
1975	20.3	6.4	9.8	36.5	55.6%	17.5%	26.8%
1980	21.2	6.2	9.3	36.7	57.8%	16.9%	25.3%
1985	22.4	6.4	9.2	38.0	58.9%	16.8%	24.2%
1990	21.6	6.9	9.9	38.4	56.3%	18.0%	25.8%
1995	20.4	8.0	10.1	38.6	52.8%	20.7%	26.2%
2000	18.0	7.6	9.9	35.5	50.7%	21.4%	27.9%
2005	19.6	8.4	10.3	38.3	51.2%	21.9%	26.9%
2007	19.4	8.4	10.6	38.3	50.7%	21.9%	27.7%
2008	20.7	8.7	10.9	40.3	51.4%	21.6%	27.0%
2010	19.0	9.7	11.0	39.8	47.8%	24.5%	27.7%
2012	18.4	9.2	10.2	37.9	48.7%	24.4%	26.9%
2015	16.8	9.0	9.7	35.5	47.4%	25.3%	27.3%
2018	16.7	8.9	9.3	34.8	47.8%	25.5%	26.6%

Source: US Bureau of Census, *Statistical Abstract* and *Annual Census of State and Local Governments*; and Budget of the United States Government, as presented in usgovernmentspending.com.

total government spending rose fairly steadily from the mid-1950s, averaging about 38% of GDP from 1985 through 2007 before hitting a peak of about 40% in 2008. Government outlays have risen as a percentage of GDP at all levels of government, although since about 1970 most of the increase has occurred at the state and local level. Throughout the period, local expenditures have exceeded state outlays (Figure 10.2). Federal expenditures ranged from about 50% to 62%

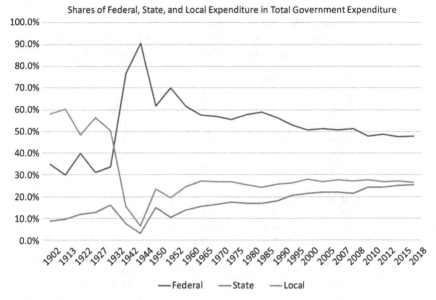

Figure 10.2.   Shares of federal, state, and local expenditure in total government sector outlays.

of total sector outlays from 1960 through 1990, declining to about 48% in 2018. Local outlays have ranged from 24% to 27% of total government expenditures since 1960, while state government outlays have grown from about 15% of the total in 1960 to more than 25% in 2017 and 2018.

As noted earlier, a key feature of the US fiscal system is the need for most states to approve balanced current budgets. Thus, most of the recorded deficits in the US government sector come from the federal budget. As shown in Table 10.5, between 1992 and 2018, the overall balance for the general government sector, as a percent of GDP, ranged from a combined surplus of 1.5% to an aggregate deficit of 11.0%. During this period, most of the variance occurred in the federal budget deficit (Figure 10.3), where the balance, as a percent of GDP, ranged from a surplus of 2.4% to a deficit of 9.9%. In most years, state and local government budgets recorded small deficits of about of 1–2% of GDP, reflecting some local deficits and the ability of states to borrow for capital outlays. In 2008, because of the 2007–2009 financial crisis,

Table 10.5.   United States: Government sector budget
balance, 1992–2018 (in percent of GDP).

	Total sector	Federal	State and local
1992	−5.9	−4.7	−1.2
1993	−5.1	−3.9	−1.2
1994	−3.7	−2.9	−0.8
1995	−3.3	−2.2	−1.1
1996	−2.3	−1.4	−0.9
1997	−0.9	−0.3	−0.6
1998	0.3	0.8	−0.5
1999	0.7	1.4	−0.7
2000	1.5	2.4	−0.9
2001	−0.6	1.3	−1.9
2002	−4.0	−1.5	−2.5
2003	−5.0	−3.4	−1.6
2004	−4.4	−3.5	−0.9
2005	−3.3	−2.6	−0.7
2006	−2.2	−1.9	−0.3
2007	−2.8	−1.2	−1.6
2008	−6.5	−3.2	−3.3
2009	−11.0	−9.9	−1.1
2010	−10.6	−8.6	−2.0
2012	−7.6	−6.7	−0.9
2015	−3.2	−2.4	−0.8
2018	−4.3	−3.8	−0.5

Sources: OECD Economic Outlook 87 Database; Economic
Report of the President; IMF, Fiscal Monitor April 2019; and
usgovernmentspending.com

the combined deficits for the state and local governments jumped to
3.3% of GDP, although they declined to about 1.1% of GDP in 2009
and 0.5% of GDP in 2018.

10.5.3. India

India presents an especially interesting case study of fiscal federalism.
India's constitution prescribes certain revenue sources to the central
government and others to state governments. However, residual
revenue functions and spending obligations belong to the central
government, rather than the states. This is in contrast to to the United

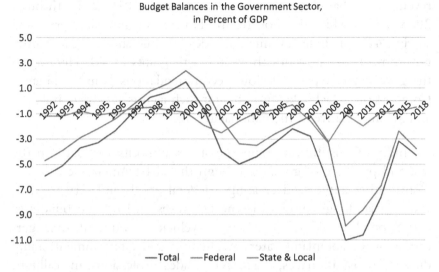

Figure 10.3.   United States: Budget balances in the government sector, 1992–2018.

States, where powers not expressly granted to the federal (central) government are traditionally reserved to the states.

India's constitution grants the central government the authority to tax corporate and personal income, levy customs duties, impose excises on goods other than alcohol, and, since 2016, levy a goods and services tax, which is coordinated with the states. A certain percentage of the main taxes (all revenues except the union surcharge, cess levied for specific purposes, and a few small excises) is to be shared with the states. As noted earlier, a Finance Commission recommends how the main revenues are to be shared, and India's Parliament generally accepts the recommendations. Since adoption of the Eightieth Amendment to the Constitution in 2000, the Finance Commission has recommended that a certain percentage of these revenues be transferred to the states. The Eleventh Finance Commission, governing fiscal years 2000/2001– 2005/2006, proposed that 29.5% of the main central taxes be shared. The Twelfth Finance Commission, covering fiscal years 2005/2006– 2010/2011, recommended that 30.5% of the main taxes be shared. The Thirteenth Finance Commission proposed that 32% of these revenues be shared for the period from fiscal 2010/2011 through 2015/2016, while the Fourteenth Finance Commission proposed sharing 42% of these revenues. Besides revenue sharing, the central government also provides the states with grants in aid. Here again the government typically follows recommendations from the Finance Commission, which take into account such factors as state population and income relative to the national average.

India's Constitution grants the states authority for taxes on the sale and purchase of goods (although the 101st Amendment to the Constitution authorized creating a federal goods and services tax), taxes on land, agricultural income tax, taxes on land and buildings, excises on alcoholic beverages, motor vehicles, goods and passengers carried by road or inland waterways, luxuries and entertainment, stamp duty and registration fees, and taxes on trades, professions, and callings. Of these, sales taxes were the most important. From 2005, virtually all states replaced their sales taxes with a value-added tax (VAT). States generally imposed a rate of 12.5% on most goods, with a lower 4% rate applied to selected items. In 2017, the central government replaced state VATs and several other levies with a single goods and services tax, administered concurrently by the central and state governments, with rates of 0.5%, 12%, 18%, or 28%, depending on the item.

On the expenditure side, the Indian Constitution assigns the central government responsibility over most functions. These include defense, foreign affairs, railways, posts and telecom, national highways, shipping, inland waterways, air transport, external trade, interstate trade and commerce, corporate matters spanning more than one state, banking, insurance, stock exchanges, control of industries declared by Parliament to be of public interest, oil fields, and mines of public interest. The states have responsibility for public order (and, where not controlled by the localities, police services), public health and sanitation, agriculture, irrigation, land rights, fisheries, and non-Union List industries. The central government and the states have concurrent responsibility for criminal law, marriage and divorce, contracts, economic and social planning, population control and family planning, trade unions, social security, and education, although central laws override conflicting ordinances made by the states. Local governments have authority over police services, urban transport, and internal pollution issues. All residuary issues lie within the exclusive domain of the central government.

The broad expenditure responsibilities of the states, combined with their relatively narrow tax base, makes them heavily dependent on revenue transfers from the central government. In 2002–2003, state expenditures totaled about 58% of those made by the central government, while the state's own revenues were only 38% of those collected by the center. Over time, the share of own revenues covering state expenditures has declined.[21] This helps explain the rising percentages of central government-shared revenue transferred to the states during the past decade.

With expenditures falling far short of own revenues and no prohibitions against state borrowing, India's states have periodically accumulated considerable debt. India's Ministry of Finance estimated total state debt at 24.8% of GDP during the 2009–2010 fiscal year, after netting out state holdings of central government securities.[22] Traditionally, the states have borrowed from the central government; doing so in principle precludes their undertaking other borrowing. In practice, however, some states have been able to evade the restriction, for example, by establishing state-established banks and then borrowing from them.

The accumulation of state debts to the center has prompted periodic moves by the center to address state debts, and various commissions have recommended debt rescheduling or other methods

---

[21] See Fraschini, A. (2006), "Fiscal Federalism in Big Developing Countries: China and India," Working Paper No. 66, Department of Public Policy and Public Choice, University of Eastern Piedmont "Amadeo Avogadro," Alessandria, Italy (January), p. 8, http://polis.unipmn.it/pubbl/RePEc/uca/ucapdv/fraschini66.pdf.

[22] Ministry of Finance, India (2010), "Government Debt: Status and Next Steps," (November), http://pib.nic.in/archieve/others/2010/nov/d2010110301.pdf.

to reduce the current burden of state debts. The Twelfth Finance Commission, for example, proposed linking debt relief with the enactment of fiscal responsibility laws at the state level, and since the 2005–2006 fiscal year at least 21 Indian states have done so. The fiscal responsibility laws appeared to improve performance at the state government level, at least until the onset of the 2008–2009 recession. Total debt of the states is estimated to have fallen from 32.5% of GDP in fiscal year 2004/2005 to 27.6% in fiscal year 2007/2008.[23] By fiscal year 2017/2018, total state debt was about 20% of GDP, based on IMF data.[24]

10.6. Summary

Many countries have federalized fiscal systems, as a result of separate central, state or provincial, and local governments. A federal structure can allow both the level and composition of expenditures to vary, thus permitting a closer match between public expenditures and local preferences. However, federalism also makes it harder to achieve broad targets for the entire government sector, unless subnational governments have tight borrowing and financing constraints. Because regional and local governments have narrower tax bases, lower levels of government often need transfers from above to fund their expenditures. However, each unit of government needs dedicated revenue sources for its financial base.

---

[23] Thirteenth Finance Commission, India (2010), "Report of the Thirteenth Finance Commission," Chapter 4, Table 4.7, p. 50, http://fincomindia.nic.in/ShowContentOne.aspx?id= 28&Section=1.

[24] IMF (2018), *India: Article IV Consultation-Press Release; Staff Report; and Statement by the Executive Director for India*, data derived from Tables 4 and 5, pp. 41 and 41, https://www. imf.org/en/Publications/CR/Issues/2018/08/06/India-2018-Article-IV-Consultation-Pre ss-Release-Staff-Report-and-Statement-by-the-Executive-46155.

Chapter Eleven: Fiscal Policy for Promoting Growth and Alleviating Poverty and Inequality

As noted in Chapter One, an economy's growth rate can vary considerably over time, partly because firms and households have incentives to behave pro-cyclically, spending more as the economy expands and less as it contracts. Thus, the government can use counter-cyclical fiscal policy to stabilize the economy, cooling activity during expansions and reviving it during recessions. In addition, the choice of certain tax and spending programs can promote growth over the medium term. The government can also address severe inequities in the distribution of income and wealth that a market economy may generate by creating a publicly funded social safety net and taking other measures to reduce economic inequality. A variety of tax and spending measures can help alleviate poverty, lessen inequality, and reduce the costs of unemployment. This chapter addresses both growth enhancement and the alleviation of poverty and economic inequality.

11.1. Using Fiscal Policy to Promote Growth

The government's approach to fiscal policy, including its choice of revenue instruments and how funds are spent, can affect an economy's growth rate. Although taxes on their own tend to reduce growth by lowering after-tax profits and income, certain taxes inhibit growth less than others. Similarly, while government spending generally increases demand, some types of spending are more likely to promote sustained growth, because of their impact on economy-wide productivity. Government debt can also affect the rate of economic growth. High debt levels can reduce growth by raising interest rates and crowding out funds for private investment. Thus, a moderate level of taxation may actually raise growth, if it allows government to finance growth-enhancing outlays while limiting the rise in public debt.

11.1.1. *Revenue policy*

On the revenue side of the budget, governments can best raise growth through an investment-friendly tax policy. Typically, this means having moderate tax rates, compared to other places investors consider when deciding where to invest. High corporate tax rates often discourage investment, although the availability of tax rebates, concessions, and other special features can offset the impact of a high rate. Moreover, the corporate tax rate is but one part — and on average, less than half — of the total tax burden that firms incur.[1] Thus, investors often consider an array of tax information when assessing the attractiveness for investment of a particular site.

The World Bank's Doing Business website, which includes a section providing corporate tax information on some 190 economies,[2] provides an estimate of the profit, labor, and other taxes that a small-to medium-sized firm would pay in each one. The data also indicate the number of tax payments to be made, on average, during the year, and the estimated number of hours during a year needed to make these payments. Summary data for late 2018 showed a wide range in estimated total tax rates at the national level, with regional averages ranging from about 32% in Eastern Europe and Central Asia to 47% in Sub-Saharan Africa (Table 11.1). Total tax rates for individual countries varied even more widely, from less than 8% in Brunei Darussalam and Vanuatu to estimated rates of more than 100% in Argentina and Comoros. Estimated total tax rates in Singapore and Hong Kong SAR, often cited as among the more competitive high-income countries,

---

[1] See PriceWaterhouseCoopers (2010), *Paying Taxes 2011: The Global Picture*, p. 4, www.pwc.com/payingtaxes.

[2] See World Bank (2018), "Paying Taxes 2019" (November), https://www.doingbusiness.org/content/dam/doingBusiness/media/Special-Reports/PwC—Paying-Taxes-2019—Smaller-19112018.pdf.

Table 11.1.   Comparative company taxes, by region, late 2018 (tax rates in pct.)

Region	No. of tax pmts.	Hours needed	Total tax rate
East Asia & Pacific	21.2	180.9	33.5
Eastern Europe & Central Asia	16.6	214.8	32.3
Latin America & Caribbean	27.1	330.0	46.7
Middle East & North Africa	17.7	196.7	32.7
OECD	11.2	159.4	39.8
South Asia	27.6	274.8	43.5
Sub-Saharan Africa	37.4	280.6	46.8

Source: World Bank (2019), "Doing Business — Paying Taxes," https://www.doingbusiness.org/en/data/exploretopics/paying-taxes. Tax rate includes taxes on profits, employer contributions to social insurance, and all other taxes paid by firms.

were about 21% and 23%, respectively, at end of 2018. Total tax rates in the United States were about 41% in Los Angeles, CA and 46% in New York City, slightly above the average of 40% for all OECD countries.

Besides ensuring that corporate tax rates are competitive, several other features can make a revenue system more growth-enhancing. These include the following:

1. *Keeping the overall tax burden moderate.* Although the ratio of total taxes to GDP is but one element affecting growth, for much of the postwar period, among OECD countries, those with lower total tax burdens, such as Japan and the United States, grew faster than those with generally higher burdens, such as many of the countries in Western Europe, at least through the 1990s.[3] There is also evidence that many OECD countries with high levels of human development, as measured by the World Bank's Human Development Index (HDI), have lowered their levels of government expenditure (and, thus, total taxes) since the start of

---

[3] See Tanzi, V., and L. Schuknecht (2000), *Public Spending in the 20th Century: A Global Perspective* (Cambridge: Cambridge University Press).

the 21st century with little damage to their HDI scores.[4] Finally, lower tax burdens can help draw investment to a country, if other economic characteristics are comparable. The relatively modest total tax burdens in Singapore and Hong Kong SAR, for example, have contributed to the growth of these economies and the influx of high-income residents migrating from higher tax jurisdictions such as China and India.

2. *Relying more on consumption than income and profit taxation.* As noted in Chapter Six, income taxes impose a double taxation on saving, because not only income but also the proceeds of income used for saving are taxed. Similarly, most corporate income taxes impose a double taxation of dividends, because profits are taxed initially at the corporate level, while dividends are taxed again at the level of the recipient unless special exemptions or rebates are provided. Relying more on consumption taxes avoids these problems. It may also encourage investment, by allowing lower profit and income tax rates that increase the competitiveness of the country's or region's business climate. Finally, relying more on consumption taxation shifts part of the local tax burden onto visitors, who pay consumption taxes on goods and services they buy. For all these reasons, shifting the tax burden toward consumption can promote growth and investment, although it may also make the tax system less progressive and increase inequality. In 2007, Singapore raised its goods and services (VAT) tax from 5% to 7%, while cutting its corporate profits tax rate to 18%, as a way of shifting more of its tax burden onto consumption. At the same time, it provided temporary rebates for lower income households, to cushion the effect of the increase in GST on the most vulnerable of its population. In 2010, Singapore reduced the corporate tax rate further, to 17%.[5]

---

[4]See Tanzi, V. (2005), "Economic Role of the State in the 21st Century," *Cato Journal,* vol. 25 (Fall), pp. 617–638, Table 2, p. 623, http://www.cato.org/pubs/journal/cj25n3/cj25n3-16. pdf.

[5]GuideMe Singapore (2019), "Singapore Corporate Tax Guide," https://www.guide mesingapore.com/business-guides/taxation-and-accounting/corporate-tax/singapore-corpor ate-tax-guide.

Besides the foregoing points, relying more heavily on consumption taxes can contribute to higher employment, if the shift in tax policy allows lower payroll taxes. Although most economists believe that employees ultimately bear the burden of payroll taxes, reducing payroll taxes, particularly for employers, can make workers appear less costly to hire. This is especially true when employment taxes apply only to the initial or lowest component of earnings, in which case some firms may find it cheaper to give existing workers overtime than to expand employment. For this reason, Singapore has regularly adjusted the contribution rate required from employers for its Central Provident Fund, reducing the rate during recessions as a way of encouraging firms to minimize layoffs and then restoring it after the economy returns to a more normal level of output.

11.1.2. Expenditure policy

Governments can also promote growth through spending policies that direct outlays toward certain activities. In general, government spending on productive goods and services that support the private sector can help promote growth, particularly if they alleviate inefficiencies or help raise the productivity of the national or regional economy. Examples of growth-promoting expenditure include the following:

1. *Education.* Outlays for education that support well-designed and effective schooling can be among the most productive expenditures governments undertake. A well-trained populace, with relevant skills, is critical for providing the labor force needed to staff private factories and offices. In low-income countries, spending for primary education that achieves literacy is often considered the most productive form of education expenditure. In middle-income and emerging market countries, spending for primary and secondary education, including vocational education that provides employable skills to those completing school, can be highly productive. In high-income countries, specific program elements may be more important than the overall level of expenditure for achieving good educational results. The United States, for example, has higher

spending per capita for primary and secondary education than most other countries but achieves poorer results, as measured on international standardized test scores, than do many other nations, because of how funds are spent. Outlays focus more on reducing class size and equalizing resources among students, rather than securing high-quality teachers or focusing resources on the neediest students.[6] The most recent Program of International Student Assessment issued by the Organization for Economic and Cultural Development (OECD), based on 2018 data, showed U.S. ranking above the average for OECD countries in science and reading and below the average in mathematics, as well as below top-scoring countries in Asia.[7] The Republic of Korea and Finland, whose students rank highly on the achievement list in reading, focus heavily on teacher training, make entry to teacher training programs quite selective, accord teachers high status, and compensate teachers well for good performance. They also focus more resources on helping weaker students and on securing better teachers, rather than reducing class size.[8]

2. *Infrastructure.* Building and maintaining high-quality infrastructure — roads, airports, electricity grids, water and sewage systems, and telecommunications services — is critical for enabling private firms and households to work effectively and efficiency. Achieving high-quality infrastructure has been important for the success of high-income countries in Western Europe and North America. It has also contributed greatly to Singapore's rapid growth and ascent to advanced economy status. Likewise, China's earlier and greater investment in infrastructure helped it achieve higher growth rates than India for many years.

---

[6]See ED.gov Blog (2010), "International Education Rankings Suggest Reform Can Lift U.S.," http://www.ed.gov/blog/2010/12/international-education-rankings-suggest-reform-can-lift-u-s/.

[7]See OECD (2019), *PISA 2018: Country Note – United States*, https://www.oecd.org/pisa/publications/PISA2018_CN_USA.pdf.

[8]See Schleicher, A. (2010), "The Importance of World Class Schools for Economic Success," testimony to US Senate HELP Committee (OECD, March 9), http://help.senate.gov/imo/media/doc/Schleicher.pdf.

In Asia, relatively high spending for infrastructure in countries such as Malaysia and Thailand, where capital outlays often account for a quarter of the budget, has contributed to high growth rates. By comparison, the slower growth of the Philippines and Pakistan can be attributed partly to lower outlays for infrastructure, as a result of higher public debt and the need to spend more on interest payments.

3. *Health care.* Developing and maintaining an effective and efficient health care system also promotes growth, by ensuring a healthy population at a moderate cost to firms and households. At the country level, the challenges resemble those for education: having enough spending to support decent primary care in low-income countries; ensuring access to good care for the bulk of the population, in middle-income countries; and obtaining high-quality and efficient care, in high-income countries. As with education, more spending does not always mean better quality. The United States spends about 18% of its GDP on health care,[9] far above the 11–12% of GDP recorded in the next highest countries (France and Switzerland).[10] However, health indicators such as life expectancy and infant mortality are poorer in the United States than in some other countries with much lower ratios of health expenditures to GDP, such as Japan and Switzerland. Thus, in high-income countries, achieving more efficient health care delivery is a key concern.

4. *Legal system.* Maintaining and developing an impartial, efficient, and highly regarded judicial system provides many benefits to a country. Investors appreciate knowing that legal disputes can be resolved quickly and fairly through the courts or arbitration. Indeed, the World Bank's Doing Business website lists enforcing contracts

---

[9]See US Department of Health and Human Services, Centers for Medicare and Medicaid Services (2018), "National Health Expenditure Data — Historical," https://www.cms.gov/Research-Statistics-Data-and-Systems/Statistics-Trends-and-Reports/. NationalHealthExpendData/NationalHealthAccountsHistorical.html (data for 2017).

[10]Statista (2019), "Health expenditure as a percentage of gross domestic product in selected countries in 2017," https://www.statista.com/statistics/268826/health-expenditure-as-gdp-percentage-in-oecd-countries/.

(dispute resolution) as among the criteria for assessing a country's attractiveness for investment.[11]

Providing adequate funding for courts is but one element in creating an effective legal system. Securing an adequate number of well-trained judges, establishing efficient legal procedures, and ensuring impartiality also matter. Singapore has benefitted from having a well-regarded set of judges and procedural reforms that have cut the average number of days for resolving a business dispute in Singapore to 164, although the average cost is about 26% of the claim. In the United States, by comparison, less efficient procedures, including legal rules offering many opportunities for delay, have kept the average time of resolution in New York City at 370 days, although the relative cost is low — on average, about 23% of the actual claim in dispute.[12]

5. *Regulatory system.* An effective and efficient regulatory system can also spur economic growth by increasing confidence in the business climate while keeping regulations from becoming too burdensome. Research has shown, for example, that a legal and regulatory environment that protects minority shareholder interests and deters fraud is associated with stronger financial systems.[13]

Developing an effective regulatory environment requires adequate funding for regulatory agencies, along with the willingness to allow these agencies to operate impartially, with limited political oversight. A key issue in many countries is paying salaries high enough to deter corruption and retain an adequate number of officials once they have been trained. For this reason, some countries have developed special pay scales for customs officials, bank examiners, and tax officers, to promote impartiality and retention.

---

[11] See World Bank (2019), "Doing Business — Enforcing Contracts," http://www. doingbusiness.org/data/exploretopics/enforcing-contracts.

[12] *Ibid.* (see country data table).

[13] See, for example, La Porta, R. *et al.* (2008), "The Economic Consequences of Legal Origins," *Journal of Economic Literature*, vol. 46, pp. 285–332, http://www.aeaweb.org/atypon.php? return_to=/doi/pdfplus/10.1257/jel.46.2.285.

11.2. Using Fiscal Policy to Alleviate Poverty, Inequality, and Unemployment

Fiscal policy can also help countries alleviate poverty, inequality, and unemployment by creating an efficient and effective social safety net and taking additional measures to reduce inequality. A country's tax system can be designed to minimize the tax burden on low-income households while also ensuring that higher income taxpayers pay an appropriate rate of income tax and face measures to limit the inheritance, and possibly also the accumulation, of massive wealth. Where administrative services allow, the tax system can also be used to provide income support, using subsidies paid out through the tax code to qualifying citizens who file tax returns. On the expenditure side of the budget, a wide variety of programs can be developed to help the poor and unemployed. In addition, governments can promote the growth of low-income areas through special programs aimed at creating jobs and improving the quality of public services, including schooling.

11.2.1. Revenue measures to assist the poor and address inequality

The two main ways countries can use revenue policy to assist the poor involve setting a minimum income for tax liability and using the tax system to provide cash benefits to the poor.

1. *Minimum tax liability threshold.* Countries with personal income taxes can make these taxes pro-poor by establishing a minimum income for tax liability. Personal exemptions are typically used for this purpose, and most countries include such provisions in their income tax laws. Exemption levels vary from country to country. In some countries, the minimum income for tax liability is relatively high. In Singapore, for example, only those with S$22,000 of income (about US$15,750 in late 2019) — about one quarter of per capita GDP — need file an income tax return. In India, the first 250,000 rupees (about US$3,540), roughly 1.7 times per

capita GDP, are exempt from income tax. In the United States, by comparison, the threshold for liability in 2019 for those under age 65 was US$12,000 for single taxpayers and US$24,000 for married taxpayers filing a joint return — well under half the US per capita GDP. However, many taxpayers earning more were able to use special tax credits to avoid paying any income tax.

2. *Providing tax subsidies to the poor.* In countries where administrative measures can effectively identify low-income individuals and households, the tax system can also be used to transfer income to the poor. Provisions can be added to the tax code authorizing cash rebates to taxpayers whose incomes fall below certain levels. Because these provisions allow taxpayers to receive money from, rather than pay to, the government, they are sometimes called "negative income taxes."

Among the best-known programs using the tax system to provide cash transfers to individuals is the *Earned Income Credit* (EIC) of the United States. The EIC allows citizens and permanent residents with earned income below certain levels to receive a credit against their income tax due. If their incomes are sufficiently low, this credit is paid out as a tax refund — in effect, a cash transfer to the taxpaying unit. In 2019, the EIC provided credits for childless individuals with incomes below US$15,570, childless couples with incomes below US$21,370, and single and married taxpayer units with children and maximum incomes of US$50,162 to US$55,952, depending on the taxpayer status (single or married) and the number of children. The amount of the credit depends on the taxpayer's income, family status, and number of children. For 2019, the maximum credit was US$6,557, for taxpaying units with three or more children, with the amount declining as income exceeds a certain level. To claim the credit, individuals or couples must file tax returns, have social security numbers for themselves and their children, and meet certain eligibility criteria about their residence and that of their children.[14]

---

[14]For details, see Nerdwallet (2019), "Earned Income Tax Credit (EIC): What It Is and How to Qualify," https://www.nerdwallet.com/blog/taxes/can-you-take-earned-income-tax-credit/; and US Internal Revenue Service (2019), "EITC Central," https://www.eitc.irs.gov/.

Revenue policy can address inequality through a combination of measures to boost the incomes of low- and moderate-income taxpayers and policies to raise tax rates for high-income and wealthy households. Policies such as the EIC could be expanded to benefit taxpayers higher on the income scale, for example, those earning up to 33% or 40% of median incomes. Another option would be a refundable tax credit for those with children or dependent relatives living at home. At the high end of the income scale, reforms could eliminate tax expenditures benefitting mainly those at the top end of the income scale, raise tax rates on capital gains, eliminate salary ceilings on social insurance contributions and taxes, and raise marginal tax rates on high-income taxpayers (e.g., to 45–50% in countries where current rates are lower). Taxes on estates or inheritances could be imposed, or the floor on taxable estates reduced — in the United States, for example, returning it to the US$2.0 million applicable in 2008. Finally, countries could consider enacting a national wealth tax, separate from local property taxes, for example, a 2% tax on wealth above US$50 million, as some US presidential candidates proposed during 2019–2020.

11.2.2. *Expenditure measures to address poverty and inequality*

In most countries, expenditure programs offer the main vehicles for assisting the poor. Governments have many ways to do so. These include providing grants of cash or specific goods and services, providing subsidies for the purchase of specific items, subsidizing employment in the private sector, and creating government jobs. Governments can also help the poor by aiding poor regions.

1. *Providing grants of cash or specific items.* Arguably the most direct way to help low-income households is to provide cash or specific goods and services. Many countries have programs offering poor families and individuals cash grants. In 2005, for example, Indonesia created a program of family allowances, ultimately set at about US$30 per month, for low-income families, in part to offset

inflationary consequences of reducing fuel subsidies.[15] During the mid-1990s, Romania introduced a system of cash transfers to low-income families, to replace a set of relatively inefficient subsidies. Several countries in Latin America have developed cash transfer programs designed also to improve school attendance and other desirable behaviors among the poor. Brazil's Bolsa Familia program, for example, provides families with significant cash grants, provided their children meet standards for attending school, receiving vaccinations, and visiting health clinics.[16] Mexico has a similar program called Opportunidades.[17] Most high-income countries also provide cash transfers to low-income families and other vulnerable groups. This includes temporary support for unemployed workers. Since the 1930s, the United States has had income support programs for poor families with children, the best known of which was the Aid to Families with Dependent Children (AFDC) program, which for many years provided cash grants to low-income, single-adult households with children. In 1996, the Personal Responsibility and Work Opportunity Act (often called the "Welfare Reform" law) replaced AFDC with the Temporary Cash Assistance for Needy Families (TANF) program, which tightened conditions for receiving cash assistance, limiting the duration of benefits and imposing requirements for work or job training.[18] Besides cash grants, the United States provides various forms of housing assistance, including access to limited amounts of publicly built or subsidized housing. These programs are separate from unemployment insurance, which provides income support for a

---

[15] For details, see Widjaja, M. (2009), "An Economic and Social Review on Indonesian Direct Cash Transfer Program to Poor Families Year 2005," https://www.appam.org/conferences/international/singapore2009/sessions/downloads/1101.pdf.

[16] See, for example, "Brazil's Bolsa Familia: How to get children out of jobs and into school," *Economist Magazine* (July 29, 2010), http://www.economist.com/node/16690887.

[17] See Shanghai Poverty Conference (2004), Case Study Summary, "Mexico's Opportunidades Program," http://info.worldbank.org/etools/docs/reducingpoverty/case/119/summary/Mexico-Opportunidades\%20Summary.pdf.

[18] For details, see the program description at U.S. Department of Health and Human Services, Office of Family Assistance (2020), "About TANF," https://www.acf.hhs.gov/ofa/programs/tanf/about.

limited period to those losing jobs. Most European countries also provide unemployment insurance and offer special cash transfers for low-income citizens.

Governments often use cash transfer programs because they provide funds directly to eligible households, without involving the need to purchase other goods or services or create jobs, which raises the cost of providing assistance. Cash transfers also give recipients maximum flexibility, letting them determine the mix of purchases (food, clothing, shelter, utilities, health care, and transportation to work) that best meets their needs. However, the very flexibility of cash grants has led some countries to restrict the use of payments, so that recipients cannot use them for socially disapproved items such as alcoholic beverages or tobacco products. Unconditional cash transfers have also been criticized for discouraging work effort, especially if benefits end abruptly when household income exceeds the limit for eligibility. For this reason, some countries like the United States have imposed work or training requirements, while Singapore opted for an earnings supplement program, paid out on the expenditure side of the budget and linked to its Central Provident Fund (Singapore's main vehicle to accumulate savings for retirement and health care expenses). Likewise, unemployment benefits can prolong joblessness if benefits are set at too high a percentage of previous earnings, thereby discouraging the unemployed from accepting new jobs quickly.

2. *Subsidies for specific goods and services.* Another way governments assist low-income families is to subsidize certain goods and services. Some countries provide subsidies for basic foods or other items, such as cooking oil and petroleum products. The petroleum subsidies of Indonesia and Malaysia are examples of general price subsidies, as is Egypt's classic bread subsidy, which keeps the price of bread extremely low (some of which is said to be resold at twice the official price).[19] Because general subsidies are available to everyone, they are quite expensive and relatively inefficient as ways of assisting only

---

[19] See Slackman, M. (2008), "Egypt's Problem and Its Challenge: Bread Corrupts," *New York Times* (January 17), http://www.nytimes.com/2008/01/17/world/africa/17bread.html.

the poor. In the mid-2000s, Egypt's bread subsidy, for example, cost the government the equivalent of more than US$2.5 billion per year, or more than 1% of GDP.[20]

To improve efficiency, many countries have attempted to limit subsidies to low-income households. Doing so requires developing an effective means to identify the poor and screen out others. One example in the developing world was Sri Lanka's earlier food subsidy program, which gave eligible households booklets with photo identification that allowed them to purchase limited amounts of rice, flour, and cooking oil at subsidized prices. A more recent example, involving an emerging market country, is Ukraine's utility assistance program, adopted in 1995 to accompany a rise in utility prices. Under this program, families who could show that more than 15% (from 1999 onward, 20%) of their income was spent on such costs received a payment from the government equal to the utility payments above that amount.[21] Among high-income countries, the Supplementary Nutrition Assistance Program (SNAP) or "food stamp" program of the United States provides families whose income and assets fall below certain levels to receive an electronic benefit card that can be used to purchase food at grocery and convenience stores. Benefit levels are set by assuming that families use 30% of their income to purchase food.[22] The United States also offers housing assistance, in the form of rent subsidies for qualifying housing units, to eligible low-income households.[23] As with the provision of public housing, the limited amount of funding and qualifying housing units greatly restricts the amount of assistance available.

---

[20]*Ibid.*

[21]For details, see Fankhouser, S. *et al.* (2008), "Utility Payments in Ukraine: Afford- ability, Subsidies and Arrears," University College, London, Center for the Study of Social Change in Europe, Economics Working Paper No. 87, http://discovery.ucl.ac.uk/17458/1/17458.pdf.

[22]For details on the SNAP program, see United States Department of Agriculture, Food and Nutrition Service (2020), "Supplemental Nutrition Assistance Program," https://www.fns.usda.gov/snap/supplemental-nutrition-assistance-program.

[23]For information, see US Department of Housing and Urban Development (2020), "Rental Assistance," https://www.hud.gov/topics/rental_assistance.

Compared to simple cash transfers, subsidies for specific goods and services have the advantage of allowing donor governments to determine which items are subsidized. Doing so may have political advantages, because it avoids the risk of recipients using the benefits for unacceptable items, such as tobacco products. However, such subsidies can result in recipients having a less desired pattern of overall spending than if they could allocate funds themselves — for example, spending a larger share of their budget on food or housing than if they received cash.

3. *Subsidizing employment in the private sector.* Another strategy some governments use is to subsidize jobs at private firms. To boost employment, governments may offer firms a subsidy equal to a certain percentage of the wages paid for new employees. This lowers the cost of hiring new workers and may encourage firms to expand employment. Among high-income countries, Germany and Spain provide such grants on the expenditure side of the budget, as do several state governments in the United States. Some governments also provide employment credits on the revenue side of the budget. For example, in its 2009 budget, Singapore introduced a temporary jobs tax credit that gave employers a cash payment equal to the first S$2,500 of monthly salary for each employee. The credit was extended through mid-2010.[24] The federal government of the United States also provides tax credits to promote employment, most recently for select groups in the labor force. The Work Opportunity Tax Credit provides tax credits for hiring new workers from certain population groups identified as having special difficulties in finding work, including disabled military veterans, youth from so-called empowerment zones (low-income neighborhoods), and persons who have received TANF benefits for an extended period.[25]

---

[24]For information, see Inland Revenue Authority of Singapore (2010), "Singapore Budget — Tax Changes — Jobs Credit Scheme," http://www.iras.gov.sg/irashome/jobscredit.aspx.

[25]For information, see United States Department of Labor, Employment and Training Administration (2020), "Work Opportunity Tax Credit," https://www.doleta.gov/business/incentives/opptax/.

Research suggests that job creation subsidies are often a costly way to expand employment. In some cases, firms use the subsidies to reduce wage costs of existing employees. Thus, some programs limit subsidies to employment above a previous level. Despite these efforts, other factors can also lower the efficiency of job creation subsidies. A 2010 study of the German job creation program, for example, found that the subsidies had no discernible effect on regional employment. One reason may have been that the rise in job opportunities created by the program induced some existing employees to leave their previous jobs to seek other work.[26]

4. *Government job creation.* Another option some governments pursue involves creating public sector jobs, by expanding government positions or by creating temporary employment programs open to designated groups, such as the unemployed. Some developing and emerging market countries have used this approach during economic downturns, creating temporary jobs in fields such as construction as a way of providing income to the unemployed without distorting work incentives. The United States did the same during the 1930s, establishing agencies such as the Civilian Conservation Corps (CCC) and the Works Progress Administration (WPA) to hire workers for conservation and infrastructure projects. A number of countries, including Australia, Canada, and the United States, also create temporary summer jobs in government agencies for students. Finally, a few countries, such as India, have periodically created temporary government jobs for hard-to-employ laborers. Sometimes, however, these programs have lasted far longer than expected, imposing large burdens on government budgets.

Government job creation programs offer a way to provide income to otherwise unemployed workers without compromising work incentives. The most effective of such programs pay wages below those generally available in the private sector and create jobs that are clearly temporary, so that participants have an incentive to

---

[26]See Steinwender, C. (2010), "Job Creation Subsidies and Employment. Empirical Evidence for Germany," summary presented at http://www.diw.de/en/diw_01.c.100353.en/about_us/department_of_the_executive_board/events/events.html.

seek regular employment in the private sector. Nevertheless, these programs are a relatively costly way to provide funds to low-income households, because work projects need to be created at significant expense. To minimize the cost, governments may wish to have some projects in reserve that can quickly be implemented using temporary workers. In this way, the programs can be viewed more as an expansion of other activities, such as providing infrastructure, where non-wage costs are normally incurred.

5. *Promoting poor regions.* Still another way that governments can help the poor is to provide additional spending to areas with high poverty rates. Investing in schools, health facilities, and infrastructure in poor regions can stimulate investment and promote employment, thereby boosting incomes of the poor (and others) in these regions. As noted earlier, many countries, including China and Thailand, have used this method as part of their poverty reduction programs. It is particularly efficient in countries with regions where most residents are poor — for example, Brazil's *favelas* and mountainous areas in countries like Albania. Directing spending to poor areas is less effective when the poor are less concentrated, because the resulting growth will likely benefit people at all income levels.

To address income inequality, besides the measures described above, governments can fund or expand benefits helpful at reducing living costs for moderate- and middle-income households. Paid parental working leave, for example, and generous subsidies for child care, or creating state-funded child care agencies as in France, can help reduce child-care expenses for moderate- and middle-income families. Greater subsidies for health care expenses would also help, as would measures to reduce the cost of post-secondary education. In addition, governments could consider creating a financial endowment that young adults can access on reaching age 18 or 21, to help fund higher education or starting a business, such as the proposal for "baby bonds" advocated by US Senator Cory Booker in 2019.[27]

---

[27] Committee for a Responsible Federal Budget (2019), "Cory Booker's 'Baby Bonds' Plan," (December), http://www.crfb.org/blogs/cory-bookers-baby-bonds-plan.

11.3. Summary

Fiscal policy can be used to promote growth and alleviate poverty and unemployment. To promote growth, countries should strive toward a moderate tax burden that allows government spending to be financed with minimal public debt over the business cycle. Revenues should be focused more on consumption than income and profits, while spending should concentrate on providing goods and services that support private sector activity. These include efficient and effective spending for education, health care, legal and judicial services, and infrastructure, and a regulatory system that addresses externalities without imposing onerous burdens on firms and households.

Alleviating poverty and unemployment requires government to establish an efficient and effective social safety net. These measures can include cash transfers to the poor and disabled, unemployment benefits, subsidies for specific goods and services, job creation subsidies, and temporary jobs in the public sector. Where certain regions have high poverty rates, governments can promote employment by providing additional spending for education, health, or infrastructure in these regions. Each of these options has advantages and disadvantages, and the effectiveness of different programs depends on the quality of administration, among other factors. The most effective programs include mechanisms to target benefits toward low-income households, although this complicates program administration.

To address inequality, the above measures should be supplemented by policies to boost after-tax incomes of low- and moderate-income households and raise taxes on those with high income and wealth. Revenue measures could include expanded tax credits for earned income and for dependents along with higher taxes on the very affluent, including the elimination of tax expenditures benefitting mainly those at high-income levels, higher marginal tax rates on top incomes and the elimination of income ceilings on social insurance taxes and contributions, greater taxation of large estates and inheritances, and possibly the imposition of a national wealth tax on those with very high assets. On the spending side, measures could include expanded paid parental leave and increased subsidies for child care, larger subsidies for health care, greater support to low- and moderate-income households for post-secondary education, and possibly the creation of a program to provide financial endowments that young adults could use to fund education or starting a business on reaching age 18 or 21.

Chapter Twelve: Fiscal Policy and Aging: Public Pension Programs

Governments around the world provide income support to the elderly. In low-income countries, these programs typically cover only civil servants. In higher income countries and some emerging market economies, the programs cover most or all of the population. The nature of these programs differs considerably from one country to another, although all are publicly mandated.

12.1. Justifications for Public Pension Programs

Both market failures and other considerations have been used to justify public pension programs.

12.1.1. Market failures

1. *Myopia.* People commonly have short time horizons, and younger people typically discount the likelihood that they will eventually age and find it hard working for an income. As life spans have grown, however, governments can reasonably forecast that many of their citizens will live to become senior citizens and find it increasingly hard to work. Thus, there is a case for having governments compel those of working age to make financial provision for retirement, whether by establishing mandatory savings plans or by imposing taxes that fund pensions for the elderly.
2. *Distributional concerns.* Private markets yield a tremendous range of incomes. Between 1993 and 2017, income gains in the United States were concentrated among those in the highest income

brackets, leaving most families and households with marginal or even negative growth in real incomes.[1] Income inequality has also grown in many other OECD countries and some emerging market economies since the 1980s, although there is evidence that inequality has leveled off in China more recently.[2] Government can reduce market-generated inequality by providing income support to the less affluent, including the elderly with below-average incomes. For example, government programs can provide supplementary benefits to senior citizens with low or below-average incomes.

3. *Adverse selection.* Because individual life spans vary and those with shorter life expectancies are less likely to purchase annuities (investments that provide income streams for the rest of the purchaser's life), *adverse selection* characterizes the private market for annuities. Thus, those interested in these products will find them overpriced relative to a fair market in which the entire population participated. By requiring all citizens (or residents) to participate in a public retirement program, the government can offer an actuarially fair retirement program whose payouts reflect the average life span of the entire population and overcome the adverse selection problem.

4. *Imperfections in information.* Financial products can be complex, and many individuals, particularly those with limited education, may have trouble choosing among different investment vehicles and protecting themselves against fraud. To the extent that a government pension program is efficiently and honestly administered, it can offer participants clarity and greater assurance about the measures used to develop retirement savings and, in some cases, the benefits these programs offer.

5. *Moral hazard.* Moral hazard arises when insured individuals behave with greater risk than the uninsured. Thus, those who believe they have a secure pension have less incentive to accumulate additional retirement savings. This can pose a problem to those employed

---

[1]See Saez, E. (2019), "Striking It Richer: Evolution of the Top Incomes in the United States", https://eml.berkeley.edu/~saez/saez-UStopincomes-2017.pdf.
[2]See OECD (2008), "Growing Unequal: Income Distribution and Poverty in OECD Countries," summary at http://www.oecd.org/dataoecd/45/42/41527936.pdf; and Jain-Chandra, S. *et al.* (2018), "Inequality in China — Trends, Drivers and Policy Debates, IMF Working Paper No. 18/127 (Washington: International Monetary Fund, June).

in the private sector, where firms can go bankrupt or terminate their pension programs with little advance warning. Thus, public pension programs may serve as a useful "backstop" to private programs, as may public agencies such as the Pension Benefit Guaranty Corporation in the United States, which underwrite the safety of private pension plans.

12.1.2. Other considerations

1. *Efficiency.* Pension programs may exhibit economies of scale, in that the administrative costs per person decline with the number of enrollees. In this case, because individual private programs will inevitably cover only part of the population, a single public program may have lower administrative costs. Cost savings will be reduced or possibly negated, however, if public program managers prove less efficient than their counterparts in the private sector.
2. *Insuring families against the cost of aging relatives.* Aging can impose costs not only on the elderly themselves but also on their families, because family members often feel obliged to provide financial and other forms of assistance to older relatives. Public pension programs can help reduce the financial burden on family members by requiring the elderly to have amassed some savings and, in the case of public pension programs, spreading the cost of support over a larger population.
3. *Regulation and oversight of private pensions.* As with the rest of the financial sector, the market for private pensions exhibits imperfect information that can lead to adverse selection, moral hazard, and opportunities for fraud and abuse of less knowledgeable consumers. Thus, one can justify government regulation and oversight of private pension instruments and programs for the same reasons as for other financial products and institutions.

12.2. Types of Public Pension Programs

Public pension programs come in two broad types: *funded systems* and *pay-as-you-go programs* (PAYGs).

In *funded systems,* enrollees accumulate assets in government-approved accounts, and benefits depend on the amount of contributions, plus any interest or other earnings received. Although a public agency often holds and administers enrollees' accounts, as is done in Malaysia and Singapore, the accounts can also be privately managed (with public oversight), as in Chile. In either case, however, the accounts are funded with individual and employer contributions mandated by law. Because they assure only the amount of contributions and earnings in these accounts, funded programs represent a public sector version of the *defined contribution* plans that many private firms have introduced in recent years. Chile, Malaysia, Singapore, and Hong Kong SAR are examples of economies with funded systems.

In *PAYG programs,* contributions (tax payments) from current earners fund the benefits provided to current retirees. Current earners, in turn, may expect to receive benefits funded by those working when they retire. PAYG programs typically provide benefits based on the enrollee's years of service, age, and level of contributions. Thus, they represent a kind of *defined benefit* pension plan, similar to plans that many large corporations offered earlier on and that still characterize the pension plans for employees of some government and public sector agencies. Benefits are designed to replace a certain percentage of pre-retirement earnings. Thus, initial benefit levels are often indexed to average earnings, which rise in time with growth and inflation. Subsequent benefits are usually indexed for inflation, using a consumer price index. Most of the leading OECD nations, including Canada, France, Germany, Italy, Spain, the United Kingdom, and the United States, have PAYG programs, although the UK program pays only a basic retirement benefit.

Partially funded programs have features of each type of program. The main part of Sweden's pension system (the *inkomstpension*), for example, is considered a partially funded program, because benefits are based on a buffer fund plus contributions from present earners, and benefits adjust if payment liabilities fall below available funds. Under the *inkomstpension,* individual pension benefits are indexed (adjusted upward) yearly by the percentage increase in an income index, less 1.6%. The degree of indexing is reduced if payment liabilities exceed the available funds, and benefits remain below the "index line" until anticipated revenues rise enough for available funds to again equal or exceed liabilities. Thus, the Swedish system avoids dipping into the buffer fund, although the parliament can vote to supplement benefits or modify slightly the indexation formula, as occurred in 2010.[3] Some observers have also considered the US Social Security system a partially funded program, because contributions from workers that exceed benefits paid to current retirees accumulate in a trust fund, to help finance benefits for future retirees. However, the US system can run short of funds, requiring a cut in benefits, if the trust funds are depleted and contributions from earners fall below the benefits due for the retirees.

12.3. Advantages and Risks of Different Types of Public Pension Systems

Fully funded and PAYG pension programs each have their advantages and risks.

12.3.1. *Fully funded systems*

Fully funded systems address the myopia problem by compelling young and middle-aged workers to accumulate funds for retirement. Moreover, they do so in a way that does not automatically impose a financial burden on the government sector. Pension benefits depend on the amounts accumulated in individual pension accounts, so the government need not provide benefits that exceed what enrollees have paid into the system. By compelling enrollees to save for their retirement, fully funded systems also reduce the financial burdens on families to provide for elderly relatives.

---

[3]See International Social Security Association (2010), "Impact of the Economic and Financial Crisis on the Swedish Pension System," http://www.issa.int/News-Events/News2/Impact-of-the-financial-and-economic-crisis-on-the-Swedish-pension-system.

Fully funded systems, like defined contribution pension plans in the private sector, place the risk of investment on the contributor. Some programs, like the core programs in Malaysia's and Singapore's provident funds, provide an assured (but modest) rate of return on contributions in standard accounts. However, enrollees bear the financial responsibility if they choose to invest amounts above the minimum in assets whose values can vary. In the case of Singapore, the typical enrollee has often lost money on such investments.[4] However, the main risk with fully funded systems is that the required contributions and earnings on them may be too small to provide a "reasonable" income for retirees. This is especially true if, as in Singapore's plan, enrollees may draw on their accounts to fund expenses other than retirement — for example, servicing mortgage loans on apartments purchased from Singapore's Housing Development Board (HDB). Singapore's Central Provident Fund requires enrollees to accumulate a minimum amount — set at S$181,000 for those turning 55 in 2020 who do not want to put a pledge on their property — for retirement purposes, an amount that provides a monthly annuity of S$1,350 to S$1,450.[5] While guaranteed for life under the CPF Life program, this is a small sum of money for a country where median household earnings averaged about S$9,425 (about US$6,930) a month in 2019.

12.3.2. *PAYG systems*

PAYG systems, like fully funded programs, address the myopia problem and reduce the burden on family members of providing financial support to elderly relatives. In addition, PAYG systems can address distributional problems by skewing benefits in favor of low-income retirees, so that payments cover a larger percentage of pre-retirement

---

[4]Koh, S. K. B. *et al.* (2007) found that, in 2006, three-quarters of those participating in the Investment Scheme of Singapore's Central Provident Fund lost money or earned less than the assured 2.5% rate of return on ordinary fund balances. See "Investment Patterns in Singapore's Central Provident Fund," Pension Research Council Working Paper No. 2006–12 (University of Pennsylvania, Wharton School: May), http://papers.ssrn.com/sol3/papers.cfm?abstract_id=933332.

[5]Poh, J. (2019), "CPF Retirement Sum — How Does It Work and How Much Do You Need," *Moneysmart*, November 7, https://blog.moneysmart.sg/budgeting/cpf-retirement-sum/.

earnings for the less affluent than for higher income enrollees. PAYG systems also relieve enrollees of having to decide how to invest their accumulated savings, since they receive a defined benefit based on their contributions and years of enrollment in the program. In addition, PAYG programs can give retirees a higher benefit than they might have earned in a fully funded system, if average contributions from earners rise faster than benefits over time. The reason is that the effective "rate of return" in a PAYG system depends on both the rate of population (labor force) growth, which raises the number of earners contributing to the system, and the rate of productivity growth, which (if earnings rise with productivity) raises the average wage rate and, thus, the average contribution per worker. In mathematical terms:

Rate of return $= ((1 + $ rate of population growth$/100)$

$*(1 + $ rate of productivity growth$/100) - 1)*100$

$$(12.1)$$

As with the defined benefit programs in the private sector, PAYG systems face the *risk of underfunding*. If contributions from current workers fall short of current benefit obligations, the government must make up the shortfall — by raising revenues or transferring funds from other programs to fund public pension benefits. If the government cannot (or refuses to) do this, then retiree benefits must be reduced. This problem becomes acute as the population ages, because the number of those working and contributing to the system falls relative to the number of retirees. Thus, as Figure 12.1 shows, the retirement systems in many OECD countries face growing financial burdens as the ratio of retirees to workers increases.

PAYG systems have additional problems. These include the following:

1. *Adverse consequences of high contribution rates.* To obtain reasonable funding, many country programs impose contribution rates of 20% or more. Although research shows that employment taxes on employers are largely or fully shifted to employees in the form of

Population 65+ as % of those in working age

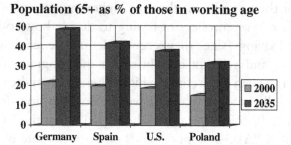

Figure 12.1. The public pension time bomb: Rising ratio of retirees to workers in key OECD nations.
Source: OCED and UN Population Division Projections.

lower wages,[6] high tax rates for insurance make it costlier for firms to hire workers and can depress employment, particularly when social insurance taxes are levied only on the lowest segment of earnings. In this case, some firms may find it cheaper to limit hiring and instead make existing employees work overtime.

2. *Discouraging private retirement savings.* Some economists have argued that the availability of public pensions reduces the incentives for private retirement savings.[7] Other economists have challenged this point, and matter remains under debate. One 2005 review of the evidence showed some support for the hypothesis, although the econometric results were not robust across different specifications.[8]

3. *Eligibility rules sometimes allow early retirement at high costs.* A number of countries have pension systems that allow workers in physically arduous occupations, such as mining, to retire at an

---

[6]See, for example, Brittain, J. (1971), "Incidence of Social Security Payroll Taxes," *American Economic Review*, vol. 61, pp. 110–125, http://profluming.com/Article/UploadFiles/201008/2010081807331083.pdf; and Sendlhofer, R. (2001), "Incidence of Social Security Contributions and Taxes, Evidence from Austria," Institute of Public Economics, University of Innsbruck, Discussion Paper 2001/1, http://homepage.uibk.ac.at/c40414/fiwidp200101.pdf.

[7]See, for example, Feldstein, Martin (1980), "Effect of Social Security on Private Savings: The Times Series Evidence," Working Paper No. 0314 (Cambridge, MA: National Bureau of Economic Research, April), http://papers.ssrn.com/sol3/papers.cfm?abstract_id=247708.

[8]See Pfau, W. D. (2005), "The Effects of Social Security on Private Savings: A Reappraisal of the Time Series Evidence," *Sophia International Review*, vol. 27, no. 1, pp. 57–70, http://ideas.repec.org/p/pra/mprapa/19032.html.

early age, usually after completing a minimum number of years of service. Although these rules enable those whom this work renders ill to receive pensions, they also allow others in good health to obtain benefits for much longer than is common for those in other industries. This raises program costs.

4. *Different retirement ages for men and women.* The public pension programs of a number of countries, including some of the formerly centrally planned economies of central and Eastern Europe and, until recently the United Kingdom, allow women to qualify for a pension at an earlier age than men. Because women typically live longer than men, such provisions inevitably increase program costs.

5. *Problems with tax collection at small firms and independent contractors.* A number of countries, including Greece and Turkey, have found it difficult to collect the required employment taxes from small firms and independent contractors. Where the system allows automatic eligibility on the basis of age, rather than on a minimum amount of contributions, governments have made strenuous efforts to collect employment taxes. In the United States, this has included efforts to collect taxes from employers of household employees such as maids and child care workers.

6. *Unintended intergenerational transfers.* Many PAYG systems benefit the first generation of recipients, who receive benefits without having contributed for as many years as enrollees in later generations. Geanakoplos and colleagues (1998) have estimated that participants in the US Social Security program born before 1938 received net transfers equivalent to about US$10 trillion. By comparison, participants born between 1938 and 1977 are estimated to face negative transfers of about US$2.5 trillion.[9]

Maintaining financial balance in PAYG systems requires satisfying the following mathematical relationship:

$$sWL = PN \qquad (12.2)$$

---

[9] See Geanakoplos, J. *et al.* (1998), "Would a Privatized Social Security System Really Pay a Higher Rate of Return?" Cowles Foundation Working Paper No. 1002 (New Haven: Yale University), http://cowles.econ.yale.edu/~gean/art/p1002.pdf.

where s is the contribution (tax) rate on earnings, W is the average nominal wage (or earnings), L is the number of workers, P is the average pension, N is the number of pensioners.

Thus, the product of (1) the average contribution per earner and (2) the number of earners in the system must equal the average pension times the number of persons drawing a pension. If the number of earners declines relative to the number of pensioners, either the average contribution per worker (sW) must rise or pension payouts must be cut by reducing the average pension or the number of persons eligible to receive pensions (by increasing the retirement age, for example).

The above relationship also implies the following relationship among the critical parameters:

$$(sW/P) = (N/L) \tag{12.3}$$

The above equation holds that the ratio between the average contribution and the average pension payment must equal the ratio of the number of pensioners (N) to the number of earners contributing to the system (L). Thus, if the ratio of pensioners to earners increases, for example, because of population aging, the ratio of the average pension payment to the average contribution per earner must also fall.

12.3.3. *Population aging and fully funded systems*

Although the risks from population aging are clearest with PAYG pension systems, fully funded systems can also encounter difficulties. The problem arises because retirees in fully funded systems accumulate financial assets but in fact want real goods and services. If aging leads to a shrinking workforce and less output per person, prices of goods and services will rise and the real value of retirees' financial assets will decline. Thus, some analysts contend that choosing a fully funded program over a PAYG system does not fundamentally prevent the adverse effects on retirees of an aging population. Instead, countries need to address the aging problem by increasing productivity or

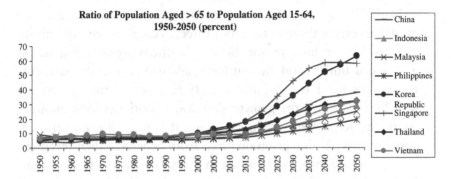

Figure 12.2.   Population aging in selected Asian countries.
Source: United Nations (2009), *World Population Prospects: The 2008 Revision.*

expanding immigration, to increase the ratio of workers to retirees.[10] This suggests that aging is also a concern in Asia, where several countries have fully funded systems (see Figure 12.2).

12.3.4. *Risks affecting all pension systems*

Both fully funded and PAYG systems face additional risks, as a result of uncertainty. These include the following:

1. *Risks from adverse macroeconomic shocks.* All public pension systems run the risk of diminished revenues when economic growth slows or the economy experiences recession (negative growth). With fully funded systems, slower growth or recession means lower earnings and/or less employment, reducing the contributions made into individual retirement accounts. In addition, lower account balances mean smaller interest earnings. Together, the two factors reduce the funds enrollees can draw on when they reach retirement age. Thus, enrollees directly bear the impact of a growth slowdown.

---

[10]See Barr, N. (2000), "Reforming Pensions — Myths, Truths, and Policy Choices," Working Paper No. 00/139 (Washington: International Monetary Fund), http://www.imf.org/external/pubs/ft/wp/2000/wp00139.pdf; and Barr, N. and P. Diamond (2006), "Economics of Pensions," *Oxford Review of Economic Policy*, vol. 22, no. 1, pp. 15–39, http://eprints.lse.ac.uk/2630/1/economics_of_pensions_final.pdf.

In PAYG systems, slower growth and recession reduce the contributions of those in the labor force, as employment diminishes and taxable earnings decline. So long as the retirement system has a financial buffer, and the buffer is allowed to shrink, payments to retirees need not be affected. If reserves in the system are low, however, or if the growth slowdown continues long enough, payments to retirees could be reduced, unless the government supplements pension program funds from general budget revenues.

Unexpected increases in inflation will also affect pension systems. With fully funded systems, retirees bear the risk of seeing the real value of their accumulated contributions decline. With inflation-indexed PAYG systems, higher inflation rates will increase the required payouts. If wages rise at about the same rate as prices, however, and employment is not diminished, revenues can keep pace with payments, leaving the net position of the system unchanged.

2. *Demographic risks.* As noted earlier, an aging population and other demographic risks can pose difficulties for both PAYG and fully funded systems. The risks are clearer with PAYG systems, because an aging population means a decline in the ratio of workers to retirees, so that revenues fall relative to payments. Balancing the system will require some combination of higher contributions from the remaining workers (i.e., higher tax rates for social insurance), a higher retirement age, and lower benefits for retirees. With a fully funded system, the risk comes from a decline in output available to retirees. As noted earlier, if population aging means fewer consumer goods and services per retiree, the prices of these goods will increase, lowering the real value of retirees' financial assets. As a result, retirees will suffer a real decline in living standards, even if the nominal value of their accumulated assets remains unchanged.

3. *Political risks.* Any public pension system bears the risk of political mismanagement, although the dangers appear greater with PAYG regimes. In some developing and emerging market countries, unscrupulous governments have appropriated some or all of the accumulated balances in national pension funds to finance other government activities. Others have invested the funds poorly, rendering programs bankrupt. In either case, enrollees have faced

the possibility of receiving little or nothing from participating in the system. The bankruptcy of the previous state-run pension program was an important reason why Chile developed its current, fully funded system, which involves mandatory contributions to privately administered pension accounts.[11] Higher income countries have proved less susceptible to this type of problem. However, a number of individual states in the United States have been guilty of failing to make the required contributions to pension programs for their own employees, in order to fund other programs and balance the state budget. As a result, the pension schemes for government employees in these states are not fully funded, and future state governments will need either to make up the shortfall or reduce promised retirement benefits to state employees.[12]

Thus far, fully funded systems have proved less susceptible to political risk. Nevertheless, questions have arisen about some programs. Some analysts, for example, have asked whether Singapore's policy of providing a fixed rate of return on the ordinary fund balances in the Central Provident Fund allows the government or government-linked enterprises to appropriate the difference between actual earnings on these balances and the interest paid on these accounts. This issue is highly controversial, and Singapore's CPF Board has noted that the interest rates paid on CPF balances match the earnings on Special Singapore Government Securities in which CPF funds are invested.[13]

4. *Management risk.* All pension programs, whether private or public, face the risk of being poorly managed. In the public sector, the problem would involve unnecessarily high administrative costs. While any pension plan requires administration, experience has shown that large pension plans can achieve considerable economies

---

[11] See, for example, Universia, Knoweldge@Wharton (2005), "Chile's Pension Reform: An Inspiration to Others," http://www.wharton.universia.net/index.cfm?fa=viewfeature&language=english&id=937.

[12] See, for example, Pew Charitable Trusts (2019), "State Pension Funding Gap: 2017" (June), https://www.pewtrusts.org/-/media/assets/2019/06/statepensionfundinggap.pdf.

[13] See Central Provident Fund Board (2019), "Interest Rates," https://www.cpf.gov.sg/Members/AboutUs/about-us-info/cpf-interest-rates.

of scale. For example, the old age and survivor's insurance portion of the US Social Security system routines achieves administrative expenses of less than 1% of all benefit payments. In 2019, the Social Security trustees reported administrative expenditures at 0.4% of benefits for this part of the Social Security system during the year 2018.[14]

Administrative expenses have been higher in some fully funded systems. In 2005, estimates of the administrative fees and commissions in Chile's system ranged from about 1.6% of payrolls[15] to 2.3% of payrolls.[16] A more recent estimate puts administrative fees at 1.25% of payrolls.[17] Administrative expenses are said to have been even higher in some other Latin American countries.

5. *Investment risk.* Investment risk, the risk that pension fund assets will perform poorly, has typically been more of a problem for private than for public pension programs. The reason is that assets of PAYG pension programs are usually invested in government securities. So long as the government remains solvent, the interest rates on government securities keep pace with inflation, and the country's currency does not collapse, these assets should retain their real values. The core assets of Asia's fully funded systems, those of Hong Kong SAR, Malaysia, and Singapore, have also preserved their value. In the case of Singapore, this reflects the prudent investment strategy of the CPF. However, the fixed annual rate of return paid on ordinary account balances limits the benefits that enrollees receive.

---

[14]See US Social Security Administration (2019), "Social Security Administrative Expenses," https://www.ssa.gov/oact/STATS/admin.html.

[15]Soto, M. (2005), "Chilean Pension Reform: The Good, the Bad, and the In-Between," Issue in Brief 31 (Boston College: Center for Retirement Research, June), http://crr.bc.edu/images/stories/Briefs/ib_31.pdf.

[16]Universia, Knoweldge@Wharton (2005), *op. cit.*

[17]*Economist* (2019), "Chile Tinkers with Its Ground-Breaking Pension System" (June 8), https://www.economist.com/the-americas/2019/06/08/chile-tinkers-with-its-ground-breaking-pensions-system.

Investment risk presents more of a problem with systems like those of Chile, which involve mandatory-funded, privately managed individual accounts. Although the enrollees in Chile's pension system have a limited range of investment choices, each of which is professionally managed, pension assets can perform poorly if the asset managers select poor investments or if the economy does badly (which limits the return on all investments.) Fortunately, Chile's economy performed extraordinarily well for the first 21 years of the current system, yielding an average real return of about 10.3% a year on pension fund assets during 1983–2004[18] and about 8% annually through 2018.[19] This performance reflects in part the impact on Chile's capital markets of the new pension system, which provided massive funding for what turned out to be highly productive investment in an environment of strong economic reform. With economic growth slowing to 1–2% during 2014–2017 and projected at 2–3% from 2019 onward,[20] pension fund assets will likely grow more slowly, creating more risk that assets will prove insufficient to provide much income during retirement. Accordingly, the government may want (or feel compelled) to provide some floor under pension earnings, to protect enrollees whose pension assets perform poorly from facing poverty on retirement. The Chilean program provides a minimum benefit, equal to 25% of average wages (about 75% of the minimum wage), for those who meet the minimum 20-year contribution requirement, and about half this benefit to those over age 65 who have not met the minimum. These benefits, funded by general revenues, are estimated to cost up to 1.5% of Chile's GDP.[21] In mid-2019, the government-funded pension provided a benefit equal to about US$154 monthly in mid-2019 to 600,000 retirees and topped up pensions for another 900,000.[22]

---

[18] Soto (2005), *op. cit.*, p. 4.

[19] *Economist* (2019), *op. cit.*.

[20] International Monetary Fund (2019), World Economic Outlook Database, October 2019.

[21] Soto (2005), *op. cit.*, p. 6.

[22] *Economist* (2019), *op. cit.*

12.4. National Pension Programs: Illustrative Examples

Before turning to strategies for addressing the problems facing different types of pension systems, it is useful to review the features of some typical national pension programs.

12.4.1. *Fully funded systems: Malaysia and Singapore*

Malaysia and Singapore have similar public pension systems, perhaps reflecting their common origin as British colonies that were politically united before the separation of Malaysia and Singapore into different countries. In both systems, employers and employees each contribute a stipulated percentage of wages into individual accounts whose balances can be drawn for retirement income and other approved expenses. When workers attain the legal retirement age, they may draw their funds for retirement, either as a lump sum or through an annuity that provides a monthly payment.

1. *Malaysia.* Malaysia's Employees Provident Fund (EPF) is intended to cover all Malaysian employees.[23] As of 2019, employees earning more than RM 5,000 monthly were required to contribute 11% of their monthly salaries, and employers another 12% (13% for workers with monthly salaries of RM 5,000 or less), into their balances with the EPF through age 59. From age 60 to 75, the required contributions declined to 6% for employers and 5.5% for employees. The above amounts can change, based on government policy. The levies apply to most salary components, with overtime, gratuities, and retirement benefits being the main exceptions. Contributions are split between two sub-accounts, called "account one" and "account two." Seventy percent goes into account one, which funds

---

[23]Except where indicated otherwise, information for this paragraph is drawn from the description provided by the Employees Provident Fund at http://www.kwsp.gov.my/index.php?ch=p2members.

retirement benefits and can only be drawn when the enrollee reaches 55, becomes incapacitated, dies, or leaves the country. Enrollees are allowed to invest part of this account at their own risk. Account two receives the remaining 30%, which can be used to finance the down payment on a home, service a home mortgage, fund family members' education expenses, pay for medical expenses, or at age 50, begin making preparations for retirement. Total EPF contributions represent a sizable amount of savings, estimated at nearly 50% of GDP in 2006.[24] At age 55, balances in accounts one and two are combined into an account labeled 55 and can be withdrawn for retirement. Amounts not withdrawn are put into an account called "emas." At age 60, amounts in this account and account 55 may be withdrawn for retirement. In 2018 the OECD estimated that the accumulated balances provide retirement benefits of about 69% of individual gross wages (and 85% of net wages) for average male earners.[25]

2. *Singapore.* Singapore's CPF is intended to cover all Singaporean employees. Both employers and employees contribute to the employee's CPF account. The amounts have varied considerably over the years, because Singapore has used the CPF contribution rate as an element of macroeconomic policy, lowering the employer's contribution during recessions to make it easier for employers to minimize layoffs. As of 2020, for all workers up to age 55 in the private sector, employers contributed 17%, and employees contributed 20%, of the first S$6,000 of monthly wages.[26] The required contributions decline after age 55; for example, employers contribute 13%, and employees contribute 13%, of the first S$6,000 of earnings for workers age 55–60. Somewhat different contribution rates apply to public sector employees with state pensions. As in

---

[24] See Park, D. (2009), "Ageing Asia's Looming Pension Crisis," ADB Economics Working Paper No. 165 (July), p. 12, www.adb.org/Documents/Working-Papers/.../Economics-WP165.pdf.

[25] OECD (2018), *Pensions at a Glance Asia/Pacific 2018*, pp. 23 and 25, https://www.oecd.org/publications/pensions-at-a-glance-asia-pacific-23090766.htm.

[26] Except where indicated otherwise, information in this section comes from materials presented by Singapore's Central Provident Fund Board at http://mycpf.cpf.gov.sg/Members/Gen-Info/mbr-Gen-info.htm.

Malaysia, CPF contributions are divided among sub-accounts. The largest portion goes to the ordinary account, which can be used to fund retirement, finance housing or certain education needs, and purchase CPF insurance. Another part goes to the special account, which funds retirement and special investments. The third portion goes to the Medisave account, which can be used to help finance expenses for hospital care, some insurance policies, and care for certain chronic medical conditions such as diabetes. The allocation of contributions to the three accounts varies by age. Contributions to the various accounts receive interest, with the rate changing over time. As of late 2019, interest of 4% was paid on balances in all special, Medisave, and retirement accounts, with an additional 1% interest paid on the first S$60,000 of CPF account balances and a further 1% on balances up to S$30,00 for those aged 55 and older.[27] CPF enrollees are required to maintain minimum balances in certain accounts. As of 2020, the required "full retirement sum" in the ordinary account was S$181,000. A smaller "basic retirement sum" of S$88,000 would apply for those willing to incur a charge or pledge on their property. The basic retirement or full retirement sums allow a monthly payment for life beginning at age 65, with the payment depending on the amount in the account. Payouts can be delayed until age 70, with the payout rising by 6% to 7% annually for each year of deferment.[28]

As of 2006, CPF savings were estimated at nearly 60% of GDP.[29] Based on data from that time, several outside observers estimate that CPF retirement benefits replace a very low percentage of earnings. Park estimated the amount at about 20%, and the OECD and World Bank

---

[27] Central Provident Fund Board and Housing & Development Board (2019) at https://www.gov.sg/~/sgpcmedia/media_releases/cpfb/press_release/P-20190920-1/attachment/Government%20Extends%20Minimum%204%20Per%20Cent%20Interest%20Rate%20Floor%20on%20SMRA%20Monies%20until%2031%20December%202020.pdf.
[28] Ministry of Manpower, Singapore (2019), "How You can use Your CPF," https://www.mom.gov.sg/employment-practices/central-provident-fund/how-you-can-use-your-cpf.
[29] Park (2009), *op. cit.*, p. 12.

estimated the amount at less than 15%.[30] A more recent analysis, based on data for 2016, suggested that CPF payouts would replace about 53% of the gross earnings and 59% of the net earnings for average male earners and somewhat less for women (47% of gross and 52% of net earnings).[31] However, this would likely require having more than the minimum sum in the ordinary account at the time of retirement. The minimum sum requirement is designed to ensure that enrollees have a minimum balance from which to finance retirement. In practice, however, minimum sum and amounts similar to it will finance only small monthly payouts — S$1,350 to S$1,450, for those retiring at age 65, according to the CPF Board,[32] compared with median monthly earnings of S$9,425 in 2019.[33]

12.4.2. PAYG Systems: United Kingdom and United States

Both the United Kingdom and the United States have PAYG public pension schemes. However, the systems differ considerably, reflecting reforms implemented in the UK during the Thatcher era. The UK's PAYG system provides only a minimum benefit, while the US scheme provides benefits linked to income and contribution levels during employment.

1. *United Kingdom.*[34] Since 2016, the UK has had a multi-tiered public pension system. The basic tier, now called the State Pension, pays a flat weekly amount to each eligible retiree or couple. This program replaced an earlier system incorporating a Basic State Pension and, for many pensioners, an earnings-related Additional State Pension. This program applies to men born before April 6, 1951 and women born

---

[30]Park (2009), *op. cit.*, p. 16, and OECD and World Bank, *op. cit.*, p. 29.

[31]OECD (2018), *Pensions at a Glance Asia/Pacific 2018, op. cit.*

[32]Ministry of Manpower, Singapore (2019), *op. cit.*

[33]Statistics Singapore (2020), *Key Household Income Trends, 2019*, pp-s26, p. 3, https://www.singstat.gov.sg/-/media/files/publications/households/pp-26.pdf.

[34]Much of the information in this section is drawn from "Your Rough Guide to UK Pensions," available at http://www.pensionsorter.co.uk/UK_pensions_guide.cfm.

before April 6, 1953.[35] People become eligible for the State Pension after contributing for 10 years and reaching the minimum age: 65 as of November 2018, rising to 66 in October 2020, with further increases planned after 2025.[36] Those with 35 years' worth of credits can receive GBP 168.60 per week.[37] Those with fewer years of credit receive proportionately less. For example, those with only 10 years of credits receive GDP 48 per week. In 2019/20 the Basic State Pension was GBP 129.20 for a single person or GBP 258.40 for a couple. These amounts fall below the British poverty line, set at 60% of median income, or about GBP 284 a week in 2019/20. If retirees on the Basic State Pension have no other income and their savings fall below GBP 10,000, they can receive a pension credit to boost their weekly benefits to about GBP 167 for an individual. Even these amounts are low for an advanced economy (GBP 334 a week translated into about US$22,750 a year at late-2019 exchange rates).

Besides the State Pension, those working in the United Kingdom have the opportunity to enroll in supplementary pension systems, many of which are offered by employers. First, citizens can establish *personal pensions*, which benefit from substantial tax benefits (annual contributions and any earnings are tax free). These include a special subset of pension instruments called *stakeholder pensions*, which provide flexibility and some limits on management fees. Individuals can also have *occupational pensions*, if their employers offer them. These pensions, which can include both defined benefit and defined contribution schemes, again offer beneficial tax treatment. Pensions classified for "automatic enrollment" must meet particular rules about enrollment. Certain staff must be enrolled; others must be granted the right to enroll or to enroll in another registered pension scheme, although not

---

[35]See UK Government (2019), "The new State Pension," https://www.gov.uk/new-state-pension.

[36]Mayer, B. (2019), "Pensions & Benefits in the United Kingdom," https://www.lexology.com/library/detail.aspx?g=4ff74f3a-ebd2-4385-8f36-0c5cf07caa5f.

[37]See Roberts, A. (2019), "State Pension," Money Saving Expert.com, https://www.moneysavingexpert.com/savings/state-pensions/#previous.

necessarily one to which the employer contributes.[38] Individuals can have multiple pensions, so long as total contributions in a year do not exceed GBP 255,000. Contributions above that level do not receive tax benefits.

In 2005, 71.2% of the population age 15–65, and 93.2% of the labor force, were covered by the UK's mandatory pension scheme.[39] As of 2018, benefits for the mandatory segment were estimated to replace about 22% of gross earnings and about 28% of the net (after-tax) earnings, for those receiving average earnings. Including voluntary pensions, benefits on average covered about 51% of the gross earnings and 61% of the net earnings.[40]

2. *The United States*.[41] The Old Age and Survivors Insurance part of the US Social Security System, typically called Social Security, provides an earnings-related pension to all who have earned and made a minimum level of contributions for at least 40 calendar quarters (10 years). The minimum earnings requirement rises over time. In 2020, it was US$1,410 per quarter. Social Security contributions are set at 12.4%, divided equally between employers and employees, on all income up to a stipulated maximum (US$137,700 in 2020) that also rises over time.[42] Benefits are based on a formula aimed at replacing a certain percentage of the enrollee's average monthly earnings (indexed for wage growth) during the period in which contributions were made. Benefits are skewed so as to replace 90% of the lowest portion of earnings (US$968 a month in 2020), 32% of the next portion (US$5,785 a month in 2020), and 15% on all additional earnings up to the maximum on which contributions are collected. Benefits are

---

[38] Mayer B. (2019), *op. cit.*

[39] OECD (2018), *Pensions at a Glance Asia/Pacific 2018*, Table 2.5, p. 33.

[40] OECD (2019), *Pensions at a Glance 2019 — OECD and G20 Indicators*, Tables 5-3 and 5-5, pp. 151 and 155.

[41] Unless otherwise indicated, information in this section is drawn from the retirement website of the US Social Security Administration, http://www.socialsecurity.gov/pgm/retirement.htm.

[42] In addition to Social Security taxes, individuals also pay 2.9% of all earnings (no limit) in Medicare taxes, divided equally between the employer and the employee.

then adjusted up or down, depending on when the enrollee retires, relative to their "full retirement age," which depends on their birth year (as of 2020, 66 for those born before 1955, rising to 67 for those born after 1959). Enrollees can draw benefits beginning at age 62; benefits are reduced by 25% for those who begin drawing at that age. Benefits are raised by 8% for each year an enrollee defers claiming benefits after full retirement age, up to age 70. The enrollee's spouse who has reached age 62 or is caring for a minor child can also receive payments of up to half of the enrollee's benefit. In 2005, the Social Security System was estimated to cover roughly 92% of the US labor force and about 71% of those aged 15–65.[43] About 88% of the population aged 20 and above was covered in 2018.[44] For those with average earnings, benefits are estimated to replace about 39% of gross earnings (49% of net earnings). Including voluntary pensions, benefits replaced an average 69% of gross and 84% of net earnings for average earners.[45]

Besides the mandatory Social Security system, the United States provides substantial tax benefits for those establishing supplementary retirement accounts. Individuals can choose between accounts for which contributions up to stated limits are tax-deductible, earnings are tax exempt, and withdrawals (which must be made by age $70\frac{1}{2}$) are taxed; and other accounts for which contributions do not provide tax deductions, but earnings and subsequent withdrawals are tax-exempt. Benefits also accrue to certain types of employer-sponsored pension plans. As of 2018, about 55% of all workers outside the federal government participated in some type of workplace retirement plan.[46] However, about half of all US elderly persons received half

---

[43] OECD (2018), *Pensions at a Glance Asia/Pacific 2018*, Table 5, p. 33.

[44] US Social Security Administration (2019), "Fast Facts & Figures about Social Security, 2019: OASI Status — Insured Population, 1970–2018," https://www.ssa.gov/policy/docs/chartbooks/fast_facts/2019/fast_facts19.html.

[45] OECD (2019), *Pensions at a Glance 2019 — OECD and G20 Indicators*, Tables 5-3 and 5-5, pp. 151 and 155.

[46] Pension Rights Center (2019), "How Many American Workers Participate in Workplace Retirement Plans?" https://www.pensionrights.org/publications/statistic/how-many-american-workers-participate-workplace-retirement-plans.

or more of their income from Social Security.[47] In 2016, about 52% of all US households had retirement savings, with median assets of US$60,000.[48]

12.5. Population Aging and the Outlook for Public Pension Programs

As noted earlier, populations around the world are aging, and the decline in the ratio of workers to retirees poses severe strains for traditional PAYG pension plans. As shown in Figure 12.3, in 2010 the European Union expected public pension expenditure, as a share of GDP, to rise from about 10% in 2007 to about 13% in 2060, with much larger increases in Luxembourg and Greece (24%) and Spain and Belgium (15%).[49] For the United States, in 2019 the Congressional Budget Office (CBO) forecast that Social Security expenditures would rise from about 4.9% of GDP in 2019 to about 6.2% from 2030 to 2093.[50] Based on the CBO's alternative forecast, the average shortfall of the system over the 75-year period through 2093 was estimated at about 4.6% of taxable payrolls, or about 1.5% of GDP.[51] IMF staff members have estimated that, across the G7 countries, aging would have raised pension spending by about 3.2% of GDP from 2010 to 2030, but that pension reforms already enacted, along with a more normal employment outlook, will limit the actual increase to about 1% of GDP.[52]

---

[47] Center on Budget and Policy Priorities (2019), "Top Ten Facts about Social Security," https://www.cbpp.org/sites/default/files/atoms/files/8-8-16socsec.pdf.

[48] Bricker, J. *et al.* (2017), "Changes in US Family Finances from 2013 to 2016: Evidence from the Survey of Consumer Finances," *Federal Reserve Bulletin*, vol. 103, No. 3 (September), Table 3, p. 18, https://www.federalreserve.gov/publications/files/scf17.pdf.

[49] Rehn, O. (2010), "Conference on the Green paper on Pensions: Key Data," slide 4, http://ec.europa.eu/social/BlobServlet?docId=6217&langId=enhttp://ec.europa.eu/social/BlobServlet?docId=6217&langId=en.

[50] See US Congressional Budget Office (2019), *The 2019 Long-Term Budget Outlook* (Washington: June), Tables 1-1, p. 6 (through 2049), and 1-3, p. 22 (through 2093), https://www.cbo.gov/system/files/2019-06/55331-LTBO-2.pdf.

[51] *Id.*, p. 22.

[52] Cottarelli, C. and A. Schaecter (2010), "Long-Term Trends in Public Finances in the G-7 Economies," IMF Staff Position Note 10/13 (Washington, September), p. 15, http://www.imf.org/external/pubs/ft/spn/2010/spn1013.pdf.

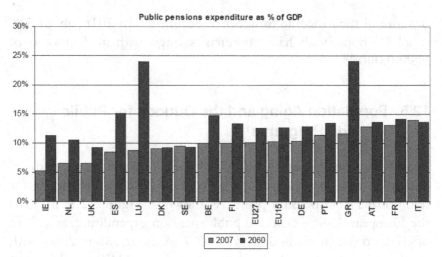

Figure 12.3.　Forecast trends in public pension expenditure in selected European Union countries.

Source: Rehn (2010).

Of the main countries with PAYG pension systems, only two — Sweden and the UK — have thus far avoided the problem of sharply rising expenditures as a percentage of GDP. As noted earlier, the benefit mechanisms in both countries' systems have elements that curb the rise in outlays. For Sweden, the automatic reduction in benefit indexing helps limit the ratio of expenditures to GDP. For the UK, reformulating the system to provide only a low, basic benefit has limited expenditures, although in 2010 an analysis by EU Commissioner Olli Rehn suggested that British pension outlays might rise over the next 50 years to approach the 10% of GDP average for the EU countries generally.[53]

Advanced economies in general, and G7 countries in particular, have experienced a sharp rise in gross and net public debt, reflecting both the deterioration in public finances following the 2007–2009 financial crisis and pressures from the impact of aging on public pension and health care expenditure. According to IMF data, average gross

---

[53]Rehn (2010), *op. cit.*

public debt in advanced economies rose from about 70% of GDP in 2001 to 102% in 2018, with a further increase to 104% projected for 2024.[54] For G7 countries, average gross debt rose from about 75% of GDP in 2001 to about 116% in 2018 and is projected to exceed 120% in 2024. Average net public debt is projected to rise from about 70% in 2010 to about 80% in 2024 for advanced economies as a whole and from 80% to 92% for G7 countries.[55]

If major economies are to return to more traditional ratios of public debt to GDP, fiscal balances will need to improve significantly. Although revenue increases can help fill part of the gap, to maintain competitiveness with expanding economies elsewhere, most of the adjustment will probably have to involve expenditure cuts. These can include additional reforms to public pension programs. In line with Equation (12.1), a combination of a further increase in the normal retirement age, a downward revision in future benefit levels (possibly through more modest indexing of benefits), and higher social insurance taxes can reduce net public pension expenditures in future years. Different combinations are possible, and partisans will likely disagree on the appropriate mix of benefit cuts and revenue increases. Nevertheless, some adjustment would contribute both to lower public debt levels and to more sustainable public pension programs.

12.6. Reforming Public Pension Programs: A General Approach

How can existing public pension programs be made more sustainable while providing more income support for the elderly? One approach involves reformulating pension systems to incorporate five different elements, or pillars, to income support.[56]

---

[54]IMF Data Mapper (2019), "General Government Gross Debt," https://www.imf.org/external/datamapper/GGXWDG_NGDP@WEO/OEMDC/ADVEC/WEOWORLD.

[55]International Monetary Fund (2019), *Fiscal Monitor, October 2019*, Table A8, p. 54, https://www.imf.org/en/Publications/FM/Issues/2019/09/12/fiscal-monitor-october-2019.

[56]See Holzmann, R. and R. P. Hinz (2005), *Old Age Income Support in the 21st Century: An International Perspective on Pension Systems and Reform* (Washington: World Bank), esp.

The *five-pillar approach* contends that countries can more effectively provide income support for the elderly through a multiplicity of elements that reduces the burden on any one measure. Such an approach offers a way to develop financial resources for retirement throughout the economy, without imposing so great a burden on public finances. As will be seen, the various pillars incorporate features of many existing public pension programs.

The *first pillar* (sometimes called the "zero" pillar in the literature) involves a flat, basic income grant designed to keep the elderly from falling into poverty. Like the UK's State Pension (with the income supplement offered to those with limited assets), payments for the zero pillar are set at about the national poverty line. Unlike the British system, however, the first pillar is financed directly from the state budget and requires no contributions from individuals. Thus, it is available to all citizens (and possibly permanent residents), regardless of their involvement in the formal sector of the economy.

The *second pillar* involves a mandatory, publicly managed pension plan, with the goal of replacing a certain percentage of pre-retirement earnings. Financing would come from contributions, with the goal of creating either a defined benefit system (like most current PAYG programs) or a notional defined contribution system (in which individuals have accounts related to, but not strictly based on, their contributions), as in Sweden. As with the US Social Security System, benefits in the second pillar could be set to replace a higher share of pre-retirement income for those with lower earnings. Because of the first pillar, however, benefit levels could be set below those in current PAYG systems, thus improving the solvency of this part of the system.

The *third pillar* involves mandatory, individual retirement accounts, similar to the provident funds in Malaysia and Singapore. To supplement benefits provided through the first and second pillars,

---

Table 5.1, p. 119, http://siteresources.worldbank.org/INTPENSIONS/Resources/Old_Age_Income_Support_FM.pdf.

the government would establish, for each individual, a retirement savings account to which individuals must make regular contributions, arguably at rates linked to earnings. Balances in these accounts could be drawn on retirement and add to the funds available from the first two pillars. The mandatory savings accounts in the third pillar would contribute to national savings and bolster the domestic funds available to finance investment. Unlike the first and second pillars, the third would not have a redistribution element.

The *fourth pillar* involves voluntary, individual savings accounts. As in the UK and United States, these could be either personal or occupationally linked. Depending on the government's fiscal position and public preferences, subsidies such as tax credits or a government match for the first increment of savings could be provided to create incentives for savings. Like the third pillar, this component would promote national savings.

The *fifth pillar* incorporates a variety of other elements aimed at supporting the elderly. These include informal support from family members, common in most societies and particularly important in low-income and emerging economies; support from other social programs, including government-provided health care; and other individual financial and non-financial assets, including the value of owner-occupied homes. As in Singapore and the United States, reverse mortgages, which allow the elderly in effect to pre-sell their homes in return for a steady income stream during their lifetimes, could be part of the fifth pillar.

The creators of the five-pillar approach recognize that certain pillars will be more appropriate for some countries than for others. Low-income countries with large informal sectors, for example, may have trouble establishing a second pillar, because of the difficulty of securing compliance with the tax system. Similarly, some countries with existing PAYG or fully funded systems may prefer to maintain either the second or the third pillar, but not both. The five-pillar system, however, has the advantage of allowing countries with PAYG systems to offer income replacement rates similar to their current systems while reducing PAYG benefit levels, and thus deficits, so long as general revenues covered the difference. Similarly, introducing a zero pillar could allow countries with fully funded systems to supplement the resources available to retirees from their existing savings accounts. Doing so, of course, would require these countries to finance additional pillars, either through general revenues or a supplementary scheme with dedicated taxation or contributions.

12.7. Summary

Market failures and other considerations can justify government programs to address the income needs of retirees, whether through public pension programs or through measures that encourage individuals to accumulate private savings. Most advanced economies, and a growing number of emerging market countries, have done so, usually through a combination of public pension programs and incentives to promote retirement savings.

Different types of public pension programs have different advantages and disadvantages. PAYG programs, the most common pension program, have the advantage of facilitating redistribution toward lower income households. However, an aging population can threaten their financial sustainability, if the programs try to replace a considerable share of pre-retirement earnings, as the ratio of retirees to earners rises. Fully funded pension systems can avoid sustainability problems. However, they may have trouble replacing a high percentage of pre-retirement earnings, particularly if enrollees can use their savings balances for non-retirement purposes, such as financing health care or housing.

Many countries with PAYG schemes have reformed their systems to increase sustainability, through a combination of raising the retirement age, curbing benefit increases, and raising social insurance taxes (contributions). Some of the fully funded systems have periodically addressed benefit limitations by offering bonus interest payments on accumulated savings. To go further, experts from the World Bank suggest that countries consider moving to a multi-pillar approach that combines elements of both regimes, along with a universal, basic payment to prevent poverty, support for voluntary savings, and recognition of additional resources, such as informal support from family members.

Chapter Thirteen: Fiscal Policy and Health Care

Governments around the world devote sizable resources to health care. In part, this reflects important shortcomings in the private market for health care services. However, it also reflects the universal importance of good health, the difficulty many people have in affording care, and the growing demand for health care services as populations age. This chapter reviews some of the basic characteristics of health care and the market for health care services. It then discusses the kinds of health care activities that governments undertake and the challenges health care poses for fiscal policy.

13.1. Basic Characteristics of Health Care

Before discussing fiscal activity involving health care, it is worthwhile reviewing some essential characteristics of health care, the market for health care services, and the role of health insurance.

13.1.1. *General characteristics of health care and the market for health care services*

1. *Preventive versus acute care.* To begin, health care can be described as falling into one of two categories: preventive and acute care. *Preventive care* represents the provision of non-urgent medical and dental services. Preventive services can typically be postponed, and consumers find it easier to decide on the nature of care they wish. As a result, the market for preventive care can be analyzed more like that of other goods and services. Sometimes, however, deferring preventive care can lead to higher total medical expenses over time, because the failure to get preventive care causes underlying

conditions to deteriorate, requiring more care in the future. Thus, some preventive medical services, such as well-baby care and periodic physical examinations, have positive externalities over time, and encouraging people to get such care can be worthwhile.

Acute care, the care provided when an individual encounters serious illness or injury, typically cannot be postponed. Thus, patients are normally less sensitive to price differences than with preventive care or other goods and services. In addition, because of the complexities associated with health care, patients often cannot judge what services they need. Thus, they rely far more on providers — the supply side of health care — to determine what services they receive than is true of most other goods and services. Together, urgency and ignorance make the provision of acute care highly susceptible to manipulation by health care providers, and patients can easily be persuaded to accept care that other knowledgeable providers might question. For this reason, countries around the world regulate the provision of health care, requiring providers to meet certain standards of competence through licensing and the requirement of continued learning. Policing the health care market is difficult, however, so even these tools may not prevent individual practitioners from providing inappropriate and excessively costly care.

2. *Health care spending is concentrated among a small group of people.* Most health care spending comes from a small fraction of the population. In the typical country, 1% of the population accounts for 20–25% of all expenditures, and 5% accounts for about half the total.[1] Moreover, a high percentage of all spending takes place during the last year of a person's life, as health status deteriorates rapidly and more services are used to address sudden ailments or try

---

[1]For example, in the United States, in 2016, the top 1% of the population accounted for 22% of all expenditures, and the top 5% accounted for 50%. See Sawyer, B. and G. Claxton (2019), "How Do Health Expenditures Vary Across the Population?" Peterson-KFF Health System Tracker, https://www.healthsystemtracker.org/chart-collection/health-expenditures-vary-across-population/#item-start.

to prevent death.[2] For a variety of reasons, this seems particularly true in the United States.

3. *The supply side plays a major role in health care costs.* Because of the urgency attached to acute care and the difficulty most consumers have in determining appropriate care, health care providers — the supply side of the market — play an unusually large role in determining health care expenditures and the cost of care. The *extreme asymmetry of information* between consumers and providers means that patients usually empower providers to decide what care is appropriate. Thus, more than in most other markets, providers determine what services consumers purchase.

4. *Uncertainty, lumpiness, and insurance.* Medical emergencies are hard to predict, and when they occur the cost of care can be very high (what economists call "lumpiness"). This creates a *demand for medical insurance*, to guard against the cost of sudden expenditures. However, having insurance creates its own consequences. Besides reducing the sensitivity of consumers to medical costs, by allowing consumers to afford more care insurance allows providers to increase the use of medical services. Thus, medical insurance can spur additional health care expenditures unless other mechanisms restrain this tendency.

5. *Technology and the unlimited desirability of care.* More so than for most other goods and services, consumers find it hard determining when health care services are not worth the cost. Except perhaps for cosmetic medical and dental care, almost all services, particularly acute care, seem worthwhile if recommended by a health care provider. Moreover, advances in technology mean that new treatments to prolong life and reduce suffering regularly become available. Widespread insurance thus creates a ready demand for additional services. This, in turn, can lead to a steady rise in health care spending — and in the share of income devoted to health care — unless measures are taken to contain expenditures.

---

[2]See Heller, P. and W. Hsiao (2007), "What Macroeconomists Should Know about Health Care Policy," Working Paper No. 07/13, http://www.imf.org/external/pubs/ft/wp/2007/wp0713.pdf.

6. *Health care spending is heaviest among the young and the elderly.* Perhaps because they are the most frail and susceptible to illness, the young and the elderly require more health care services and account for a larger share of total outlays, than those between these age groups. In high-income countries, expenses rise especially rapidly among the elderly, although the degree varies from country to country. Relative to those in late middle-age (ages 50–64), expenses among the elderly range from about double in Austria, Germany, Spain, and Sweden to four times in Japan and Australia (see Figure 13.1). In the United States, the ratio averages much higher — more than eleven times that for persons in late middle age, in the case of persons aged 80–100.[3] This may reflect the much greater availability of health insurance for those over age 64 and medical practices favoring aggressive spending towards the last days of life.

13.1.2. *Special aspects of health insurance*

Health insurance has particular characteristics and has important implications for the market for health care services.

1. *Moral hazard.* As noted in Chapter One, having insurance can give rise to *moral hazard*, in that those with coverage can demand and afford more care. Insurance can also reduce the sensitivity of the insured to health care prices. To limit this tendency, many policies include *deductibles*, which require patients to pay the first part of any expenses, and *co-insurance* or *co-payments*, which requires them to cover a certain percentage of costs after paying the required deductible.
2. *Adverse selection.* As with some other types of coverage, the private market for health insurance is characterized by *adverse selection*. Unless everyone must have insurance, those most needing care

---

[3]See Hagist, C. and L. Kotlikoff (2006), "Health Care Spending: What the Future Will Look Like," National Center for Policy Analysis Report No. 286 (Dallas, TX: June), Table II, p. 2, http://www.ncpa.org/pdfs/st286.pdf.

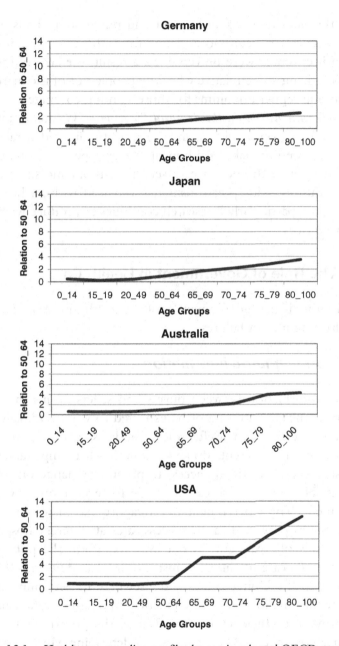

Figure 13.1. Health care spending profiles by age in selected OECD countries.

Source: Reproduced from Hagist, C., and L. Kotlikoff (2005), "Who's Going Broke? Healthcare Spending in Ten OECD Countries," NBER Working Paper 11833, Figure 1, pp. 21–23, https://www.nber.org/papers/w11833.pdf.

are the ones most likely to want and purchase it. Thus, insurers can expect to incur more claims from those seeking insurance than if coverage were universal. As a result, the cost of insurance rises, driving some relatively healthy people out of the market and requiring higher premiums for those wanting coverage.

3. *Health insurance and the demand for services.* Greater demand for care, reliance on providers, and the almost unlimited attractiveness of care together make health insurance an especially potent source of inflation in the health care sector. Without measures to limit expenditures, widespread insurance can lead to high health care spending, particularly if research continues to produce worthwhile new services.

13.2. The Role of Government in Health Care

As with other issues, government's role in health care should be based on addressing market failures.

13.2.1. *Asymmetric information*

Unequal information between buyers and sellers means that private markets for health care cannot be expected to work optimally. Thus, government can play a useful role in addressing the asymmetry of information. Governments do so by adopting licensing standards for professionals and restricting access to potentially dangerous pharmaceuticals. However, a case can be made for even more government involvement. The Government of Singapore and many states in the United States publish data on success rates at different hospitals for certain types of treatment, as one way to inform the public about the quality of care at different institutions. In addition, efforts are underway in the United States and elsewhere to determine and disseminate information about best practices in treating certain ailments, to improve the efficiency of care. Where the government provides insurance coverage, public agencies can determine which procedures insurance will cover, although this can be controversial if patients are denied care they would like.

13.2.2. Externalities

Another justification for government involvement arises where medical care has positive (or negative) externalities. Because the benefits to the general population are so great, governments often require that children receive certain vaccinations in order to attend school. In most countries, governments also take steps to ensure that citizens have access to clean water and sanitation services, even if provided by private contractors. In many tropical countries, governments mount campaigns to combat malaria, sleeping sickness, dengue fever, and other ailments. In the United States, chain restaurants with at least 20 locations must provide nutritional information about the food they serve, as part of a broader campaign to provide calorie and nutrition information about food sold by restaurants and vending machines.[4] In addition, many school districts are taking steps to improve the nutritional quality of meals served in public schools.

13.2.3. Distributional concerns

A third basis for government involvement arises from concerns about access to health care for low-income households. Many health care services are quite expensive, making them hard for those with limited incomes to afford. To extend health care to the poor, many governments establish public health care facilities — hospitals and medical clinics — that provide services at modest cost. In low-income countries, these facilities often provide the only health care services available to those in sparsely populated or poor regions. In middle- and high-income countries, these public facilities frequently offer more affordable care than that available from private hospitals and medical and dental offices. In addition, in most high-income countries the government provides or organizes health insurance so that virtually all citizens have coverage for a wide range of medical and dental

---

[4]US Food and Drug Administration (2018), "Menu and Vending Machine Labeling," https://www.fda.gov/food/food-labeling-nutrition/menu-and-vending-machine-labeling.

services. The form of coverage varies from country to country.[5] In the United Kingdom, the government's National Health Service provides medical services, while in Canada the government funds care provided by private practitioners. In France, Germany, and Japan, government-supervised networks of health insurers provide coverage for care dispensed mainly at private medical and dental offices. In the United States, the government's Medicare program provides the elderly insurance for a wide variety of medical services, while Medicaid covers care for those in qualifying low-income households, although low reimbursement rates mean that not all doctors will accept Medicaid patients. Military veterans have access to government-run Veterans Hospitals. Those not covered by these programs often receive coverage through their employers or have access to coverage through policies offered on federal or state websites through the US Patient Protection and Affordable Care Act, enacted in 2010. Nevertheless, as of 2018, about 8.5% of US residents lacked health insurance coverage, mainly those under age 65.[6]

13.3. Trends in Health Expenditures

Health care expenditures have risen as a share of GDP in most advanced countries, as shown in Figure 13.2.[7]

The increase has been largest for the United States, where outlays rose from 7% of GDP in 1970 to an estimated 17% in 2018. However, most other countries have also experienced increases. The one exception appears to be Singapore, where health care expenditures have remained at about 4% of GDP from 1995 through 2016.[8] Health

---

[5]For an informative discussion of medical insurance practices around the world see Reid, T. R. (2009), *Healing of America* (New York: Penguin Press).

[6]Berchick, E. R. *et al.* (2019), *Health Insurance Coverage in the United States: 2018*, US Bureau of Census, Current Population Reports, P60-267 (RV), November, p. 2, https://www.census.gov/content/dam/Census/library/publications/2019/demo/p60-267.pdf.

[7]OECD (2019), "Health Expenditure and Financing," OECD.Stat, https://stats.oecd.org/Index.aspx?ThemeTreeId=9.

[8]For 2009–2016, see theGlobalEconomy.com (2019), "Singapore: health spending as per-cent of GDP," https://www.theglobaleconomy.com/Singapore/health_spending_as_percent_

Figure 13.2.   Health care outlays as percent of GDP in selected OECD countries, 2010–2018.
Source: OECD (2019), "Health Expenditure and Financing," OECD.Stat, https://stats.oecd.org/Index.aspx?ThemeTreeId=9.

care outlays also rose as a percentage of GDP in several low- and middle-income countries in Asia, including India, Indonesia, and Malaysia (Figure 13.3). Expenditures as a share of GDP have risen further, to about 3.1%, in Indonesia in 2018.[9]

Why have health expenditures risen as a percentage of GDP? *Aging populations* provide one reason. As Figure 13.4 indicates, countries with higher proportions of elderly residents (as measured by the *elderly dependency ratio* — the ratio of those age 65 or more to those age 15–64) on average spend a higher share of GDP on health care. In addition, health care expenditures have risen during a period when the elderly dependency ratio has risen in OECD countries (Figure 13.5). To date, aging has been less evident in developing and emerging market

of_gdp/. Because multinational firms contribute an important share of Singapore's GDP, some might argue that using GDP as a denominator understates the true burden of health care expenditures on the Singaporean economy. Thus, some would propose measuring health care expenditures as a percentage of indigenous GDP, which is less than the total GDP and would yield a higher health care spending ratio. Unless the share of indigenous GDP is declining, replacing total GDP with indigenous GDP will not change the relatively flat trend of health care expenditures as a share of total economic activity, however. Data show that between 2006 and 2010 Singapore's indigenous GDP remained at about 56–58% of its total GDP. The share of indigenous gross national income (GNI) in total GNI was larger — above 70% — although the share was somewhat less during 2008–2010, in the range of 72–73%, than before the crisis (75–79%), possibly reflecting the decline in overseas earnings by Singaporeans because of the weak global economy. However, the ratio has been fairly steady since 2008. For details, see Statistics Singapore (2011), *Yearbook of Statistics Singapore, 2011*, http://www.singstat.gov.sg/pubn/reference/yos11/statsT-income.pdf."
[9]OECD (2019), "Health Expenditure and Financing," OECD.Stat, https://stats.oecd.org/Index.aspx?ThemeTreeId=9.

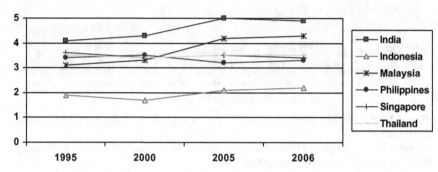

Figure 13.3.   Health care expenditure as a percent of GDP in selected Asian countries, 1995–2006.

Source: World Health Organization, Health systems statistics database.

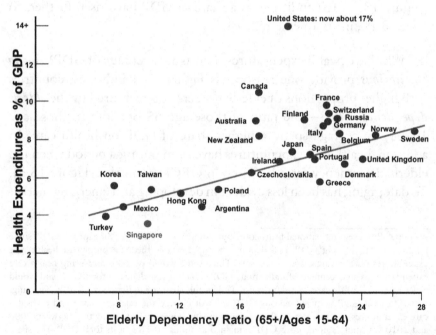

Figure 13.4.   Health care expenditure as a percentage of GDP and the elderly dependency ratio.

Source: Dr. Phua Kai Hong, National University of Singapore.

Old-Age Dependency Ratios for Seven OECD Countries

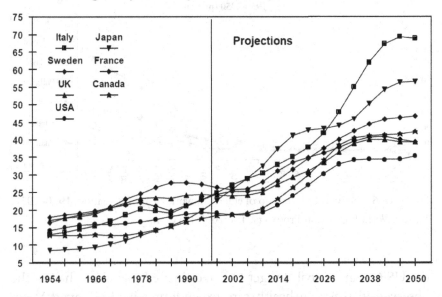

Figure 13.5.   Old-age dependency ratios in seven OECD countries, 1950–2050.
Source: Fougère, Maxime, and Marcel Mérette (1998), "Population ageing and economic growth," Department of finance, Canada, Working Paper No. 98–03, p. 7, http://epe.lac-bac.gc.ca/100/200/301/finance/working_papers-ef/1998/1998-03/98-03e.pdf.

countries, although in Asia aging is already becoming apparent in advanced economies such as Singapore and South Korea (Figure 13.6).

The *development of new technology* offers another explanation. New medical equipment, treatment protocols, and pharmaceuticals have mushroomed since the 1960s, making it possible to treat many ailments previously considered incurable. While some innovations have reduced costs, on balance new technology has increased outlays for health care. The effect of new technology has likely been most pronounced in high-income economies, where health care systems have been quick to adopt innovations. Estimating the size of the impact is hard, however, and most studies have tried to do so by attributing to technology the share of cost increases that cannot reasonably be attributed to more easily identified factors. A 2008 literature review by staff at

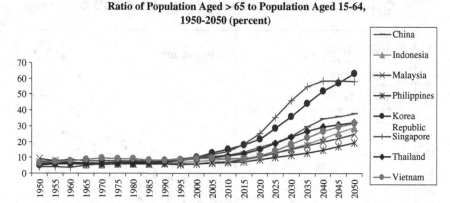

Figure 13.6.   Asia: Trends in ratio of elderly to working age population, 1950–2050.
Source: World Population Prospects: The 2008 Revision.

the US Congressional Budget Office estimated that about half of the observed increases in health care expenditures in the United States during the period 1965–2005 could be attributed to technological advances.[10] A study by Martins and Maisonneuve (2006) of public sector health care expenditures in OECD countries noted that, of the average increase of 3.6% of GDP in public health care expenditures between 1981 and 2002 across all OECD countries, only 0.3% could be attributed to aging. Another 2.3 percentage points were linked to higher incomes, leaving a residual of about 1 percentage point, much of which may be linked to technological innovation. The size of the residual varied noticeably across countries, however: from negative amounts in Denmark, Sweden, and some Eastern European countries to large positive figures (more than half of the observed total increase) for Switzerland, the United States, and some of the newer OECD members, such as Mexico and Turkey.[11]

---

[10]Congressional Budget Office (2008), *Technological Change and the Growth of Health Care Spending*, http://www.cbo.gov/ftpdocs/89xx/doc8947/01-31-TechHealth.pdf.

[11]Martins, J. O. and C. de la Maisonneuve (2006), "The Drivers of Public Expenditures on Health and Long-Term Care: An Integrated Approach," *OECD Economic Studies*, vol. 43, No. 2, pp. 116–154, Table 1, p. 122, http://www.oecd.org/dataoecd/62/19/40507566.pdf.

Despite these general observations, the rise in health care expenditures as a percentage of GDP has varied tremendously across countries. This suggests that some countries have been more successful at containing the growth in expenditures than others. In this regard, it is worth analyzing the experience of Singapore, which has succeeded in keeping health care expenditures virtually constant as a percentage of GDP since the 1970s (although the ratio rose slightly from 2000 to 2016, from about 3.0% of GDP to just under 4.5%[12]).

13.4. Singapore: Avoiding the Rise in Health Care Expenditures as a Percentage of GDP

Among high-income countries, Singapore is unique in having kept health care expenditures almost unchanged as a percentage of GDP since 1970. Health care outlays were just below 4% of GDP in 1970. Recorded data show a similar figure for 2007 (Figure 13.3), with a slight increase after that.

External assessments would suggest that quality has not been an issue. The World Health Organization ranked Singapore as sixth among nations in its 2000 assessment of overall health system performance.[13] Many of Singapore's hospitals have international reputations, and foreign nationals, including US government staff located overseas, routinely choose Singapore to receive emergency medical care.

Instead, Singapore has pursued a multi-pronged strategy to contain expenditures while preserving quality. Several elements stand out.

1. *Limitations on health insurance.* Unlike in most other high-income countries, health insurance in Singapore is linked to individual

---

[12]theGlobalEconomy.com (2019), "Singapore: Health Spending as Percent of GDP," https://www.theglobaleconomy.com/Singapore/health_spending_as_percent_of_gdp/.
[13]See World Health Organization (2000), "Health Performance Rank by Country," http://www.photius.com/rankings/world_health_performance_ranks.html.

accounts in the country's social insurance system, the Central Provident Fund (CPF). Part of each person's CPF deposits goes to fund a Medisave account, whose balances can be used to help finance hospital care and treatment for a very few chronic conditions, such as kidney failure. Medisave funds can also cover premiums for the Medishield Life program, which covers very large hospital bills. Strict rules limit the portion of any medical bills that Medisave balances or Medishield Life can cover. Because few Singaporeans have supplementary health insurance, almost everyone faces a significant out-of-pocket cost for every hospital bill. A 2009 study, for example, reported that about 75% of the average hospital bill was paid either through out-of-pocket payments or the Medisave funds from the patient and other family members.[14] In addition, outpatient doctor and dentist bills and the cost of prescription medicines are largely paid out of pocket (Singapore civil servants get very modest sums toward some dental care). Singaporeans thus have a financial incentive to monitor health care expenses, and providers realize that the funds backing most patients are limited. This helps to constrain costs.

2. *Competition from government institutions.* Although private institutions deliver a large share of health care in Singapore, the government has also created a system of public hospitals and polyclinics that help restrain costs in the private sector. The public hospitals have good reputations, and private institutions realize that their clientele may shrink if their costs rise substantially above those in the public sector. Private physicians feel the same pressure from government-managed polyclinics, which provide care similar to that offered by general practitioners (GPs). These institutions do not have the same stigma as do many public clinics in the United States, so they provide a check on private medical fees.

3. *Information on typical costs for medical procedures.* Singapore's Ministry of Health publishes data on typical charges at government

---

[14]Abeysinghe, T. (2009), "Singapore's Health Care System," lecture delivered at 2009 Singapore Economic Policy Conference. Abeysinghe's study showed out-of-pocket payments covered about 7 percent of the typical bill.

hospitals for a wide array of medical ailments. The data indicate the volume of procedures performed and the bill at the 50th percentile of costs, based on the type of hospital room (from single-bedded rooms to multiple-bed wards).[15] Patients can use this information when deciding which hospital to use, if they have a choice, and public as well as private hospitals keep track of this information. Thus, it can help discipline costs.

4. *Advance information about fees.* Singapore' Private Hospitals and Medical Clinics Act and Regulations require private practitioners to advise patients, before a consultation begins, on the fees for the consultation, examination, and any treatment. Until April 2007, the Singapore Medical Association maintained a schedule of recommended fees for different services. Many practitioners were said to post these recommendations in order to comply with the above-mentioned Act. The Association withdrew the schedule when advised that it might contravene provisions of Singapore's Competition Act, which took effect in 2006. Surveys suggest that the fee schedule helped center fees around recommended levels, although some fees were reported to be below or above the guidelines.[16] The Ministry of Health later reversed its position and in late 2018 published a list of fee benchmarks for a number of surgical procedures.[17]

5. *Careful planning about the volume of hospital facilities and number of practitioners.* Besides providing a variety of methods to promote price sensitivity among consumers and concern for competitiveness among providers, Singapore limits the volume of hospital beds and physicians, in line with claims that allowing more facilities and providers will generate additional expenditures.

---

[15] See Ministry of Health Singapore (2019), "Fee Benchmarks and Bill Amount Information," https://www.moh.gov.sg/cost-financing/fee-benchmarks-and-bill-amount-information/DescriptionTextSearch.

[16] See Lim, M. K. (2007), "Deregulation of Doctors' Fees," *Health Policy Monitor*, http://www.hpm.org/en/Surveys/University_of_Singapore_-_Singapore/09/Deregulation_of_doctor_fees.html;jsessionid=0AEA73A7D1F0E6C363A84E699AD75532.

[17] Ministry of Health, Singapore (2018), *Fee Benchmarks Advisory Committee Report,* Annex D, https://www.moh.gov.sg/docs/librariesprovider5/pressroom/press-releases/fee-benchmarks-advisory-committee-report.pdf.

13.5. Strategies for Containing Fiscal Costs for Health Care

Although many low-income countries could benefit from additional spending on health care, economists at the International Monetary Fund have noted that already high health care outlays are expected to rise still further in advanced economies during the period through 2030. Public health care outlays are forecast to rise by about 3% of GDP in Europe and $4^1/_2$% of GDP in the United States. Moreover, the increase in the United States could rise by a further 1% of GDP during this period if planned Medicare payment reductions are not achieved, or if subsidies (for example, for purchasing coverage on insurance exchanges) prove more expensive than currently foreseen.[18] These increases in forecast represent an important part of the rise in public debt in advanced economies that the IMF staff has forecast for the coming decades. A 2010 report warned that the average net government sector debt in advanced economies could rise from 77% of GDP in 2011 to 200 percent of GDP in 2030,[19] although more recent forecasts in the IMF's Fiscal Monitor series project average net public debt rising more gradually, to about 80% of GDP, and gross debt to nearly 106%, in 2024.[20]

Containing the rise in health care spending could play an important role in preventing a further jump in the ratio of public debt to GDP in advanced economies. Thus, countries may want to consider various options to limit the growth in public health care outlays. Several European countries have introduced measures to curb the rise in costs for pharmaceuticals. However, IMF economists believe that these efforts will have only a modest effect in containing costs, because

---

[18] See International Monetary Fund (2010), *Fiscal Monitor: November 2010*, Box 3.1, p. 56, http://www.imf.org/external/pubs/ft/fm/2010/fm1002.pdf.

[19] See Cottarelli, C. and A. Schaecter (2010), "Long-Term Trends in Public Finances of the G-7 Economies," IMF Staff Position Note 10/13 (Washington: September 1), Figure 11, p. 18, www.imf.org/external/pubs/ft/spn/2010/spn1013.pdf.

[20] International Monetary Fund (2019), *Fiscal Monitor, October 2019*, Tables A7 and A8, pp. 53 and 54.

pharmaceuticals only account for about 15% of health care spending across OECD countries.[21] Apart from technological breakthroughs, policy options that would change provider incentives or reduce the demand for health care could provide significant help. On the supply side, replacing traditional fee-for-service payments with case-based payments or providing global budgets for care could alter the incentives for providers to deliver more services, rather than economize on care. Further efforts at managed care, despite their unpopularity, could also help. On the demand side, reducing subsidies to purchase health insurance and increasing co-insurance could help moderate the demand for services. Quantifying the impact of these measures is difficult. However, firm steps in these directions could help slow the anticipated skyrocketing of public debt in advanced economies over the foreseeable future.

13.6. Summary

Health care, like pensions, represents an important part of government expenditure, and government outlays for health care are likely to rise further in coming decades, as a result of aging populations, technological developments, and insurance policies that raise the demand for health care. Among advanced economies, only Singapore has maintained a steady ratio of health care expenditures as a percentage of GDP. The ratio has risen steadily in most other advanced economies. In the United States, the rise has been exceptional: from about 7% of GDP in 1970 to nearly 18% in 2018. Several emerging market countries, including India and Malaysia, have also seen health care spending rise as a share of GDP in recent years, although by smaller amounts.

Because providers play a key role in determining the volume of health care outlays, creating incentives for suppliers to economize on health expenditures while maintaining high-quality care will be

---

[21] International Monetary Fund (2010), *op. cit.*, pp. 56–57. Policy suggestions in this paragraph are drawn from this reference.

important. Moving from fee-for-service reimbursement to case-based payments or global budgets may help in this regard. Countries could also benefit by providing more information about typical costs for medical procedures at different hospitals, as Singapore has done. On the demand side, countries may also wish to consider modifications to health insurance that will raise the price sensitivity of consumers, such as introducing more cost sharing and reducing subsidies for the purchase of health insurance.

Chapter Fourteen: Fiscal Rules

Fiscal rules impose quantitative limits on specific budgetary aggregates, such as the overall budget balance or the ratio of government debt to GDP, with the aim of strengthening fiscal discipline. In some ways, they resemble the inflation targets that some countries adopt for monetary policy. Fiscal rules create numerical targets for specific fiscal indicators, in a way that can be readily used, explained to the public, and monitored. Unlike inflation targets, they are typically binding. They also tend to be expressed as simple numerical figures, rather than point estimates with a range. Examples of fiscal rules include the 3% ceiling on budget deficits and 60% maximum on the ratio of public debt to GDP for countries adopting the Euro under the Maastricht Treaty, and the constitutional requirement to adopt (or, in some cases, achieve) a balanced current budget (budget excluding capital spending) in 49 of the 50 states of the United States. According to an EXCEL file accessible from the IMF's Fiscal Rules website, as of December 2016 at least 96 countries had national or supra-national fiscal rules, versus only six in 1985 and seven in 1986.[1]

14.1. Kinds of Fiscal Rules and Their Implications

14.1.1. *Types of rules*

IMF staff economists have noted that countries have created a variety of rules applying to different fiscal indicators.[2] These include the following:

---

[1]IMF Fiscal Affairs Department (2017), "Fiscal Rules Data Set, 1985–2015", EXCEL file, https://www.imf.org/external/datamapper/fiscalrules/matrix/matrix.htm.

[2]Lledó, V. *et al.* (2017), "Fiscal Rules at a Glance — Background Paper," p. 8, IMF (March), https://www.imf.org/external/datamapper/fiscalrules/matrix/matrix.htm.

1. *Rules for the budget balance.* Budget balance rules impose restrictions on the overall fiscal balance, the cyclically adjusted balance, structural balance, or the "balance over the cycle," where the rule specifies a definition for the business cycle. In some countries or jurisdictions, rules apply only to the primary fiscal balance (balance excluding interest payments) or the current balance.

2. *Rules for public debt.* Debt rules typically prescribe ceilings for the ratio of government or public debt to GDP, as a way of attaining fiscal sustainability. However, they are not binding if the debt-to-GDP ratio is well below the ceiling.

3. *Rules for revenues.* Some rules impose floors or ceilings on revenues, either as percent increases or in percent of GDP. Ceilings are often designed to limit the tax burden, while floors aim toward achieving certain revenue objectives. By themselves they cannot be used to achieve public debt objectives, because they do not constrain expenditures.

4. *Rules for expenditures.* Expenditure rules typically impose limits on total, primary, or current outlays, either as absolute amounts or, more commonly, as growth rates or as a percentage of GDP. Such rules are often designed to limit the size of government. As with revenue rules, they cannot, by themselves, achieve a particular objective for public debt sustainability.

14.1.2. Implications of different rules

1. *Efficacy of specific rules for different objectives.* Certain rules seem better suited for achieving some fiscal objectives than others. As noted in Table 14.1, reproduced from a 2009 IMF staff study on fiscal rules,[3] rules for debt ceilings appear most closely linked to achieving public debt sustainability objectives, followed by rules for the overall balance, cyclically adjusted balance, and balance

---

[3]International Monetary Fund (2009), "Fiscal Rules — Anchoring Expectations for Public Finances" (Washington, December 16), p. 7, http://www.imf.org/external/np/pp/eng/2009/121609.pdf.

Table 14.1. Relative effectiveness of different fiscal rules for achieving different objectives.

| | Objectives | | |
Type of fiscal rule	Debt sustainability	Economic stabilization	Government size
Overall balance	++	−	0
Primary balance	+	−	0
Cyclically adjusted balance	++	−	0
Balanced budget over the cycle	++	+++	0
Public debt-to-GDP ratio	+++	−	−
Expenditure	+	++	++
Revenue			
Revenue ceilings	−	−	++
Revenue floors	+	+	−
Limits on revenue windfalls	+	++	++

Notes: 1/Positive signs (+) indicate stronger property, negative signs (−) indicate weaker property, zeros (0) indicate neutral property with regard to objective.
Source: Reproduced from IMF (2009), *op. cit.*, Table 1, p. 6.

"over the cycle." Rules for the budget balance "over the cycle" seem best suited for achieving stabilization objectives, followed by the cyclical budget balance, expenditure rules, and rules limiting revenue windfalls. Rules on expenditures, revenue ceilings, and limits on the size of revenue windfalls seem best designed to limit the size of government (as a share of GDP).

2. *Issues of flexibility.* Some rules are more flexible than others in responding to economic shocks. The least flexible rules prescribe *absolute ceilings* for the overall budget balance or the ratio of public or government debt to GDP. Likewise, *expenditure* rules do not allow for discretionary stimulus through spending. A rule for the *cyclical balance* allows for changes in the fiscal balance attributable to the business cycle, although not for discretionary fiscal stimulus. Under this rule, the observed or forecast fiscal balance is adjusted to reflect deviations of GDP from potential output, lowering the deficit indicator when GDP falls below potential and raising it when GDP exceeds potential. The *structural balance* allows both for cyclical effects and for other shocks not linked to the business cycle, such

as changes in the exchange rate or global interest rates. The most flexible rules are those that apply *over the cycle*, since automatic and discretionary stimulus measures can be accommodated if they are offset by tightening during the subsequent recovery.

Revenue and expenditure rules tend to be less flexible. Revenue floors do not take into account the effect of automatic stabilizers during a downturn. Revenue ceilings are similarly inflexible during upturns, while expenditure ceilings constrain discretionary spending for stimulus during a recession. Because the business cycle tends to affect revenue more than expenditure, particularly in developing and emerging market countries, revenue rules by themselves can have a *pro-cyclical* effect on fiscal policy. In some states of the United States with ceilings on revenue or revenue growth, the ceiling restrains tax increases during upturns while requiring expenditure cuts during downturns, if the budget is also subject to a ceiling on the overall balance or current balance.

3. *Taking account of inflation.* Inflation can affect how fiscal rules operate. For example, with a nominal expenditure target, inflation reduces the real level of allowed spending. Inflation-adjusted targets avoid this problem. However, adjusting fully for inflation can limit the effectiveness of a fiscal rule where large deficits have been an important source of inflation and, thus, need addressing. Inflation can also undermine the effectiveness of a debt-to-GDP rule, by raising nominal interest rates, which in turn increases debt service costs and adds to the overall deficit. In this case, using an inflation-adjusted fiscal target, such as the operational balance (which removes the inflationary, but not the real, component of interest payments from the overall balance), could be useful.

14.2. Effectiveness of Fiscal Rules

Although fiscal rules can help offset the short-term bias of fiscal policy and the effects on the entire budget of special interest provisions, these rules can also have drawbacks.

1. Establishing rules without sufficient political commitment or the institutions needed for their success can undermine the credibility of fiscal policy.

2. Some rules, as noted earlier, can impart a pro-cyclical bias to fiscal policy, for example, constraining stimulus during economic downturns while having no impact during expansionary periods.

3. Rules may harm the quality of fiscal policy, because they typically leave governments free to decide how to adjust the budget. This can lead to adjustment based on easier measures with adverse long-run consequences, such as cutting capital projects and spending for operations and maintenance.

4. Complying with fiscal rules may divert attention or effort from achieving longer term reforms, such as reorienting spending from current to capital outlays.

5. Rules may encourage governments to adopt dubious accounting methods and move some expenditures off-budget as a way of achieving compliance.

Despite the above concerns, there is evidence linking fiscal rules with better economic performance. According to IMF staff economists, in the European Union stronger fiscal rules have been associated with improvement in cyclically adjusted primary balances, although not debt-to-GDP ratios (which may suggest the use of creative accounting in cutting deficits). In addition, budget balance and debt rules, more than expenditure rules, have been linked to better budget outcomes. For countries generally, rules at the national level seem to have worked better than those for sub-national governments. Research also suggests that in countries that have achieved large fiscal adjustment, the size of the adjustment was larger, and more front-loaded, where fiscal rules were in place. Indeed, of 24 episodes of large fiscal adjustment in OECD, EU, and G20 countries, in only three (in Korea, South Africa, and Turkey) were no fiscal rules in place before, during, or after the episode.[4] Finally, some research suggests that

---

[4] *Id.*, pp. 16–17.

fiscal rules need not be incompatible with achieving macroeconomic stabilization.[5]

14.3. Fiscal Rules as Part of the Framework for Fiscal Policymaking

Fiscal rules have often been adopted in the context of broader reforms designed to strengthen the "framework" for fiscal policymaking. The reforms typically include the following elements[6]:

1. Legislating broad principles to guide the development of fiscal policy;
2. Requiring "rolling" budget plans and fiscal projections for the short-, medium-, and longer term;
3. Establishing mechanisms to limit "deficit bias," including requirements for top-down budgeting, assessing projects via cost-benefit analysis, and limiting budget amendments or supplements; and
4. Instituting requirements for transparency and public oversight, including the required publication of regular reports with multiyear fiscal projections and other key information.

These reforms have sometimes been strengthened by establishing *independent fiscal agencies* to monitor and assess fiscal developments. A number of emerging market and advanced economies have created such agencies, including Chile, Hungary, the Netherlands, Sweden, and the United States. In addition, the reforms have sometimes included the introduction of *fiscal responsibility laws* (FRLs). Besides creating procedures to improve policy formulation, many of these laws include fiscal rules, sometimes with "escape clauses," along with penalties for infractions. Table 14.2, reproduced from the previously-cited

---

[5]Andres, J. and R. Domenech (2006), "Fiscal Rules and Macroeconomic Stability," *Hacienda Publica Espanola*, vol. 176-1, pp. 9–41, http://iei.uv.es/docs/wp_internos/RePEc/pdf/iei_0501.pdf.
[6]International Monetary Fund (2009), *op. cit.*, p. 12.

Table 14.2. Fiscal rule elements of leading fiscal responsibility laws.

Country and date	Original law	Procedural rules	Numerical targets in FRL[a]	Coverage[b]	Escape clauses	Sanctions
Argentina federal regime of fiscal responsibility (2004)	1999, 2001	Yes	ER; DR	CG[c]	Yes	Yes
Australia: Charter of budget honesty (1998)		Yes	–[c]	CG	No	No
Brazil: Fiscal responsibility law (2000)		Yes	–[e]	PS	Yes	Yes
Colombia: Organic law on fiscal Transparency and responsibility (2003)	1997, 2000	Yes	BBR; ER; DR	NFPS[f]	No	Yes
Ecuador: Fiscal responsibility law (2005)	2002	Yes	BBR; ER; DR	PS	No	Yes
India: Fiscal responsibility and budget management act (2003)		Yes	BBR	CG[c]	Yes	No
New Zealand: Public finance (state sector management) Bill (2005)	1994[d]	Yes	–[e]	GG	No	No
Pakistan: Fiscal responsibility and debt limitation act (2005)		Yes	BBR;DR	CG	Yes	No
Panama: Law no. 2 on economic activity promotion and fiscal responsibility (2002)		No	BBR; DR	NFPS	No	No
Peru: Fiscal responsibility and transparency law (2003)	1999	Yes	BBR; ER[g]	NFPS	Yes	Yes
Spain: Budget stability law (2007)		Yes	BBR	NFPS	Yes	Yes
Sri Lanka: Fiscal management responsibility act (2003)	2001	Yes	BBR; DR	CG	Yes	No
United Kingdom: Code for fiscal stability (1998)		Yes	–[e]	PS	No	No

Notes: [a] ER Expenditure rule; BBR Budget balance rule; DR Debt rule; RR Revenue rule.
[b] CG Central government; GG General government; PS Public sector; NFPS Non-financial public sector.
[c] Also adopted by some subnational governments.
[d] Fiscal responsibility act (1994) (and Fiscal responsibility amendment act, 1998).
[e] These countries operate (*de facto*) rules, which are however not spelled out in the FRL.
[f] Fiscal rules set out in the FRL only apply to subnational governments.
[g] Some subnational rules are set out in the fiscal decentralization law.
Sources: Corbacho and Schwartz (2007), and country documents. Reproduced from IMF (2009), *op. cit.*, Table 2, p. 14.

IMF staff paper, highlights fiscal rule elements in a number of FRLs as of 2009.[7]

A few countries, notably Australia and New Zealand, have strengthened their fiscal institutions without adopting formal rules. In these countries, transparency, including the regular publication of fiscal reports, has been critical in achieving objectives for budget deficits and public debt sustainability.

14.4. Developing Effective Fiscal Rules

14.4.1. General considerations

IMF staff economists suggest that three features are paramount for developing effective fiscal rules[8]:

1. A clear and steady relationship between the quantitative rule and the ultimate objective, such as public debt sustainability.
2. Enough flexibility to respond to temporary shocks, without losing the ability to help policy adjust to permanent shocks (e.g., loss of mineral resources).
3. A clear mechanism that fosters the correction of temporary deviations from targets within a reasonable time period, including explicit enforcement procedures and penalties for deviations.

On this last subject, the method adopted by Switzerland is worth noting. Switzerland stores deviations from its structural balance rule in a "notional account." Under Swiss law, policy must respond once the sum of negative deviations (i.e., excess deficits) exceeds 6% of outlays; the sum must be reduced to less than 6% within 3 years. Germany, by comparison, in 2011 opted for a straightforward rule, requiring the

---

[7] *Id.*, p. 14.
[8] *Id.*, p. 20.

Federal government to reduce any structural fiscal balance to 0.35% of GDP by 2016 and the *länder* to achieve structural balance by 2020.[9]

14.4.2. Which indicator to target

Good indicators have a clear connection to the ultimate policy objective, are controllable, and can be easily monitored. Although the debt-to-GDP ratio is more closely linked to public debt sustainability, targeting the overall budget balance (which is linked to sustainability) has advantages because of its transparency and controllability. A cyclical balance or structural balance rule can be useful for providing flexibility to respond to output shocks. More flexible still is to require balance over the business cycle. To be effective, however, countries must tighten sufficiently during upturns to correct for deviations during downturns. As noted earlier, a structural balance rule can take into account factors besides the business cycle, such as changes in world interest and exchange rates. For commodity exporters, a factor taking into account shocks to commodity prices or export volumes can be useful.

To implement a structural balance rule, countries need to have (1) a numerical target for the structural balance; (2) an estimate of the *output gap* (the deviation of GDP from potential output); and (3) estimates of the elasticities of revenues and expenditures to changes in real GDP. The third element allows the government to adjust actual (or forecast) revenues and expenditures to what they might be at potential output, so as to calculate the structural balance. Various methods are available to estimate potential GDP and the output gap, including the Hodrick–Prescott and other filters, although doing so requires technical expertise. Estimating revenue and expenditure elasticities can also be challenging. Given the technical requirements, an independent fiscal agency can be helpful in providing the requisite estimates for the output gap and the structural balance or in furnishing an independent set of estimates, much as the Congressional Budget Office in the United

---

[9]Lledó *et al.* (2017), *op. cit.*, p. 32.

States, which provides budget estimates separate from those made by the Office of Management and Budget, which reports to the US President.

14.5. Recent Experience with Fiscal Rules

One way to assess the value of fiscal rules is to assess their operation during the Global Financial Crisis of 2007–2009. A survey conducted by IMF staff economists[10] suggested that 31 countries, including a majority of those with nationally set fiscal rules, managed to observe the rules during the crisis. Many of these rules allowed flexibility in achieving numerical limits or the time needed for adjustment, or included "escape clauses." Another 16 countries changed or suspended their rules, while a further group of 25 did not change their rules but appeared to experience conflict between the rules and fiscal outcomes. Regarding supranational rules, excessive deficit procedures were implemented in 20 of the 27 European Union countries, although most of these allowed a relatively long time period for the compensating adjustment. As might be expected, those countries with more flexible rules — typically advanced and emerging economies — found it easier to implement countercyclical measures. Among lower income countries, flexible numerical constraints and "escape clauses" were more important for providing scope to implement countercyclical stimulus.

Under some circumstances, fiscal rules may also prove useful for countries aiming to restore public debt sustainability following a crisis. Countries needing only modest adjustment may find that adopting a fiscal rule (with the necessary political and institutional support) can help in guiding fiscal policy. By comparison, those requiring large adjustments may find that the corrections required in a new or existing rule are too large to be implemented. Countries in this position may want first to establish and implement a medium-term plan for fiscal adjustment, backed by appropriate sanctions. At the same time, work

---

[10] *Id.*, Table 6, p. 35.

could start on developing a fiscal rule to be adopted once sustainability is restored.

14.6. Summary

Fiscal rules are laws or constitutional provisions designed to strengthen the fiscal discipline by constraining key fiscal aggregates. Fiscal rules typically impose quantitative limits on the overall or current budget balance, government debt, revenues, or expenditures, either in absolute terms, in terms of growth, or as percentages of GDP. Although many rules impose limits on the actual budget balance, others are specified in terms of the cyclical or structural balance or the balance over the business cycle. These alternative rules allow some flexibility for the budget balance to respond to cyclical factors. A structural balance rule can also provide for flexibility to certain other factors, such as shocks to interest or exchange rates or, for commodity producers, to commodity prices.

Evidence suggests that fiscal rules have been associated with better budget performance in the European Union, and with stronger and more front-loaded adjustment in countries undertaking major fiscal consolidation. Nevertheless, fiscal rules can be counter-productive, if the unwillingness to enforce them undermines the credibility of government, or if they lead governments to use creative accounting or make politically expeditious but economically undesirable choices in trying to comply. Fiscal rules may prove more effective when adopted as part of a broader package of reforms aimed at strengthening the framework for making fiscal policy, which may also include fiscal responsibility laws and the creation of independent fiscal institutions that can analyze, project, and monitor fiscal performance in an objective and transparent manner.

Effective fiscal rules tend to have a clear and steady relationship between the rule and the ultimate fiscal objective; enough flexibility to respond to temporary shocks; and a mechanism fostering the correction of temporary deviations within a reasonable time period, including enforcement procedures and sanctions. Controllability, ease of monitoring, and a clear connection to debt sustainability make the overall budget balance a desirable indicator for fiscal rules. Using the cyclical balance or structural balance rather than the actual balance allows for flexibility in responding to shocks in output, as does a rule for the budget balance over the cycle. Implementing a cyclical or structural balance rule requires estimating the output gap and the elasticities of revenue and expenditure to changes in real GDP, along with a clear target for the cyclical or structural balance. An independent fiscal agency can be useful in providing objective estimates for these politically sensitive but technically complex indicators.

Experience during the 2007–2009 Global Financial Crisis suggests that fiscal rules, particularly those with elements of flexibility, can be observed during recessions. In addition, fiscal rules can play a useful role in helping countries needing small adjustments to achieve sustainable debt-to-GDP ratios implement the necessary measures. Rules may be harder to implement in countries requiring large reductions in debt-to-GDP ratios, where recession and economic uncertainty may make it difficult to impose large adjustments in a short time. These countries may do better undertaking a medium-term fiscal strategy to achieve debt sustainability while developing a fiscal rule that could be implemented later on, once more normal debt-to-GDP ratios are attained.

Chapter Fifteen: Fiscal Reforms

Many countries undertake fiscal reform programs. Sometimes they do so to avoid anticipated problems or to correct long-standing inefficiencies. More often, reforms are implemented in response to crises, such as a balance of payments and exchange rate crisis triggered by a loss of confidence after years of unsustainable fiscal deficits. Whatever their origins, fiscal reforms can have massive effects on the size and composition of revenues, expenditures, and budget financing. After reviewing various objectives and measures that can be considered in developing reform programs, this chapter discusses a number of specific programs that countries at various income levels have introduced since the mid-1980s.

15.1. Goals of Fiscal Reform Programs

Fiscal reform programs can be undertaken for a variety of reasons.

1. *Achieving sustainability.* Many countries undertake reform programs to reach a sustainable fiscal position — one where the ratio of public sector or government debt-to-GDP stabilizes at a "safe" level. As discussed in Chapter Five, "safe" levels can differ, depending on the country's income level and history. In general, however, developing and emerging market countries may want to target the maximum public debt-to-GDP ratio at 40–50%. Recent history suggests that advanced economies may be able to sustain higher ratios. In late 2010, the International Monetary Fund estimated the fiscal adjustments needed for advanced

economies (other than Japan) to return to ratios of 60% or less by 2030.[1]

2. *Reducing deficits for other reasons.* Apart from sustainability concerns, governments may wish to improve fiscal balances to allow more credit to the private sector without requiring faster monetary growth or to reduce pressure on the bond market arising from a steady increase in government debt. For governments that rely heavily on foreign financing, reducing deficits would lessen the need for foreign borrowing to support the budget.

3. *Reallocating government expenditure, to improve efficiency or achieve different spending objectives.* In some cases, government may want to shift expenditures to more productive activities, for example, cutting poorly targeted subsidies to afford more spending for infrastructure. Other countries may want to trim old programs to provide funds for new spending needs, for example, cutting defense spending to finance additional outlays for education or health care.

4. *Reforming the tax system.* Governments with poorly performing revenue systems may want to review their tax laws and administrative systems to see how best to increase revenues, minimize the distortions created by existing taxes, and address distributional concerns. In some countries, governments may want to scale back tax expenditures and eliminate "nuisance" taxes that raise little money but occupy tax administrators' resources that could more productively be assigned to major revenue raisers. In other countries, the goal may be to simplify tax codes by eliminating complex provisions and multiple rates. Still other countries may want to update their tax administration systems in order to increase efficiency, simplify compliance, and strengthen auditing systems, all of which may bolster collections.

---

[1] See International Monetary Fund (2010), *Fiscal Monitor, November 2010*, Appendix Table 1, p. 128, https://www.imf.org/en/Publications/FM/Issues/2016/12/31/Fiscal -Exit-From-Strategy-to-Implementation. For Japan, the adjustment was designed to return net debt to 80 percent of GDP.

15.2. Potential Revenue Reforms

Many options are available for countries wanting to reform their revenue systems.

15.2.1. *Broadening the tax base, to allow lower rates*

Many countries suffer from narrow tax bases, the result of widespread exemptions, exclusions, and other allowances that reduce the productivity of the tax system. These provisions require tax rates to be higher than otherwise, to raise a targeted amount of revenue. Measures to broaden the tax base include the following:

1. *Removing costly exclusions.* Many national income taxes exclude non-cash income, such as parking or health insurance provided at no charge by employers. Others exclude capital gains or subject these gains to highly preferential rates. Scaling back these exclusions could generate new revenues.
2. *Limiting exemptions and tax allowances.* Many corporate income taxes include generous tax holidays that substantially reduce revenues, compared to the cost of more targeted subsidies linked to new investment. Some personal income taxes provide costly deductions for homeownership, raising demand and increasing prices for housing, at the expense of other possible investments. Many European value-added taxes (VATs) have important exemptions or dual rates that significantly reduce revenues. Trimming these various allowances could reduce distortions while raising additional revenues.
3. *Redesigning poorly targeted tax subsidies.* Some national income taxes provide deductions for certain expenses, thereby giving larger tax subsidies to higher income taxpayers when tax rates are progressive. Converting these deductions to credits would provide equal rates of subsidies to taxpayers at all income levels. Reducing credits as income rises would concentrate subsidies on less-affluent households, promoting equality in income. Both reforms could raise revenues if the average rate of subsidy declined.

15.2.2. Adopting new taxes with good potential for raising revenue

Several countries, such as the United States, do not yet have a VAT. Others have only a limited personal income tax, with enforcement effectively restricted to those working at large firms and agencies. Both kinds of taxes have proved to be effective revenue generators, and several studies have contended that the United States could easily raise considerable new revenue by enacting a VAT or national sales tax. In 2010 the Bipartisan Policy Commission estimated that the United States could raise close to 1.9% of GDP by enacting a 6.5% "domestic sales tax."[2] William Gale of the Brookings Institution has estimated that a broad-based 10% VAT at the federal level would raise federal revenue by 2.6% of GDP yearly in the United States.[3] A third option to raise revenue would involve introducing a carbon tax. In 2019 Gale estimated that a tax set initially at US$30 per ton of carbon content, rising at 5% over inflation each year, would add 1.5% of GDP annually to federal revenue in the United States.[4]

15.2.3. Adjusting other taxes and non-tax revenues

Many countries lose significant revenue by not maintaining accurate, up-to-date registries of property values. Improving property records through regular surveys of property sales could raise substantial additional funds for real property taxes. Similarly, many countries could increase revenues from non-tax sources by periodically updating fees, charges, and penalties to keep pace with inflation. Restructuring state enterprises to increase profitability could allow these agencies to increase profit transfers to government budgets.

---

[2]Calculations based on data in Bipartisan Policy Center, Debt Reduction Tax Force (2010), *Restoring America's Future*, pp. 126–127, http://bipartisanpolicy.org/sites/default/files/FINAL%20DRTF%20REPORT%2011.16.10.pdf.
[3]Gale, W. G. (2019), *Fiscal Therapy* (New York: Oxford University Press), p. 245.
[4]*Id.*, pp. 15 and 259.

15.3. Potential Expenditure Reforms

As with revenues, many options are available for reforming or trimming expenditures.

15.3.1. *Current expenditures*

1. *Rationalize government hiring.* Many lower income countries continue to devote a large share of personnel expenditure to hiring low-skilled workers, in effect acting as a long-term employer of last resort. Replacing such programs with limited duration workfare projects, along with job training that prepares low-skilled workers for existing private sector jobs, could allow savings. In addition, reforming wage structures could facilitate hiring skilled policy and budget analysts, keeping tax and customs administrators honest, and retaining trained bank examiners.

2. *Improve government contracting and streamlining publications.* Improving government contracting, by replacing sole-source contracts with formal bidding and arms-length negotiations, could reduce the cost of supplies for many government activities and diminish opportunities for corruption. Putting more documents on the Internet could provide savings by reducing publication and printing expenses, while making information easier to access.

3. *Target subsidies.* Targeting subsidies on the intended beneficiaries could save substantial funds while allowing higher benefits for those eligible. Options could include replacing across-the-board food subsidies with subsidies limited to the poor and restricting farm subsidies to low-income farmers, in both cases using ID cards or other screening mechanisms to deter fraud.

4. *Limit entitlements.* Many higher income countries could reduce transfers to persons by restricting programs offering open-ended benefits to those meeting eligibility qualifications. For example, pension programs for those in difficult occupations could limit early retirement to those with poor health.

5. *Restrict government guarantees.* Many countries with financially troubled state enterprises could reduce the risk of future debt

service obligations by enacting and enforcing tight limits on the debt obligations that government can guarantee.

15.3.2. *Capital expenditures*

Governments that have not yet done so could require cost-benefit assessments for all capital projects, rank projects by net present value, and limit undertakings to the most highly rated projects. Savings could also come from ensuring that current projects can be finished before starting new ones.

15.4. Potential Reforms for State Enterprises

Countries with loss-making state enterprises can consider a number of options to reduce losses.

1. *Require enterprises to earn profits or limit the size of losses.* Government transfers to loss-making state enterprises could be reduced, and government dividends from profitable state enterprises increased, if the government introduced policies to limit losses and require that enterprises operate in a commercial manner wherever possible. As noted in Chapter Eight, such reforms may require limiting political interference in state enterprise management, allowing enterprises to restructure and adjust prices, and possibly establishing management or performance contracts.

2. *Impose hard budget constraints by cutting subventions and ready access to bank loans.* Governments can accelerate enterprise restructuring by cutting access to automatic budget subventions (transfers). Bank regulators can help by insisting that banks assess borrowing requests from state enterprises without favoritism, presumably with the same standards they would use for comparable private firms.

3. *Privatize enterprises where public operation does not seem essential.* Governments could realize money by privatizing non-essential public enterprises. In addition, selling or closing loss-making enterprises could reduce costly government transfers and subsidies.

15.5. Potential Reforms in Tax Administration and Public Expenditure Management

Governments can also raise revenues and cut expenditures by strengthening tax administration and expenditure management.

15.5.1. Tax administration

1. *Ensure that all current and potential taxpayers have tax identification (ID) numbers.* Requiring that all firms and, at least potentially, all individuals have tax ID numbers makes it easier to cross-check tax filings, monitor applications for government benefits, and audit taxpayers when needed. The ID number can be linked to enrollment in the government's social insurance or provident fund account, making it easier to check the eligibility of applicants for benefits.

2. *Restructure tax administration to promote efficiency.* Governments at all income levels can benefit by reviewing current tax administration methods and structures, assessing management, installing new equipment, and creating taxpayer tools (such as online forms and instructions and telephone access to basic tax information) that enable administrators to focus on the most difficult and potentially lucrative cases. Current research suggests that reorganizing administration based on the size of taxpayer units, starting with creation of a large taxpayer unit, can boost revenues, because most revenue typically comes from a small group of very large taxpayers (large firms and wealthy individuals).

15.5.2. Public expenditure management

1. *Create a Treasury and monitor all expenditures.* Many countries have found it expeditious to establish a central Treasury, to manage payments (and, in some cases, receipts). Doing so can ensure that all payments meet government accounting standards. It can also facilitate the careful recording of all government expenditures. Monitoring spending in all ministries and agencies is also critical to keep track of outlays and assess budget performance against targets.

2. *Eliminate off-budget expenditures.* Eliminating off-budget expenditures can improve expenditure management by compelling all spending either to be recorded on budget or eliminated. This can be particularly useful in countries where expenditure overruns are frequent because certain ministries, such as defense, keep some outlays "off the books." Countries with significant off-budget expenditures or special treatment for certain outlays during 2007–2010 included India (off-budget spending for oil subsidies) and the United States (Iraq War spending given special status in budget resolutions).

Table 15.1.   New Zealand: Key reporting requirements under the fiscal responsibility act of 1994.

Box 1: Key reports required under the Fiscal Responsibility Act 1994

The Budget Policy Statement is published by the end of March and is required to set out:

- Long-term fiscal objectives for Crown operating expenses, revenues and balance, debt and net worth.
- Short-term fiscal intentions for the above variables for the Budget year and the following two financial years.
- Broad strategic priorities for the coming Budget.

The Fiscal Strategy Report is tabled with the Budget and must include:

- A comparison of the fiscal forecasts in the Budget Economic and Fiscal Update with the short-term fiscal intentions in the BPS.
- Progress Outlook projections for 10 or more years of the variables specified for the long-term fiscal objectives.
- Assessment of the Progress Outlooks with the long-term fiscal objectives in the BPS.

Inconsistencies between the BPS and/or the FSR and the immediately preceding Statement or Report must be explained and justified by the Government.

The Treasury is required to prepare:

- An Economic and Fiscal Update at the time of the Budget and each December.
- A Pre-election Economic and Fiscal Update before each general election.

The Updates provide short-term forecasts for variables such as GDP, consumer price inflation, unemployment and the current account of the balance of payments. Fiscal information includes forecasts of the Crown financial statements.

Source: Reproduced from Janssen (2001), *op. cit.*, Box 1, p. 12.

3. *Improve budget transparency.* Many countries could benefit from greater budget transparency, including more publications about budget performance. New Zealand's Fiscal Responsibility Act of 1994, among the first of such laws, requires the government to publish (1) a budget policy statement before presenting the budget; (2) a fiscal policy report with 10-year projections at the time of the budget; and (3) periodic economic and fiscal forecasts (see Table 15.1). All statements must be prepared in accordance with Generally Accepted Accounting Practice (GAAP) standards.[5]

4. *Curb quasi-fiscal expenditures.* Budget transparency will improve and the public sector borrowing requirement may decline if quasi-fiscal expenditures (fiscal-like activities performed by the monetary authorities and other public agencies, outside the government budget) are reduced. The first step toward curbing these outlays involves recognizing and publicizing them, through an appendix or other mention in the government budget.

15.6. Achieving Fiscal Reform

Achieving fiscal reform generally requires major effort, because most changes create losers as well as winners. Often, reforms provide small benefits to many people but impose heavy losses on each of a relatively few firms and individuals. For example, broadening the tax base without losing revenue requires trimming existing tax preferences, such as tax holidays. Those who previously benefited — for example, persons who had invested heavily in sectors that will now lose their tax holidays — may find that the investment projects will become unprofitable, creating huge losses. By comparison, each of the taxpayers benefiting from the reduction in tax rates may realize only modest savings, although the many beneficiaries make the total savings as great, or greater, than the benefits lost by the few. Because those losing benefits will each lose heavily, they will likely fight hard to keep their preferences.

---

[5]Janssen, J. (2001), "New Zealand's Fiscal Policy Framework: Experience and Evolution," Working Paper No. 01/25 (Wellington: December), pp. 9–10, http://www.treasury.govt.nz/publications/research-policy/wp/2001/01-25.

Sustaining reform is also difficult. Sometimes governments implement adjustment measures, such as cutting operations and maintenance outlays, that are hard to continue for prolonged periods. Others, such as cuts in subsidies, may be reversed if a major shock, such as a jump in food prices, occurs. More than one IMF-supported adjustment program failed because the government agreed to sensitive policy measures that were reversed after riots and demonstrations. In Ghana, for example, the government rescinded the introduction of a VAT following public protests.[6] In January 2011, the Pakistani government reversed a rise in petroleum prices introduced as part of an IMF-supported adjustment program following protests from opposition leaders.[7] In the United States, a massive letter writing campaign to members of Congress after implementation of a withholding tax on interest and dividends in 1982 led to its repeal and replacement by "backup withholding" the next year. Under the Interest and Dividends Tax Compliance Act of 1983, financial institutions simply report earnings and dividends to the Internal Revenue Services, to allow checking against tax returns.[8]

15.6.1. *Why reforms are implemented*

Fiscal reforms are typically implemented under several circumstances. These include the following:

1. *Economic crises.* In many countries, economic crises have been the trigger for major fiscal reforms. In Brazil, for example, the balance of

---

[6]See Leite, S. (2000), *Ghana: Economic Development in a Democratic Environment*, Occasional Paper 199 (Washington: International Monetary Fund), p. 38, http://books.google.com.sg/books?id=8e2H_6n4vD0C&pg=RA1-PT37&lpg=RA1-PT37&dq= IMF+program+rescind+price+increase&source=bl&ots=IVoLAB-Rz&sig=YPeOsTFcYIMJT-HVNk_EXy7o_mw&hl=en&ei=3rxETeiPKoaglAeVxuRI&sa=X&oi=book_result&ct=result&resnum=9&ved=0CEkQ6AEwCA.

[7]See, for example, Reuters (2011), "IMF Criticizes Petrol Price Hike Reversal," *Express Tribune and International Herald Tribune* (January 7), http://tribune.com.pk/story/100321/imfcriticises-petrol-price-hike-reversal.

[8]See Tax Policy Center (2010), "Tax Legislation — Major Tax Legislation Enacted 1980–89," http://www.taxpolicycenter.org/legislation/1980.cfm\#Interest1983.

payments crisis of 2002 gave rise to major fiscal reforms that led to a dramatic turnaround in the nation's economy. Likewise, Turkey's 2000–2001 financial crisis led to fiscal reforms that finally brought inflation under control and led to steady growth for much of the period through 2018. Among high-income countries, Canada's near crisis in 1993–1994 led to major reforms that turned large deficits into surpluses within 2 years and a sharp improvement in the public debt-to-GDP ratio. These changes helped stabilize the currency and provide a strong foundation for later growth.

2. *Political change.* In many countries, major political changes have instigated fiscal reforms. In Eastern Europe, the inauguration of Poland's reform-minded, Solidarity-led government in 1989 brought a comprehensive reform of all aspects of economic management, including a substantial scaling back and restructuring of fiscal activity, that ultimately brought a dramatic transformation of Poland's economy. On a lesser scale, the change in political administration in the United States in 1993 led to the passage of tax increases that strengthened the federal budget, encouraged the Federal Reserve Board to lower interest rates, and contributed to fiscal surpluses during the final years of the 1990s.

3. *Confluence of interests.* On occasion, shared objectives among different interests have led to fiscal reform. In the United States, for example, the long-standing desire among Democrats and fiscal reformers to eliminate poorly targeted and inefficient tax allowances, and President Reagan's desire to lower tax rates, led to passage of the Tax Reform Act of 1986, which removed many tax preferences and used the resulting savings to reduce marginal rates.

15.6.2. *Why reforms sometimes fail*

Reform programs can also fail, however, often for one or more of the following reasons:

1. *Lack of program ownership.* Many low-income and emerging market countries have approached the International Monetary Fund and

World Bank for financial assistance. IMF loans are generally linked to implementation of an agreed macroeconomic adjustment program, while Structural Adjustment loans and credits from the World Bank require introducing agreed policy changes. While countries negotiate with both institutions on the terms of the program, they often rely heavily on the IMF and the World Bank to develop specific program measures. As a consequence, country leaders may feel less committed to implementing the agreed policy reforms than if they had developed them on their own and then approached these institutions for financial support. The IMF's Poverty Reduction and Growth Facility, which replaced earlier facilities for assisting low-income countries and was in existence through 2009, addressed program ownership by having countries seek input from a broad set of interested groups, including civil society, while developing the poverty reduction strategy paper guiding their IMF-supported adjustment program.[9]

2. *Strong opposition and lack of political will.* Often, political opposition coupled with reluctance by country leaders to accept the political costs of enforcing controversial measures will derail a fiscal reform program. A recent example is the above-mentioned rollback of fuel price increases in Pakistan in early 2011. Pakistan's government may have been reluctant to maintain an unpopular hike in petroleum prices given the stress already experienced from continuing violence and terrorist activities within the country and in neighboring Afghanistan. A second example may be the cool response of political leaders in the United States to the policy recommendations of the National Commission on Fiscal Responsibility and Reform, appointed by President Obama.[10] Although

---

[9]See International Monetary Fund (2009), "Factsheet: The Poverty Reduction and Growth Facility," http://www.imf.org/external/np/exr/facts/prgf.htm. As of 2019, the IMF was providing concessional lending to low-income countries through various facilities funded by the Poverty Reduction and Growth Trust (PRGT). See International Monetary Fund (2019), "IMF Support for Low-Income Countries," https://www.imf.org/en/About/Factsheets/IMF-Support-for-Low-Income-Countries.

[10]See National Commission on Fiscal Responsibility and Reform (2010), "Moment of Truth," http://www.fiscalcommission.gov/news/moment-truth-report-national-commission-fiscal-responsibility-and-reform.

11 of the 18 commissioners voted to support the Commission's recommendations, five of the 11 were not elected officials, and two more were members of Congress who decided not to seek re-election in 2010. Six of the 10 continuing members of Congress on the Commission voted against the recommendations.[11] In addition, President Obama, while urging the US Congress to work with him in reducing the federal budget deficit, noted in his January 2011 State of the Union Message that he, too, did not agree with all the Commission's recommendations.

3. *Government officials lack the technical ability to implement the program.* Occasionally fiscal reform programs include technical elements that, as time progress, turn out to be technically harder to implement than envisioned or that raise unexpected pitfalls. In the Ghanaian example cited earlier, the authorities failed to exempt small businesses from the newly introduced VAT, although these firms would have contributed little to overall revenue. The resulting political outcry led to a rollback of the VAT.[12] In some countries, the Finance Ministry's inability to monitor and control all expenditures has led to expenditure overruns — for example, where the Defense Minister is accustomed to determining the Ministry's outlays. In some countries, the existing apparatus has contributed to failure. During the early 1990s in Romania, for example, the Finance Ministry had to rely on other government agencies to prepare a macroeconomic forecast, and delays in updating and transmitting new information to the Ministry meant that budgets were often based on outdated macroeconomic projections. Finally, reforms in tax administration can fail because the authorities lack enough staff and equipment, or because internal conflicts make it impossible to reorganize the tax administration office for greater efficiency.

4. *Inadequate or unsuccessful technical assistance.* Technical assistance can be critical for implementing fiscal reforms, particularly in low-income and emerging market countries. Civil servants in

---

[11] See *Economist* (2010), "The President's Deficit Commission: No Cigar," December 9, http://www.economist.com/node/17679788.

[12] See Leite (2000), *op. cit.*

these countries are often poorly paid, and governments may have difficulty attracting and retaining enough officials with the training and experience needed for basic fiscal policy management, let alone reform programs. Thus, training and on-going technical assistance may be needed for countries to introduce and sustain reforms in taxation, spending, and administration. The IMF, World Bank, and regional development banks all maintain active training programs. They also have staffs of technical experts to provide specialized assistance on fiscal issues ranging from tax policy and administration to expenditure management and budget financing. In addition, many IMF-supported adjustment programs and World Bank structural adjustment loans and credits have provisions for technical assistance, including stationing experts for short and medium terms in the country. Despite these facilities, resources are limited, technical assistance requested or provided is not always well matched to country needs, and countries do not always implement the recommendations of technical assistance teams they request from these institutions. Institutions like the IMF and the World Bank periodically review their technical assistance activities to make them more effective.[13] Nevertheless, these activities can always be improved, and countries do not always have the technical support needed to implement reform programs.

15.6.3. Research on reform programs

As noted in earlier chapters, academic research on *high-income countries* indicates that cuts in subsidies, transfers, and the government's wage bill tend to produce more durable reforms than do cuts in capital expenditures and tax increases.[14] According to Alesina and Perotti,

---

[13] See, for example, International Monetary Fund (2010), "Technical Assistance Evaluation Program: Findings of Evaluations and Updated Program," http://www.imf.org/external/np/pp/eng/2010/060910.pdf.

[14] See Alesina, A. and R. Perotti (1996), "Fiscal Adjustments in OECD Countries: Composition and Macroeconomic Effects," NBER Working Paper No. 5730 (Cambridge, MA: National Bureau of Economic Research), available on the Internet at http://www.j-bradford-delong.net/movable_type/refs/Mozilla_Scrapbook/w5730.pdf.

the reason is that spending for government employment and social welfare programs has tended to increase automatically and during the 30 years prior to the mid-1990s had been rising as a share of public outlays. In 13 episodes (16 years) of successful adjustment, which these authors defined as yielding an average decline of at least 2% of GDP in the cyclically adjusted budget deficit and an average reduction of at least 5% of GDP in the public debt-to-GDP ratio for the 3 years after adjustment, cuts in the pubic wage bills, subsidies, and transfers accounted for more than 60% of the expenditure reductions, with cuts in public investment contributing only 20%. By comparison, in 46 episodes of failed adjustment, more than 60% of the spending reductions came from cuts in capital expenditure, compared with less than 25% for cuts in government wages, subsidies, and transfers.[15] Cuts in capital spending, while easy to introduce in the short run, were hard to maintain because of the inevitability of having to maintain an "adequate level" of public infrastructure through new capital projects. As for tax increases, countries appear to have had more success in preserving tax increases on firms than in raising taxes on household incomes or increasing levies for social insurance.[16]

In *emerging market countries*, research by IMF staff shows that cuts in subsidies and transfers and robust levels of revenue are associated with a greater likelihood of sustained adjustment.[17] Cuts in wages and salaries are also linked with more steadfast adjustment, although the evidence is less clear. In addition, countries with a higher share of capital expenditures in total outlays have a higher chance of sustaining adjustment. Interestingly, higher ratios of revenue-to-GDP appear associated with more success in sustaining fiscal adjustment, unlike in higher income countries.[18] The reason is that ratios of revenue-to-GDP are typically lower in emerging market countries, and many

---

[15] *Id.*, Table 6, p. 15.
[16] *Id.*, Table 9, p. 18.
[17] Gupta, S. *et al.* (2003), "What Sustains Fiscal Consolidations in Emerging Market Countries?" Working Paper No. 03/224 (Washington: International Monetary Fund, November), http://www.imf.org/external/pubs/ft/wp/2003/wp03224.pdf.
[18] *Id.*, p. 13.

governments have struggled to achieve sufficient revenues to support essential public services. In low-income countries, where revenue-to-GDP ratios can be less than 15 percent, adjustment is associated with increased revenues, which can come from better tax administration, fewer exclusions, and reduced tax evasion, as well as higher tax rates.[19]

15.7. Case Studies of Fiscal Reform

15.7.1. *Countries of the former Soviet Union*

Shortly after the former Soviet Union (FSU) split into 15 individual states, each of which joined the International Monetary Fund and World Bank, many of the newly independent countries approached the IMF and received support for economic reform programs. Fiscal adjustment was a major part of most countries' programs. The various programs committed the governments to reduce their budget deficits through expenditure cuts and reorganization, in part to accommodate the decline in revenues anticipated as these countries transitioned to market economies, and many state enterprises would need to shrink or close. Although the countries recorded noticeable declines in *cash* budget deficits, in many cases deficits fell because the governments used *sequestration* to delay payments on continuing expenditure obligations, including salary payments.[20] Fiscal balances measured on an *accrual* basis improved far less, however. During this period, countries such as the Russian Federation and Ukraine became known for incurring large wage arrears, as governments lacked the cash to pay salaries on time and were often several months late in meeting salary obligations. Because unpaid spending obligations would eventually need to be settled, it was not clear how much genuine fiscal adjustment had occurred in many of these countries.

---

[19]Gupta, S. *et al.* (2002), "Expenditure Composition, Fiscal Adjustment, and Growth in Low-Income Countries," Working Paper No. 02/77 (Washington: International Monetary Fund, April), p. 27, http://www.imf.org/external/pubs/ft/wp/2002/wp0277.pdf.

[20]For details, see Cheasty, A. and J. Davis (1996), "Fiscal Transition in Countries of the Former Soviet Union — An Interim Assessment," Working Paper No. 96/61 (Washington: International Monetary Fund, June).

Following the mid-1990s, fiscal performance in most of these countries improved. The average fiscal deficit declined from about 5% of GDP in 1996 to 1% in 2002, with four countries (Estonia, Kazakhstan, Ukraine, and the Russian Federation) achieving budget surpluses that year.[21] Indeed, in the three Baltic countries of Estonia, Latvia, and Lithuania, economic reforms advanced sufficiently that fiscal problems appeared to be largely resolved, and all three countries were welcomed into the European Union in 1999. Of the remaining 12 countries, nine (Armenia, Azerbaijan, Georgia, Kazakhstan, Kyrgyz Republic, Moldova, Russia, Tajikistan, and Ukraine) showed clear fiscal improvement, although their fiscal positions remained less secure than in the Baltic countries. *Revenue* rose as a share of GDP in eight of the countries, with four countries (Azerbaijan, Kazakhstan, Kyrgyz Republic, and Tajikistan) recording increases of at least 4% of GDP during the period. Higher petroleum revenue, due in part to higher oil prices, contributed to improved revenue performance in Kazakhstan and Azerbaijan. Indeed, strong oil earnings eventually enabled Kazakhstan to record budget surpluses and establish a sovereign wealth fund. *Expenditure cuts* were more important in other countries. Expenditure fell in six of the nine countries, and average outlays declined by 2.5% of GDP over the period. Expenditure cuts were particularly important in Moldova, where spending declined by 13% of GDP, enough to offset a decline in revenue of about 6% of GDP. In Armenia, where revenue rose by only about 1% of GDP during the period, spending cuts of nearly 6% of GDP were critical to cutting the overall deficit by 7% of GDP. In the Russian Federation, both revenue increases and spending cuts contributed to a dramatic improvement in the government's fiscal balance. Revenue rose by about 3% of GDP, largely because of higher oil revenues. However, expenditure fell by 7% of GDP. Thus, the overall budget balance moved from a deficit of nearly 9% of GDP in 1996 to a surplus of about 1% in 2002. Data for public debt ratios confirm that

---

[21]Gershenson, D. and J. Greene (2006), "Fiscal Reforms in the BRO Countries, 1996–2002," *Problems and Perspectives in Management*, vol. 2006, no. 1, pp. 5–21, http://www.businessperspectives.org/journals_free/ppm/2006/PPM_EN_2006_01_Gershenson.pdf

adjustment occurred in a number of these countries, with public debt-to-GDP ratios declining to about 46% for Armenia, 35–36% for Russia and Ukraine, and less than 25% for Azerbaijan and Kazakhstan.[22]

15.7.2. India

India has faced less pressure to reform than many other countries with its level of gross public debt, which exceeded 80% of GDP in the early 1980s and remained near 70% in 2018.[23] The reason is that India has a deep capital market and a relatively large volume of "captive savings," as the banking sector's long willingness to acquire and hold public debt has effectively led many private firms to seek other financing alternatives, including self-financing, for investment projects.[24] In addition, high fiscal deficits have not triggered the type of macroeconomic instability observed in many other countries with persistent, large budget deficits. Instead, inflation has generally remained moderate, and only once between independence and 2010 did India encounter a serious balance of payments crisis, during 1991–1992.

Despite this relatively good fortune, India has periodically undertaken fiscal adjustment, most recently from 2000 onward. In 2003, after three years of deliberation, India inaugurated its Fiscal Responsibility and Budget Management Act (FRBM), which set forth objectives for the central government to eliminate the revenue (current) budget deficit and reduce the overall budget deficit to 3% of GDP, initially by March 2008 (the deadline was later postponed). The law also required that successive budgets reduce the anticipated revenue deficit by at least 0.5% of GDP, and the overall deficit by at least 0.3% of GDP, each year.

---

[22] *Id.*, Tables 1, 3, 4, and 7, pp. 6, 9, and 11.

[23] Data drawn from the IMF's World Economic Outlook database for October 2019.

[24] Hausmann, R. and C. Purfield (2004), "The Challenge of Fiscal Adjustment in a Democracy: The Case of India," Working Paper No. 04/168 (Washington: International Monetary Fund, September), http://www.imf.org/external/pubs/ft/wp/2004/wp04168.pdf.

Table 15.2. India: Key fiscal indicators, 2005/2006–2009/2010 (in pct. of GDP).

	2005/06	2006/07	2007/08	2008/09	2009/10
Gen. Govt. Rev.	19.6	21.2	22.1	19.9	18.5
o/w: Cen. Govt.	10.1	10.9	12.0	10.0	9.1
Gen. Govt. Expend.	26.4	26.5	26.0	28.2	28.3
o/w: Cen. Govt.	14.2	14.4	14.5	16.1	15.5
Gen. Govt. Balance*	−7.2	−6.3	−4.4	−9.0	−9.9
o/w: Cen. Govt.	−4.1	−3.5	−3.1	−6.8	−6.5
o/w: States	−2.5	−1.9	−1.4	−2.1	−2.9**
Gen. Govt. Debt	84.0	80.8	74.6	75.4	71.3
o/w: Cen. Govt.	63.0	61.5	59.4	59.3	55.5

Notes: *IMF definition. Treats divestment receipts as financing and subsidy-related bonds issued as expenditure.
**Authorities' definition, which treats divestment proceeds and land sales as capital receipts.
Source: IMF (2010), *India: 2009 Article IV Consultation — Staff Report*, Tables 5 and 6; and IMF (2012), *India: 2012 Article IV Consultation — Staff Report*, Tables 5 and 6.

The FRBM, along with implementing recommendations of recent Finance Commissions and strong economic growth, helped India make major progress toward the FRBM objectives. Central government revenue rose from 10.1% of GDP during the 2005/2006 fiscal year to 12.0% in 2007/2008, while total expenditure rose by only 0.3 percentage point, to 14.5% of GDP (Table 15.2). As a result, the overall budget deficit fell to 3.1% of GDP, and the revenue (current) deficit fell from 2.5% of GDP to 0.6%.[25] The Central Government's debt-to-GDP ratio declined from 63.0% at the end of March 2006 to about 59.4% at the end of March 2008.

India's states have also taken steps toward fiscal reform. After many years of consideration, following a meeting in June 2004 of State Finance Ministers, Indian states began to introduce VATs to replace less efficient state sales taxes. By the 2006/2007 fiscal year, most states and Union territories had done so, establishing a two-tier rate structure

---

[25] International Monetary Fund (2010), *India: 2009 Article IV Consultation — Staff Report*, Table 5, p. 18, http://www.imf.org/external/pubs/ft/scr/2010/cr1073.pdf.; and International Monetary Fund (2012), *India: 2012 Article IV Consultation — Staff Report*, Table 5, p. 36, https://www.imf.org/external/pubs/ft/scr/2012/cr1296.pdf.

with rates of 4% and 12.5%. India's central government reported that, during 2006/2007, state tax revenues in those states that had adopted VATs rose 21% over those of the previous fiscal year. States with VATs registered a further revenue increase of about 15% during the first half of fiscal year 2007/2008, relative to the first half of 2006/2007.[26] Besides enacting VATs, most states have enacted Fiscal Responsibility Laws (FRLs), in response to the Twelfth Finance Commission's call for the Central Government to forgive part of the debt from those states that introduced reform measures, including the introduction of FRLs. Together, these measures helped reduce the consolidated deficits for states and union territories from 2.5% of GDP in fiscal year 2005/2006 to 1.4% in 2007/2008. The improved position of the states contributed to reducing total debt of the India's government sector from 84.0% of GDP at the end of March 2006 to 74.6% at the end of March 2008.[27]

The Global Financial Crisis interrupted India's progress toward fiscal adjustment. As noted in Table 15.2, central government revenue fell to 10.0% of GDP in fiscal year 2008/2009 and 9.1% in 2009/2010, while central government outlays rose to 16.1% of GDP in 2008/2009 and 15.5% in 2009/2010 because of measures to soften the economic slowdown. These figures exclude the off-budget issuance of bonds to finance oil and other subsidies. Once they are included and divestment receipts are treated as budget financing, the central government's fiscal deficit reached 6.8% in 2008/2009 and 6.1% in 2009/2010. The central government's debt-to-GDP ratio reached 59.3% at the end of 2008/2009 but improved to 55.5% a year later with good economic growth. As with the central government, the consolidated deficits of the states and Union territories were estimated to have risen, to 2.1% of GDP in 2008/2009 and 2.9% of GDP in 2009/2010, reflecting the financial crisis. However, general government debt, after reaching

---

[26]Business Portal of India (2009), "Taxation: Value Added Tax," http://business.gov.in/taxation/vat.php.
[27]International Monetary Fund (2010), *op. cit.*, Table 6, p. 19; and International Monetary Fund (2012), *op. cit.*, Table 6, p. 37.

75.4% of GDP at the end of 2008/2009, declined to 71.3% at the end of 2009/2010.

India's government voiced its desire to reduce the central government budget deficit by 5.5% of GDP in 2011/2012 and by 4.0% the following fiscal year. The actual deficits were 6.1% and 5.5%, although the deficit narrowed during the next few years, reaching 3.7% of GDP in 2016/2017. The replacement of the central government's sales tax (CST) and individual state VATs with a single goods and services tax (GST), with revenues shared by the central government and the states, became effective in July 2017 and should ultimately boost revenues. However, the initial implementation proved challenging for a variety of reasons, including a reluctance of some states to tax petroleum and other sensitive items.[28] On the expenditure side, rationalizing subsidy programs, including the possible replacement of certain subsidies on food and fertilizer with direct transfers to low-income farmers and households, could provide savings while improving the targeting of benefits toward the poor.[29]

15.7.3. *Pakistan*

Pakistan has undertaken fiscal reforms periodically, often in the context of broader adjustment programs supported by the IMF. Among the more recent efforts was one inaugurated in late 2001, as part of a three-year arrangement under the IMF's Poverty Reduction and Growth Facility. That arrangement aimed to reduce Pakistan's high debt-to-GDP ratio, which had approached 100% during the late 1990s, by strengthening revenue performance, in part through curbing the liberal use of tax exemptions, and by improving public expenditure management, including smaller losses at state enterprises. Despite a challenging security situation and delays in implementing structural

---

[28]See, for example, Sharma, S. N. and S. Layak (2019), "GST: The Challenges Before India's Largest Indirect Tax Reform," *Economic Times*, September 29, https://economictimes. indiatimes.com/news/economy/policy/gst-the-challenges-before-indias-largest-indirect-tax-re form/articleshow/71353710.cms.

[29]International Monetary Fund (2010), *op. cit.*, p. 13.

Table 15.3.   Pakistan: Key fiscal indicators, 2000/2001–2006/2007 (in pct. of GDP).

	2000/ 01	2001/ 02	2002/ 03	2003/ 04	2004/ 05	2005/ 06	2006/ 07
Revenue	14.3	16.1	17.2	14.6	14.1	14.8	15.2
Expenditure	17.2	18.8	18.5	16.4	18.4	18.7	19.2
Overall balance	−3.3	−3.6	−1.3	−1.8	−3.7	−4.0	−4.0
Primary balance	2.4	2.0	2.9	1.7	−0.6	−0.2	1.2
Government debt	88.8	80.2	74.5	67.8	62.9	57.3	54.6

Sources: IMF, Staff Reports for the 2005 and 2007 Article IV Consultations with Pakistan.

reforms, Pakistan's government achieved major successes under the program. As shown in Table 15.3, the central budget deficit fell from 3.3% of GDP in fiscal year 2000/2001 to 1.3% in 2002/2003. Improving tax administration, introducing self-assessment, and scaling back exemptions helped raise revenues from 14% to 17% of GDP, while tight control over spending kept the rise in total outlays to about 1% of GDP. Thus, the budget achieved primary surpluses each year. With higher growth and continued low real interest rates, the public debt ratio fell steadily, reaching 74.5% at the end of the 2002/2003 fiscal year. The following year, Pakistan succeeded in limiting the deficit to 1.8% of GDP, despite a decline in revenue performance, because less-than-expected defense spending and lower interest payments curbed total outlays. Thus, the debt-to-GDP ratio fell further, to 68.7% of GDP. Relatively high growth rates, exceeding 6% a year, enabled Pakistan to continue reducing its debt-to-GDP ratio in subsequent years, despite a rise in budget deficits to about 4% of GDP. By the end of fiscal year 2006/2007, with revenue performance improving slightly, the ratio of public debt-to-GDP had fallen to 54.6%.

A marked deterioration in public finances during the 2007/2008 fiscal year, largely reflecting government efforts to shield the population from rising food and energy prices, triggered higher inflation, a rise in the public debt-to-GDP ratio, and a balance of payments crisis. The public debt-to-GDP ratio rose to 58.4% at the end of the fiscal year, and Pakistan requested IMF financial assistance later in 2008. The new arrangement included a variety of measures aimed at boosting revenue and rationalizing expenditure, including a cut in energy subsidies to allow higher spending on poverty reduction programs. Despite an augmentation of the arrangement, progress proved challenging, and the authorities requested an extension of the arrangement to 2011 to allow more time to implement planned reforms. While Pakistan succeeded in completing four program reviews, drawing the equivalent of US$7.3 billion of a potential US$10.7 billion in support,[30] the authorities were unable to complete the terms of the arrangement. Economic performance subsequently deteriorated, and Pakistan entered into an extended arrangement covering much of 2013–2016. With the economy remaining weak, and with reserves remaining under three months of the upcoming years' imports and projected to decline further, Pakistan approached the IMF for assistance again and entered into a new, three-year Extended Fund Facility arrangement, potentially providing support of about US$6.0 billion, in July 2019.[31]

15.7.4. Brazil

Since the late 1990s, Brazil has implemented major fiscal reforms that have substantially improved the overall balance of the public sector and reduced its public debt-to-GDP ratio. These reforms took place in the context of broader macroeconomic adjustment programs supported by the IMF, following balance of payments crises in late 1998 to early 1999 and again in 2002 that led to sharp depreciations in the currency and significant increases in the ratios of foreign and total public debt-to-GDP. As part of these adjustment programs, the government committed to achieve primary surpluses of more than 3%

---

[30] International Monetary Fund (2010), *Pakistan: Fourth Review under the Stand-By Arrangement*, Table 3b, p. 26, http://www.imf.org/external/pubs/ft/scr/2010/cr10158.pdf.
[31] International Monetary Fund (2019), *Pakistan: Request for an Extended Arrangement under the Extended Fund Facility — Press Release; Staff Report; and Statement by the Executive Director for Pakistan*, https://www.imf.org/en/Publications/CR/Issues/2019/07/08/Pakistan-Request-for-an-Extended-Arrangement-Under-the-Extended-Fund-Facility-Press-Release-470 92.

Table 15.4. Brazil: Key indicators for public sector, 1998–2008, in pct. of GDP.

	Primary balance	Overall balance	Net public debt
1998	−0.1	−7.2	38.9
1999	3.0	−5.2	44.5
2000	3.4	−3.3	47.0
2001	3.2	−3.2	51.5
2002	3.2	−4.4	60.0
2003	3.2	−5.2	54.3
2004	3.7	−2.9	50.2
2005	3.7	−3.5	48.0
2006	3.2	−3.6	46.5
2007	3.2	−2.7	44.6
2008	3.8	−1.5	37.6

Source: International Monetary Fund (2019), IMF World Economic Outlook October 2019 database.

of GDP for the entire public sector. Because of initially high levels of debt and interest rates, the public sector recorded large overall deficits, which peaked at 7.2% in 1998 and 5.2% in 1999 (Table 15.4). After 2002, smaller interest payments and higher primary surpluses reduced the overall deficit to 2.9% in 2004 and 2.7–3.6% in the next three years. By 2008, with the primary surplus near 4%, the overall deficit had fallen to 1.5%.[32]

Important to the success of Brazil's fiscal adjustment was the passage in 2000 of the country's Fiscal Responsibility Law (FRL), along with an accompanying "Fiscal Crimes" Law that established penalties for officials who violated the FRL. The FRL limited the share of personnel outlays in total expenditures to 50% for the federal government and 60% for state and local governments; restricted new borrowing to the amount of capital expenditures; prohibited government officials from enacting during their last year of office spending commitments lasting more than one budget period; required

---

[32]National Treasury (2009), Public Debt: The Brazilian Experience (Brasilia: August), Statistical Annex, http://www.tesouro.fazenda.gov.br/english/public_debt/downloads/book/Statistical_annex.pdf; and International Monetary Fund (2019), IMF WEO October 2019 database.

publication of tax exemptions and abatements, along with measures to offset their impact; barred public institutions from lending to any of their shareholders; and prohibited bank lending to any state that exceeded debt or deficit ceilings set by the Brazilian Senate or that was in default to any creditor. Other provisions established procedures to ensure transparency and promote compliance by publishing lists of government units violating the law and establishing other sanctions. The law provides for certain contingencies but requires that action be taken to correct budgetary overruns within a year.[33]

The FRL appeared to have affected Brazil's state governments most. According to one study, the consolidated balance of Brazil's state governments moved from repeated deficits during the period 1993–1999 to consistent surpluses averaging 4% of GDP from 2000 to 2007.[34] Provisions in the FRL allowed the federal government to impose tight constraints on the states, limiting their borrowing and forcing them to comply with budget limits. However, the federal government also contributed to the improved fiscal outcome. Much of the reform involved raising contributions for various social programs funded mainly at the federal level, including pensions and health insurance. Combined federal, state, and local revenues rose by more than 5% of GDP between 1999 and 2005. Moreover, many special allowances were removed from federal income and profit taxes, allowing a cut in tax rates.[35]

The Global Financial Crisis, which hit Brazil late in 2008, led the govern- ment to introduce stimulus measures in 2009. However, rapid recovery enabled Brazil to scale back spending in 2010.[36] Fiscal

---

[33] See Melo, M. *et al.* (2010), "The Political Economy of Fiscal Reform in Brazil: The Rationale for the Suboptimal Equilibrium," Inter-American Development Bank Working Paper No. 117 (Washington, February), Annex No. 6, p. 75, http://www.iadb.org/research/pub_desc.cfm?pub_id=IDB-WP-117.

[34] *Id.*, pp. 6–7.

[35] *Id.*, pp. 11–13.

[36] International Monetary Fund (2010), "IMF Executive Board Concludes 2010 Article IV Consultation with Brazil," Press Information Notice No. 10/111 (Washington, August), http://www.imf.org/external/np/sec/pn/2010/pn10111.htm.

performance improved through 2013, with the general government budget deficit narrowing to 3.0% of GDP. However, the deficit subsequently widened to 6.0% in 2014 and 10.3% in 2015, with some improvement to about 7% in subsequent years.[37] With gross debt of the nonfinancial public sector reaching 89.5% of GDP at the end of 2019, Brazil faces continued fiscal challenges.

15.7.5. Canada

Canada is one of several advanced economies that has implemented major fiscal reforms since 1990 to address burgeoning public debt levels. Unlike New Zealand and Australia, it did so without enacting a fiscal responsibility law. In the early 1990s, Canada faced severe fiscal problems. As shown in Table 15.5, during 1992–1994, budget deficits for the entire government sector averaged more than 8% of GDP, and net public debt exceeded 67% of GDP by 1995.

In 1995, the Canadian government introduced significant fiscal reforms to address the situation. Because Canadian revenue levels were already relatively high, averaging more than 40% of GDP, the authorities decided to focus on cutting expenditure. Between 1995 and 2000, government expenditure fell by more than 7 percentage points of GDP, while revenues remained in the range of 43–44% of GDP. The overall balance for the general government sector moved from a deficit of more than 5% of GDP in 1995 to budget balance in 1997. By 2000, the balance recorded a surplus of nearly 3% of GDP. The improved fiscal position, together with resumed economic growth, reduced the net public debt-to-GDP ratio from nearly 68% in 1995 to about 44% at the end of 2000.

From 2001 to 2008, the Canadian government undertook reforms to reduce the tax burden, lowering revenue collections from 44% to 39% of GDP. To maintain a sound fiscal position, expenditures were further reduced, and the broad government sector recorded surpluses

---

[37] International Monetary Fund (2020), *Fiscal Monitor, April 2020*, Table A15.

Table 15.5. Canada: Key fiscal indicators (in percent of GDP).

	Revenue	Expenditure	Overall balance	Net public debt
1992	43.3	52.5	−9.2	58.1
1993	42.5	51.5	−8.9	62.9
1994	42.1	49.0	−6.9	66.1
1995	42.2	47.7	−5.5	67.6
1996	42.8	45.9	−3.1	67.3
1997	43.5	43.5	0.0	63.3
1998	43.5	43.4	0.1	59.1
1999	43.4	41.8	1.7	52.4
2000	43.2	40.6	2.6	43.8
2001	41.6	41.1	0.5	41.4
2002	40.2	40.4	−0.2	39.2
2003	40.1	40.3	−0.1	36.9
2004	39.9	39.1	0.8	32.4
2005	40.1	38.5	1.6	28.5
2006	40.5	38.7	1.8	25.7
2007	40.3	38.5	1.8	22.2
2008	39.0	38.8	0.2	18.8
2009	39.5	43.4	−3.9	24.7
2010	38.3	43.1	−4.7	27.1
2011	38.3	41.6	−3.3	27.6
2012	38.4	40.9	−2.5	29.0
2013	38.5	40.0	−1.5	29.8
2014	38.5	38.4	0.2	28.6
2015	40.0	40.0	−0.1	28.5
2016	40.1	40.6	−0.4	28.8
2017	39.9	40.3	−0.3	27.6
2018	40.3	40.7	−0.4	26.8
2019	40.8	41.2	−0.4	25.9

Source: IMF, World Economic Outlook Database, April 2020.

in six of the eight years and deficits of only 0.1% of GDP in the other two. The strong fiscal performance reduced the ratio of net public debt-to-GDP to about 22% at the end of 2008. To counteract the effects of the Global Financial Crisis, Canada temporarily boosted expenditures in 2009 and 2010, raising net public debt to nearly 28% of GDP at the end of 2011. Nevertheless, Canada's many years of fiscal restraint enabled it to implement stimulus with little risk to fiscal sustainability, and debt and deficits remained low through the end of 2019.

The particular economic and political circumstances facing Canada encouraged the implementation of fiscal reforms. Economic growth was low at the start of the decade, with real GDP falling by 2.1% in 1991 and rising by only 0.9% in 1992 and 2.3% the following year. In addition, large public deficits and a public debt-to-GDP ratio approaching 70% put pressure on the Canadian dollar, particularly following the emergence of currency crisis in Mexico. Between March 1993 and the end of December 1994, the Canadian dollar depreciated by more than 10%, from about Can$1 = US$0.80 to less than Can$1 = US$0.71.[38] These developments, and recognition that expansionary fiscal policy was not restoring growth, encouraged the government to reorient fiscal policy.

The political situation also favored reform. The government elected in 1993 felt pressure to cut the budget, because large deficits and poor economic performance had contributed to the defeat of the previous government. Moreover, the main opposition party also advocated fiscal restraint. Because a left-of-center party was in charge, the government was thought more likely to implement adjustment in a "fair" way than if a more conservative government were in power.[39] These circumstances enabled the government to undertake a serious review of government programs and cut spending generally while preserving key safety net programs. Following the review, foreign aid and subsidies for agriculture and transport were sharply reduced, while other categories of spending were preserved or increased. For example, assistance for the elderly rose by more than 15%.[40]

Once surpluses emerged and the economy began to revive, the government made achieving surpluses, particularly at the federal level, a priority. Strong economic growth during the last half of the 1990s also helped. Between 1995 and 2000, real GDP growth averaged 3.9% a year, partly because of the booming US economy and the favorable

---

[38] Data from Bank of Canada, http://www.bankofcanada.ca/cgi-bin/famecgi_fdps.

[39] Lewis, T. (2003), *In the Long Run We're All Dead: The Canadian Turn to Fiscal Restraint* (Vancouver: UBC Press), Ch. 8.

[40] Halpern, D. and J. Myers (2009), "Think Tank: A Model of Brutality Britain can Build On," *Sunday Times*, May 3, http://www.timesonline.co.uk/tol/comment/article6210977.ece.

results of the North American Free Trade Agreement (NAFTA). Even after 2000, the Liberal-led Canadian government continued to pursue fiscal surpluses, partly as a way of promoting Canadian productivity, and Canada earned plaudits from the IMF and other international organizations.[41]

15.7.6. *United States*

Passage of the US Tax Reform Act of 1986 (TRA86), Public Law 99–514, provides an example of how the confluence of interests between normally opposed political leaders can yield economic reform. TRA86 began as a conventional tax bill for the United States. Particularly in the US Senate, many special interest groups proposed, and tentatively received, benefits in the form of additional allowances and other tax breaks. At one point, the bill, which in the US House had favored simplification and base-broadening, threatened to make the US tax code even more riddled with special interest provisions.

After several weeks of this activity, the then head of the Senate Finance Committee, Senator Robert Packwood, stepped back from the process and decided that something entirely different was needed. Heeding suggestions from Democratic Senator Bill Bradley, who along with Representative Dick Gephardt and leading public finance economists of the day had championed eliminating many special interest provisions, Packwood adopted a new strategy. Under his direction, the bill was rewritten to broaden the tax base so that tax rates could be cut while keeping tax revenues and the distribution of the tax burden across different income groups largely unchanged.[42] This new approach attracted support from then President Reagan, who strongly supported lowering tax rates. It also reflected public opinion, which had come to consider the existing tax code especially unfair, as a result of special interest provisions. By combining base broadening with rate

---

[41]For more on Canada's fiscal reforms, see Mauro, P. ed. (2011), *Chipping Away at Public Debt* (New York: Wiley), ch. 1. A version of the chapter appears online at https://media.wiley.com/product_data/excerpt/83/11180433/1118043383-20.pdf.

[42]Birnbaum, J. H., and A. S. Murray (1987), *Showdown at Gucci Gulch* (New York: Random House).

reductions and broad distributional neutrality, the new law succeeded in addressing the concerns of many different legislative actors.[43] The result was a reworking of the US income tax, one of the few such reform bills to have been enacted in recent years.

The final version of the law lowered the top marginal tax rate from 50% to 28%, while raising the lowest rate from 11% to 15% — unique in the history of the US income tax. In addition, capital gains were now treated in the same way as ordinary (e.g., wage and salary) income. The law also eliminated the deductibility of interest on consumer loans (other than for housing) and state and local sales taxes, while raising the personal exemption and standard deduction (which helped lower income taxpayers.)

TRA86 also increased incentives favoring investment in owner-occupied housing relative to rental housing by increasing the home mortgage interest deduction. The imputed income an owner receives from an investment in owner-occupied housing has always escaped taxation in the US federal tax code, but TRA86 changed the treatment of imputed rent, local property taxes, and mortgage interest payments to favor homeownership, while phasing out many investment incentives for rental housing. Because these changes could have decreased the supply of housing accessible to low-income households, who tend more to rent than own homes, a low-income housing tax credit was added to provide some balance and encourage investment in multifamily housing for the poor.

By removing tax shelters, especially for real estate investments, TRA86 significantly reduced the value of many such investments, which had been held more for their tax-advantaged status than for their inherent profitability. TRA86 thus contributed to the end of the real estate boom of the early to mid-1980s, and, by helping lower property prices, to the US Savings and Loan crisis. However, most economists consider the net long-term effect of eliminating tax shelters and other

---

[43]Weiss, R. D. (2006), "How Did the Tax Reform Act of 1986 Attract So Much Support?" Testimony before the U.S. Senate Finance Committee, pp. 6–7, http://finance.senate.gov/.

distortions to have been positive, by redirecting assets toward the most inherently profitable investments.

Tax legislation since TRA86 has undone many of the law's accomplishments. The political attractiveness of using the tax code to provide benefits has led to a proliferation of new tax incentives favoring a wide array of objectives, from subsidizing adoption, university enrollment, and retirement saving to the production of ethanol. Despite calls for tax simplification, competing objectives have led to a more complex tax code. Thus, it may take an even broader goal, such as promoting US competitiveness, to persuade the US Congress and President to agree on legislation to again simplify the tax code as a way of reducing tax rates. In 2010, several of the proposals for long-term budget reform of the United States included such proposals. For example, the National Commission on Fiscal Responsibility and Reform offered proposals that would reduce marginal tax rates and the US corporate tax rate by phasing out many tax allowances and exclusions.[44] The Bipartisan Policy Center's Deficit Task Force also recommended tax reform as part of its long-term program to reduce the US federal budget deficit.[45] Neither of these proposals was ultimately implemented. As of 2020, the United States continued to face significant public debt problems.[46]

15.8. Conclusions

Population aging and the need to restore public debt ratios to more sustainable levels will create pressures for fiscal reform, particularly in advanced economies. The experiences of countries at different income levels show that governments seeking fiscal adjustment have many options, both to reduce deficits and make fiscal policy more supportive of economic growth. On the revenue side, governments can consider reforms that broaden the tax base, to allow lower tax rates with no loss in revenues. Adopting a VAT, for countries that do not have one,

---

[44] See National Commission on Fiscal Responsibility and Reform (2010), *op. cit.*, pp. 28–35.

[45] See Bipartisan Policy Center, Deficit Reduction Task Force (2010), *op. cit.*, pp. 31–45.

[46] See, e.g., Congressional Budget Office (2020), *Federal Debt: A Primer*, https://www.cbo.gov/system/files/2020-03/56165-CBO-debt-primer.pdf.

and scaling back the use of multiple rates in countries that already have VATs, can raise revenues in a way less antagonistic to growth than a rise in personal or corporate income taxes. Adjusting fees and charges and strengthening tax administration can also help. Although expenditure cuts have tended to be more durable in advanced economies, in emerging market and developing countries with relatively low ratios of revenue-to-GDP, revenue-raising measures can be a useful component of a broader reform package.

On the expenditure side, research shows that cuts in the government wage bill, subsidies, and transfers have generally proved more sustainable than cuts in capital expenditure. Accordingly, governments seeking reform may want to consider measures to rationalize government hiring, target subsidies more effectively on the intended beneficiaries, and limit entitlement programs. Governments can also curb spending by improving expenditure management, through measures such as eliminating off-budget outlays and curbing quasi-fiscal expenditures.

Experience shows that countries often implement reform programs in response to crises, political change, or when many political actors stand to benefit. By comparison, programs fail when they lack political ownership, face strong opposition, or when governments lack the technical ability or support to implement them. Case studies show that reform programs have succeeded in countries at a variety of income levels. Favorable shocks, such as high oil prices, have helped countries such as Kazakhstan and Russia sustain reforms. In others, such as Brazil and Canada, making success a priority has proved important. Reforms can be fragile, however, particularly in countries susceptible to adverse political and economic shocks, such as Pakistan, or where political and institutional pressures can easily overwhelm forces promoting reform, as in India and the United States. This may explain why many countries undertake reform only when it seems unavoidable. Thus, the realization that current fiscal positions are unsustainable may provide the impetus for countries facing unfavorable demographic trends to implement serious fiscal reform.

Glossary

Accelerated depreciation: Under an income or profit tax, the ability to claim depreciation expenses at a rate faster than the true rate of depreciation for an asset.

Acute care: Health care provided in response to illness or injury.

Addition approach: Value added tax (VAT) in which tax is based on the value of all incomes paid by the taxpayer.

Adverse selection: The situation where imperfect information about potential customers enables those needing insurance to apply disproportionately for coverage, thereby raising costs.

Aggregate demand: The total demand for goods and services in an economy.

Allocation: In public finance, the provision of goods and services by government.

Arrears: Spending for which government is late in paying; can also apply to overdue tax obligations.

Asset exchange: An exchange of assets between a government and a financial institution that typically involves providing government debt in return for impaired financial assets.

Asset management company: A public entity designed to recapitalize financial institutions by purchasing their impaired assets and, where possible, arranging for their repayment or resolution.

Automatic stabilizers: Tax revenues and certain expenditure programs such as unemployment benefits, which automatically adjust to the level of the economy; revenues contract and spending rises when the economy weakens, while revenues expand and spending contracts when the economy strengthens.

Bank financing: Budget financing provided by commercial banks.

Benefit principle: The idea that those benefitting from a public good or service should finance it.

Block grants: Transfers by one level of government to another that can be used for any purpose within a broad functional area such as health or education spending.

Bond financing: Budget financing provided by selling bonds and other securities.

Budget balance: The difference between government (budgetary) revenue and expenditure.

Budget financing: The amount of new debt issued by the government to cover the shortfall of revenue from expenditure. Budget financing is positive if the budget is in deficit and negative if it is in surplus.

Buoyancy/tax buoyancy: The percent change in actual revenues divided by the percent change in the observed tax base, without any adjustment for changes in tax law or administration.

Capital expenditure: Spending for goods and services presumed to last more than a year; includes outlays for development projects and building military installations, but not other military spending.

Capital gains: Rise in the value of assets such as housing, corporate stock (equity), and bonds.

Central bank financing: Budget financing provided by a country's monetary authority (central bank).

Consolidated public sector: The combined activity of all levels of government and all state enterprises.

Consumer subsidies: Subsidies provided to consumers (e.g., spending that lowers the cost of food).

Contingent expenditures: Spending that can arise if a possible event occurs (e.g., default on a guarantee).

Conventional (cash) budget balance: Cash revenues and grants less expenditures paid in cash.

Countercyclical policy: Policy that moves contrary to the business cycle, thus promoting stabilization.

Credibility: The confidence of financial markets that a government will act as claimed.

Credit invoice approach: Value added tax (VAT) in which tax for each party in the production chain is based on the volume of sales, less tax paid on inputs for which the party has receipts proving tax paid.

Current expenditure: Government spending for items presumed to be used within a year; includes wages and salaries, most other purchases, most military outlays, subsidies, transfers, and interest.

Customs (import) duty: Tax levied on imports.

Debt-stabilizing primary balance: The primary balance that leaves the public debt-to-GDP ratio constant.

Decreasing average costs: A condition in which firms face a limited fixed cost and the marginal cost of serving an additional customer is very low, causing the average cost per customer to decline as the number of customers increases. In this situation, supply by a single producer (monopoly) is the most efficient form of production.

Dedicated revenue source: Tax or other revenue used to fund a specific program or level of government.

Demographic risk: Risk to the funding of public pension programs from population aging, which reduces the ratio of contributors to beneficiaries in a pay-as-you-go pension program.

Direct sale: Sale of state enterprise directly to a specific private party without using an auction or tender.

Direct taxes: Taxes on income, profits, and property, which fall directly on a taxpayer's income or assets.

Discretionary expenditures: Spending that the legislature can set freely during each fiscal period.

Distribution: Government policies to achieve a more acceptable distribution of income and wealth.

Divestiture: Transferring ownership of a state enterprise from government to a private party.

Domestic financing: Budget financing from domestic sources (banks and other purchasers of debt).

Double taxation of dividends: Dividends are paid from after-tax company income and then subject to personal (or corporate) income tax when received by a taxpayer.

Double taxation of savings: An income tax imposes tax both on the income that gives rise to savings and on the earnings that result from those savings.

Drawing down official foreign exchange reserves: Using the country's official reserves to finance a budget deficit, for example, by using reserves of the central bank to finance development projects.

Earmarking: Dedicating a particular revenue source to funding a specific type of expenditure.

Economic classification of expenditures: Classification of government spending based on economic criteria; aggregates spending across different programs into current outlays (for wages and salaries, other purchases, subsidies and transfers, and interest), capital outlays (development), and net lending.

Effective tax rate: The ratio of actual government receipts from a tax to the relevant tax base.

Elastic revenue system: A revenue system in which total revenues grow at least as fast as GDP.

Enterprise restructuring: Reforming or reorganizing an enterprise while maintaining public ownership.

Entitlement: Automatic benefit to which a person is entitled because of specific characteristics.

Estimated (advance) tax payments: Tax payments made in advance, toward total tax due for the year.

Excise tax: Special sales tax imposed on specific products, most often petroleum, alcohol, and tobacco.

Expenditure productivity: The ratio of benefits from a particular expenditure to the amount of spending.

Expenditures: Spending undertaken by a government.

Externalities: Benefits or costs accruing to those neither producing nor consuming a good or service.

Fiscal decentralization: Dispersing the responsibility for delivering public services among multiple institutions and levels of government.

Fiscal dominance: The condition when fiscal deficits and the resulting need for financing effectively control the direction of monetary policy.

Fiscal federalism: Using multiple levels of government to deliver public services.

Fiscal policy: The use of the government budget to promote macroeconomic objectives.

Fiscal responsibility law: A law specifying the rules and procedures for the accountability, transparency, and stability of government budgeting.

Fiscal rules: Laws and constitutional provisions that impose quantitative limits on specific budgetary aggregates, such as the overall budget balance or the ratio of government debt to GDP, with the aim of strengthening fiscal discipline.

Fiscal space: The availability of budget resources to finance worthwhile activities without prejudicing the government's financial position.

Fiscal sustainability: The ability of government to maintain the current fiscal policy without threat of a crisis; usually implies a condition in which the ratio of public debt to GDP does not appear to rise without limit.

Fiscal vulnerability: Structural weaknesses in revenue or expenditure policy and administration.

Five-pillar approach: A proposal by World Bank economists to provide income security to the elderly using five different elements, including an initial, non-contributory element to prevent poverty; a mandatory, publicly managed plan to replace a certain percentage of prior earnings; mandatory, individual retirement accounts; voluntary, individual savings accounts; and other measures, including support from family members.

Foreign (external) financing: Budget financing provided by foreign institutions and persons.

Free rider: Someone able to benefit from a public good or service without paying for it. The "free rider" problem arises because of the difficulty of excluding those who do not pay from access to public goods.

Fully funded systems: Pension programs in which benefits are fully funded by participants' own contributions and earnings on the balances in individual accounts.

Functional classification of expenditures: Classification of government spending by program category (e.g., health, education, administration).

General purpose grants: Transfers by one level of government to another that can be used for any purpose.

Globalization: Growing connectivity and interdependence of markets and economic activity worldwide.

Government savings (current balance): Cash revenues and grants less current expenditure paid in cash.

Grants: Non-repayable transfers to government, usually provided by foreign countries or organizations.

Hard budget constraint: Enterprises cannot count on transfers, subsidies, or loans to cover losses.

Horizontal equity: Condition in which taxpayers in similar circumstances pay similar rates of tax.

Impaired (troubled) assets: Loans and other financial assets held by a bank that are not being serviced as scheduled or whose market value is significantly below face value.

Incidence of a tax: The amount of tax obligations that a party actually bears and cannot shift onto others.

Indirect taxes: Taxes levied on a taxpayer's use of income or assets, such as sales and excise taxes.

Information failures: Market failures resulting from the lack of full and equivalent information among buyers and sellers for a good or service.

Infrastructure: Public facilities for transport, power, water and sewerage, and the like.

Intergenerational transfers: Transfers from one generation to another, often resulting from social insurance programs benefiting the elderly but funded by younger, current workers.

Investment risk: Risk of a loss in market value of the assets in which pension funds are invested.

Liquidity support: Providing loans, subsidies, or transfers to enable financial institutions to meet the current financial obligations, including payments to depositors.

Liquidity/illiquidity: The ability (inability) of government to meet the current debt service obligations.

Lock-in effect: When capital gains are taxed only when realized (i.e., when assets are sold), the incentive for taxpayers to avoid selling assets so as not to pay capital gains tax.

Lumpiness: The high cost of many forms of acute health care, which creates a demand for insurance to reduce the cost at the time of incidence.

Management contract: A contract authorizing individuals or a firm to manage a state enterprise.

Management risk: Risk that pension benefits may be compromised from poor or inefficient management.

Management/employee buyout: Sale of a state enterprise to its managers or employees.

Mandatory expenditures: Spending a government is required to make, because of continuing programs; also includes interest payments.

Marginal tax rate: Rate of tax on the taxpayer's last (highest) portion of income or profit.

Marriage penalty: In a progressive income tax, the additional tax a married couple pays when their combined income pushes them into a higher marginal tax bracket, compared to what they would pay if they could file as single taxpayers.

Mass privatization: Transferring ownership of a large percentage of state enterprises by distributing vouchers to the populace that can be used to obtain shares in privatized firms.

Matching grants: Transfers by one level of government to another that require the receiving government to contribute a stipulated percentage of total program expenses.

Medium-term budgeting framework: A document that establishes medium-term objectives for fiscal policy and uses these to guide annual budgets and the choice of specific spending programs.

Merit goods: Goods whose benefits are thought to exceed their market price; usually applied to cultural activities considered to have positive externalities.

Minimum tax liability threshold: The minimum level of income or profit at which a taxpayer is required to pay tax.

Minimum tax: A tax usually imposed on small taxpayers to replace filing and paying a regular tax.

Mobile tax base: A tax base that can change location to escape taxation; tax bases differ in their mobility.

Moral hazard: Incentives created by insurance for those covered to engage in riskier behavior.

Natural monopolies: Industries in which having a single supplier is the most efficient form of production, generally because of decreasing average costs.

Net lending/borrowing (2001 GFS): Net operating balance minus net capital investment.

Net lending: Loans extended by government for public purposes, less repayments of principal received from past loans of this type.

Net operating balance (2001 GFS): Government revenues less expenses (outlays excluding net lending and the purchase of non-financial assets).

Neutrality (of a tax): Condition in which a particular tax does not favor specific types of transactions.

Non-bank financing: Budget financing provided by persons and by institutions other than banks.

Non-cash income: Income paid in kind, rather than in cash; for example, free company parking or employer payments toward health insurance.

Non-debt-creating inflows: Supplementary government revenues, such as privatization proceeds, that do not create public debt.

Non-discretionary expenditure: Spending that the legislature cannot freely set, because of legal obligations; includes interest payments.

Non-tax revenue: Revenues other than taxes; typically includes fees, charges, and state enterprise profits.

Off-budget expenditures: Spending by government that takes place outside the official budget.

Operational balance: Cash revenues and grants less that part of cash expenditures excluding the real component of interest payments (only that part of interest payments representing inflation is excluded).

Partially funded programs: Pension programs in which past contributions in excess of past benefits supplement financing for pensioners from current contributors.

Pay-as-you-go-(PAYG) programs: Pension programs in which contributions from those currently working fund benefits for current retirees.

Performance contract: A contract, typically with current managers, requiring that certain performance standards be met.

Political risk: Risk that political leaders may misappropriate funds from a public pension program.

Presumptive levy (tax): Tax calculated on presumed income or receipts, based on the assumed levels of output and observed product prices.

Preventive care: Health care provided in advance of illness or injury to reduce the likelihood of future medical problems and the associated need for health care services; includes periodic medical check-ups and routine dental examinations and cleaning.

Primary (fiscal) balance: Cash revenues and grants less that part of cash expenditures excluding interest.

Principal-agent problem: Situation in which agents act to benefit themselves, rather than the party (the principal) they are supposed to represent.

Privatization: Sale or transfer of shares in a public enterprise to a private party.

Pro-cyclical policy: Policy that moves in the same direction as the business cycle, with government expenditure typically rising as an economy expands and slowing as an economy contracts.

Producer subsidies: Subsidies provided to producers (e.g., spending that lowers the cost of fertilizer).

Program grants: Transfers by one level of government to another to fund specific programs.

Progressive tax: Condition in which the marginal tax rate rises with a taxpayer's income.

Proportional tax: Condition in which taxpayers at all income levels face the same marginal tax rate.

Proxy tax base: A measurable approximation to the true legal base on which a tax is levied.

Public debt: The total amount of public sector securities outstanding. Government debt is the total of government securities outstanding. Public debt includes the debt outstanding of state (public) enterprises.

Public debt sustainability: The ability of government to service and, in principle, eventually repay public debt; in practice, a condition in which the ratio of public debt to GDP does not rise without limit.

Public goods: Goods and services to which everyone has access if anyone does, and for which one person's consumption does not reduce the amount available for others to consume.

Public pension programs: Government-managed or -supervised programs providing a pension to qualifying citizens or residents.

Public sale: Sale of state enterprise shares through auction or publicly announced tender.

Public sector borrowing requirement: The combined deficit of the government sector and all state (public) enterprises.

Public-private partnership: Use of a privately organized entity to fund the construction of a public project or service, often with the entity receiving fees or income in return for delivering the service.

Quasi-fiscal expenditure: Outlays similar to government spending that take place outside the regular budget, by a non-governmental public institution.

Recapitalizing institutions: Providing loans or transfers to financial institutions to increase their capital.

Regressive tax: Condition in which the marginal tax rate falls with a taxpayer's income, causing the burden of a tax to fall more heavily on lower income households.

Revenue elasticity: Percent change in revenue for each 1 percent change in the tax base (or GDP).

Revenue sharing: Required distribution to one level of government of part of the revenue collected by another level of government.

Revenue structure: The composition of revenues.

Revenues: All government receipts, excluding grants, that need not be repaid.

Sales tax: Tax levied on a company's sales; most often applied to retail sales.

Social assistance programs: Similar to social insurance; often include programs to raise incomes to a minimum level.

Social insurance: An insurance program mandated or carried out by government to provide assistance to vulnerable groups in the population, which can include the elderly, disabled, unemployed, and poor.

Social safety net: The set of government policies designed to provide income support to the unemployed, disabled, and elderly, to prevent or alleviate poverty.

Soft budget constraint: Ready availability of government transfers, subsidies, and bank loans to cover losses at state enterprises.

Solvency/insolvency: The ability (inability), in principle, of government eventually to repay public debt.

Stabilization: The use of monetary, fiscal, and exchange rate policy to moderate business cycles, with the goal of achieving low inflation and high employment.

State (public) enterprises: Government-owned entities that operate like independent firms or institutions, with their own mandates, revenues, and budgets.

State-owned (public) enterprises: Government-owned entities that operate outside the state budget.

Stress testing: Assessing the effect of shocks to key macroeconomic parameters, such as the inflation or GDP growth rate, on the ratio of public debt to GDP.

Subsidies: Government benefits that reduce the price of a good or service.

Subtraction approach: Value added tax (VAT) in which each party's tax is based on the difference between receipts and the value of allowed expenses.

Supportive legal framework: A legal environment that encourages investment by protecting property rights, including those of minority shareholders, and providing ready access to impartial courts.

Tanzi diagnostic test: A set of eight questions designed to measure the quality of tax administration.

Targeting: Directing program benefits toward a specific group of persons or institutions.

Tax allowance: A tax provision that reduces tax liability for a specific type of income or expenditure.

Tax elasticity: The "built-in" responsiveness of revenue to a change in the relevant tax base, typically measured as a percent change in revenue from a 1 percent change in the relevant tax base, adjusted to reflect a consistent set of tax laws and administration over time.

Tax expenditure: Special benefit provided to persons, households, or firms through the tax code, rather than legislated expenditure; is equivalent to budgetary expenditure but does not appear in the budget.

Tax harmonization: Reconciling the tax provisions of different jurisdictions to provide similar tax treatment to specific transactions or taxpayers.

Tax haven: A country or other jurisdiction offering unusually low tax rates.

Tax holiday: A provision that exempts a company or investor from all tax obligations for a specified time.

Tax incentive: A tax provision encouraging behavior by offering a special deduction, credit, or exemption.

Tax revenue: Compulsory and unrequited receipts collected by government for public purposes.

Tax shifting: A firm's ability to shift the burden of a corporate income (profit) tax to consumers (forward shifting) or employees (backward shifting).

Transfer payments: Government payments to individuals or institutions with specified characteristics.

Transfer pricing: Setting prices for inputs produced in one country and used for production in another so as to minimize a company's national or global tax liability.

Treasury: Government office, typically located in a finance ministry, providing centralized payments for all government activities.

Turnover tax: A tax on total company receipts.

Unproductive expenditure: Government spending whose benefits are low relative to the size of outlays.

User fee: Charge levied for the use of a public good or service, such as admission to a national park.

Value-added tax (VAT): Tax levied separately on the value added (revenues less production expenses) at each stage of the production, distribution, and retail sale of a good or service.

Vertical equity: Condition in which a taxpayer's effective tax rate rises with income.

Wagner's Law: The ratio of public expenditure to GDP should rise as an industrial economy develops.

Windfall gains and losses: Gains or losses in income or profit, usually from jumps in commodity prices.

Withholding (at source): When tax is withheld before paying a taxpayer income, interest or profit earned.

Bibliography

Abeysinghe, T. (2009), "Singapore's Health Care System," Lecture delivered at 2009 Singapore Economic Policy Conference.

Afonso, A. *et al.* (2008), "Fiscal Policy Responsiveness, Persistence, and Discretion," Working Paper No. 954, European Central Bank (October), http://www.ecb. europa.eu/pub/pdf/scpwps/ecbwp954.pdf.

Akerlof, G. A. (1970), "The market for 'lemons': Quality uncertainty and the market mechanism," *Quarterly Journal of Economics* Vol. 84, no. 3, 488–500.

Akerlof, G. A., and R. J. Shiller (2015), *Phishing for Phools* (Princeton, NJ: Princeton University Press).

Akitoby, B. *et al.* (2004), "Cyclical and Long-Term Behavior of Government Expenditures in Developing Countries," IMF Working Paper No. 04/202 (Washington: International Monetary Fund, October), http://www.imf.org/external/pubs/ ft/wp/2004/wp04202.pdf.

Alesina, A. and G. Tabellini (2005). "Why is fiscal policy often pro- cyclical?" Harvard Institute for Economic Research Discussion Paper No. 2090 (August), http://www.cesifo-group.de/portal/page/portal/DocBase_Content/WP/WP -CESifo_Working_Papers/wp-cesifo-2005/wp-cesifo-2005-10/cesifo1_wp155 6.pdf.

Alesina, A., and R. Perotti (1996), "Fiscal Adjustments in OECD Coun- tries: Composition and Macroeconomic Effects," NBER Working Paper No. 5730 (Cambridge, MA: National Bureau of Economic Research), http://www. j-bradford-delong.net/movable_type/refs/Mozilla_Scrapbook/w5730.pdf.

Alesina, A., and R. Perotti (1997), "Fiscal adjustments in OECD countries: Composition and macroeconomic effects," *International Monetary Fund Staff Papers*, Vol. 44, pp. 210–248.

Alesina, Alberto and Silvia Ardanga (1998), "Tales of fiscal adjustments," *Economic Policy*, Vol. 27 (October).

Alm, J. and M. A. Khan (2008), "Assessing Enterprise Taxation and the Investment Climate in Pakistan," International Studies Program, Working Paper No. 08-10 (Atlanta: Georgia State University), http://aysps.gsu.edu/isp/files/ ispwp0810(2).pdf.

American Road and Transportation Builders Association (2019), "2019 Bridge Report," https://artbabridgereport.org/reports/2019-ARTBA-Bridge-Report. pdf.

Andres, J., and R. Domenech (2006), "Fiscal Rules and Macroeconomic Stability," *Hacienda Publica Espanola*, Vol. 176–1, no. 9–41, http://iei.uv.es/docs/wp_ internos/RePEc/pdf/iei_0501.pdf.

Arreaza, A. *et al.* (1998), "Consumption Smoothing Through Fiscal Policy in OECD and EU Countries," NBER Working Paper No. 6372 (Cambridge, MA: National Bureau of Economic Research).

Auerbach, A. (2005), "Who Bears the Corporate Income Tax: A Review of What We Know," paper presented at the NBER Tax Policy and the Economy Conference, http://www.econ.berkeley.edu/auerbach/bearstax.pdf.

Auerbach, A. and W. Gale (2009), "The Economic Crisis and the Fiscal Crisis: 2009 and Beyond," *Tax Notes*, October 5, 2009, pp. 101–130.

Baig, T. *et al.* (2007), "Domestic Petroleum Product Prices and Sub- sidies: Recent Developments and Reform Strategies," Working Paper No. 07/71 (Washington, DC: International Monetary Fund, March), http://www.imf.org/external/pubs/ft/wp/2007/wp0771.pdf.

Baker, B. D. *et al.* (2010), *Is School Funding Fair? A National Report Card* (Rutgers University), http://www.schoolfundingfairness.org/National_Report_Card.pdf.

Baldacci, E. *et al.* (2010), "Restoring Debt Sustainability After Crisis: Implications for the Fiscal Mix," Working Paper No. 10/232 (Washington: International Monetary Fund, October).

Ballard, C. L. *et al.* (1985), "Replacing the Personal Income Tax with a Progressive Consumption Tax," in Ballard, C. L. *et al.* (eds.), *A General Equilibrium Model for Tax Policy Evaluation* (Cambridge, MA: National Bureau of Economic Research), Ch. 9, pp. 171–187.

Bank of Canada (2010), "CAN$/US$ Exchange Rate Lookups," http://www.bankofcanada.ca/cgi-bin/famecgi_fdps.

Barr, N. (2000), "Reforming Pensions — Myths, Truths, and Policy Choices," Working Paper No. 00/139 (Washington: International Monetary Fund), http://www.imf.org/external/pubs/ft/wp/2000/wp00139.pdf.

Barr, N. and P. Diamond (2006), "Economics of pensions," *Oxford Review of Economic Policy*, Vol. 22, no. 1, pp. 15–39, http://eprintsr.lse.ac.uk/2630/1/economics_of_pensions_final.pdf.

Basle Committee on Banking Supervision (1988), *International Convergence of Capital Measurement and Capital Standards*, http://www.bis.org/publ/bcbs04a.pdf.

Bellafiore, R. (2018), "Summary of the Latest Federal Income Tax Dara, 2018 Update," Tax Foundation, Fiscal Fact No. 622 (Washington: November), https://files.taxfoundation.org/20181113134559/Summary-of-the-Latest-Federal-Income-Tax-Data-2018-Update-FF-622.pdf.

Berchick, E. R. *et al.* (2019), *Health Insurance Coverage in the United States: 2018*, U. S. Bureau of Census, Current Population Reports, P60-267 (RV), November, https://www.census.gov/content/dam/Census/library/publications/2019/demo/p60-267.pdf.

Bipartisan Policy Center, Debt Reduction Task Force (2010), *Restoring America's Future* (Washington), http://www.bipartisanpolicy.org/sites/default/files/FINAL%20DRTF%20REPORT%2011.16.10.pdf.

Birnbaum, J. H. and A. S. Murray (1987), *Showdown at Gucci Gulch* (New York: Random House).

Blejer, M. and A. Cheasty (1993), *How to Measure the Fiscal Deficit* (Washington: IMF).

Blum, W. J. and H. Kalven, Jr. (1953), *Uneasy Case for Progressive Taxation* (Chicago: University of Chicago Press).

Blumberg, L. (2009), "Improving Health Insurance Markets and Promoting Competition under Health Care Reform," Committee on Ways and Means, House of Representatives (April 22), http://www.urban.org/uploadedpdf/901246_improving%20healthinsurance.pdf.

Board of Governors of the Federal Reserve System (2019), "What are the Federal Reserve's Objectives in Conducting Monetary Policy?" https://www.federalreserve.gov/faqs/money_12848.htm (March).

Bricker, J. *et al.* (2017), "Changes in U.S. Family Finances from 2013 to 2016: Evidence from the Survey of Consumer Finances," *Federal Reserve Bulletin*, vol. 103, no. 3 (September), https://www.federalreserve.gov/publications/files/scf17.pdf.

Brittain, J. (1971), "Incidence of social security payroll taxes," *American Economic Review*, vol. 61, pp. 110–125, http://profluming.com/Article/UploadFiles/201008/2010081807331083.pdf.

Brondolo, J. *et al.* (2008), "Tax Administration Reform and Fiscal Adjustment: The Case of Indonesia (2001–07)," Working Paper No. 08/129 (Washington: International Monetary Fund), http://www.imf.org/external/pubs/ft/wp/2008/wp08129.pdf.

Business Portal of India (2009), *Taxation: Value Added Tax*, http://business.gov.in/taxation/vat.php.

California Department of Tax and Fee Administration, "California City & County Sales and Use Tax Rates," https://www.cdtfa.ca.gov/taxes-and-fees/sales-use-tax-rates.htm.

Calomiris, C. W. (1989), "Deposit insurance: Lessons from the record," *Economic Perspectives* (May), Federal Reserve Bank of Chicago, pp. 10–30.

Carroll, A. E. and A. Frakt (2017), "The Best Health Care System in the World: Which One Would You Pick?" *New York Times*, September 18, https://www.nytimes.com/interactive/2017/09/18/upshot/best-health-care-system-country-bracket.html.

Centers for Disease Control and Prevention, National Center for Health Statistics (2010), *FastStats: Health Insurance Coverage*, http://www.cdc.gov/nchs/fastats/hinsure.htm.

Central Provident Fund Board (2010), "Changes in CPF Minimum Sum, Medisave Minimum Sum and Medisave Contribution Ceiling from 1 July 2010," May 24, http://mycpf.cpf.gov.sg/CPF/News/News-Release/N_14May2010.htm.

Central Provident Fund Board (2010), "General Information," http://mycpf.cpf.gov.sg/Members/Gen-Info/mbr-Gen-info.htm.

Central Provident Fund Board (2010), "Interest Rates," http://mycpf.cpf.gov.sg/Members/Gen-Info/Int-Rates/Int-Rates.htm.

Central Provident Fund Board (2019), "CPF Statistics — Balances," https://www.cpf.gov.sg/Members/AboutUs/about-us-info/cpf-statistics.

Central Provident Fund Board (2019), "Interest Rates," https://www.cpf.gov.sg/Members/AboutUs/about-us-info/cpf-interest-rates.

Chand, S. K. and A. Jaeger (2000), *Aging Populations and Public Pension Schemes*, Occasional Paper 147 (Washington: International Monetary Fund).

Chang, T. (2002), "Econometric test of Wagner's law," *Applied Economics*, vol. 34, pp. 1157–1169.

Cheasty, A. and J. Davis (1996), "Fiscal Transition in Countries of the Former Soviet Union — An Interim Assessment," Working Paper No. 96/61 (Washington: International Monetary Fund, June).

Chew, V. (2009), "First Drawdown of National Reserves," Singapore Infopedia, National Library of Singapore (March 19), http://infopedia.nl.sg/articles/SIP_1489_2009-03-20.html.

Chin, K. K. (2002), "Road Pricing — Singapore's Experience," *Singapore Land Transport Authority*, http://www.imprint-eu.org/public/Papers/IMPRINT3_chin.pdf.

Chudik, A. *et al.* (2015), "Is there a Debt Threshold Effect on Output Growth?" IMF Working Paper No. 15/197 (Washington: International Monetary Fund, September), https://www.imf.org/external/pubs/ft/wp/2015/wp15197.pdf.

Citigroup (2007), "Indonesia Outlook" (May).

Claessens, S. *et al.* eds. (2010), *Financial Sector Taxation — The IMF's Report to the G-20 and Background Material* (Washington: September), http://www.imf.org/external/np/seminars/eng/2010/paris/pdf/090110.pdf.

Coady, D. *et al.* (2019), "Global Fossil Fuel Subsidies Remain Large: An Update Based on Country-Level Estimates," Working Paper No. 19/89 (Washington, DC: International Monetary Fund, May), https://www.imf.org/en/Publications/WP/Issues/2019/05/02/Global-Fossil-Fuel-Subsidies-Remain-Large-An-Update-Based-on-Country-Level-Estimates-46509.

Commission on Fiscal Responsibility and Reform (2010), *Moment of Truth* (Washington), Figure 17, p. 65, http://www.fiscalcommission.gov/sites/?scalcommission.gov/files/documents/TheMomentofTruth12_1_2010.pdf.

Commission on Growth and Development (2008), "Highlights of the Growth Report" (Washington: World Bank), http://www.growthcommission.org/storage/cgdev/documents/Report/ReportHighlights.pdf.

Commission on Growth and Development (2008), *Growth Report* (Washington: World Bank), http://cgd.s3.amazonaws.com/GrowthReportComplete.pdf.

Committee for a Responsible Federal Budget (2019), "Cory Booker's 'Baby Bonds' Plan," December, http://www.crfb.org/blogs/cory-bookers-baby-bonds-plan.

Congressional Budget Office (1982), *Reducing the Federal Budget: Strategies and Examples, Fiscal Years 1982–1986* (Washington: U.S. Government Printing Office), http://www.cbo.gov/doc.cfm?index=11171.

Congressional Budget Office (1997), *Economic Effects of Comprehensive Tax Reform* (Washington: July), http://www.cbo.gov/ftpdocs/0xx/doc36/taxrefor.pdf.

Congressional Budget Office (2008), *Technological Change and the Growth of Health Care Spending*, http://www.cbo.gov/ftpdocs/89xx/doc8947/01-31-TechHealth.pdf.

Congressional Budget Office (2019), *2019 Long-Term Budget Outlook*, June, https://www.cbo.gov/publication/55331.

Congressional Budget Office (2019), *Updated Budget Projections: 2019–2029*, May, https://www.cbo.gov/system/files/2019-05/55151-budget_update_0.pdf.

Congressional Budget Office (2019), *Federal Investment, 1962–2018*, https://www.cbo.gov/system/files/2019-06/55375-Federal_Investment.pdf.

Congressional Budget Office (2020), *Federal Debt: A Primer*, https://www.cbo.gov/system/files/2020-03/56165-CBO-debt-primer.pdf.

Congressional Budget Office (2020), *2020 Long-Term Budget Outlook*, September, https://www.cbo.gov/publication/56516.

Cottarelli, C. and A. Schaecter (2010), "Long-Term Trends in the Public Finances of the G-7 Economies," Staff Position Note 10/13 (Washington: International Monetary Fund, September), http://www.imf.org/external/pubs/ft/spn/2010/spn1013.pdf.

Davis, J. *et al.* (2000), *Fiscal and Macroeconomic Impact of Privatization*, Occasional Paper 194 (Washington: International Monetary Fund).

Dell'Erba, S. *et al.* (2014), "Medium-Term Fiscal Multipliers during Protracted Recessions," IMF Working Paper No. 14/213 (Washington: December).

Dhasmana, I. (2017), "What is GST, how is it different from now: Decoding the Indirect tax regime," Business Standard, 17 April, https://www.business-standard.com/article/economy-policy/what-is-gst-how-is-it-different-from-now-decoding-the-indirect-tax-regime-117041700033_1.html.

Economist (2010), "Brazil's Bolsa Familia: How to get children out of jobs and into school," *Economist Magazine*, July 29, http://www.economist.com/node/16690887.

Economist (2010), "The President's Deficit Commission: No Cigar," December 20, http://www.economist.com/node/17679788.

Economist (2019), "Chile Tinkers with Its Ground-Breaking Pension System," June 8, https://www.economist.com/the-americas/2019/06/08/chile-tinkers-with-its-ground-breaking-pensions-system.

ED.gov Blog (2010), "International Education Rankings Suggest Reform Can Lift U.S.," http://www.ed.gov/blog/2010/12/international-education-rankings-suggest-reform-can-lift-u-s/.

Eichengreen, B. *et al.* (2005), "The Mystery of Original Sin," in Barry, E. and R. Hausmann (eds.), *Other People's Money: Debt Denomination and Financial Instability in Emerging-Market Economies* (Chicago: University of Chicago Press).

Employees Provident Fund Website (2010), http://www.kwsp.gov.my/index.php?ch=p2members.

Fankhouser, S. (2008), "Utility Payments in Ukraine: Affordability, Subsidies and Arrears," University College, London, Center for the Study of Social Change in Europe, Economics Working Paper No. 87, http://discovery.ucl.ac.uk/17458/1/17458.pdf.

Fatás, A. and I. Mihov (2003), "The case for restricting fiscal policy discretion," *Quarterly Journal of Economics*, vol. 118, pp. 1419–1447.

Feldstein, M. (1980), "Effect of Social Security on Private Savings: The Times Series Evidence," Working Paper No. 0314 (Cambridge, MA: National Bureau of

Economic Research, April), http://papers.ssrn.com/sol3/papers.cfm?abstract_id=247708.

Fernandes, A. L. and P. Santana (2018), "Reforms of Fiscal Relations in Brazil" (OECD, November). https://www.oecd.org/tax/federalism/reforms-of-fiscal-relations-in-brazil.pdf.

Fiorito, R. (1997). "Stylized Facts of Government Finance in the G-7," IMF Working Paper No. 97/142.

Fiscal Affairs Department (2004), *Public–Private Partnerships* (Washington: International Monetary Fund, March), http://www.imf.org/external/np/fad/2004/pifp/eng/031204.pdf.

Fiscal Affairs Department (2009), "State of Public Finances Cross Country Fiscal Monitor: November 2009," Staff Position Note 09/25 (Washington: International Monetary Fund), http://www.imf.org/external/pubs/ft/spn/2009/spn0925.pdf.

Fougère, M. and M. Mérette (1998), "Population Ageing and Economic Growth," Department of Finance, Canada, Working Paper No. 98-03, http://epe.lac-bac.gc.ca/100/200/301/?nance/working_papers-ef/1998/19 98-03/98-03e.pdf.

Fraschini, A. (2006), "Fiscal Federalism in Big Developing Countries: China and India," Working Paper No. 66, Department of Public Policy and Public Choice, University of Eastern Piedmont "Amadeo Avogadro," Alessandria, Italy (January), http://polis.unipmn.it/pubbl/RePEc/uca/ucapdv/fraschini66.pdf.

Frassinelli, M. (2010), "Governor Christie Cancels ARC Tunnel for Second Time," *Newark Star-Ledger*, October 27, http://www.nj.com/news/index.ssf/2010/10/gov_christie_cancels_arc_tunne.html.

Freedman, C. *et al.* (2009), "The Case for Global Fiscal Stimulus," Staff Position Note 09/03 (Washington, DC: International Monetary Fund, March), http://www.imf.org/external/pubs/ft/spn/2009/spn0903.pdf.

Frenkel, J. *et al.* (2011), "Fiscal Policy in Developing Countries: Escape from Procyclicality," VoxEU (June).

Galal, A. *et al.* (1994), *Welfare Consequences of Selling Public Enterprises: An Empirical Analysis* (New York: Oxford University Press).

Gale, W. G. (2019), *Fiscal Therapy* (New York: Oxford University Press).

Galí, J. (1994), "Government size and macroeconomic stability," *European Economic Review*, vol. 38, no. 1, pp. 117–132.

Galí, J. (2005), "Modern perspective of fiscal stabilization policies," *CESifo Economic Studies*, vol. 51, no. 4, 587–599.

Galí, R. and P. Jordi (2003), "Fiscal Policy and Monetary Integration in Europe," *Fiscal Policy*, vol. 18, (October) pp. 533–572.

Gandhi, S. (2010), *Audit the Tax Code: Doing What Works for Tax Expenditures* (Washington: Center for American Progress, April), http://www.american-progress.org/issues/2010/04/pdf/dww_tax_framing_execsumm.pdf.

Geanakoplos, J. *et al.* (1998), "Would a Privatized Social Security System Really Pay a Higher Rate of Return?" Cowles Foundation Working Paper 1002 (New Haven: Yale University), http://cowles.econ.yale.edu/~gean/art/p1002.pdf.

Gershenson, D. and J. Greene (2006), "Fiscal Reforms in the BRO Countries, 1996–2002," *Problems and Perspectives in Management*, vol. 2006, no. 1, pp. 5–21, http://www.businessperspectives.org/journals_free/ppm/2006/PPM_EN_2006_01_Gershenson.pdf.

Government of India (2009), "Financial Performance of Indian Railways," *Economic Survey 2009–10*, Table 2.15, http://indiabudget.nic.in/es2009-10/chapt2010/tab215.pdf.

Government of Pakistan, Finance Division (MTBF Secretariat), "Medium Term Budgetary Framework: Frequently Asked Questions," http://www.mtbf-pakistan.gov.pk/pdf/MTBF%20FAQs-FINAL.pdf.

Government of Singapore (1994), *Competitive Salaries for Competent & Honest Government: Benchmarks for Ministers & Senior Public Officers: White Paper [Cmd. 13 of 1994]*, Singapore: Prime Minister's Office.

Government of Singapore, "GST Offset Package," http://www.gstoffset.gov.sg/Overview.html.

Greene, J. (2018), *Macroeconomic Analysis and Policy: A Systematic Approach* (Singapore: World Scientific).

Grinberg, I. (2009), "Where Credit is Due: Advantages of the Credit-Invoice Method for a Partial Replacement VAT," paper prepared for the American Tax Policy Institute Conference (Washington, DC, February 18–19), http://www.americantaxpolicyinstitute.org/pdf/VAT/Grinberg.pdf.

GuideMeSingapore (2019), "Singapore Corporate Tax Guide," https://www.guidemesingapore.com/business-guides/taxation-and-accounting/corporate-tax/singapore-corporate-tax-guide.

Gupta, S. *et al.* (1999), "Privatization, Social Impact, and Social Safety Nets," Working Paper No. 99/68 (Washington: International Monetary Fund: May), http://www.imf.org/external/pubs/ft/wp/1999/wp9968.pdf.

Gupta, S. *et al.* (2001), "Privatization, labor, and social safety nets," *Journal of Economic Surveys*, vol. 15 (December), pp. 647–670.

Gupta, S. *et la.* (2002a), "The Effectiveness of Government Spending on Health Care and Education in Developing and Transition Economies," *European Journal of Political Economy*, vol. 18, pp. 717–737, http://www.appg-popdevrh.org.

Gupta, S. *et al.* (2002b), "Expenditure Composition, Fiscal Adjustment, and Growth in Low-Income Countries," Working Paper No. 02/77 (Washington: International Monetary Fund, April), p. 27, http://www.imf.org/external/pubs/ft/wp/2002/wp0277.pdf.

Gupta, S. *et al.* (2003), "What Sustains Fiscal Consolidations in Emerging Market Countries?" Working Paper No. 03/224 (Washington: International Monetary Fund, November), http://www.imf.org/external/pubs/ft/wp/2003/wp03224.pdf.

Gupta, S. *et al.* (2004), "The persistence of fiscal adjustments in developing countries," *Applied Economics Letters*, vol. 11, pp. 209–212.

Hagist, C. and L. Kotlikoff (2005), "Who's Going Broke: Comparing Healthcare Costs in Ten OECD Countries," Working Paper 11833 (Cambridge, MA: National Bureau of Economic Research, December), https://www.nber.org/papers/w11833.pdf.

Hagist, C. and L. Kotlikoff (2006), "Health Care Spending: What the Future Will Look Like," National Center for Policy Analysis Report No. 286 (Dallas, TX: June), Table II, p. 2, http://www.ncpa.org/pdfs/st286.pdf.

Halpern, D. and J. Myers (2009), "Think Tank: A Model of Brutality Britain Can Build On," *Sunday Times*, May 3, http://www.timesonline.co.uk/tol/comment/article6210977.ece.

Hardin, G. (1968), "The Tragedy of the Commons," *Science*, vol. 162(3859), pp. 1243–1248, http://www.garretthardinsociety.org/articles/art_tragedy_of_the_commons.html.

Hardin, R. (2008), "The Free Rider Problem," *Stanford Encyclopedia of Philosophy* (Fall Edition), http://plato.stanford.edu/archives/fall2008/entries/free-rider/.

Hausmann, R. and C. Purfield (2004), "The Challenge of Fiscal Adjust- ment in a Democracy: The Case of India," IMF Working Paper No. WP/04/168 (Washington, DC: International Monetary Fund), http://www.imf.org/external/pubs/ft/wp/2004/wp04168.pdf.

Heilbroner, R. and L. Thurow (1998), *Economics Explained* (New York: Simon and Schuster).

Heller, P. (2005), "Understanding Fiscal Space," IMF Policy Discussion Paper 05/4 (Washington: International Monetary Fund, March), http://www.imf.org/external/pubs/ft/pdp/2005/pdp04.pdf.

Hemming, R. *et al.* (2002), "The Effectiveness of Fiscal Policy in Stimulating Economic Activity: A Review of the Literature," IMF Working Paper No. 02/28 (Washington: International Monetary Fund), http://www.imf.org/external/pubs/ft/wp/2002/wp02208.pdf.

Hercowitz, Z. and M. Strawczynski (2004), "Cyclical Ratcheting and Government Spending: Evidence from the OECD," *Review of Economics and Statistics*, vol. 86(1), pp. 353–361.

Holtzmann, R. and R. Hinz (2005), *Old Age Income Support in the 21st Century* (Washington: World Bank), http://siteresources.worldbank.org/INTPENSIONS/Resources/Old_Age_Inc_Supp_Full_En.pdf.

Honohan, P. and D. Klingebiel (2000), "Controlling Fiscal Costs of Banking Crises," World Bank Policy Research Paper 2441 (Washington: May), http://elibrary.worldbank.org/content/workingpaper/10.1596/1813-9450-2441.

Hsiao, W. and P. Heller (2007), "What Macroeconomists Should Know about Health Care Policy," Working Paper No. 07/13 (Washington, DC: International Monetary Fund, January), http://www.imf.org/external/pubs/ft/wp/2007/wp0713.pdf.

Hughes, J. (2005), "Amtrak Fires David Gunn as Railroad's Chief Executive (Update Five)," *Bloomberg*, November 9, http://www.bloomberg.com/apps/news?pid=newsarchive&sid=a7O0SxbxAgos.

Ilzetzki, E. and C. A. Végh (2008), "Procyclical Fiscal Policy in Developing Countries: Truth or Fiction?" NBER Working Paper No. 14191 (Cambridge, MA: National Bureau of Economic Research).

IMF Data Mapper (2019), "General Government Gross Debt," https://www.imf.org/external/datamapper/GGXWDG_NGDP@WEO/OEMDC/ADVEC/WEOWORLD.

IMF Fiscal Affairs Department (2017), "Fiscal Rules Data Set, 1985–2015," https://www.imf.org/external/datamapper/fiscalrules/matrix/matrix.htm.

IMF Staff Team led by D. S. Hoelscher and M. Quintyn (2003), *Managing System Banking Crises*, Occasional Paper 224 (Washington: International Monetary Fund).

IMF Staff (2010), "A Fair and Substantial Contribution by the Financial Sector," in Claessens *et al.* (eds), (2010), Ch. 1.

Inland Revenue Authority of Singapore (2010), "Singapore Budget — Tax Changes — Jobs Credit Scheme," http://www.iras.gov.sg/irashome/jobscredit.aspx.

International Monetary Fund (1995), "Unproductive Public Expenditures: A Pragmatic Approach to Policy Analysis," IMF Pamphlet No. 48, http://www.imf.org/external/pubs/ft/pam/pam48/pam4801.htm.

International Monetary Fund (2006), *Government Finance Statistics Yearbook 2006* (Washington).

International Monetary Fund (2009), *Vietnam: 2008 Article IV Consultation — Staff Report; Staff Statement and Supplement; Public Information Notice on the Executive Board Discussion; and Statement by the Executive Director for Vietnam* (IMF Country Report 09/110).

International Monetary Fund (2010), *India: 2009 Article IV Consultation — Staff Report*, http://www.imf.org/external/pubs/ft/scr/2010/cr1073.pdf.

International Monetary Fund (2012), *India: 2012 Article IV Consultation — Staff Report*, https://www.imf.org/external/pubs/ft/scr/2012/cr1296.pdf.

International Monetary Fund (1986), *Manual on Government Finance Statistics, 1986* (Washington).

International Monetary Fund (2001), *Government Finance Statistics Manual 2001* (Washington).

International Monetary Fund (2014), *Government Finance Statistics Manual 2014* (Washington).

International Monetary Fund (2003), "Public Debt in Emerging Markets: Is It Too High?" in *World Economic Outlook* (Washington: IMF, September 2003), Chapter III, pp. 113–152, http://www.imf.org/external/pubs/ft/weo/2003/02/pdf/chapter3.pdf.

International Monetary Fund (2005), *Lao People's Democratic Republic: Selected Issues and Statistical Appendix*, IMF Country Report 05/09 (Washington), http://www.imf.org/external/pubs/ft/scr/2005/cr0509.pdf.

International Monetary Fund (2005), *Pakistan: 2005 Article IV Consultation and Ex Post Assessment of Longer-Term Program Engagement — Staff Reports; Staff Supplement; Public Information Notice on the Executive Board Discussion; and Statement by the Executive Director for Pakistan*, IMF Country Report 05/409 (Washington, November), http://www.imf.org/external/pubs/ft/scr/2005/cr05409.pdf.

International Monetary Fund (2008), *Pakistan: 2007 Article IV Consultation — Staff Report; Staff Statement; Public Information Notice on the Executive Board Discussion; and Statement by the Executive Director for Pakistan*, IMF Country Report 08/21 (Washington, January).

International Monetary Fund (2009), "Factsheet: The Poverty Reduction and Growth Facility," http://www.imf.org/external/np/exr/facts/prgf.htm.

International Monetary Fund (2009), "Fiscal Rules — Anchoring Expectations for Public Finances" (Washington, December 20), http://www.imf.org/external/np/pp/eng/2009/121609.pdf.

International Monetary Fund (2009), *Zimbabwe: 2009 Article IV Consultation — Staff Report; Public Information Notice on the Executive Board Discussion; and Statement by the Executive Director for Zimbabwe*, http://www.imf.org/external/pubs/ft/scr/2009/cr09139.pdf.

International Monetary Fund (2010), *Fiscal Monitor May 2010*, http://www.imf.org/external/pubs/ft/fm/2010/fm1001.pdf.

International Monetary Fund (2018), *Fiscal Monitor October 2018*, https://www.imf.org/en/Publications/FM/Issues/2018/10/04/fiscal-monitor-october-2018.

International Monetary Fund (2010), "IMF Executive Board Concludes 2010 Article IV Consultation with Brazil," Press Information Notice No. 10/111 (Washington: August), http://www.imf.org/external/np/sec/pn/2010/pn10-111.htm.

International Monetary Fund (2010), "Pakistan: Fourth Review under the Stand-By Arrangement," http://www.imf.org/external/pubs/ft/scr/2010/cr10158.pdf.

International Monetary Fund (2010), "Technical Assistance Evaluation Program: Findings of Evaluations and Updated Program," http://www.imf.org/exterrnal/np/pp/eng/2010/060910.pdf.

International Monetary Fund (2010), *Fiscal Monitor: November 2010*, https://www.imf.org/en/Publications/FM/Issues/2016/12/31/Fiscal-Exit-From-Strategy-to-Implementation.

International Monetary Fund (2010), *World Economic Outlook*, October 2010, http://www.imf.org/external/pubs/ft/weo/2010/02/index.htm.

International Monetary Fund (2013), "Staff Guidance Note for Public Debt Sustainability Analysis in Market Access Countries" (Washington, July), https://www.imf.org/external/np/pp/eng/2013/050913.pdf.

International Monetary Fund (2018), "Debt Sustainability Analysis for Market Access Countries," https://www.imf.org/external/pubs/ft/dsa/mac.htm.

International Monetary Fund (2018), *India: Article IV Consultation-Press Release; Staff Report; and Statement by the Executive Director for India*, https://www.imf.org/en/Publications/CR/Issues/2018/08/06/India-2018-Article-IV-Consultation-Press-Release-Staff-Report-and-Statement-by-the-Exec utive-46155.

International Monetary Fund, *Philippines: 2018 Article IV Consultation: Press Release; Staff Report; and Statement by the Executive Director for Philippines* (Washington: IMF, September), Country Report 18/287.

International Monetary Fund (2018), *Thailand: 2018 Article IV Consultation — Press Release; Staff Report; and Statement by the Executive Director for Thailand* (Washington: IMF, June), Country Report 18/143.

International Monetary Fund (2018), "Debt Sustainability Framework for Low-Income Countries, July, https://www.imf.org/external/pubs/ft/dsa/lic.htm.

International Monetary Fund (2019), "Joint World Bank-IMF Debt Sustainability Framework for Low-Income Countries (March)," https://www.imf.org/en/About/Factsheets/Sheets/2016/08/01/16/39/Debt-Sustainability-Framewo rk-for-Low-Income-Countries.

International Monetary Fund (2019), IMF Country Focus, "Greece: Economy Improves, Key Reforms Still Needed," March, https://www.imf.org/en/News/Articles/2019/03/11/na031119-greece-economy-improves-key-refor ms-still-needed.

International Monetary Fund (2019), *Fiscal Monitor*, April 2019, https://www.imf.org/en/Publications/FM/Issues/2019/03/18/fiscal-monitor-april-2019.

International Monetary Fund (2019), *Fiscal Monitor*, October 2019, https://www.imf.org/en/Publications/FM/Issues/2019/09/12/fiscal-monitor-octob er-2019.

International Monetary Fund (2019), "IMF Support for Low-Income Countries," https://www.imf.org/en/About/Factsheets/IMF-Support-for-Low-Income-Countries.

International Monetary Fund (2019), *Pakistan: Request for an Extended Arrangement under the Extended Fund Facility — Press Release; Staff Report; and Statement by the Executive Director for Pakistan*, IMF Country Report 19/212, https://www.imf.org/en/Publications/CR/Issues/2019/07/08/Pakistan-Re quest-for-an-Extended-Arrangement-Under-the-Extended-Fund-Facility-Press-Release-47092.

International Monetary Fund (2019), *Singapore: 2019 Article IV Consultation — Press Release; Staff Report; and Statement by the Executive Director for Singapore*, July, Country Report 12/233, https://www.imf.org/en/Publications/CR/Issues/2019/07/15/Singapore-2019-Article-IV-Consultation-Press-Release-Staff-Re port-and-Statement-by-the-47119.

Irwin, N. (2009), "Bernanke Presses for Fiscal Restraint," *Washington Post*, June 4.

Jacobs, J. (2010), "U.S. Schools Adopt Singapore Math," October 10, http://www.joannejacobs.com/2010/10/u-s-schools-adopt-singapore-math.

Jain-Chandra, S. *et al.* (2018), "Inequality in China — Trends, Drivers and Policy Debates," IMF Working Paper No. 18/127 (Washington: International Monetary Fund, June).

Janssen, J. (2001), "New Zealand's Fiscal Policy Framework: Experience and Evolution," Working Paper No. 01/25 (Wellington: December), http://www.treasury.govt.nz/publications/research-policy/wp/2001/01--25.

Johnson, W. (2005), "Are Public Subsidies to Higher Education Regressive?" *Education Finance and Policy*, vol. 1, pp. 288–315.

Joint Committee on Taxation (2018), "Estimates of Federal Tax Expenditures for Fiscal Years 2018–22" (Washington: U.S. Govt. Printing Office, October), https://www.jct.gov/publications.html?id=5148&func=startdown.

Kagan, J. (2019), "Value–Added Tax — Tax Definition," April, Investopedia, https://www.investopedia.com/terms/v/valueaddedtax.asp.

Kaminsky, G. *et al.* (2004), "When It Rains, It Pours: Procyclical Capital Flows and Macroeconomic Policies," NBER Working Paper No. 10780 (Cambridge, MA: National Bureau of Economic Research).

Kasek, L. and D. Webber, eds. (2009), *Performance-Based Budgeting and Medium Term Expenditure Frameworks in Emerging Europe* (World Bank), http://siteresources.worldbank.org/INTECA/Resources/WBperformanceBud getingTEF.pdf.

Keen, M. and A. Simone (2004), "Tax Policy in Developing Countries: Some Lessons from the 1990s and Some Challenges Ahead," in Gupta, S. *et al.* (eds.), *Helping Countries Develop: The Role of Fiscal Policy* (Washington: International Monetary Fund).

Keen, M. and B. Lockwood (2007), "Value Added Tax: Its Causes and Consequences," Working Paper No. 07/183 (Washington: International Monetary Fund, July), p. 27, http://www.imf.org/external/pubs/ft/wp/2007/wp07183.pdf.

Keen, M. and S. Smith (2007), "VAT Fraud and Evasion: What Do We Know, and What Can Be Done?" Working Paper No. 07/31 (Washington: International Monetary Fund, February).

Kessides, I. N. (2004), *Reforming Infrastructure: Privatization, Regulation, and Competition* (Washington: World Bank), http://www.iumsp.ch/Enseignement/ postgradue/Besancon/docs/rapport_WB_sur_reorg.pdf.

Kharas, H. *et al.* (2001), "An analysis of Russia's 1998 meltdown: Funda- mentals and market signals," *Brookings Papers on Economic Activity*, #1, 2001.

Kidd, M. (2010), "Revenue Administration: Functionally Organized Tax Administra- tion," Technical Notes and Manuals (Washington: International Monetary Fund, June), http://blog-pfm.imf.org/files/fad-technical-manual-17.pdf.

Kikeri, S. and J. Nellis (2004), "An Assessment of Privatization," *World Bank Research Observer*, vol. 19(Spring), pp. 87–118.

Kile, J. (2008), "Issues in Infrastructure Investment," presentation to National Tax Association, September 26, http://www.cbo.gov/ftpdocs/98xx/doc9817/ NTA_Conf_9-26-08_Final.pdf. U.S.

Knowledge @ Wharton, 2005, "Reform of China's Banks, Burdened by Bad Loans, Is Priority for Government," June 1, http://knowledge.wharton.upenn.Edu/ article.cfm?articleid=1202.

Koh, S. K. B. *et al.* (2007), "Investment Patterns in Singapore's Central Provident Fund," Pension Research Council Working Paper No. 2006-12 (University of Pennsylvania, Wharton School: May), http://papers.ssrn.com/sol3/papers.cfm? abstract_id=933332.

Koo, R. C. (2009), *The Holy Grail of Macroeconomics: Lessons from Japan's Great Recession* (New York: Wiley).

Koveos, P. and P. Yourougou (2009), "Public–Private Partnerships in Emerging Mar- kets," *QFinance*, http://www.qfinance.com/contentFiles/QF02/gjbkw9a0/ 17/0/publicprivate-partnerships-in-emerging-markets.pdf.

La Porta, R. *et al.* (2008), "The economic consequences of legal origins," *Journal of Economic Literature*, vol. 46, pp. 285–332, http://www.aeaweb.org/atypon. php?return_to=/doi/pdfplus/10.1257/jel.46.2.285.

Lane, P. R. (2003), "Cyclical Behavior of Fiscal Policy: Evidence from the OECD," *Journal of Public Economics*, vol. 87(December), pp. 2661–2675.

Lank, A. G. (1997), "A Conversation with Tom Bata," Family *Business Review*, vol. 10(Fall), pp. 211–220, http://www.decon.unipd.it/info/sid/materiale8/ bel_bata.semiario-9-4.pdf.

Lawsky, S. B. (2011), "On the Edge: Declining Marginal Utility and Tax Policy," *Minnesota Law Review*, vol. 95, pp. 904–52, http://papers.ssrn.com/sol3/ papers.cfm?abstract_id=1760050.

Leite, S. (2000), *Ghana: Economic Development in a Democratic Environment*, Occasional Paper 199 (Washington: International Monetary Fund), http:// books.google.com.sg/books?id = 8e2H_6n4vD0C&pg = RA1-PT37&lpg=RA1- PT37&dq = IMF+program+rescind+price+increase&source = bl&ots = IVoLAB- bRz&sig=YPeOsTFcYIMJT-HVNk_EXy7o_mw&hl = en&ei=3rxETeiPKoaglAe VxuRI&sa=X&oi=book_result&ct=result&resnum=9&ved=0CEkQ6AEwCA.

Lewis, T. (2003), *In the Long Run We're All Dead: The Canadian Turn to Fiscal Restraint* (Vancouver: UBC Press).

Ley, E. (2003), "Fiscal (and External) Sustainability," updated version at http://mpra. ub.uni-muenchen.de/13693/.

Ley, E. (2009), "Fiscal (and external) Sustainability," unpublished (Munich Personal RePEc Archive, February 28), http://mpra.eub.uni-muenchen.de/13693/1/ MPRA_paper_13693.pdf.

Lim, M. K. (2007), "Deregulation of Doctors' Fees," *Health Policy Monitor*, http://www.hpm.org/en/Surveys/University_of_Singapore_-_Singapore/09/ Deregulation_of_doctor_fees.html;jsessionid = 0AEA73A7D1F0E6C363A84E6 99AD75532.

Ljungwall, S. *et al.* (2009), "Central Bank Financial Strength and the Cost of Sterilization in China," Stockholm School of Economics, http://swopec.hhs.se/ hacerc/papers/hacerc2009-008.pdf.

Lledó, V. *et al.* (2017), "Fiscal Rules at a Glance — Background Paper," IMF (March), https://www.imf.org/external/datamapper/fiscalrules/matrix/matrix.htm.

Loevy and Loevy (2007), "Tax Fraud," https://loevy.com/whistleblower- protection/.

Mann, G. (2018), "Central Transfers to States: Role of the Finance Commission," *PRS Blog*, April 11, https://www.prsindia.org/theprsblog/ central-transfers-states-role-finance-commission.

Mankiw, N. G. (2006), *Macroeconomics* (New York: Worth Publishers).

Martins, J. O. and C. de la Maisonneuve (2006), "The Drivers of Public Expenditures on Health and Long-Term Care: An Integrated Approach," *OECD Economic Studies*, vol. 43(2), pp. 116–154, http://www.oecd.org/dataoecd/62/19/ 40507566.pdf.

Matheson, T. (2010), "Taxing Financial Transactions: Issues and Evidence," in Claessens *et al.*, eds., Ch. 8.

Mauro, P. (1996), "The Effects of Corruption on Growth, Investment, and Gov- ern-
ment Expenditure," IMF Working Paper No. 96/98 (Washington: International
Monetary Fund).

Mauro, Paulo, ed. (2011), *Chipping Away of Public Debt* (New York: Wiley).

Mayer, B. (2019), "Pensions & Benefits in the United Kingdom," https://www.
lexology.com/library/detail.aspx?g=4ff74f3a-ebd2-4385-8f36-0c5cf07caa5f.

McGill, D. M. *et al.* (2010), *Fundamentals of Private Pensions*, Ninth Edition (New
York: Oxford University Press).

Megginson, W. L. and J. M. Netter (2001), "From State to Market: A Survey of
Empirical Studies on Privatization," *Journal of Economic Literature*, vol. 39(June),
pp. 321–389.

Melo, M. *et al.* (2010), "The Political Economy of Fiscal Reform in Brazil:
The Rationale for the Suboptimal Equilibrium," Inter-American Development
Bank Working Paper No. 117 (Washington: February), http://www.iadb.org/
research/pub_desc.cfm?pub_id=IDB-WP-117.

Michel, F. (2008), "A Primer on Public–Private Partnerships," Public Financial Management Blog (Washington: International Monetary Fund), http://blog-pfm.
imf.org/pfmblog/2008/02/a-primer-on-pub.html.

Ministry of Finance, India (2010), *Government Debt: Status and Next Steps* (November), http://pib.nic.in/archieve/others/2010/nov/d2010110301.pdf.

Ministry of Health, Singapore (2010), "Singapore Healthcare System," http://www.
ahp.mohh.com.sg/singapore_healthcare_system.html.

Ministry of Health, Singapore (2018), *Fee Benchmarks Advisory Committee Report*,
https://www.moh.gov.sg/docs/librariesprovider5/pressroom/press-releases/
fee-benchmarks-advisory-committee-report.pdf.

Ministry of Health, Singapore (2019), "Fee Benchmarks and Bill Amount Information," https://www.moh.gov.sg/cost-financing/fee-benchmarks-and-bill-amo
unt-information/DescriptionTextSearch.

Ministry of Health, Singapore (2019), "Medisave," https://www.moh.gov.sg/
cost-financing/healthcare-schemes-subsidies/medisave.

Ministry of Manpower, Singapore (2019), "How You Can Use Your CPF,"
https://www.mom.gov.sg/employment-practices/central-provident-fund/how
-you-can-use-your-cpf.

Musgrave, R. A. and P. B. Musgrave (1989), *Public Finance in Theory and Practice*,
5th Edition (New York: McGraw Hill).

National Commission on Fiscal Responsibility and Reform (2010), *Moment of Truth*,
http://www.fiscalcommission.gov/news/moment-truth-report-national-comm
ission-fiscal-responsibility-and-reform.

National Conference of State Legislatures (2020), "Remote Sales Tax Collection,"
https://www,ncsl.org/reserach/fiscal-policy/e-fairness-legislation-overview.
aspx (March).

National Treasury (2009), *Public Debt: The Brazilian Experience* (Brasilia, August),
Statistical Annex, http://www.tesouro.fazenda.gov.br/english/public_debt/
downloads/book/Statistical_annex.pdf.

National Treasury (2009), *Public Debt: The Brazilian Experience*, http://www.
tesouro.fazenda.gov.br/english/public_debt/book_divida.asp.

Nerdwallet (2019), "Earned Income Tax Credit (EIC): What It Is and How to Qualify," https://www.nerdwallet.com/blog/taxes/can-you-take-earned-inco me-tax-credit/.

New Jersey State League of Municipalities (2010), "A Short and Simple Glimpse at the Property Tax in New Jersey," http://www.njslom.org/tax_brochure.html.

OECD (2008), *Growing Unequal: Income Distribution and Poverty in OECD Countries*, http://www.oecd.org/dataoecd/45/42/41527936.pdf.

OECD (2008), "Keeping Government Contracts Clean," *Policy Brief*, http://www.oecd.org/dataoecd/63/21/41550528.pdf.

OECD (2009), "Following G20 OECD Delivers on Tax Pledge," http://www.oecd.org/document/57/0,3343,en_2649_34487_42496569_1_1_1_1,00.html.

OECD (2010), "PISA Education Rankings 2009," http://www.oecd.org/dataoecd/54/12/46643496.pdf.

OECD, Economic Outlook 87 Database. OECD, Forum on Tax Administration, Compliance Sub-Group (2009), "Information Note — Withholding & Information Reporting Regimes for Small/Medium- Sized Businesses & Self-Employed Taxpayers," (Paris, August), http://www.oecd.org/dataoecd/49/16/43728416.pdf.

OECD (2018), *Pensions at a Glance Asia/Pacific 2018*, OECD Publishing, Paris, https://www.oecd.org/publications/pensions-at-a-glance-asia-pacific-23 090766.htm.

OECD (2018), *Revenue Statistics 1965–2017*, 2018 Edition, Table 3.9, https://read.oecd-ilibrary.org/taxation/revenue-statistics-2018_rev_stats-2018-en#page71.

OECD (2019), "Health Expenditure and Financing," OECD.Stat, https://stats.oecd.org/Index.aspx?ThemeTreeId=9.

OECD (2019), *Pensions at a Glance 2019 — OECD and G20 Indicators*.

OECD (2019), *PISA 2018: Country Note — United States*, https://www.oecd.org/pisa/publications/PISA2018_CN_USA.pdf.

OECD (2019), *Revenue Statistics 1965–2018*, OECD Publishing, Paris, http://dx.doi.org/10.1787/888934054645.

OECD (2020), "International Collaboration to End Tax Avoidance," https://www.oecd.org/tax/beps/.

Oregon Health Authority (2019), *Prioritized List of Services*, https://www.oregon.gov/oha/HSD/OHP/Pages/Prioritized-List.aspx.

Ouanes, A. and S. Thakur, 1997, *Macroeconomic Analysis and Accounting in Transition Economies* (Washington: International Monetary Fund).

Padmanabhan, A. (2007), "Tracking the Indian Railways' Turnaround Saga," *Business Times*, July 21, http://indiainteracts.in/columnist/2007/07/21/Tracking-the-Indian-Railways-turnaround-saga.

Park, D. (2009), "Ageing Asia's Looming Pension Crisis," ADB Economics Working Paper No. 165, July, www.adb.org/Documents/Working-Papers/.../Economics-WP165.pdf.

Pechman, J. A., ed. (1980), *What Should Be Taxed: Income or Expenditure?* (Washington: Brookings).

Pensionsorter (2010), *Your Rough Guide to UK Pensions*, http://www.pension-sorter.co.uk/UK_pensions_guide.cfm.

Pension Rights Center (2019), "How Many American Workers Participate in Workplace Retirement Plans?" https://www.pensionrights.org/publications/statistic/how-many-american-workers-participate-workplace-retirement-plans.

Perotti, R. (1998), *Fiscal Policy in Good Times and Bad* (New York: Columbia University), http://didattica.unibocconi.it/mypage/upload/49621_20090119_052630_BADTIMES.PDF.

Pescatori, A. *et al.* (2014), "Debt and Growth: Is There a Magic Threshold?" IMF Working Paper No. 14/34 (Washington: International Monetary Fund, February), https://www.imf.org/external/pubs/ft/wp/2014/wp1434.pdf.

Petri, M. *et al.* (2002), "Energy Sector Quasi-Fiscal Activities in the Countries of the Former Soviet Union," Working Paper No. 02/60 (Washington: International Monetary Fund), Figure 1, http://www.imf.org/external/pubs/ft/wp/2002/wp0260.pdf.

Pew Charitable Trusts (2019), "State Pension Funding Gap: 2017," June, https://www.pewtrusts.org/-/media/assets/2019/06/statepensionfundinggap.pdf.

Pfau, W. D. (2005), "The Effects of Social Security on Private Savings: A Reap-Praisal of the Time Series Evidence," *Sophia International Review*, vol. 27(1), pp. 57–70, http://ideas.repec.org/p/pra/mprapa/19032.html.

Poh, J. (2019), "CPF Retirement Sum – How Does It Work and How Much Do You Need," *Moneysmart*, November 7, https://blog.moneysmart.sg/budgeting/cpf-retirement-sum/.

PriceWaterhouseCoopers (2010), *Paying Taxes 2011: The Global Picture*, www.pwc.com/payingtaxes.

PriceWaterhouseCoopers (2019), "Value-Added Tax (VAT) Rates," http://taxsummaries.pwc.com/ID/Value-added-tax-(VAT)-rates.

Purfield, C. (2004), "The Decentralization Dilemma in India," Working Paper No. 04/32 (Washington: International Monetary Fund, February), http://www.imf.org/external/pubs/ft/wp/2004/wp0432.pdf.

Rehn, O. (2010), *Conference on the Green paper on Pensions: Key Data*, http://ec.europa.eu/social/BlobServlet?docId=6217&langId=enhttp://ec.europa.eu/social/BlobServlet?docId=6217&langId=en.

Reid, T. R. (2009), *Healing of America* (New York: Penguin Press).

Republic of Poland, Ministry of Finance (2010), *Tax Expenditures in Poland* (Warsaw: November), p. 5, http://www.mofnet.gov.pl/_files_/english/fiscal_system/tax/report_tax_expenditures_in_poland_english_version.pdf.

Reuters (2011), "IMF Criticizes Petrol Price Hike Reversal," *Express Tribune and International Herald Tribune*, January 7, http://tribune.com.pk/story/100321/imf-criticises-petrol-price-hike-reversal.

Reuters, "Greece Concludes Early Repayment of IMF Loans," https://www.reuters.com/article/us-greece-economy-imf/greece-concludes-early-repayment-of-imf-loans-idUSKBN1XZ23V.

Roberts, A. (2019), "State Pension," Money Saving Expert.com, https://www.moneysavingexpert.com/savings/state-pensions/\#previous.

Rosen, H. and T. Gayner (2009), *Public Finance*, 9th Edition (New York: Irwin).

Rudowitz, R. *et al.* (2019), "Medicaid Financing: The Basics," kff.org, https://www.kff.org/report-section/medicaid-financing-the-basics-issue-brief/.

Saez, E. (2019), "Striking It Richer: Evolution of the Top Incomes in the United States", https://eml.berkeley.edu/~saez/saez-UStopincomes-2017.pdf.

Saez, E. and G. Zucman (2019), *Triumph of Injustice* (New York: W.W. Norton & Co.).

Samuelson, P. (1954), "The Pure Theory of Public Expenditure," *Review of Economics and Statistics*, vol. 36(4), pp. 387–389.

Saving, J. L. (1998), "Privatization and the Transition to a Market Economy," *Federal Reserve Bank of Dallas Economic Review*, Fourth Quarter, http://www.dallasfed.org/research/er/1998/er9804b.pdf.

Sawyer, B. and G. Claxton (2019), "How Do Health Expenditures Vary Across the Population?" Peterson-KFF Health System Tracker, https://www.healthsystemtracker.org/chart-collection/health-expenditures-vary-across-population/#item-start.

Schenk, A., *et al.* (2015), *Value Added Tax: A Comparative Approach, Second Edition* (Cambridge, UK: Cambridge University Press).

Scherer, R. (2007), "Bridge Collapse Highlights America's Deferred Maintenance," *Christian Science Monitor*, August 3, http://www.csmonitor.com/2007/0803/p01s05-usgn.html.

Schleicher, A. (2010), "The Importance of World Class Schools for Economic Success," testimony to U.S. Senate HELP Committee (OECD, March 9), (http://help.senate.gov/imo/media/doc/Schleicher.pdf.

Schultze, C. (1977), *The Private Use of Public Interest* (Washington: Brookings Institution.

Sendlhofer, R. (2001), "Incidence of Social Security Contributions and Taxes, Evidence from Austria," Institute of Public Economics, University of Innsbruck, Discussion Paper 2001/1, http://homepage.uibk.ac.at/~c40414/fiwidp200101.pdf.

Serra, J. and J. R. R. Afonso (2007), "Fiscal Federalism in Brazil: An Overview," *CEPAL Review*, vol. 91 (April), pp. 29–51, http://www.eclac.org/publicaciones/xml/8/29498/lcg2333iSerra.pdf.

Setser, B. and A. Pandey (2009), "China's $1.7 Billion Bet" (New York: Council of Foreign Relations Working Paper No. 6), http://www.cfr.org/content/publications/attachments/CGS_WorkingPaper_6_China.pdf.

Shafik, N. (1995), "Making a Market: Mass Privatization in the Czech and Slovak Republics," *World Development*, vol. 23, 1143–1156.

Shanghai Poverty Conference (2004), Case Study Summary, "Mexico's Opportunidades Program," http://info.worldbank.org/etools/docs/reducingpoverty/case/119/summary/Mexico-Oportunidades%20Summary.pdf.

Sharma, S. N. and S. Layak (2019), "GST: the challenges before India's largest indirect tax reform," *Economic Times*, September 29, https://economictimes.indiatimes.com/news/economy/policy/gst-the-challenges-before-indias-largest-indirect-tax-reform/articleshow/71353710.cms.

Sheshinski, E. and L. F. Lopez-Calva (2003), "Privatization and its benefits," *CESifo Economic Studies*, vol. 49, pp. 429–459.

Shirley, M. and P. Walsh (2001), "Private vs. Public Ownership: The Current State of the Debate," World Bank Research Paper 2420, http://papers.ssrn.com/sol3/papers.cfm?abstract_id=261854.

Slackman, M. (2008), "Egypt's Problem and Its Challenge: Bread Corrupts," *New York Times*, January 17, http://www.nytimes.com/2008/01/17/world/africa/17bread.html.

Slemrod, J. (2009), "Old George Orwell Got It Backward: Some Thoughts on Behavioral Tax Economics," CESifo Working Paper No. 2777, p. 2, http://www.ifo.de/portal/pls/portal/docs/1/1186062.PDF.

Slemrod, J. and J. Bakija (2008), *Taxing Ourselves*, 4th Edition (Cambridge, MA: MIT Press).

Social Security Association (2010), "Impact of the Economic and Financial Crisis on the Swedish Pension System," http://www.issa.int/News-Events/News2/Impact-of-the-financial-and-economic-crisis-on-the-Swedish-pension-system.

Soto, M. (2005), "Chilean Pension Reform: The Good, the Bad, and the In- Between," *Issue in Brief 31* (Boston College: Center for Retirement Research, June), http://crr.bc.edu/images/stories/Briefs/ib_31.pdf.

Spilimbergo, A. *et al.* (2008), "Fiscal Policy for the Crisis," Staff Position Note 08/01 (Washington, DC: International Monetary Fund, December), http://www.imf.org/external/pubs/ft/spn/2008/spn0801.pdf.

Spilimbergo, A. *et al.* (2009), "Fiscal Multipliers," Staff Position Note 09/11 (Washington, DC: International Monetary Fund, May), http://www.imf.org/external/pubs/ft/spn/2009/spn0911.pdf.

Statista (2019), "Health Expenditure as a Percentage of Gross Domestic Product in Selected Countries in 2017," https://www.statista.com/statistics/268826/health-expenditure-as-gdp-percentage-in-oecd-countries/.

Statistics Singapore (2011), *Yearbook of Statistics Singapore, 2011*, http://www.singstat.gov.sg/pubn/reference/yos11/statsT-income.pdf.

Statistics Singapore (2019), "Singapore Economy — GDP 2018 at Current Market Prices," https://www.singstat.gov.sg/modules/infographics/economy.

Statistics Singapore (2020), *Key Household Income Trends, 2019*, pp-s26, https://www.singstat.gov.sg/-/media/files/publications/households/pp-26.pdf.

Steinwender, C. (2010), "Job Creation Subsidies and Employment. Empirical Evidence for Germany," http://www.diw.de/en/diw_01.c.100353.en/about_us/department_of_the_executive_board/events/events.html.

Stults, T. (2004), "Tax Harmonization versus Tax Competition: A Review of the Literature," entry to the 2004 Moffatt Prize in Economics, http://economics.about.com/cs/moffattentries/a/harmonization.htm.

Summers, L. H. and V. P. Summers (1989), "When Financial Markets Work too Well: A Cautious Case for a Securities Transactions Tax," *Journal of Financial Services Research*, vol. 3, pp. 261–286.

Sunley, E. (2009), "Comments on Itai Grinberg's Paper," http://www.american-taxpolicyinstitute.org/pdf/VAT/Sunley.pdf.

Talvi, E. and C. A. Végh (2005), "Tax base variability and procyclical fiscal policy," *Journal of Economic Development*, vol. 78(1), pp. 156–190.

Tanzi, V. (1996), "Globalization, Tax Competition, and the Future of Tax Systems," Working Paper No. 96/141 (Washington: International Monetary Fund).

Tanzi, V. (2005), "Economic Role of the State in the 21st CENTURY," *Cato Journal*, vol. 25(Fall), pp. 617–638, http://www.cato.org/pubs/journal/cj25n3/cj25n3-16.pdf.

Tanzi, V. and H. Davoodi (1997), "Corruption, Public Investment, and Growth," Working Paper No. 97/39 (Washington: International Monetary Fund, October), http://www.imf.org/external/pubs/ft/wp/wp97139.pdf.

Tanzi, V. (xxxx), "Globalization, Technological Developments, and Fiscal Termites," Working Paper No. 00/181 (Washington: International Monetary Fund, November), http://www.imf.org/external/pubs/ft/wp/2000/wp00181.pdf.

Tanzi, V. and L. Schuknecht (2000), *Public Spending in the 20th Century: A Global Perspective* (Cambridge, UK: Cambridge University Press).

Tax Policy Center (2010), *Tax Legislation — Major Tax Legislation Enacted 1980–1989*, http://www.taxpolicycenter.org/legislation/1980.cfm\#Interest1983.

Tax Policy Center (2019), "Briefing Book — Who Bears the Burden of the Corporate Income Tax?" https://www.taxpolicycenter.org/briefing-book/who-bears-burden-corporate-income-tax.

TheGlobalEconomy.com (2019), "Singapore: Health Spending as Percent of GDP," https://www.theglobaleconomy.com/Singapore/health_spending_as_percent_of_gdp/.

The Nation (2005), "Excise Tax Raised for Hard Liquor," September 7, http://www.phuket-info.com/forums/news-articles/9077-nation-excise-tax-raised-hard-liquor.html.

Thirteenth Finance Commission, India (2010) *Report of the Thirteenth Finance Commission*, http://fincomindia.nic.in/ShowContentOne.aspx?id=28&Section=1.

Transport for London (2003), "Congestion Charging Six Months On," http://web.archive.org/web/20060515194436/http://www.tfl.gov.uk/tfl/downloads/pdf/congestion-charging/cc-6monthson.pdf.

U.K. Government (2019), "The New State Pension," https://www.gov.uk/new-state-pension.

U.S. Bureau of Census, Statistical Abstract, http://www.usgovernmentspending.com/.

U.S. Council of Economic Advisers (2010), *Economic Report of the President*, http://www.gpoaccess.gov/eop/2010/2010_erp.pdf.

U.S. Department of Agriculture, Food and Nutrition Service (2019), "Supplemental Nutrition Assistance Program," https://www.fns.usda.gov/snap/supplemental-nutrition-assistance-program.

U.S. Department of Health and Human Services (2009), *Federal Financial Participation in State Assistance Expenditures*, http://aspe.hhs.gov/health/fmap11.htm.

U.S. Department of Health and Human Services, Centers for Medicare and Medicaid Services (2018), "National Health Expenditure Data — Historical," https://www.cms.gov/Research-Statistics-Data-and-Systems/Statistics-Trends-and-Reports/NationalHealthExpendData/NationalHealthAccountsHistorical.html.

U.S. Department of Health and Human Services, Office of Family Assistance (2020), "About TANF," https://www.acf.hhs.gov/ofa/programs/tanf/about.

U.S. Department of Housing and Urban Development (2019), "Rental Assistance," https://www.hud.gov/topics/rental_assistance.

U.S. Department of Labor, Employment and Training Administration (2019), "Work Opportunity Tax Credit," https://www.doleta.gov/business/incentives/opptax/.

U.S. Department of Transportation, Federal Transit Administration, *Major Capital Investments* (*New Starts & Small Starts*), http://www.fta.dot.gov/funding/grants/grants_financing_3559.html.

U.S. Food and Drug Administration (2018), "Menu and Vending Machine Labeling," https://www.fda.gov/food/food-labeling-nutrition/menu-and-vending-machine-labeling.

U.S. Internal Revenue Service (2019), "EITC Central," https://www.eitc.irs.gov/.

U.S. Social Security Administration (2011), "Retirement," http://www.socialsecurity.gov/pgm/retirement.htm.

U.S. Social Security Administration (2019), "Fast Facts & Figures about Social Security, 2019: OASI Status — Insured Population, 1970–2018," https://www.ssa.gov/policy/docs/chartbooks/fast_facts/2019/fast_facts19.html.

U.S. Social Security Administration (2019), "Social Security Administrative Expenses," https://www.ssa.gov/oact/STATS/admin.html.

U.S. Treasury Staff (1977), *Blueprints for Basic Tax Reform* (Washington: U.S.G.P.O), http://www.treasury.gov/offices/tax-policy/library/blueprints.

United Nations (2009), *World Population Prospects: the 2008 Revision*, http://esa.un.org/unpp/index.asp?panel=2.

Universia, Knoweldge@Wharton (2005), "Chile's Pension Reform: An Inspiration to Others," http://www.wharton.universia.net/index.cfm?fa=viewfeature&language=english&id=937.

USAID and PriceWaterhouse Coopers (1998–1999), *Final Report — Ukraine Mass Privatization Project*, http://pdf.usaid.gov/pdf_docs/PDABR432.pdf.

Varsano, R. (2003), *Tax Reform in Brazil: The Long Process in Progress* (Washington: Inter-American Development Bank), http://www.fiscalreform.net/library/pdfs/u_Tax%20Reform%20in%20Brazil.pdf.

Viard, A. A. (2019), "Wealth Taxation: An Overview of the Issues," in *Maintaining the Strength of American Capitalism*, M. S. Kearney and A. Ganz (eds.) (Aspen Institute Economic Strategy Group).

VisualEconomics (2010), *Health Care Costs Around the World*, http://www.visualeconomics.com/healthcare-costs-around-ther-world_2010-03-01 (slightly different data for U.S. health care expenditures).

Walter, J. R. (1991), "Loan Loss Reserves," *Federal Reserve Bank of Richmond Economic Review*, vol. 77(July), pp. 20–30.

Weiss, R. D. (2006), "How Did the Tax Reform Act of 1986 Attract So Much Support?" Testimony before the U.S. Senate Finance Committee, http://finance.senate.gov/imo/media/doc/9231ORWTEST1.pdf.

Widjaja, M. (2009), "An Economic and Social Review on Indonesian Direct Cash Transfer," Program to Poor Families Year (2005), https://www.appam.org/conferences/international/singapore2009/sessions/downloads/1101.pdf.

Wolff, E. N., "Wealth Taxation in the United States," National Bureau of Economic Research Working Paper No. 26555 (Cambridge, MA: December).

World Bank (1995), *Bureaucrats in Business: The Economics and Politics of Government Ownership* (Washington: October).

World Bank (2019), "Doing Business — Enforcing Contracts," http://www.doingbusiness.org/data/exploretopics/enforcing-contracts.

World Bank (2019), "Doing Business — Paying Taxes 2011," http://www.doingbusiness.org/reports/special-reports/paying-taxes-2011.

World Bank (2019), "Doing Business — Measuring Business Regulation," http://www.doingbusiness.org.

World Bank (2019), "Worldwide Governance Indicators," https://info.worldbank.org/governance/wgi/.

World Bank (2018), *Paying Taxes 2019*, November, https://www.doingbusiness.org/content/dam/doingBusiness/media/Special-Reports/PwC- - -Paying-Taxes-2019- - -Smaller-19112018.pdf.

World Health Organization (2000), *Health Performance Rank by Country*, http://www.photius.com/rankings/world_health_performance_ranks.html.

World Health Organization, Health Systems Statistics Database.

Index

Printed in the United States
by Baker & Taylor Publisher Services